Victims' Rights and Advocacy at the International Criminal Court

Victims' Rights and Advocacy at the International Criminal Court

T. MARKUS FUNK

OXFORD
UNIVERSITY PRESS

OXFORD
UNIVERSITY PRESS

Oxford University Press, Inc., publishes works that further Oxford University's objective of excellence in research, scholarship, and education.

Oxford New York
Auckland Cape Town Dar es Salaam Hong Kong Karachi Kuala Lumpur Madrid Melbourne
Mexico City Nairobi New Delhi Shanghai Taipei Toronto

With offices in
Argentina Austria Brazil Chile Czech Republic France Greece Guatemala Hungary Italy
Japan Poland Portugal Singapore South Korea Switzerland Thailand Turkey Ukraine
Vietnam

Published by Oxford University Press, Inc.
198 Madison Avenue, New York, New York 10016

Library of Congress Cataloging-in-Publication Data

Funk, T. Markus.
Victims' rights and advocacy at the International Criminal Court /
T. Markus Funk.
p. cm.
Includes bibliographical references and index.
ISBN 978-0-19-973747-5 (hardback : alk. paper)
1. International Criminal Court—Rules and practice. 2. War victims—Legal status, laws, etc. I. Title.
KZ6311.F858 2010
341.6'7—dc22

2009047948

2 3 4 5 6 7 8 9

Printed in the United States of America on acid-free paper

Note to Readers
This publication is designed to provide accurate and authoritative information in regard to the subject matter covered. It is based upon sources believed to be accurate and reliable and is intended to be current as of the time it was written. It is sold with the understanding that the publisher is not engaged in rendering legal, accounting, or other professional services. If legal advice or other expert assistance is required, the services of a competent professional person should be sought. Also, to confirm that the information has not been affected or changed by recent developments, traditional legal research techniques should be used, including checking primary sources where appropriate.

(Based on the Declaration of Principles jointly adopted by a Committee of the American Bar Association and a Committee of Publishers and Associations.)

We must establish incredible events by credible evidence.

— Nuremberg Trial United States Chief Prosecutor,
United States Supreme Court Justice Robert Jackson,
June 7, 1945

Where the personal interests of the victims are affected, the Court shall permit their views and concerns to be presented and considered at stages of the proceedings determined to be appropriate by the Court and in a manner which is not prejudicial to or inconsistent with the rights of the accused and a fair and impartial trial . . . .

— Rome Statute of the International Criminal Court,
Article 68(3)

Contents

The International Criminal Court
The Hague, Netherlands

Foreword

As T. Markus Funk in this groundbreaking book illustrates so compellingly, the broad crimes punishable by international criminal law generate a disturbing number of real flesh-and-blood victims.

However, for a very long time, such victims of the most serious crimes of concern to the international community were, as a group, viewed as mere witnesses. In the aftermath of the Second World War, for example, the International Military Tribunals of Nuremberg and Tokyo never considered the lot of victims, except through the repression of the crimes giving rise to the harms they suffered.

Some international humanitarian agreements, including the four Geneva Conventions of 12 August 1949, and their additional Protocols of 8 June 1977, provided for the effective punishment of persons who committed, or ordered to be committed, any grave breaches of their provisions, but they did not accord any kind of compensation rights to victims. Moreover, these international agreements neglected to provide for any right of victims to trigger judicial proceedings against the authors of war crimes, nor did they provide a right for victims to intervene in the criminal proceedings or to obtain reparation.

The human rights conventions, and the evolution of human rights in general, progressively brought to the forefront of international law the idea that victims are entitled to compensation for their prejudice. Accordingly, the International Covenant on Civil and Political Rights of 19 December 1966, the European Convention on Human Rights of 4 November 1950, as well as various regional conventions, provided for the right to access justice and to claim reparations for victims whose fundamental rights had been violated. These rights can also be found in specialised conventions such as the United Nations Convention against Torture, which prompted the creation of the Voluntary Fund for Victims of Torture.

International recognition of victims' rights took a decisive step forward with the adoption of the Declaration of Basic Principles of Justice for Victims of Crime and Abuse of Power, passed by the General Assembly of the United Nations on 29 November 1985. This unique declaration provides a general survey of the rights of victims, at least under domestic law. These rights include: the right to access justice, right to fair treatment, the right to restitution, and the right to medical, psychological, and social assistance.

However, when the International Criminal Tribunals for the former Yugoslavia and Rwanda were created, victims were again left apart. Victims did not have *locus standi* in these courts, nor were they empowered to claim reparation for the harms they suffered.

It is only with the adoption of the Rome Statute of the International Criminal Court that victims were finally placed at the heart of international criminal justice. Henceforth, the rights and interests of victims have been fully recognised at the international level.

Pursuant to the Rome Statute, victims now are able to substantively participate in the Court's proceedings at any stage. This, of course, does not mean victims now have the right to initiate proceedings or a *constitution de partie civile*, but it does amount to a critical development for victims since victims are now entitled to present to the Court their views and concerns where their personal interests are affected.

The goal of facilitating victims' participation should be to champion the issues victims consistently have described as most important to them. A review of the literature produced on this subject suggests that, among the most important interests of victims in the context of their interaction with a criminal justice system, well beyond even the right to reparations, is the right to receive information regarding their case. Victims also value information and clarity concerning their particular role in the criminal proceedings, and need to feel that the system gives them the appropriate amount of respect. Finally, and perhaps most fundamentally, victims are more likely to be satisfied with the criminal justice system if they feel their voices are being heard.

Involvement of victims in criminal proceedings indeed also requires taking into account the realities of each specific country situation, as well as factors involved in the prosecution of complex and lengthy trials, likely involving hundreds or thousands of victims, in locations far from where the relevant crimes have occurred. As this book commendably points out, victim advocates must take great measures to avoid creating in the victims erroneous hopes and expectations that cannot be fulfilled, or that will leave victims otherwise frustrated.

The legal instruments of the Court, however, unfortunately do not explicitly detail the modalities of victims' participation in the proceedings. According to Rule 89(1) of the Rules of Procedure and Evidence, for example, "*the Chamber shall* [. . .] *specify the proceedings and manner in which participation is considered appropriate*." Moreover, Article 68(3) of the Rome Statute specifies somewhat vaguely that "*[w]here the personal interests of victims are affected, the Court shall permit their views and concerns to be presented and considered at stages of the proceedings determined to be appropriate by the Court and in a manner which is not prejudicial to or inconsistent with the rights of the accused and a fair and impartial trial*." Determining the meaning of these provisions has resulted in considerable legal controversy.

The first proceedings before the Court have shown how complex the victim-related legal framework is, and have demonstrated that effective and meaningful participation of victims in the proceedings depends mainly on the Chambers' interpretation of the legal texts' provisions. The deeply challenging questions of what the purpose of victims' participation in the context of the ICC proceedings scheme is (or should be), and how it should be implemented, are the very ones this book addresses.

In light of these considerable challenges, this important book contributes significantly to practitioners' efforts to illuminate what has been described as the main novelty of the Rome Statute: participation of victims in the proceedings.

The book, for example, skillfully explores the legacy of abuse and suffering which specifically led to the creation of the ICC and to a more comprehensive development of victims' rights under international law. It also carefully details the proceedings before the ICC, lays out the role of different actors, and finally identifies alternative avenues for the effective implementation of victims' rights in the proceedings before the Court.

The author's considerable experience and competence in international criminal law and litigation allow him to adroitly analyze crucial issues on both a theoretical and practical level that is understandable to practitioners, but also of great value to the non-specialized public. The result is a book which expertly provides the reader with an insight into the profound issues at stake, as well as with a comprehensive picture of the proceedings before the ICC, and the challenges faced by both the Court and actors in said proceedings.

This book in the end leads to a dramatically-improved comprehension of victims' rights by significantly advancing the debate on victims' participation within the framework of the Rome Statute, and by enhancing our shared understanding of how to most effectively and responsively address victims' needs, as well as their interest in participating in the proceedings.

—Paolina Massidda
Principal Counsel of the International Criminal Court's Office of Public Counsel for Victims

November 26, 2009
The Hague, Netherlands

About the Author

T. MARKUS FUNK is a federal prosecutor in Chicago, Illinois, in the Organized Crime and Public Corruption section of the United States Attorney's Office. Mr. Funk previously served in the Major Cases and Narcotics/Cartel sections in Chicago. In 2008, Mr. Funk received the United States Department of Justice's Attorney General's Award (the "John Marshall Award"), the Department's highest trial performance award. Mr. Funk received the award for the prosecution of the landmark mob-murder racketeering conspiracy known as "Operation Family Secrets."

From 2004–2006, Mr. Funk served as the United States Department of Justice Resident Legal Advisor for Kosovo, providing training and advice to international war crimes judges, defense attorneys, victim advocates, investigators, and prosecutors throughout the Balkans. During this time, Mr. Funk published the *Kosovo Trial Skills Handbook*, which remains the most cited source in Kosovo's *Compilation of Applicable Criminal Laws*. For his service abroad, the United States Department of State awarded Mr. Funk the Superior Honor Award. After returning to the United States, Mr. Funk was appointed the Co-Chair of the American Bar Association's Human Trafficking and Organized Crime Committee, and joined the ABA's Darfur Task Force.

Prior to joining the Department of Justice in 2000, Mr. Funk was a Lecturer in Law at Oxford University (St. Catherine's College), as well as a law clerk to the Honorable Morris S. Arnold, United States Court of Appeals for the 8th Circuit, and the Honorable Catherine D. Perry, United States District Court, St. Louis, Missouri. Mr. Funk has also taught at the University of Chicago School of Law, Northwestern University School of Law, the University of Pristina (Kosovo), the University of Arkansas at Little Rock Law School, Loyola University of Chicago, and the United States Department of Justice's National Advocacy Center, and has authored numerous popular and academic articles and book chapters on a variety of legal and non-legal topics.

Mr. Funk thanks the leadership, management, and staff of the International Criminal Court, including members of the Office of the Prosecutor, Office of

Public Counsel for the Defense, Office of Public Counsel for Victims, and legal officers of the Court, for meeting with him and candidly discussing various issues examined in this book. Mr. Funk, moreover, is grateful to M. Cherif Bassiouni, Amar S. Bhachu, Andrew S. Boutros, Antonio Cassese, Patsy Engelhard, Alexandra Guhr, Pierre St. Hilaire, William R. Hogan, Brianne McGonigle, Dastid Pallaska, David Scheffer, and Brenda Sue Thornton for their valuable insights and comments on earlier drafts of the book.

Although the author has obtained written permission from his employer, the United States Department of Justice, to write and publish this book, the views expressed herein are the personal views of the author, and do not necessarily reflect the views or positions of the United States Department of Justice. Any errors or omissions are the author's alone.

PART I

Introduction

WAR AND ITS ACCOMPANYING ATROCITIES have been part of the human experience since the earliest days of man. Although the refined, reassuring language of modernity and diplomacy may now ring familiar, as a practical matter, war's severity and toll on humankind have hardly relented. Indeed, since World War II there have been some 250 conflicts throughout the world, leading to an estimated 70–170 million victims.[1] Experts estimate that during the twentieth century, warlords and military leaders subjected approximately four times more civilians to crimes against humanity and war crimes than the combined total of soldiers killed in all international wars during the same time. Unlike diseases or natural disasters, the injuries and tragedies of war are largely self-inflicted.

With the advent of the modern media, however, the world has become increasingly sensitive to episodes of organized and methodical state-sponsored killing, maiming, mutilating, raping, and torturing of civilians. Such conduct, often broadcasted live, is now near-universally condemned as out of bounds, striking at the very heart of civilized society. In response to well-documented outrages committed openly and notoriously in now-familiar places like Rwanda, Cambodia, Bosnia, and Kosovo, the international

1. *See generally* M. Cherif Bassiouni, *International Recognition of Victims' Rights*, 6 HUMAN RIGHTS L. REV. 203, 209–10 (2006) ("Despite the post-WWII human rights conventions, within 50 years of WWII conflicts of an international and non-international character resulted in casualties double those of the two World Wars. An estimated 70–170 million people have died since WWII in over 250 conflicts around the world."); *see also* STÉPHANE COURTOIS, *ET AL.*, THE BLACK BOOK OF COMMUNISM: CRIMES, TERROR, REPRESSION 4 (1999) (providing an exhaustive chronicle of crimes perpetrated to advance communist political ideology); RUDOLPH RUMMEL, DEATH BY GOVERNMENT 9 (1994) (examining some 8,000 reports of government-caused death—which Rummel terms "democide"—and estimating that during the approximately 250 post-World War II conflicts, governments killed some 169 million of their own people).

community in the late 1990s joined together to establish the International Criminal Court ("ICC").[2]

The ICC is the first permanent juridical body with the stated purpose of bringing to justice perpetrators of "atrocity crimes" such as genocide, war crimes, and crimes against humanity.[3] The ICC, however, does not, as observers often assume, sit above all other courts as the world's supreme adjudicator of atrocity crimes. Instead, the ICC is designed to function more like an "international catch-all court," capturing those cases that fall through the cracks when domestic legal systems are unwilling or unable to investigate and prosecute them. The Court's mandate is, therefore, to deliver justice when no other mechanisms are available.

Despite a slow and rocky start, the ICC's efforts to hold the perpetrators of atrocity crimes accountable have intensified in recent years. But beyond simply investigating and prosecuting humanity's most ruthless villains, the ICC has ambitiously sketched out a broader restorative mandate for itself.[4] More specifically, the ICC, itself a first-of-its-kind institution, among its many innovative missions singularly enshrined the rights of atrocity crime victims to participate directly in the actual proceedings instituted against their alleged victimizers. The ICC empowers victims to participate in the proceedings of, and to seek recompense from, those who terrorized and abused them. This book focuses on these considerable efforts to stanch human

---

2. The ICC is alternatively referred to herein as "the Court."

3. The term "atrocity crime" is an all-inclusive reference to the four so-called "core crimes" (war crimes, genocide, crimes against humanity, and the as-of yet undefined crime of aggression), and, in this context, was coined by Ambassador David Scheffer. *See generally* David Scheffer, *The Future of Atrocity Law*, 25 SUFFOLK TRANSNAT'L L. REV. 389 (2002); *see also* David Scheffer, *The Merits of Unifying Terms: 'Atrocity Crimes' and 'Atrocity Law'*, 2 GENOCIDE STUD. & PREVENTION 91, 91–96 (2007); David Scheffer, *Genocide and Atrocity Crimes*, 1 GENOCIDE STUD. & PREVENTION 229, 229–50 (2006).

4. "Restorative justice" refers to a theory of criminology dating back centuries in which the crime and wrongdoing are considered acts against the individual, rather than against the state or the collective (more on this later). Advocates of restorative justice posit that the person harmed must play the central role in the criminal justice process, and that the person who culpably did the harming should be accountable and accept personal responsibility for his conduct. Although the traditional criminal justice systems seek to determine what laws were broken, who broke those laws, and what sentence the law-breaker should receive, restorative justice's aim is to determine who was harmed, what that person's needs are, and who should be obligated to meet those needs. Restitutional sanctions, intended to force the wrongdoer to "make whole" the person wronged, are therefore a traditional, and indeed ancient, restorative aspect of criminal justice systems.

suffering and piece together the lives of the victims of unspeakable affronts to human dignity.

Invoking its undoubtedly noble purpose, proponents of the ICC steadfastly demand that the world community take the Court seriously, both as a model of reform and as a crime-fighter. Why, ask Court supporters, would any country interested in justice and world peace not support the Court's mission by signing on as a State Party?

One of the challenges, however, is that the international community's track record for bringing to justice the world's most notorious criminals and their henchmen has sadly, on the whole, been somewhat underwhelming.[5] The ICC, for reasons discussed later, at present arguably provides no exception to this percieved broader deficiency.[6]

Sceptics may, as a consequence, be tempted to reject out of hand the ICC's victim-centric efforts as yet another example of the international community's much-talk-little-action routine. Well-intentioned rhetoric, deployed by diplomats often possessing only the vaguest understanding of what it takes to achieve a criminal conviction, is, after all, not a substitute for professionally-conducted investigation and prosecution leading to the imprisonment of the world's premier wrongdoers. Indeed, threats and promises not followed up by concrete action can, in the long run, become justice's most devastating enemy. To the sceptic, the significant, and often quite obvious, institutional flaws discussed herein reveal a Court ill-equipped to handle the monumental task it is facing. The Court, the sceptic's argument goes, is,

---

5. Consider, for example, the International Criminal Tribunal for the Former Yugoslavia ("ICTY"), with a broad jurisdiction covering four separate bloody conflicts (namely, Croatia, Bosnia-Herzegovina, Kosovo, and the Former Yugoslav Republic of Macedonia), and as of 2009 employing more than 1,100 persons. As discussed in more detail in Part II, since becoming operational some sixteen years ago, the ICTY has spent over $1.5 billion pursuing Balkan war criminals. To date, however, the ICTY has only sentenced 61 individuals (in rough numbers, this equates to a present total expenditure of some $25 million per final sentence). Moreover, although convicted of genocide, war crimes, and crimes against humanity, more than a third of the 60 men (and one woman) with "completed cases" received prison sentences of *less* than ten years. Indeed, only *ten* received sentences in excess of twenty years. It is, therefore, debatable to what extent the ICTY has truly lived up to its own motto of "[b]ringing war criminals to justice, bringing justice to victims." *See* www.icty.org.

6. The ICC has a present annual budget of approximately $150 million, with more than 700 employees. Despite its significant resources, and a plethora of worthy targets, in its first seven years of operation, the Court has not issued a single verdict, sentence, or victim reparations order. For a discussion of some of the likely causes of this present lack of more tangible results, as well as suggestions for reform, *see* Part IV(J).

therefore, in a particularly weak position to demand the world community's respect and dutiful adherence.

But, whatever the Court's possible present deficiencies, the answer is not to give up on it, or, even worse, to seek to chop it down. In fact, there is no indication that the young Court, despite its admittedly mixed record to date, will not continue on as international justice's focal point. Simply pointing to the Court's shortfalls, throwing one's arms in the air, and walking away from the entire enterprise is therefore not an acceptable response.

Instead of focusing purely on the more lacklustre aspects of the Court's performance, the solution this book proposes is real and meaningful reform, which, if applied in a targeted manner, can help catapult the ICC towards its full restorative potential. This is, in part, because at its core, the ICC offers something unique and unavailable anywhere else for millions of victims, namely, the opportunity for victim participation in the trials of their victimizers. The ICC, for all of its arguable shortfalls, seeks to break a new path by promising victim-centric restorative justice to those who traditionally have remained voiceless outsiders to the legal process, and by providing the legal framework and tools necessary for this undertaking.

And with millions massacred in the many post-World War II conflicts, and considering the increased visibility of such opprobrious crimes, the need for internationally coordinated victim redress indeed presses. In order to meet its restorative objectives, the ICC announced a host of ambitious and laudable victim-oriented goals. One need not look further for instances of this forward-looking agenda than the ICC's mission statement, set forth in the Rome Statute's Preamble, which describes the ICC's goal as "guarantee[ing] lasting respect for and the enforcement of international justice" by "put[ting] an end to impunity for the perpetrators of [international] crimes and thus ... contribut[ing] to the prevention of such crimes ...."

The Preamble leaves little room for doubt: The primary purpose of the ICC is to end cruelty and to bring those responsible for atrocities "to justice"—the same desires as those of the victims, of course. To effectuate the expansive aim of providing a more fulsome measure of restorative justice, and to reflect the recognition that "during this century millions of children, women, and men have been victims of unimaginable atrocities that deeply shock the conscience of humanity,"[7] the Assembly of States Parties of the ICC enacted

7. Preamble, Rome Statute. *See also* George P. Fletcher, *Justice and Fairness in the Protection of Crime Victims*, 9 LEWIS & CLARK L. REV. 547, 551 (2005) ("The purpose of the Rome Statute is to vindicate the interests of these victims.").

a host of provisions addressing the protection and restoration of atrocity crime victims.

This book shines a light on this particularly important and complex, but under-examined, aspect of the ICC's broader agenda. The goal here is to equip lawyers, victim representatives,[8] academics, victim-related non-governmental organizations (NGO's), government officials, legal advisors, and other interested parties with a meaningful understanding of the promises, and potential challenges and pitfalls, of pursuing victims' rights, and engaging in victim advocacy, at the ICC.

Referenced throughout this book is the kaleidoscope of at-times confusing ICC articles, rules, and regulations, all of which the victim representative must disentangle and understand.[9] Familiarity with these enactments is, indeed, the critical preparatory step toward competent victim advocacy. That said, the principal focus must be on sound, effective advocacy skills, not on the full range of fine nuances and idiosyncrasies of developing ICC procedure and practice. To that end, these pages will summarize key ICC rulings and provisions to illustrate current, ever-evolving ICC practices as they relate to victim advocacy. Of course, it remains the victim-representative's responsibility to conduct factual and case-specific legal research in order to determine the contemporary state of the law as it relates to a particular situation.

Effective advocacy, in the end, is both an art and a science. Diligent representation of victims' rights—whatever form these rights take over the next years, decades, and beyond—requires the representative to consider all options at his disposal suited to addressing the client-victim's personal, emotional, financial, philosophical, and legal goals. The paramount purpose of this book, therefore, is to empower victim representatives and other interested ICC participants and observers with a realistic and practical understanding of the ICC's victim-centric promises, mandates, challenges, and shortcomings. In the course of doing so, this book will attempt to advance the discussion of best practices, and will frankly raise some basic questions and concerns that, to date, have remained notably unaddressed during the otherwise heated public debate over this central international institution.

---

8. The term "victim representative" used herein is a reference to those legal advocates to whom the Chamber has granted formal recognition as in-court legal representatives of victims. The term "victim advocate," on the other hand, is a broader term referring to individuals—lawyers and non-lawyer alike—who wish to assist victims at the ICC. *See generally* Part VI.

9. Certain key victim-related provisions and materials are included in the Appendix.

PART II

A Legacy of Abuse and Suffering leads to the Birth of the ICC

THE WELL-DOCUMENTED "ROAD TO ROME," a common reference to the ICC's founding Rome Statute, was as long as it was serpentine. Well before lawyers and politicians gathered in the 1990s to begin the drafting process, there were those who, grappling with the evidence of man's capacity for inhumanity, expressed their belief in the need for a transnational tribunal with the capacity to deter atrocities and punish those who engineered and executed them.

Back in 1873, Swiss lawyer, Nobel Prize nominee, and co-founder of the International Committee of the Red Cross,[1] Louis Gabriel Gustave Moynier, presented one of the first proposals for the creation of a permanent and impartial international criminal court. Moynier, still deeply disturbed by the atrocities committed during the Franco-Prussian War, observed:

> A treaty was not a law imposed by a superior authority on its subordinates . . . [but] only a contract whose signatories cannot decree penalties against themselves since there would be no one to implement them. The only reasonable guarantee should lie in the creation of international jurisdiction with the necessary power to compel obedience. . . . The prospect for those concerned of being arraigned before the tribunal of public conscience if they do not keep to their commitments and of being ostracized by civilized nations, constitutes a powerful enough deterrent for us to believe ourselves correct in thinking it better than any other.[2]

---

1. During its early years, the Red Cross was also known as the "International Committee for Relief of the Wounded."

2. LOUIS GABRIEL GUSTAVE MOYNIER, ETUDE SUR LA CONVENTION DE GENEVE POUR L'AMELIORATION DU SORT DES MILITAIRES BLESSES DANS LES ARMEES EN CAMPAGNE 300 (1870) (English translation *in* PIERRE BOISSIER, FROM SOLFERINO TO TSUSHIMA: HISTORY OF THE INTERNATIONAL COMMITTEE OF THE RED CROSS 282 (1963)).

Moynier's proposal, however, failed to garner the support of the world community because the nations feared surrendering sovereignty to such an international adjudicating body.

Following World War I, the drafters of the 1919 Treaty of Versailles picked up on Moynier's earlier call for internationalized justice by seeking to set up an *ad hoc* international court to try German Kaiser Wilhelm II, as well as his Prussian military leaders. Kaiser Wilhelm II was Germany's third and final Kaiser, losing his throne as a consequence of Germany's defeat during World War I. This push for such a transnational system of justice, however, for a host of practical and political reasons, did not prove successful. Not only did neutral Holland provide the Kaiser (now ironic) refuge,[3] but the French and British were weary of fermenting latent public anger in Germany against the weak Weimar Republic. At bottom, the victors were concerned that hostile public sentiment would boil over in the face of such trials.

The German Supreme Court was left to handle the criminal cases that the German prosecutors brought under German penal law against the dozen mid and lower-level German officers.[4] The post-war proposal for an international court, nonetheless, was historic in its own right, as it reflected the Allied victors' belief that they had the right (if not the duty) to set up an international court for the purpose of holding to account, through law, those accused of war crimes.

The Treaty of Versailles also led to the creation of the League of Nations, which in 1920, through the Commission of Jurists, began drafting legal instruments to establish the Permanent Court of International Justice, called for by the League's Covenant.[5] In 1937, the League in fact adopted a treaty for the creation of an international criminal court. The proposal, however, as during Moynier's day, once again failed due to insufficient state support.[6] Events in history a few decades later were to provide the necessary impetus for a more robust call for "international justice."

---

3. The Kaiser in fact remained in Holland until his death in 1941.

4. *See generally* Karl Arthur Hochkammer, *The Yugoslav War Crimes Tribunal: The Compatibility of Peace, Policy, and International Law*, 29 VAND. J. OF TRANS'L L. 119, 132–40 (1995) (describing the war tribunals in Leipzig).

5. *See* Protocol of Signature Relating to the Statute of the Permanent Court of International Justice Provided for by Article 14 of the Covenant of the League of Nations Articles 1–6, December 16, 1920, 6 L.N.T.S. 380 (1921).

6. As of January 1, 1941, no state had ratified this early international criminal court treaty.

In 1948, following the atrocities of World War II chronicled so graphically at the Nuremberg trials[7] and in the Tokyo Tribunal,[8] the United Nations ("U.N.") General Assembly formally recognized the need for a permanent international court. Such a court had to be capable of addressing the type of state-sanctioned terror that, at the time, was so vividly in the minds of world leaders, as well as the world's public at large.[9]

The General Assembly in 1948 took the first steps, adopting the Convention on the Prevention and Punishment of the Crime of Genocide. The Convention called for accused war criminals to be tried "by such international penal tribunals as may have jurisdiction," and formally invited the International Law Commission ("ILC") to "study the desirability and possibility of establishing an international judicial organ for the trials of persons charged with genocide." Perhaps for the first time, the establishment of a permanent international criminal court appeared to be just over the horizon.

In the early 1950s, the ILC was, in fact, fully occupied with the serious undertaking of drafting just such a foundational statute. Gridlock caused by the Cold War, however, temporarily derailed the effort. The General Assembly abandoned the proposal pending agreement on an international Code of Crimes, as well as on an acceptable definition of the "crime of aggression."[10]

---

7. Although there were other trials held in the various German zones the Allies occupied, the most famous proceedings were the 12 held before the American court in Nuremberg.

8. The Tokyo Trials were based on the January 19, 1946, Charter for the Far East. The prosecution team charged 28 high-ranking defendants, including four premiers, three foreign ministers, and one colonel. In the end, 16 of the 28 were convicted, and 7 were sentenced to death. For a detailed accounting of the Tokyo Tribunal, *see* YUMA TOTANI, THE TOKYO WAR CRIMES TRIBUNAL: THE PURSUIT OF JUSTICE IN THE WAKE OF WORLD WAR II (2009).

9. *See* Leila Nadya Sadat, *The Establishment of the International Criminal Court: From The Hague to Rome and Back Again*, 8 J. INT'L. L. & PRAC. 97, 100–16 (1999) ("The atrocities of the Second World War rekindled interest in the establishment of a permanent international criminal court. The model statutes proposed by jurists gave way to the pressure of political events, however, and the Charters of the Nuremberg and Tokyo tribunals took their place. Although not the first international criminal trials in history, the Nuremberg and Tokyo trials are the first major precedents of our time.").

10. *See generally* Jonathan A. Bush, *"The Supreme . . . Crime" and Its Origins: The Lost Legislative History of the Crime of Aggressive War*, 102 COLUM. L. REV. 2324, 2390–91 (2002) ("But the UN congealed into the familiar Cold War blocs almost as fast as Nuremberg eased up against aggressive criminality. As a result, by 1950, both conversations about aggression were routinized. In the Security Council, the world of diplomacy and politics, aggression was a political accusation, and it was almost always log-jammed by the rigidity of the

In the intervening years, the states at the U.N. intermittently discussed the creation of a permanent institution in which to try alleged war criminals.[11]

Ironically, it took the proliferating narcotics trade of the late 1980s to cause an unlikely international prime mover, Trinidad and Tobago, to once again resurrect the long-retired concept of an international tribunal created by the world community, and purpose-built to handle international crimes. In 1989, at the request of Trinidad and Tobago's then-Prime Minister (and later President) Arthur Robinson,[12] the General Assembly requested the ILC include within its consideration of a draft code a discussion of the potential for an international criminal court or other mechanism with jurisdiction over, among other offences, what Trinidad and Tobago viewed as the evolving international crime of drug trafficking.[13]

Some five years later, in 1994, the ILC presented to the General Assembly its first draft statute establishing the ICC. The ILC, moreover, recommended that a conference be convened at which the plenipotentiaries[14] would negotiate the necessary treaties to enact the Court's statute. In response, the

---

Cold War alliances and the Security Council veto. In the other world of law schools and the International Law Commission . . ., the entity affiliated with the UN to which the General Assembly had referred Nuremberg issues and aggression for further study, aggression meant the opportunity for unrealistic proposals and pie-in-the-sky debates about improved definitions."). Defining the crime of aggression, as discussed in Part IV(C)(4), continues to be an endeavor steeped in considerable controversy.

11. *See, e.g.,* Convention on the Prevention and Punishment of the Crime of Genocide (January 12, 1951), 78 U.N.T.S. 277 (1951) (the Convention declared the need for establishing a permanent international court); United Nations Declaration of Basic Principles of Justice for Victims of Crime and Abuse of Power, G.A. Res. 40/34, Annex paras. 4, 6(b), U.N. GAOR, 40th Sess., Supp. No. 53, U.N. Doc. A/40/53 (November 29, 1985) (providing that victims should have "access to the mechanisms of justice and to prompt redress . . . for the harm they have suffered," and that the "views and concerns of victims [should] be presented and considered at appropriate stages of the proceedings"). *See also* Leila Sadat Wexler, *The Proposed Permanent International Criminal Court: An Appraisal*, 29 CORNELL INT. L. J. 665, 677 (1996).

12. President Robinson later explained his view that the purpose of the Court was to protect "the little [ordinary] people all over the world" by holding "people at the top . . . accountable, particularly in the case of gross violations of human rights and atrocities, such as those that had occurred in Rwanda, the former Yugoslavia, Cambodia and Burundi." United Nations Press Briefing (October 9, 1997), www.un.org/News/briefings/docs/1997/19971009.tnt.html.

13. *See* G.A. Res. 44/39, P 1, U.N. GAOR, 44th Sess., Supp. No. 49, U.N. Doc. A/RES/44/39 (December 4, 1989).

14. The Latin term "plenipotentiaries" translates into "full powers," and in this context refers to diplomats who are fully authorized to act on behalf of their respective governments.

General Assembly created the Ad Hoc Committee on the Establishment of the ICC. The Committee met twice in 1995. A complex treaty process unfolded, during which the participating sovereign nations negotiated the circumstances under which they would cede the primacy of their jurisdiction to an international body for the purpose of investigating, and prosecuting, alleged perpetrators of atrocity crimes.[15]

After the U.N. General Assembly reviewed the Committee's report, it organized the U.N. Preparatory Committee on the Establishment of the ICC. The Committee was tasked with generating a comprehensive draft text for the creation of an international court. Between 1996 and 1998, the Preparatory Committee met on six occasions at the U.N. headquarters in New York City.

In January 1998, the Preparatory Committee gathered for an intercessional meeting in Zutphen, Holland, to restructure and consolidate the various draft articles into a final omnibus draft. The General Assembly found promise in the Preparatory Committee's draft, and convened the U.N. Conference of Plenipotentiaries on the Establishment of an ICC in the Netherlands. The objective was to "finalize and adopt a convention on the establishment" of a permanent international court. This institution, proponents argued, would have the benefit of being free from mandates of a specific time and place, unlike the *ad hoc* tribunals with narrow jurisdictional mandates set up during the aftermath of the atrocities in Rwanda, Sierra Leone, Cambodia, the former Yugoslavia, East Timor, and elsewhere.

The purpose-built tribunals following these conflicts, after all, took years to become operational, and, to some extent, failed to garner the full measure of public support or tangible results the victims and the international community had hoped (and richly paid) for. Consider, for example, that as of March 23, 2009, the ICTY, staffed and fully operational since the early 1990's, had 1,118 employees and a generous annual budget of $342,322,300.[16] The total cash outlay for the ICTY has to date exceeded $1.5 billion, yet the Tribunal in the past 16 years has only sentenced 61 perpetrators. These 60 men and one woman with "completed cases" committed genocide, war

---

15. For a first-hand account of this treaty process, *see* David Scheffer & Ashely Cox, *The Constitutionality of the Rome Statute of the International Criminal Court*, 98 JOURNAL OF CRIMINAL LAW & CRIMINOLOGY 983, 989–93 (2008).

16. *See* www.icty.org./sid/325. The ICTY had jurisdiction over the conflicts in Croatia (1991–95), Bosnia and Herzegovina (1992–95), Kosovo (1998–99), and the Former Yugoslav Republic of Macedonia (2001).

crimes, and crimes against humanity, yet over a third of them received terms of imprisonment of 10 years or less.[17] Moreover, only ten received sentences in excess of twenty years imprisonment. To many, this relatively feeble record places into doubt whether the ICTY lived up to its self-described purpose of "bringing war criminals to justice and bringing justice to victims."[18] In any event, establishment of a permanent court, it was hoped, would lead to swifter and more sure justice by overcoming many of the deficiencies hampering *ad hoc* tribunals like the ICTY.

The now-famous June 15–July 17, 1998, "Rome Conference" involved representatives of some 160 countries, as well as countless NGOs. The negotiators hoped to overcome the omnipresent dilemma of reconciling the interests of "sovereignty" with the "international rule of law."[19] The negotiators' central agreement in this regard was the introduction of the principle of "complementarity," which was designed to ensure that the Court would only have jurisdiction over those cases which national jurisdictions were either unable or unwilling to effectively investigate and prosecute. In large part due to the considerable efforts on the part of the ILC, as well as the intense drafting negotiations among governments (including, prominently, the United States), on July 17, 1998, the negotiating countries approved the Rome Statute to thunderous applause, jubilation, handshakes, and hugs.

When the votes were tallied, 120 nations had voted in favor of adopting the Rome Statute of the ICC, with the United States, Israel, China, Iraq, Libya, Yemen, and Qatar voting against the treaty, and 21 other states abstaining. Although the United States was, as discussed below, among the handful of nations that voted against the final text, it, as one of the permanent members of the United Nations Security Council, unquestionably played a major role in creating the Court and advancing Administration objectives by being fully involved in the drafting of the ICC's Rules of Procedure and Evidence and the Elements of Crime.[20] The United States negotiation team, headed by

---

17. *See* www.icty.org./action/cases/4; www.icty.org./sections/TheCases/KeyFigures.

18. *See* www.icty.org.

19. *See generally* BRUCE BROOMHALL, INTERNATIONAL JUSTICE AND THE INTERNATIONAL CRIMINAL COURT: BETWEEN SOVEREIGNTY AND THE RULE OF LAW 68 (2003) ("The former President of the [ICTY], Antonio Cassese, describes the choice in stark terms: either one supports the international rule of law, or one supports state sovereignty. The two are not, in his view, compatible.").

20. These important documents were adopted by consensus, with the United States' approval, in June 2000. *See* Barbara Crossette, *U.S. Gains Compromise on War Crimes Tribunal*, N.Y. TIMES (June 30, 2000), at A6.

Ambassador David Scheffer, was, for example, instrumental in efforts to define "war crimes" and "crimes against humanity," and to exclude drug trafficking from the statute. [21]

The Preparatory Commission thereafter specifically tackled the task of negotiating the complementary documents, including the Rules of Procedure and Evidence, the Elements of Crimes, the Relationship Agreement between the Court and the U.N., the Financial Regulations, and the Agreement on the Privileges and Immunities of the Court. During the September 2000 Millennium Summit, U.N. Secretary General Kofi Annan, as anticipated, lent his support to this undertaking, and backed the drafters and negotiators: "I strongly urge all countries to sign and ratify the Rome Statute of the International Criminal Court. . . ."[22]

On December 31, 2000, the day marking the deadline for signature of the Rome Statute without nations' first having ratified it, United States President Bill Clinton joined the 137 other governments who signed the Rome Statute. Even though few at the time viewed U.S. ratification as likely, with the President's signature the United States could remain formally involved in the follow-on negotiations over the Court's establishment.

Next began the ratification process by the individual nations. The halfway mark for bringing the Rome Statute into force was reached on April 30, 2001, when the small, landlocked principality of Andorra became the 30th state to ratify the Rome Statute. Roughly one year later, on April 11, 2002, the much-anticipated 60th ratification was deposited during a special ceremony

---

21. *See* David J. Scheffer, *The United States and the International Criminal Court*, 93 AM. J. INT'L L. 12, 12–14 (1999) ("[United States] Administration lawyers subjected the ILC drafts to extensive internal review and analysis. U.S. objectives included a significant role for the United Nations Security Council in the referral of cases to the court, specific and properly defined war crimes in the statute of the court, exclusion of drug trafficking and the hard-to-define crime of aggression from the statute, and further study of our deep concerns about including crimes of international terrorism in the statute . . . . The U.S. delegation succeeded in its effort to broaden the complementarity regime to include a deferral to national jurisdictions at the outset of a referral of an overall situation to the ICC rather than only at a preliminary stage of the work on any particular case. We also succeeded, with the help of many governments, in restructuring the procedures of the court into a more comprehensible and rational sequence of steps. We were unsuccessful at stemming the support for the ICC prosecutor to initiate cases himself absent any referral of an overall situation by a state party or the Security Council. There was also growing opposition to any role for the Security Council in determining which situations should be referred to the court, even those situations regarding which the Council was exercising its Chapter VII responsibilities.").

22. KOFI A. ANNAN, WE THE PEOPLES: THE ROLE OF THE UNITED NATIONS ON THE 21ST CENTURY 69 (2000).

at U.N. headquarters.[23] Marking this occasion, General Assembly President Han Seung-soo stated:

> Since 1948, following the Nuremberg and Tokyo tribunals after the Second World War, the establishment of a permanent international criminal court has remained one of the most important goals of the General Assembly of the United Nations. The scope, scale, and nature of atrocities that have been committed in many parts of the world during the last 20 years reminded us of the urgency of creating a permanent mechanism to bring to justice the perpetrators of such inhuman crimes as genocide, ethnic cleansing, sexual slavery, and maiming.[24]

On May 6, 2002, however, United States President George W. Bush, concerned in large part with the possibility of ICC prosecutions of American soldiers, military leaders, and government officials, informed the U.N. that the United States no longer considered itself bound by the Treaty as a signatory nation. President Bush formally rendered inactive the United States signature.[25]

---

23. The countries depositing their treaty instruments during this ceremony were Bosnia & Herzegovina, Bulgaria, Cambodia, Democratic Republic of Congo, Ireland, Jordan, Mongolia, Niger, Romania, and Slovakia.

24. *United Nations Press Release*, GA/SM/292 L/T/4367 (November 4, 2002).

25. The United States Congress, concerned with American involvement in the ICC, passed the American Service Members Protection Act. *See* 22 U.S.C. § 7421(9) ("In addition to exposing members of the Armed Forces of the United States to the risk of international criminal prosecution, the Rome Statute creates a risk that the President and other senior elected and appointed officials of the United States Government may be prosecuted by the International Criminal Court. Particularly if the Preparatory Commission agrees on a definition of the Crime of Aggression over United States objections, senior United States officials may be at risk of criminal prosecution for national security decisions involving such matters as responding to acts of terrorism, preventing the proliferation of weapons of mass destruction, and deterring aggression. No less than members of the Armed Forces of the United States, senior officials of the United States Government should be free from the risk of prosecution by the International Criminal Court, especially with respect to official actions taken by them to protect the national interests of the United States."). The Act not only prohibited United States cooperation with the ICC, but in fact sought to punish those nations that joined the ICC. In 2007, however, the United States Congress repealed the punitive measures of this Act. *See* John Warner National Defense Authorization Act for Fiscal Year 2007, Pub. L. 109-364, § 1210, 120 Stat. 2083 (amending the American Service-Members' Protection Act to remove International Military Education and Training restrictions); National Defense Authorization Act for Fiscal Year 2008, Pub. L. 110-181, § 1212, 122 Stat. 3 (amending the American Service-Members' Protection Act to eliminate restrictions on Foreign Military Financing assistance laws).

The Rome Statute took formal force and effect of law on July 1, 2002, and the Assembly of States Parties met for the first time in September 2002. September 9, 2002, marked the official opening of the ICC Article 36 nomination period to fill the judicial and prosecutorial positions (the closing date was November 30, 2002). Between March and June 2003, the Assembly swore in the first 18 judges of the ICC,[26] as well as the first prosecutor (Luis Moreno-Ocampo), and appointed the Registrar of the Court (Bruno Cathala). The initial election of 18 judges—based on anonymous ballots cast by the representatives of the State Parties—was made from a field of 43 candidates. The winning judges drew lots to determine whether they were assigned to three, six, or nine year terms (with those serving a three-year term being eligible for re-election in 2006). One hundred thirty years after Moynier's vision of an international body adjudicating atrocity crimes, the Court was ready to accept investigations and to hear cases.

The Bush Administration's concerns about United States' involvement with the ICC were, however, more nuanced than many have recognized. Consider, for example, the November 2008 statement of Department of State Legal Advisor John Bellinger:

> [E]ven if the United States is not a party to the Rome Statute, there are many ways for the United States and ICC parties to work constructively on international criminal justice issues. In recent years, this Administration has sought to steer the focus away from unnecessary wrangling over the issues that divide the ICC's supporters and opponents towards finding practical and constructive ways to cooperate in advancing our common values and our shared commitment to international justice.
>
> We've re-emphasized as a core principle of our policy our respect for the decisions of other states to join the ICC, and have acknowledged that the court can have a valuable role to play in certain cases. On this point, Darfur is exhibit A.

John B. Bellinger III, *U.S. Perspectives on International Criminal Justice, Remarks at the Fletcher School of Law and Diplomacy* (November 14, 2008), at www.amicc.org/docs/Bellinger_11_14_2008.pdf.

26. As of this writing, the judges of the Court are Sang-Hyun Song (Republic of Korea), Fatoumata Dembele Diarra (Mali), Hans-Peter Kaul (Germany), Elizabeth Odio Benito (Costa Rica), Akua Kuenyehia (Ghana), Erkki Kourula (Finland), Anita Ušacka (Latvia), Sir Adrian Fulford (United Kingdom), Sylvia Steiner (Brazil), Ekaterina Trendafilova (Bulgaria), Daniel David Ntanda Nsereko (Uganda), Bruno Cotte (France), Joyce Aluoch (Kenya), Sanji Mmasenono Monogeng (Botswana), Christine van den Wyngaert (Belgium), Cuno Tarfusser (Italy), and René Blattman (Bolivia). The sitting judges backgrounds are summarized in www.icc-cpi.int/Menus/ICC/Structure+of+the+Court/Chambers/The+Judges/. Judge Fumiko Saiga (Japan) passed away on April 24, 2009. Eight other judges have, since their 2003 elections, left the Court. Only one judge (Tuiloma Neroni Slade from Samoa) was defeated in the 2006 election. Although judges can be removed for "serious misconduct" or "a serious breach of his or her duties," a lack of legal acumen, or failure to properly perform one's judicial duties, is not an available basis for dismissal. *See* Article 46 (setting same removal standard for prosecutors, judges, the Registrar, and the Deputy Registrar).

The overriding hope shared by the signatory states at the ICC's founding continued to be that this permanent Court—with a mandate to hold accountable those responsible for the world's most serious crimes, atrocities, and mass murders—would be more effective and efficient than the predecessor after-the-fact tribunals. One of the primary wellsprings for this widespread optimism was the shared belief that the ICC would be able to more quickly respond to atrocity crimes within its jurisdiction because it was free from having to receive a special mandate from the U.N. Security Council.[27] Supporters of the Court viewed the capacity for rapid response by a permanent international court with broad jurisdiction as likely limiting the duration and extent of violent episodes, while providing a more enduring general deterrent.

Potential war criminals, proponents hoped, would reconsider carrying out their illegal plans if they knew a court was likely to hold them individually responsible, regardless of their political power and leadership position within a state.[28] In fact, supporters of the ICC considered potential atrocity crimes perpetrators to be particularly susceptible to the deterrent effect of international justice. Unlike perpetrators of "ordinary" domestic crimes, they

27. *See, e.g.*, Scheffer & Cox, *supra* note 15, at 1047–59.

28. On this point, as we shall see, there are sharply disparate view. *Compare* Sonja Starr, *Extraordinary Crimes at Ordinary Times: International Justice Beyond Crisis Situations*, 101 Nw. U. L. Rev. 1257, 1263 (2007) ("Scholarship in the field often explicitly states that the objective of international criminal justice is to respond to war crimes and mass atrocities."); Allison Marston Danner & Jenny S. Martinez, *Guilty Associations: Joint Criminal Enterprise, Command Responsibility, and the Development of International Criminal Law*, 93 Cal. L. Rev. 75, 77, 79 (2005) ("Contemporary international criminal law is largely concerned with holding individual defendants responsible for mass atrocities."); Greg Vetter, *Command Responsibility of Non-Military Superiors in the International Criminal Court*, 25 Yale J. Int'l L. 89, 92 (2000) ("Individual criminal responsibility, and command responsibility in particular, are important because, to deter human rights abuses, potential perpetrators must perceive ICC prosecution as a possible consequence of their actions."); and International Crimes, Peace, and Human Rights: The Role of the International Criminal Court xi (Dinah Shelton, ed., 2000) ("The aim of international criminal justice is essentially to deter crime and help restore international peace and security by punishing those responsible for international crimes committed during armed conflicts."); *with* David Wippman, *Atrocities, Deterrence, and the Limits of International Justice*, 23 Fordham Int'l L.J. 473, 488 (1999) (observing that international criminal prosecutions may "strengthen whatever internal bulwarks help individuals obey the rules of war, but the general deterrent effect of such prosecutions seems likely to be modest and incremental, rather than dramatic and transformative"); and Payam Akhavan, *Beyond Impunity: Can International Criminal Justice Prevent Future Atrocities?*, 95 Am. J. Int'l L. 7, 31 (2001) ("No one should entertain the illusion that the relative success of the ICTY, the ICTR, and the ICC process, or the engagement of national and foreign courts, has somehow exorcised the specter of genocide and other massive crimes from our midst.").

hypothesized, war criminals as a group are not "hardened criminals," but rather are "politicians or leaders of the community that have up until now been law-abiding people.... If people in leadership positions know there's an international court out there, that there's an international prosecutor, and that the international community is going to act as an international police force, [they will] think twice as to the consequences...."[29]

Whether creating this dichotomy between political and apolitical criminals is justified, and whether the presence of the ICC is likely to have the desired deterrent impact, will be explored in Part IV. Suffice it to say that, given the performance of the ICC to date, it is arguably unlikely that the leader of a rogue state engaged in mass murder, as well as organized mutilations, rape, and torture, will concern himself all that deeply with today's ICC. The somewhat remote chance that the Office of the Prosecutor will effectively investigate and charge him, law enforcement capture him, the jurisdiction seizing him thereafter extradite him, the Trial Chamber try, convict, and then sentence him, and the Appeals Chamber affirm the conviction is unlikely to keep any but the most risk-averse and pessimistic war criminal up at night. And this is the exact sort of person who is not likely to become a war criminal to begin with. What is more likely to plague such a leader's thoughts is the tangible, and often indeed likely, possibility that he[30] will come to know death at the hands of political or military rivals.

Stated plainly, although the ICC provides the educational, symbolic, and coercive benefits discussed later, the deterrent effect of the ICC, as it presently operates, is more limited. And this is bad news for victims, their advocates, and others who desperately want to see their former tormentors convicted, and who hope that the tangible threat of international legal action will, in the long term, deter potential perpetrators of atrocity crimes from engaging in their planned abuses.

---

29. Michael P. Scharf, *The Prosecutor v. Dusko Tadic, An Appraisal of the First International War Crimes Trial Since Nuremberg*, 60 ALB. L. REV. 861, 869 (1997) (quoting former South African Constitutional Court judge and Tadic prosecutor Richard Goldstone).

30. Because strict adherence to gender-neutral language makes for awkward reading, the reader must forgive the default use of masculine antecedents.

PART III

Tracing the Development of Victims' Rights Under International Law

ALTHOUGH SOME MAY THINK of victims' rights as a fairly recent and enlightened legal innovation, the principle that individuals who have suffered personal harm or material injury as a result of another's conduct are entitled to be "made whole" is in fact quite an ancient one. Whether through a tribe, religious order, or the state, the collective traditionally provided a forum offering victim-centric dispute resolution, as well as enforcement mechanisms for judgments. In earlier cultures, however, the victim, his family, or the collective (such as his tribe or village) predominantly visited such punishment directly on the wrongdoer or his kin. Anglo-Saxon communities as early as the fifth century A.D., for example, resolved interpersonal conflicts between individuals, families, and clans through slayings and blood feuds.[1] These direct enforcement mechanisms were, indeed, part of the natural order for societies in which the family or tribe occupied a position of centrality within the political and administrative systems.

For example, following the collapse of the Roman Empire, and in the general absence of powerful central governments throughout Europe and in England, blood feuds and self-help constituted the "justice system" of the day.[2] "Public law," in the sense of centralized and state-provided justice, gave way to the private resolution of legal disputes. People of the time viewed lawbreakers as having gone to war against the victim and the victim's community, and, in so doing, subjected themselves and their property to communal responses, such as banishment, destruction of their property and houses,

1. *See* James R. Acker & Jeanna Mastrocinque, *Causing Death and Sustaining Life: The Law, Capital Punishment, and Criminal Homicide Victims' Survivors*, *in* WOUNDS THAT DO NOT BIND: VICTIM-BASED PERSPECTIVES ON THE DEATH PENALTY 141, 142–45 (James R. Acker & David R. Karp, eds., 2006).

2. *See generally* Lynne N. Henderson, *The Wrongs of Victims' Rights*, 37 STANFORD L. REV. 937, 938–40 (1985) ("The available historical work in the field of the criminal law reveals a steady evolution away from the 'private,' or individual, sphere to the 'public' or societal one.").

or death. In pre-modern societies, therefore, offenders faced both a private right of action, as well as a public one.

The earliest recorded legal systems and religious traditions—from the eighteenth century B.C. Babylonian Code of Hammurabi to the Visigothic Law Codes of the fifth century A.D.—in fact reflect the near-universal belief that those wronged *must* have a right to redress. Indeed, no justice system has refused to recognize the general principle that the system must accord the victim a right to private redress of wrongs. Providing a forum for personal and direct redress has, thus, traditionally formed the very heart of the social contract between the individual and the collective.

Tribal societies and their heirs relied on notions of social responsibility as their organizing principle, providing not only for restorative, but also for punitive, damages.[3] As such, dispute resolution between the accused and the victim was a matter to be addressed by the collective, rather than a matter left for the two parties to resolve. This, in turn, provided for individualized vindication, while at the same time cabining additional escalating violence and disturbances of the peace.[4]

Ancient customary laws worldwide, as a consequence, were almost exclusively victim-centric. A searching examination of such codes, though interesting, is, however, beyond the scope of this book. But, in order to flesh out how domestic customary laws enshrined the victim's primacy, we will examine one set of customary laws in some detail immediately below.

The *Code of Leke Dukagjini* stands as a proxy for similar ancient victim-centric codes found around the world, in that it placed the personal interests of wronged victim at the very center of the legal framework. Individual victim redress, and, relatedly, the punishment of the wrongdoer, were the *Code*'s overriding concerns, to the exclusion of any collectivist or utilitarian tendency to elevate the "communal good" over the interests of particular victims.

---

3. *See generally* HENRY MAINE, ANCIENT LAW: ITS CONNECTION WITH THE EARLY HISTORY OF SOCIETY AND ITS RELATION TO MODERN IDEAS (1861).

4. In later years, Italian criminal groups, collectively and popularly known as the "Mafia," similarly established their own polycentric legal systems to resolve disputes in the absence of real, or accepted, state power and control, and to, in theory at least, vindicate the rights of victims. With time, however, these groups moved from dispute resolution to the exploitation of their fellow citizens, and, in so doing, firmly established their corrosive and anti-social reputations.

A. Victim-Centric Justice of the 1400s—Customary Law As Exemplified by the *Code of Leke Dukagjini*

In Greek, the word *Kanun* means "rule," "measure," or "standard of excellence." By Byzantine times, the Ottoman Turks had introduced this word in to the Albanian language. Albanians soon relied on the word as common reference to the then-prevailing code of law.

The *Code of Leke Dukagjini* (the "*Kanun*")[5] deeply marked Albanian cultural and legal history. For centuries, the *Kanun* dominated economic and interpersonal relationships, providing clear (and at times somewhat unorthodox) guidelines for everyday life among the ethnic Albanian populations of what is now Albania, Kosovo, Montenegro, Macedonia, and Serbia.[6] Often referenced only in the context of legitimizing, and in fact encouraging, uncompromising blood feuds, the *Kanun* in fact was a far more nuanced code of conduct. The *Kanun* reflected the rural and anti-statist views prevalent to this day in Albania's countryside, and particularly in the mountains of northern Albania. What follows is a brief discussion highlighting some of the *Kanun*'s victim-centric provisions.

Protecting the victim's honor—considered a person's most important possession—was a central and reoccurring theme in the *Kanun*. Dishonor could be brought upon the victim in a variety of ways, including by the victim being threatened, pushed, spit on,[7] having his wife insulted or having her

---

5. The Code of Leke Dukagjini (Leonard Fox Translation, 1989). Although the *Kanun* is commonly viewed as the product of prominent and wealthy aristocrat Leke Dukagjini's (1410–1481) efforts, in reality the *Kanun* has evolved over centuries, developing long before Dukagjini was born, and continuing on after his death. Nevertheless, it was Dukagjini who collected and published what we today consider Albanian customary law.

6. The *Kanun* addresses subject matters in the following order: Offenses relating to the church, the cemetery, and church employees including the priest, *id.* at §§ 1–17; structure of the family, *id.* at §§ 18–27; the wedding and marriage, *id.* at §§ 28–55; familial rights and obligations, §§ 56–63; property division/inheritance, *id.* at §§ 64–117; relationship between master and servant, *id.* at §§ 117–31; offenses against house, livestock, and other property, *id.* at §§ 132–212; property rights, *id.* at §§ 213–88; work/employment, *id.* at §§ 289–395; hunting and fishing, *id.* at §§ 396–451; trades, *id.* at §§ 452–98; transfer of property, *id.* at §§ 499–508); promises and gifts, *id.* at §§ 511–19; oaths, *id.* at §§ 520–92; personal and social honor/hospitality, *id.* at §§ 593–694; blood and kinship, *id.* at §§ 695–734; damages, *id.* at §§ 735–65; crimes, *id.* at §§ 766–990; and judicial law, §§ 991–1220.

7. *Id.* at § 601(b).

"run off with someone,"[8] having his hospitality violated,[9] or by virtue of the offender taking his weapon.[10] The *Kanun*, indeed, treated honor as such a fragile possession that a visitor could insult the victim-homeowner by "remove[ing] the cover of a cooking pot on [the owner's] hearth."[11] According to the *Kanun*, any victim who was so dishonored was "considered dead"[12] until the "spilling of blood"[13] or "magnanimous pardon (through the mediation of good friends)"[14] removed the stain. As to the former method, which sanctioned the price of blood for dishonor, the *Kanun* clearly envisaged some form of self-help:

> The [dishonored victim] has every right to avenge his honor: no pledge is given, no appeal is made to the Elders, no judgment is needed, no fine is taken. The strong man collects the fine himself.[15]

In addition to restoring honor, the *Kanun* provided extensive guidance on criminal matters.[16] In theft cases, for example, liability followed the principal or accomplice's "participation in the crime," but, "if the theft is discovered, [those involved] must make restitution [to the victim] for the stolen object."[17] In fact, the *Kanun* provided not only for restitution, but also required punitive damages in the form of a fine. Theft of livestock, for example, required the offender to "restore" the victim's animals, as well as to pay a fine of 500 *grosh* (which was the price of a building site for a house or the price of a "good rifle"[18]).[19] Moreover, the *Kanun* proclaimed that "every stolen object is subject

8. *Id.* at § 601(d).
9. *Id.* at § 601(f).
10. *Id.* at § 601(e).
11. *Id.* at § 601(i).
12. *Id.* at § 600.
13. *Id.* at § 598.
14. *Id.*
15. *Id.* at § 599.
16. *See generally id.* at §§ 766–990.
17. *Id.* at § 768.
18. The *Kanun* even provided a non-inflationary price-schedule to reflect the value of a *grosh*: a building site or a rifle cost 500 *grosh*, a donkey cost 300 *grosh*, a "good olive grove" cost 100 *grosh*, a bee hive with bees cost 50 *grosh*, and a pair of sandals cost a mere 5 *grosh*. *See id.* at § 484.
19. *Id.* at § 790.

to double compensation."[20] Similarly, a person who stole a "bellwether" goat or ram, "wishing to cause affront or because of some hatred towards the herdsman, and is not killed on the spot, must pay a fine of 500 *grosh* and double compensation."[21] The *Kanun*, therefore, provided to the victim both restitution for the harm suffered, as well as a fine designed to punish the offender and deter similar future conduct.

In terms of enforcing the punishment, if a particular accused failed to submit to the judgment, the village could place the individual "under ban" (that is, ostracize him), and could even withdraw all legal protection from the accused who committed the act, "leaving those whom he has offended free to do whatever they like to him."[22] Moreover, in those cases in which the offender's house was ordered burned as punishment, and other property, such as vineyards, were ordered destroyed, the offender himself (or, if he was not available, someone from, or close to, the offender's family)[23] had to give the signal to begin the burning and destruction, saying "May the evils of the village and the Banner fall upon me!"[24] The offender, in the spirit of restorative justice and acceptance of personal responsibility for the harm he caused the victim, therefore, had to personally commence his own punishment.

An even deeper act symbolizing the restorative aspects of the *Kanun* occurred once "the hearts of the members of the family of the murderer and the family of the victim [had] been reconciled."[25] Upon reaching this level of forgiveness and healing, the former adversaries took two half-full glasses of *raki* (a high-proof grape alcohol), tied their little fingers together, and pricked them with a needle.[26] The two men then dropped blood from their fingers into the two half-full glasses of *raki* and mixed the *raki* and the blood.[27] Thereafter, "the two men exchange glasses and, with arms linked, they [held]

---

20. *Id.* at § 804. Note that the killing of a rooster, on the other hand, carried a fixed (and rather high, by most standards) penalty of "500 *grosh* to the owner" because the rooster was said to be "the poor man's clock." *See id.* at § 808.

21. *Id.* at § 154.

22. *Id.* at § 1183.

23. *Id.* at § 1199.

24. *Id.* at § 1198.

25. *See id.* at §§ 988–90.

26. *Id.* at § 989.

27. *Id.*

the glasses to each other's lips, drinking each other's blood."[28] This symbolic act signalled true reconciliation between the offender and the victim, as well as an end to the impending, or ongoing, cycle of violence. "Guns are fired in celebration and they become like new brothers, born of the same mother and father."[29] Even the most cynical critic of restorative justice would consider such an outcome—the creation of such a "blood brotherhood"—if sincere, to be the pinnacle of justice-system success. Righting the social equilibrium was, thus, one of the customary law's goals; but making the victim whole was primary.

B. Centralized State Power in the 1700s and 1800s, the Scientification of Criminal Law, and the Decline of Victims' Rights Under Domestic Law

Customary law, as exemplified by the *Code of Leke Dukagjini*, has, as we have seen, long put the victim at the center of the proceeding. Making the victim whole was, indeed, ancient law's paramount purpose.

Beginning in the 1700s, however, Western customary law's focus on protecting the interests of victims gave way to broader societal objectives, namely, reducing crime and consolidating state power. Regional leaders increasingly viewed customary law's private "dispute resolution" approaches as tearing at the societal fabric.

Centralized authority, accompanied by community judicial control, accelerated the influence of the state on the administration of criminal justice. Medieval kings and feudal lords restricted blood feuds by introducing tariff systems. The tariff systems required victims to petition for pecuniary compensation from offenders, instead of resorting to private vengeance. As societies became more consolidated, fines payable to the victims—and then to the king—took the place of the collective's grant of permission that victims seize or destroy the offender's property.

As kings and lords consolidated power, compensation to victims gradually became the exception to the rule. Significantly, legal systems began to view lawbreakers as having committed offenses against the "crown," the "king's peace," or "society," rather than against the particular victim. The king

---

28. *Id.* at § 990.

29. *Id.*

and his representatives punished minor crimes with fines, and relied on more serious corporal punishments for graver offenses.[30] Victims, in turn, were left to "seek justice" by testifying for the prosecution.

As the law began to embark on this slow transformation from mediator to punisher, victims became increasingly restricted in their ability to dispense punishment and collect compensation. The victim, once the central figure, now was little more than a source of evidence against the accused. As the criminal justice system's purpose shifted in this manner, the importance of restitution to victims waned to the point that restitution morphed into a fine payable to the state. The focus, unmistakably, moved from the victim's welfare to the welfare of the community at large.[31] (Private citizens, of course, retained the right to bring a private cause of action in tort against those who had injured them.) By cleaving individual claims for restitution from the perpetrator from those brought against the perpetrator by the "government," the law relegated the victim to a distinctly secondary role.[32]

By the early 1700s, governments went beyond simply consolidating the justice system's authority. Increasingly, they began elevating the study of law and the process of law-making to a "legal science." Under this re-conception of the justice system's purpose, the idea of victims' rights and victims' centrality to the justice system represented little more than an antiquated vestige of a by-gone era. European thinkers started to develop widely divergent theories on the origins of crime and the optimal methods of crime prevention. As discussed below, the one common thread running through these new modes of thinking was that none of them contemplated a meaningful role for victims.

---

30. Although customary law, as noted above, continued to play a dominant role in rural stretches of Albania, it, as a general matter, disappeared in the rest of western and central Europe.

31. *See generally* STEPHEN SCHAFER, VICTIMOLOGY: THE VICTIM AND HIS CRIMINAL 12–14 (1977) (discussing this collectivist trend in Germany and England).

32. *See generally* ROBERT REIFF, THE INVISIBLE VICTIM: THE CRIMINAL JUSTICE SYSTEM'S FORGOTTEN RESPONSIBILITY xi (1979) ("Society—sensitive to the issues of social justice for the offender—spends millions of dollars on programs for offender-oriented court reform and rehabilitation. On the other hand, society fails to protect crime victims, degrades them socially, and refuses them aid."); MARGARET O. HYDE, THE RIGHT OF THE VICTIM 4 (1983) ("[F]or the most part, victims are the innocent and neglected element in the criminal justice system.").

1. The Classical School of Criminology

The "Classical School of Criminology" was a criminological movement which emerged during the late 1700s and the early 1800s. Scholars called this school of thought "classical" because of the similarity in thinking between those scholars and early Greek philosophers such as Aristotle, Euripides, and Plato, all of whom placed great emphasis on the centrality and importance of free will. Proponents of the Classical School considered deterring crime through carefully calibrated punishment a great humanitarian reform, superior in many ways to the medieval practices it replaced. Some of the defining features of the Classical School included the idea that people acted on the basis of free will; that behavior was guided by hedonism (pleasure/pain calculation); that crime was the result of free will and hedonism; that punishment should fit the offense; and that wrongdoers were little more that the products of bad laws.

The Italian thinker and abolitionist Cesare Beccaria was one of the father's of the Classical School. In 1767, Beccaria wrote the book *On Crimes and Punishment*, which argued that the social contract forms the basis of society, in that a violation of another's liberties equates to a violation of the social contract binding all civilized people. The criminal law, the theory went, must necessarily have a restricted scope, presuming people innocent until proven guilty. The law must also be codified, and crimes must be made widely known and understood, so that all citizens are "on notice" of what conduct is proscribed. Moreover, adherents of the Classical School contended that the justice system must limit the severity of punishment so that it never exceeds that required to deter people from committing the crime (explaining why the Classical School rejected capital punishment). That said, punishment must be certain and swift, and must be popularly viewed as such. At bottom, the justice system had to accurately calculate the citizen's pleasure/pain threshold in order to incentivize "good" conduct and deter "bad" behavior.

By synthesizing and applying revolutionary Enlightenment notions of universal and self-evident rights[33] to the problems of crime, Beccaria shifted

---

33. Conceptions of rights during the Enlightenment of course were not uniform; the differences between German and French Enlightenment thinkers, for example, were significant, as were the differences between Thomas Hobbes', Jean-Jacques Rousseau's, and John Locke's conceptions of liberty and freedom. *Compare* THOMAS HOBBES, LEVIATHAN (1651) (arguing that powerful central government is the only way to bring man out of the chaotic state of nature, which is characterized by the "war of all against all") and

the focus from criminals and retribution-based punishment to crime control, reform of the criminal justice system, and the "science" of making good laws. Englishman Jeremy Bentham then took this approach to a new level in his book, *An Introduction to the Principles of Morals and Legislation*, which developed utilitarianism (Bentham's version of hedonism) as the basis for sound social governance. In this epoch of emerging socio-legal engineering, the victim's role, like the offender's role, became secondary, and achieving the broader societal objective of crime control emerged as the justice system's reason for being.

2. The Positivist School of Criminology and Beyond

During the mid 1800s and early 1900s, a social movement most closely associated with Cesare Lombroso, known as the "Positivist School," began gaining popularity. The Positivist School adopted forward-looking attitudes toward social and personal betterment, and extolled the (perhaps over-optimistic) belief in the perfectibility of both society and human nature. The aim was to explain and, more importantly, predict human behavior, much like a natural scientist observes, and then predicts, uniform patterns in the natural world. The Classical School's reliance on hedonism and utilitarianism, in contrast, fell from favor as justice officials began to view it as an over-simplified philosophy that did not adequately account for the full range of factors driving human conduct. The new focus was thus away from the Classical School's belief in the promise of legal science as a means of effective crime control, and on the inner workings of the "criminal mind." Punishment now was supposed to fit the individual, and not the crime. A scientific elite/technocracy, devoted to treating, correcting, and rehabilitating criminals, was to guide the justice system down this complex path towards a fuller understanding of what makes criminals "tick."

John Locke, Second Treatise of Government (1689) (developing a theory of political and civil society based on natural rights and contract theory) *with* Jean-Jacques Rousseau, The Social Contract, Or Principles of Political Right (1762) (arguing for direct, not representative, democracy, and contending that government can only be legitimate if it has been sanctioned by the people in the role of the sovereign). However, for our purposes it is sufficient to recognize that Enlightenment thinkers did share certain central themes.

In the 1960s, mainstream criminologists, expanding the positivist position, began to look away from the individual and towards society for answers to the question of what makes criminals criminal. Robert Merton's "Strain Theory," part of the Chicago School of Criminology, exemplifies this surging progressive criminological philosophy. Adherents hypothesized that the "lower socio-economic classes" were most vulnerable to social pressure, or "strain," resulting from the purported gap, imbalance, or disjunction between culturally-induced aspirations for economic success ("I want a nice car and designer clothes"), and limited structurally distributed possibilities of ever achieving that success ("But I don't have the high school or college education, or steady job, that will permit me to legitimately obtain the nice car and designer clothes").

The lower socio-economic classes, theorists contended, would maintain their unfulfilled economic aspirations in spite of frustration and failure. Although providing rewards for noneconomic pursuits (such as public service, family, sport, and entertainment) could stabilize the system, the stress, or "strain toward anomie," would continue. Imperfect coordination of means and ends ultimately would fatally undermine the regularity and predictability of the social structure.

This focus on societal culpability, rather than individual responsibility, made followers of the positivist position view both perpetrators and persons they wronged as victims of society. For it was society, the argument went, that left the perpetrator with no choice but to commit crime in order to bridge the gap between what modern commercial culture told him he should have, and what his meager legitimate means permitted him to acquire.

Followers of "Conflict Theory" and "Radical Criminology" later adopted this societal-blame philosophy, championing the neo-Marxist view that the criminal justice system and criminal law was, indeed, deliberately rigged to operate on behalf of rich and powerful social elites, with resulting crime control policies put into place solely as a means of controlling the poor. The criminal justice establishment's goal, their theory went, was to impose standards of morality and good behavior, as dictated by the powerful minority who directly benefitted from a permanently subjugated underclass.

Once again, the ideology of the day considered the victim of a particular crime, committed by a particular perpetrator, to be, in reality, a victim of the collective. Only this time the "collective" was comprised of the rich and powerful "ruling elite," rather than capitalist society generally. Academics and sympathetic lawmakers pushed this position beyond its natural breaking point, resulting in a public law-and-order backlash against what the citizenry understandably viewed as an unacceptable ideological trend away from crime control, and towards blanket excuses for criminal conduct.

C. Twentieth-Century Resurgence of Victims' Rights Under Domestic Law

As we have seen, the dominant criminological theory of the 1960s was rehabilitation, the central tenet of which was "fixing" perpetrators by fixing society. The rehabilitative model, with its reliance on penological experts who examined and tried to explain the offender's criminal pathology, left little room for the involvement of victims. For under this view of punishment, victims added nothing to the quasi-clinical "diagnosis" and "treatment" of offenders.

In the United States, where adherence to the philosophy of rehabilitation by the late 1960s began to give way to policies favoring retribution, the majority of states began to institute pro-victim compensation programs and the like.[34] The "victimology" movement viewed such government-paid compensation to victims as an effective way to increase victim participation in criminal prosecutions, helping victims feel that the state and society has taken an active interest in their plight.[35] Those who viewed retribution and deterrence as the true purposes of the criminal law, moreover, felt victims had been unfairly neglected by a justice system concerned chiefly with the accuseds'

34. For example, Wisconsin adopted its first compensation statue in 1975. *See* 1975 Wis. Laws ch. 344, § 3. Minnesota enacted its victim's compensation statue in 1974. *See* 1974 Minn. Laws ch. 463, § 3. New Jersey adopted victim compensation in 1971, Alaska in 1972. *See* 1971 N.J. Laws ch. 317, § 1; 1972 Alaska Sess. Laws ch. 203, § 1. Indeed, even victims' rights amendments to state constitutions became common. *See, e.g.*, Alaska Const. Article I, § 24; Ariz. Const. Article II, § 2.1; Cal. Const. Article I, §§ 12, 28; Colo. Const. Article II, § 16(a); Conn. Const. Article I, § 8(b); Fla. Const. Article I, § 16(b); Idaho Const. Article I, § 22; Ill. Const. Article I, § 8.1; Ind. Const. Article I, § 13(b); Kan. Const. Article 15, § 15; La. Const. Article 1, § 25; Md. Decl. of Rights Article 47; Mich. Const. Article I, § 24; Miss. Const. Article 3, § 26(A); Mo. Const. Article I, § 32; Neb. Const. Article I, § 28; Nev. Const. Article I, § 8(2); N.J. Const. Article I, § 22; N.M. Const. Article 2, § 24; N.C. Const. Article I, § 37; Ohio Const. Article I, § 10(a); Okla. Const. Article II, § 34; Or. Const. Article I, §§ 42–43; R.I. Const. Article I, § 23; S.C. Const. Article I, § 24; Tenn. Const. Article 1, § 35; Tex. Const. Article I, § 30; Utah Const. Article I, § 28; Va. Const. Article I, § 8-A; Wash. Const. Article 1, § 35; and Wis. Const. Article I, § 9(m).

35. *See generally* Alan T. Harland, *Monetary Remedies for the Victims of Crime: Assessing the Role of the Criminal Courts*, 30 UCLA L. Rev. 52, 64–77 (1982) (explaining use of restitution at different stages of criminal proceedings); Richard E. Laster, *Criminal Restitution: A Survey of Its Past History and An Analysis of Its Present Usefulness*, 5 U. Rich. L. Rev. 71, 71–80 (1970) (discussing history of restitution).

rights. They considered the victim a much more sympathetic figure than the accused, and, in support of their position, pointed to the failure of the environmental and sociologically-based crime control models to meaningfully predict or deter criminality.

One possible, but under-examined, explanation for the revival in concern for victims and victims' rights during the 1960s–1980s is that ordinary citizens gained a greater understanding of, and level of empathy with, victims of crime. Crime rates during this time were on the rise.[36] Moreover, television news reports and shows graphically depicted victims' suffering, rendering their plight more tangible. Put simply, victims no longer existed in the abstract. Rather, citizens sitting in their living rooms could see, and empathize with, victims in a direct manner previously impossible. As a result, the average citizen became more worried about crime and victimization than he would have been in the late 1800s or early 1900s. These factors, in turn, translated into increased pressure on the criminal justice system to better protect and treat victims.

International comparisons, however, reveal that the United States' recognition of victims' rights in the 1960s lagged behind Western Europe. In most civil-law countries, victims ("injured persons") long possessed the right to participate at various stages of the criminal process, from the pre-trial phase to the appeal. Such participatory rights included the qualified right to

---

36. For example, violent crime in England started to rise in the mid-1950s; England's contemporary violent crime rates for every type of crime, except murder and rape, have in fact surpassed the United States' rates, and the English and American murder rates are now converging, with the United States murder rate declining over the past decade, and the English murder rate increasing during the same time. *See generally* Joyce Lee Malcolm, *Lessons of History: Firearms Regulation and the Reduction of Crime*, 8 TEX. REV. L. & POL. 175, 177–79 (2003); *see also* Michael Tonry, *Preface*, CRIME AND JUSTICE (2007) ("Crime rates everywhere in Europe rose steeply from the late 1960s through the early to mid 1990s."); Tapio Lappi-Seppälä, *Trust, Welfare, and Political Culture: Explaining the Differences is National Penal Policies*, 37 CRIME & JUSTICE 313, 341 n. 14 (2008) (noting that crime rates in Scandinavian countries increased between the 1960s and 1990s); Cheryl Marie Webster & Anthony N. Doob, *Punitive Trends and Stable Imprisonment Rates in Canada*, 36 CRIME AND JUSTICE 297, 302–03 (2007) (noting steadily increasing crime rates in Canada and the United States between the 1960s and 1990s). Moreover, although Asian countries have dramatically lower crime rates relative to their level of income development, industrialization, and urbanization, they have followed the trend of increasing levels of criminality from the 1950s–1990s. With a worldwide increase in social and cultural mobility and diversity, then, came a decrease in social control, civic republicanism, communal solidarity, and inter-personal accountability; the result has been a world-wide rise in crime rates.

cross-examine witnesses, introduce evidence, brief motions, and seek additional investigation.[37]

For example, Italian victims, through their attorneys, traditionally participated on an equal basis with the *Publico Ministero* (the prosecutor) and defense counsel.[38] Natural or legal persons, as well as their heirs, who were injured could join the proceedings the public prosecutor initiated as *parte civile*. Victims injured as a result of an offense (*persona offesa dal reato*) were permitted to put forward supporting evidence, and to present to the court a statement of their case. Once the trial opened, the victim was given the right to preview for the court the evidence the victim intended to present in support of establishing certain facts. The victim also had the right under certain criminal codes, as well as civil tort law, to obtain restitution and/or reparations for injuries suffered at the hands of the offender.

In France, the justice system likewise permitted victim participation in the proceedings,[39] and allowed the victim, in some instances, to substitute for the public prosecutor. Although the French system accorded victims no participatory or other rights during the investigative stage, it provided that a victim who had suffered harm as a result of the offense could come before the court as a *partie civile*, and could opt to either join the ongoing prosecution or initiate his own prosecution.[40] If the victim joined an ongoing case (before the *juge d'instruction*), then he was permitted to demand compensation. Alternatively, the victim could bypass the public prosecutor's decision not to prosecute, or could directly accuse the defendant before the *tribunal correctionnel* or the *tribunal de police*.[41] Once at trial, the victim was permitted to produce evidence (and, interestingly, the exclusionary rules did

---

37. *See generally* William Pizzi & Luca Marafioti, *The New Italian Code of Criminal Procedure: The Difficulties of Building an Adversarial Trial System on a Civil Law Foundation*, 17 YALE J. INTL'L L. 1, 14 (1992). Note, however, that in most civil law jurisdictions, witnesses, following a short preamble, are asked to describe what occurred in an unconstructed narrative fashion (following the epistemological premise that evidence should be presented in a manner most closely approximating its "original" form). *See, e.g., Strafprozessordnung* § 69(1) (F.R.G.).

38. *Codice di Procedura Penale* Articles 410, 493, 496, 498, and 523.

39. Mario Chiavario, *Private Parties: The Rights of the Defendant and the Victim, in* MIREILLE DELMAS-MARTY & J.R. SPENCER, EUROPEAN CRIMINAL PROCEDURES 543 (2002).

40. *See generally* Proc. Code Articles 183, 197, and 217 (right to notice of rulings and hearings); *id.* Articles 198, 281, 315, 316, 346, 454, and 460 (right to be heard); and *id.* Articles 186, 186-1, and 497 (appeal rights).

41. *See generally* Valerie Dervieux, *The French System, in* MIREILLE DELMAS-MARTY & J.R. SPENCER, EUROPEAN CRIMINAL PROCEDURES 226–27 (2002).

not pertain to him, since he was not a state actor). This system of relatively broad victim participation was part of the French Code of Criminal Procedure, which stated that any

> [c]ivil action aimed at the reparation of the damage suffered because of a felony, a misdemeanor or a petty offence is open to all those who have personally suffered damage directly caused by the offence.[42]

Under the German system, certain minor offences directly impacting the privacy of the victim (*Verletzte*) required the victim first to file a complaint. The German *Privatklaeger* ("private accuser") was traditionally permitted to exercise significant quasi-prosecutorial powers (in such cases, the victim, or *Verletzte*, conducted the prosecution[43]). Victims were also permitted to nominate themselves as accessory complainants through a legal process called *Nebenklage*.[44] Those authorized to lodge such an accessory complaint included victims of bodily injury, victims of white-collar crimes, and relatives of homicide victims. These victims were permitted to join the proceedings at any time, provided they first filed a request for compensation ("*Anschlusserklaerung*").

Although the United States may have been playing catch-up with European countries in matters of victims' rights,[45] by the late 1970s a somewhat watered-down version of victim participation (providing for, among other things, the filing of victim impact statements) had become accepted. International law, however, at that point had not yet come to fully recognize victims' rights.

D. Victims' Rights Recognized as Part of International Law

The gradual movement towards "internationalized victims' rights," extending beyond private actors and individual responsibility to public actors and state responsibility, can be traced to the international community's growing

---

42. C. PR. P´EN. Article 2, available at www.legislationline.org/legislations.php?jid=19&ltid=15.

43. *Strafprozessordnung* §§ 374–94.

44. *Id.* at §§ 395–402.

45. For a thorough review of the role of victims in United States domestic courts, *see* Markus Dubber, *The Victim in American Penal Law: A Systematic Overview*, 3 BUFF. CRIM. L. REV. 3 (1999).

focus on trans-national criminal culpability following the tragic victimization and destruction of human life during the two world wars. States, after all, bore the responsibility for the large-scale human rights violations occurring during World War I and World War II. Recognizing the state and state actors as directly responsible for human atrocities provided the necessary push for a broader notion of responsibility and obligation extending beyond the traditional municipal law boundaries. No longer were individual rights and obligations solely a matter between the individual and the state, governed by local law.[46]

1. International Law's Recognition of Individual Rights

The rights of the individual that the Nuremberg Tribunal and the International Military Tribunal for the Far East, also known as the "Tokyo Trials" or the "Tokyo War Crimes Tribunal," sought to uphold were calculated to safeguard the most basic conditions of human life and human decency. The drafters of the tribunals criminal charges considered the crimes to be violations of bedrock preconditions to a "normal" life, and thus termed them "crimes against humanity." Breaches of these fundamental standards included extermination, enslavement, and forced deportation, as well as other "inhumane acts" committed against civilian populations.[47]

Following the Allied tribunal's trials of Nazi leaders on such charges of crimes against humanity, the 1945 Charter of the newly formed U.N. incorporated the notion of human rights. The U.N. Charter provided, *inter alia*,

---

46. *See generally Chorzow Factory Case*, PCIJ Reports 1927, Series A No. 8, 21 (July 26, 1927) (Permanent Court for International Justice finding that "[i]t is a principle of international law that the breach of an engagement involves an obligation to make reparations in an adequate form. Reparations therefore is the indispensable complement of a failure to apply a convention and there is no necessity for this to be stated in the convention itself"); *Selmouni v. France*, 29 EHRR 403 (1999) (European Court of Human Rights ruling that an effective remedy requires that the state conduct a thorough and effective investigation making it possible for the investigators to identify and punish those responsible for the alleged violations); *Velasquez Rodriguez* IACtHR Series C, No. 4 (1988) (Inter-American Court for Human Rights ruling in case of unresolved disappearance of individual in Honduras that states are required to "effectively ensure . . . human rights," and must investigate alleged human rights violations "in a serious manner and not as a mere formality preordained to be ineffective").
47. Charter of the International Military Tribunal, August 8, 1945, Article 6(c), 59 Stat. 1544, 82 U.N.T.S. 279.

that all signatory governments would promote the expansive objectives of "universal respect for, and observance of, human rights and fundamental freedoms."[48]

The 1948 Universal Declaration of Human Rights,[49] in contrast, was more of an aspirational document. The Universal Declaration promised the world's citizens various "rights," including the right to "rest and leisure" and "periodic holidays with pay;"[50] the right to "free choice of employment;"[51] the right to a "standard of living adequate for the health and well-being of himself and his family, including food, clothing, housing, and medical care;"[52] and the right to "enjoy the arts and to share in scientific advancement."[53] These social, political, economic, and cultural self-actualization rights amounted to a conception of the good, and as such were fundamentally different from the Nuremberg Trial's protection of rights that were basic preconditions to human life and civilized society.[54]

As a practical matter, of course, guaranteeing such expansive rights to every person in the world—including people languishing in abject poverty simply because they had the misfortunate of being born in areas of the world where industrialization is in its infancy—threatens to deprecate the goals of those seeking "international justice." Fortunately, the pursuit of more achievable rights, such as the right to vote, the right to equal pay, the right to due process, and the right to be free from cruel and unusual punishment and torture, has occupied international bodies more than the right to "rest and leisure," "periodic holidays with pay," "free choice of employment," and the enjoyment of the arts.

As international law began to subject individuals—and not just states—to criminal sanctions, it also began to vest individuals with personal rights, and to view accountability as a component of victim redress. Various post-World War II international instruments and corresponding monitoring bodies,

---

48. U.N. Charter Article 55(c).

49. G.A. Res. 217 (December 10, 1948).

50. *See id.* at Article 24.

51. *See id.* at Article 23.

52. *Id.* at Article 25(1).

53. *Id.* at Article 27.

54. The Universal Declaration, unsurprisingly, contained no enforcement mechanisms, describing itself simply as a "common standard of achievement." *Id.* at Preamble.

such as the 1948 Universal Declaration on Human Rights,[55] the 1950 European Convention for the Protection of Human Rights and Fundamental Freedoms,[56] and the 1966 International Covenant on Civil and Political Rights,[57] reflected the emergence of these rights. These documents went beyond traditional notions of simple state responsibility to other states, and increasingly provided individuals with mechanisms to press their claims against states. Individuals no longer had to go to their states of nationality to submit claims through either diplomatic channels or judicial means. The traditional (that is, pre-Nuremberg trials) notion that harm of a state citizen was solely injury to the state, in short, had begun to erode.[58]

2. Victims' Rights Under International Law

Beyond according individuals a general right to redress, the U.N. by the 1960s sought to enforce the personal rights described in the 1948 Universal Declaration (labled an "International Bill of Human Rights") through the 1966 Optional Protocols[59] of the International Covenant on Economic, Social, and Cultural Rights ("ICESCR") (seeking to protect "economic" rights, such as shelter, food, employment, education, and health care), as well as through the International Covenant on Civil and Political Rights ("ICCPR") (seeking to protect "political" rights, such as physical integrity of the

55. GA Res. 217A (December 10, 1948).

56. ETS No. 5 "ECHR".

57. G.A. Res. 2200A (December 16, 1966).

58. Under the Hague Conventions of 1899 and 1907, for example, non-combatants physically or materially harmed as a result of a state engaging in armed conflict could petition their state of nationality to request compensation on their behalf behalf from the state that is alleged to have committed these violations. Similar provisions are contained in, *inter alia*, the Geneva Convention Relative to the Treatment of Prisoners of War, the Geneva Convention Relative to the Protection of Civilian Persons in Time of War, the American Convention on Human Rights, and the International Covenant on Civil and Political Rights. These conventions require states to provide a remedy/reparations for human rights violations. *See also* Universal Declaration of Human Rights ("[E]veryone has the right to an effective remedy by the competent national tribunals for acts violating the fundamental rights granted him by the constitution or by law.").

59. *See* Optional Protocol to the International Covenant on Civil and Political Rights, adopted Dec. 16, 1966, 999 U.N.T.S. 302; Second Optional Protocol to the International Covenant on Civil and Political Rights, Aiming at the Abolition of the Death Penalty, adopted December 15, 1989, G.A. Res. 44/128, U.N. GAOR Supp. No. 49, U.N. Doc A/RES/44/128 (1989).

person, legal proceedings, free speech, and free thought rights).[60] Although the ICCPR provided a mechanism for submitting and processing complaints, and was written in mandatory language, the ICESCR did and was not.[61]

Significantly, the ICCPR's Article 2.3 provided that states must generally accord an effective remedy to any person whose rights are violated. The U.N. Human Rights Committee, a body of independent experts monitoring the implementation of the ICCPR, in turn interpreted Article 2.3 as requiring states to conduct an effective prosecution to remedy the harm caused to victims in cases involving arbitrary detentions, forced disappearances, torture, and extrajudicial executions.[62]

On June 23, 1983, the Committee of Ministers of the Council of Europe issued a regional recommendation titled "Participation of the Public in Crime Policy."[63] The bulk of the Recommendation covered topics of "social prevention," including encouraging architects and town planners to "give cities a more humane layout aimed at crime prevention."[64] Other matters of accommodation included alternatives to custodial sentences,[65] non-discrimination against offenders,[66] and publicity campaigns to increase public understanding of the penal and social consequences of criminality.[67] The recommendations suggested that the Member States' justice systems take into consideration the victims' interests. The recommendations also proposed that victims have

---

60. Adopted December 19, 1966, Sen. Exec. Doc. E, 95–2, at 23 (1978), 999 U.N.T.S. 171.

61. A discussion of this two-tier notion of human rights is beyond the scope of this book, but suffice it to say that some of the most prominent/activist human rights NGOs, such as Human Rights Watch and Amnesty International, the World Bank, and the European Bank, structure their institutional priorities in this same fashion, reflecting the belief that respecting political rights merely requires states to abstain from violating the rights, whereas meeting a population's economic needs is as practical matter impossible without huge (and unavailable) cash outlays.

62. *See, e.g., Chonwe v. Zambia*, Communication No. 821/1998, at 7 (2000), available at www.unhchr.ch/tbs/doc.nsf (attempted murder); *Vicente et al. v. Colombia*, Communication No. 612/1995, at 10 (1997), available at www.unhchr.ch/tbs/doc.nsf (arbitrary detention, torture, and forced disappearance); and *Tshiongo v. Zaire*, Communication No. 366/1989, at 7 (1993), available at www.unhchr.ch/tbs/doc.nsf (arbitrary detention and torture).

63. Recommendation of the Committee of Ministers, Doc. No. R(83) 7 (June 23, 1983).

64. *Id.* at III(B).

65. *Id.* at III(6).

66. *Id.* at III(2).

67. *Id.* at III(14).

"access to justice at all times,"[68] and that Member States establish systems of legal aid to help victims gain access to justice.[69]

The Inter-American Court on Human Rights,[70] an autonomous judicial institution based in Costa Rica and established in 1979, similarly in the 1990s began interpreting various articles of the American Convention on Human Rights as guaranteeing victims the right to the effective prosecution of their victimizers, the right to access and to be heard, the right to procedural fairness, and the right to effective recourse and reparations. The American Convention in Chapter 2 accords a comprehensive catalogue of due process, fair trial, freedom of expression, personal liberty, and other rights. Although the Convention does not expressly have much to say on the topic of victims' rights, the Inter-American Court has held that family members have the right to know what happened to their loved ones, and that a denial of this right to the truth is the equivalent of a state's denial of victim-access to effective justice and to procedural fairness.[71]

The European Court of Human Rights, established as a regional judicial body by the 1950 European Convention on Human Rights, and operational as of March 1, 1998, similarly accorded victims various procedural and substantive rights.[72] Not only can the 47 member states of the Council of Europe bring Applications against the State Parties for alleged human rights violations, but so also can individuals and other parties. The European Court on Human Rights, for example, faulted the British criminal justice system for not informing victims of the reasons the prosecutors decided to decline a case, and for failing to subject the declination decision to judicial review.[73]

---

68. *Id.* at III(29).

69. *Id.*

70. The Court both interprets and enforces provisions of the American Convention on Human Rights. Cases are brought to the Court by member states of the Organization of American States, and its functions are both advisory and adjudicatory (if the accused is a State Party accused of human rights violations that has accepted jurisdiction). Cases are referred either by the Inter-American Commission on Human Rights or a State Party. Citizens, unlike in the European human rights system, are not permitted to bring cases directly to the Court.

71. *Velasquez Rodriguez*, Inter-Am. C.H.R., Ser. C, No. 4 (1988).

72. *See* May 4, 2001, decisions in *Jordan*, 1020 Eur. Ct. H.R. 300, P 123; *McKerr*, 34 Eur. H.R. Rep. 20, P 131; *Kelly*, 2004 Eur. Ct. H.R. 240, at 117; *Shanaghan*, 1814 Eur. Ct. H.R. 400, P 107.

73. *See id.*

The Council of the European Union has similarly adopted a Council Framework Decision meant to improve victims' standing in criminal proceedings. This Decision urged Member States to ensure that victims have a "real and appropriate role in its criminal legal system."[74] These international courts and conventions laid the groundwork for the ICC's more aggressive victims' rights agenda.

Victims' rights under international law received a significant boost in 1985 with the drafting of the U.N. Declaration of Basic Principles of Justice for Victims of Crime and Abuse of Power.[75] Although the Basic Principles did not provide victims with any new rights, they embody the first formal recognition by the U.N. that, in order to comply with emerging norms of international justice, states had to "adequately recognize" victims' rights[76] by providing victims with "access to the mechanisms of justice and to prompt redress, as provided for by domestic legislation, for the harm that they have suffered."[77] The Basic Principles, moreover, defined "victims,"[78] stated that victims are entitled to access to justice and "prompt redress,"[79] emphasized the importance of keeping victims informed of case-related activities and of providing victims with assistance throughout the legal process,[80] and advised that domestic justice systems should permit victims to present their "views and concerns" at "appropriate stages of the proceedings where their personal interest are affected, without prejudice to the accused. . . ."[81] The Basic Principles, in short, sought to internationalize victim-centric rights that by the mid-1980s had received broad acceptance in many domestic justice systems.

---

74. Council Framework Decision 2001/220/JHA, 2001 O.J. (L 82) 1–4 (2001), Article 2. Indeed, the decision also urged Member States to ensure that victims may be heard during the proceedings, can supply evidence, and are informed of the status of the case. *Id.* at Articles 3, 4, and 7.

75. G.A. Res. 40/34 (November 29, 1985). *See* www.un.org/documents/ga/res/40/a40r034.htm

76. *Id.* at Preamble.

77. *Id.* at Article 4.

78. *Id.* at Article 1.

79. *Id.* at Article 4.

80. *Id.* at Articles 6(a) and 6(c).

81. *Id.* at Article 6(b).

Commenting on the December 11, 1985, adoption of the Basic Principles, Professor Bassiouni wrote:

> Victims of crime and abuse of power are by the very fact of their victimization persons whose basic human rights have been violated. . . . Throughout history, in the so-called primitive societies, victims of aggression have usually found support and assistance from their tribe, family, or village. But in modern societies, which pride themselves on their heightened levels of development and civilization, this is seldom the case. In these societies, the incidence of crime and state sponsored abuses of human rights have dramatically increased. At the same time traditional patterns of social solidarity and dependency have significantly decreased and, frequently, victims become relegated to a worse social and human position than those who have victimized them. Thus, the time has come for the world community to take a position on the rights of victims in modern society.[82]

Judges at the ICTY, commenting on the significance of the Basic Principles, similarly observed:

> While issues relating to what might generally be referred to as 'victims' rights' have been addressed in many domestic law systems for long periods of time, consideration of these issues under international law is of relatively recent vintage. In 1985, the General Assembly adopted a Declaration of Basic Principles for Victims of Crime and Abuse of Power, which has served as the cornerstone for establishing legal rights for victims under international law and has led to a number of developments relating to victims.[83]

The Basic Principles, thus, for the first time recognized a victim's right to receive information and to present his views and concerns to a domestic

---

82. M. Cherif Bassiouni, International Protection of Victims 9 (1988).

83. International Criminal Tribunal for the Former Yugoslavia, Judges' Report, Victims' Compensation and Participation, 1, CC/P.I.S./528-E (September 13, 2000), available at www.un.org/icty/pressreal/tolb-e.htm.

judicial body, as well as other rights that collectively can be described as "access to justice rights."[84]

On March 21, 2006, following a series of revisions and political compromises, the U.N. General Assembly adopted by consensus the Basic Principles and Guidelines on the Right to a Remedy and Reparations for Victims of Gross Violations of International Human Rights Law and Serious Violations of International Humanitarian Law. These "2006 Basic Principles" were intended to provide something akin to an international bill of rights, whereas the 1985 Basic Principles had focused on the rights of crimes victims under national justice systems.[85]

The 2006 Basic Principles, which make explicit reference to the Rome Statute's victims' rights provisions,[86] seek to provide "mechanisms, modalities, procedures and methods for the implementation of existing legal obligations under international human rights law and international humanitarian law. . . ."[87] Under the 2006 Basic Principles, "victims" can include the immediate family or dependents of the direct victim who have suffered harm while intervening to assist victims or to prevent victimization.[88]

The General Assembly explicitly adopted the 2006 Basic Principles so that States:

> [T]ake the Basic Principles and Guidelines into account, promote respect thereof and bring them to the attention of members of the executive bodies of government, in particular law enforcement officials and military and security forces, legislative bodies, the judiciary, victims and their

---

84. *See* Susana SáCouto & Katherine Cleary, *Victims' Participation in the Investigations of the International Criminal Court*, 17 TRANSNAT'L L. & CONTEMP. PROBS. 73, 79 (2008) ("[A]mong the rights promoted by the Victims Declaration are the right of victims to be treated with respect, the right to receive information regarding relevant judicial proceedings, and the right to present their views and concerns to a court. Although some national jurisdictions involve victims to an even greater extent in criminal proceedings, these principles—being treated with respect, receipt of information, and the opportunity to present views and concerns—are seen as fundamental to providing victims 'access to justice.'").

85. G.A. Res. 60/147 (March 21, 2006).

86. *Id.* at Preamble.

87. *Id.*

88. *Id.* at V(8).

representatives, human rights defenders and lawyers, the media and the public in general. . . .[89]

International law once considered victims to be little more than the *objects* of rights and obligations. Today, in stark contrast, both domestic justice systems and international law increasingly view victims as the *subjects* of such rights and obligations.[90] This shift in thinking is critical, and the ICC follows—and expands upon—this developing legal trend.

---

89. *Id.* at 2.

90. Consider the Geneva Convention Relative to the Treatment of Prisoners of War, the European Convention on Human Rights, the American Convention on Human Rights, the International Covenant on Civil and Political Rights 1966, the International Convention on the Elimination of All Forms of Racial Discrimination 1965, and the Universal Declaration of Human Rights. State practice has similarly increasingly begun to provide reparations to victims. *See, e.g.*, Germany's *Wieder Gut Machung* law (providing over $104 billion in compensation to victims of Nazi crimes, and continuing to provide some $624 million annually to 100,000 pensioners) and the United States' "1988 Civil Liberties Act" (providing $20,000 to each citizen of Japanese ancestry interned during WWII). That said, state practice of providing compensation to non-state actors is at best an emerging norm. *See generally* M. Cherif Bassiouni, *International Recognition of Victims' Rights*, 6 HUMAN RIGHTS L. REV. 223 (2006).

PART IV

Primer on the ICC

THE FOLLOWING IS A PRIMER to generally familiarize the reader with the ICC's functions and procedures, particularly as they relate to victims.

A. Breaking New Ground for Victims' Rights

There are, as discussed above, legitimate grounds for contending that the ICC to date has not lived up to the international community's expectations, and for believing that there remains significant room for improvement. But one promising area in which the ICC has in fact assumed a true leadership role is in the field of victims' rights. The ICC's host of victim-centric laws at bottom strive to empower victims by providing them with a substantive seat at the proverbial table. In contrast to national models of direct victim redress, such as provided by European justice systems, representative, class action-style group litigation grounds the ICC's conception of victim representation.

Being prepared to accept the considerable responsibility placed on victim representatives' shoulders requires them to carry effective and flexible advocacy techniques in their arsenal, as well as to gain an intimate familiarity with the structure and challenges of the forum in which they must advocate.[1] The ability to alter course in the face of obstacles is, therefore, this book's continuing theme. Although full trial participation may be the goal, the prepared victim representative must give plenary thought to effective alternatives having the potential of meeting the victims' needs and desires.

---

1. Outside and inside observers agree that, while the Office of Public Counsel for Victims is staffed with a small cadre of lawyers who are very familiar with the ICC's articles, rules, and regulations, the larger groups of "external" legal representatives too frequently have failed to adequately prepare themselves for this unique venue and its unusual rules of play. Relying on sheer good will and optimism about doing "the right thing," while laudable, is never a substitute for a careful reading and understanding of the applicable legal provisions.

B. The ICC's Operation

The ICC stands alone as an international organization created by treaty among sovereign nations, enjoying a recognized international legal personality, yet neither bound nor controlled by any particular government. Headquartered in The Hague (Netherlands), with a liaison office in New York City and various field offices, the Court, at its core, is a high-profile and richly funded institution with significant political clout. As of 2010, the ICC employed more than 700 attorneys and professional staff from approximately 80 different states, with an annual operating budget approaching $200 million.

Member states' contributions finance the Court. In fact, the Court employs the same method used by the U.N. to determine the amount payable by each State Party—the Court bases a state's contribution on the state's capacity to pay, which in turn reflects factors such as a national income and population. The Court, however, limits the maximum amount a single country can pay in any year to 22 percent of the Court's budget.

Pursuant to Article 34, the ICC is comprised of the Presidency,[2] the Pre-Trial Chamber,[3] the Trial Chamber,[4] the Appeals Chamber,[5] the Office of the Prosecutor,[6] and the Registry.[7] The Assembly of States Parties nominates and

---

2. The duties of the Presidency are summarized in Article 38.

3. The duties of the Pre-Trial Chamber are summarized, among other places, in Articles 56–61. Whether the Pre-Trial Chamber consists of a single judge or three judges is determined by the Pre-Trial Chamber, *see* Rule 7(1), and is governed by Article 39(2)(b)(iii) (giving option between one and three judges); Article 57(2) (same); Rule 7(1) (stating that decision to designate single judge must be made "on basis of objective pre-established criteria"); and Regulation 47(1) (listing, as non-comprehensive list of criteria for selecting a single judge, the seniority and criminal trial experience of the judge, the circumstances of the proceedings, and the workload of the individual judges). *See generally* Situation in the Democratic Republic of the Congo, Case No. ICC-01/04: *Decision on the Designation of a Single Judge of Pre-Trial Chamber I* (March 26, 2009) (justifying appointment of single judge to carry out functions of the Pre-Trial Chamber in *The Prosecutor v. Bosco Ntaganda*); *see also* Situation in Uganda, Case No. ICC-02/04: *Decision Designating a Single Judge on Victims' Issues* (March 23, 2009), at 3–5 (Pre-Trial Chamber's decision that a single judge designated to handle victims' issues was needed to "ensure proper management and efficiency in the handling of victims' issues in the proceedings before the Chamber").

4. The primary duties of the Trial Chamber are outlined in Articles 64–76.

5. The primary duties of the Appeals Chamber are outlined in Articles 81–85.

6. The Prosecutor's primary duties are outlined in, among other places, Articles 42 and 54.

7. The Registry's primary duties are outlined in Article 43 and Rules 12–16.

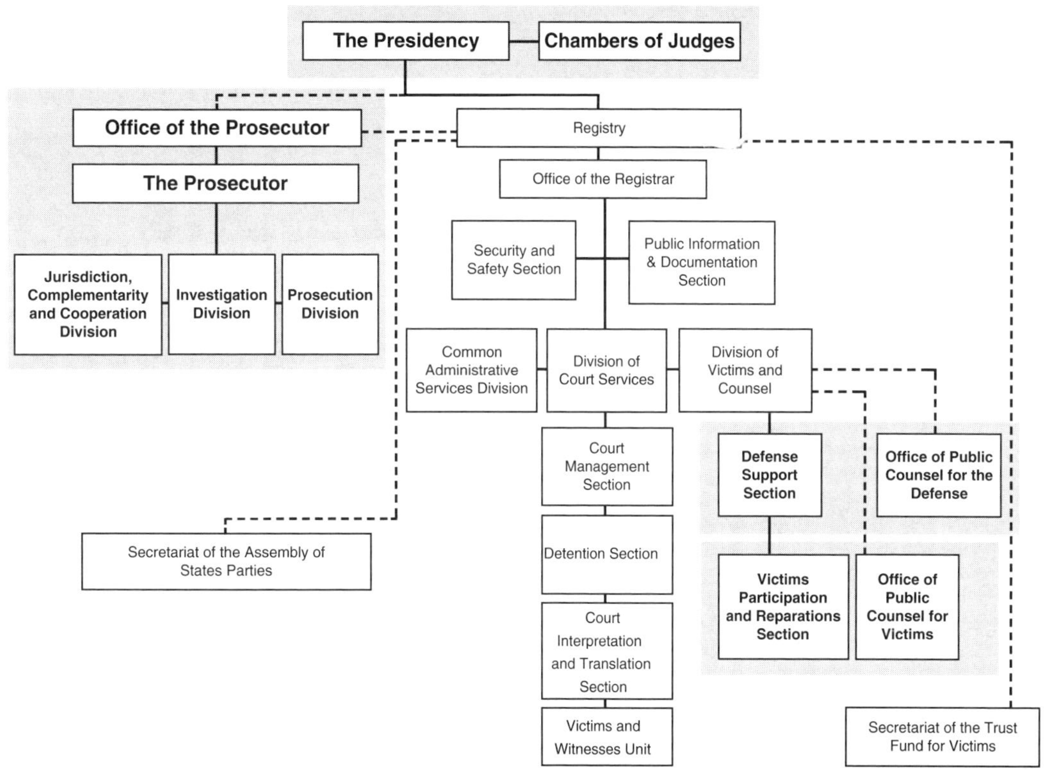

'Victims Before the International Criminal Court. A Guide for the Participation of Victims in the Proceedings of the Court.' Copyright© International Criminal Court 2006.

confirms the Prosecutor and judges who, as a group, are required to represent diverse geographic, gender, and legal backgrounds.[8] The Office of the Prosecutor, in order to preserve independence, operates as a separate organ of the Court. Some 250 lawyers, investigators, and staff are employed by the Office of the Prosecutor. The Registry, on the other hand, is responsible for all non-judicial aspects of the Court, including the Victim and Witness Unit. The Registry also set up the Office of Public Counsel for Victims, which as of this writing employs three attorneys and five staff.

Unlike the International Court of Justice ("ICJ"), the ICC is legally and functionally independent from the U.N. The "Relationship Agreement between the International Criminal Court and the United Nations" governs the arrangement between the ICC and the U.N. That said, the Rome Statute does grant certain powers to the U.N. Security Council. Article 13(b), for example, allows the Security Council to refer to the ICC situations that would not otherwise fall under the Court's jurisdiction. (The Security Council, in fact, used this legal mechanism in relation to the situation in Darfur, which the ICC could not otherwise have prosecuted because Sudan is not a State Party.) Moreover, Article 16 empowers the Security Council to require the Court to defer a case's investigation for a renewable period of 12 months. The Security Council may renew such a deferral indefinitely. The ICC also cooperates with the U.N. in many other areas, including in the exchange of information and logistical support.

C. The ICC's Limited Subject-Matter Jurisdiction

Article 5 of the Rome Statute grants the ICC jurisdiction over four broad categories of crimes, which the Article characterizes as the "most serious crimes of concern to the international community as a whole." Thus, the crimes listed under Article 5 of the Rome Statute, and defined in Articles 6, 7, and 8, all require the Prosecutor to prove specific, and more "serious," forms of intent as *mens rea* elements of the crime. The physical act of killing

8. *See* Article 36(7)-(8). As of this writing, 110 countries are State Parties (at times alternatively referred to as "States Parties") to the Rome Statute of the ICC. Thirty of the State Parties are African States, 14 are Asian States, 17 are Eastern Europe States, 24 are Latin American and Caribbean States, and 25 are Western European and other states. On October 1, 2009, the Czech Republic joined as a State Party.

somebody is, by way of example, not itself a crime within the jurisdiction of the ICC unless the physical act is also (1) "committed with intent to destroy, in whole or in part, a national, ethnic, racial or religious group" (as required to convict an accused[9] of having committed genocide under Article 6); (2) "committed as part of a widespread or systematic attack directed against any civilian population, with knowledge of the attack" (as required to convict an accused of having committed crimes against humanity under Article 7); or (3) "wilful," in the sense of being intentional (as required to convict an accused of having committed war crimes under Article 8). Academics, government officials, and international lawyers have advanced a variety of reasons for restricting the ICC's jurisdiction to such "super crimes," including the need to strengthen universal acceptance of the ICC, and to avoid overburdening it so that it can remain focused on its principal role and function.[10] As it stands, the crimes over which the ICC has jurisdiction are the least controversial, as they represent the most brazen attacks on bedrock human-rights principles.

1. The Crime of Genocide

Elements of Crime Article 6 defines the crime of genocide by reference to a number of particular acts committed "with intent to destroy, in whole or in part, a national, ethnical, racial, or religious group." These proscribed criminal acts include killing members of a group; forcibly transferring children from one group to another; imposing measures intended to prevent births within a group; inflicting conditions of life calculated to physically destroy the group; and causing serious bodily or mental harm to members of the group.

---

9. For ease of reading, the terms "accused" and "defendant" will be used somewhat interchangeably herein, even though the ICC and other international tribunals typically only use the term "accused."

10. *See* David Scheffer & Ashely Cox, *The Constitutionality of the Rome Statute of the International Criminal Court*, 98 JOURNAL OF CRIMINAL LAW & CRIMINOLOGY 1007 (2008) (discussing possibility that drug trafficking and terrorism could be "resurrected as candidates for inclusion in the ICC's subject matter jurisdiction"); *see also* David J. Scheffer, *The United States and the International Criminal Court*, 93 AM. J. INT'L L. 12, 12–13 (1999) (noting that "U.S. objectives [when considering the early ILC drafts] included . . . exclusion of drug trafficking and the hard-to-define crime of aggression from the statute").

Noteworthy is that, under Article 6's definition, the accused need not commit the crime through a government or its military, but rather can also be found guilty if he committed the offense through a terrorist or guerrilla organization, an NGO, etc. Moreover, the offence is limited to ethnic, national, racial and religious groups, which (with the exception, perhaps, of some "converted" members of religious groups) are "indelible" groups into which one is born. What is not covered by Article 6, therefore, are acts committed with the intent to destroy, say, certain ideological, political, professional, or similar groups which one typically joins as a matter of choice. Finally, the offense language requires that the Prosecutor establish the accused's intent to "destroy" the group in question, rather than to simply remove, or "cleanse," the group from a particular region.

2. Crimes Against Humanity

Elements of Crime Article 7 defines crimes against humanity as the commission of acts such as murder, extermination, enslavement, deportation, imprisonment, torture, rape, sexual slavery, enforced disappearance, and persecution constituting "part of a widespread or systemic attack directed against any civilian population." Article 7's crimes against humanity demands that the Prosecutor establish the existence, or at least the emergence, of a broader, systematic attack directed against a civilian population. Article 7 provides that the "humanity" sought to be protected contemplates the individuality of all human beings, apart from their membership in a particular group. Sudanese President Omar al-Bashir has been indicted, in part, on allegations that he committed such crimes against humanity. Specifically, al-Bashir was charged with violating Article 7(1)(a) (murder); Article 7(1)(b) (extermination); Article 7(1)(d) (forcible transfer); Article 7(1)(f) (torture); and Article 7(1)(g) (rape).[11]

3. War Crimes

Elements of Crime Article 8 defines war crimes extremely broadly to include violations of the Geneva Convention of August 12, 1949, as well as specified

---

11. *See* www.icc-cpi.int/NR/exeres/0EF62173-05ED-403A-80C8-F15EE1D25BB3.htm.

"serious violations of the laws and customs applicable in international armed conflict, within the established framework of international law," and "[o]ther serious violations of the laws and customs applicable in armed conflicts not of an international character." With regard to the requirement that the accused realize that the conduct took place in the context of, and was associated with, an international armed conflict, and that the accused was aware of the factual circumstances establishing the existence of "an" armed conflict, Article 8 provides that:

— There is no requirement for a legal evaluation by the perpetrator as to the *existence* of an armed conflict or its character as international or non-international.
— In that context, there is no requirement for awareness by the perpetrator of the facts that established the *character* of the conflict as international or non-international.[12]

Article 8's only requirement is that the accused have an awareness of the *factual circumstances* that establish the existence of an armed conflict.

4. The Crime of Aggression

Although the crime of aggression is technically "on the books," it continues to remain purposefully undefined. The ICC cannot exercise jurisdiction over the crime of aggression until such time as the State Parties agree on a definition of the crime, and set out with specificity the conditions under which it may be prosecuted.[13] Although the crime of aggression remains without definition or ICC referral procedure, in 2010 the first review conference of the Rome Statute by the State Parties is expected to take up the proposal to

---

12. Emphasis added.

13. For one generally accepted definition, *see* Report of the Special Committee on the Question of Defining Aggression, at 11, U.N. GAOR, 29th Sess., Supp. No. 19, U.N. Doc. A/9619 (March 11–April 12, 1974); *see also* Roger S. Clark, *Rethinking Aggression as a Crime and Formulating Its Elements: The Final Work-Product of the Preparatory Commission for the International Criminal Court*, 15 LEIDEN J. INT'L L. 859 (2002); Matthias Schuster, *The Rome Statute and the Crime of Aggression: A Gordian Knot in Search of a Sword*, 14 CRIM. L.F. 1 (2003).

"activate" this offense.[14] The general conduct considered for proscription involves military invasions or attacks of another state's territory without a legitimate self-defense claim.

Of course, at present the ICC has subject-matter jurisdiction over a host of crimes falling within the above-described categories. To date, however, the Court has only investigated and prosecuted a minute number of cases, when compared to the universe of perpetrators. Moreover, few in the Office of the Prosecutor will argue, either privately or on the record, that they are all that interested in adding this particularly politically-charged offense. Although much is written about the purported promise of adding the crime of aggression to the Prosecutor's arsenal, formally defining the offense, setting aside its symbolism, is politically difficult and will not likely open any new (or meaningful) avenues of prosecution.

The prosecutors have, as they will candidly concede, enough on their plates already, without also wading into the political morass of determining whether one state has committed a crime of aggression (however defined) against another. This debate thus once again highlights politicians' and diplomats' emphasis on the "symbolic" value of the ICC, while at the same time drawing into focus how unfamiliar many of them are with the existing abundance of prosecutorial legal tools, and the limits on prosecutorial resources and capacity. Adding new crimes may not be needed; increasing the number of investigations, prosecutions, and convictions, however, is very much required. Whether the crime of aggression is formally defined will, by itself, thus likely do little to address the prevailing need to enhance the ICC's efficiency and professionalism.

D. Territorial and Personal Jurisdiction Requirements

The ICC is headquartered, has its offices, and has its detention facility in the Netherlands. But its venue is effectively worldwide, as its proceedings may take place anywhere. The ICC, moreover, can exercise jurisdiction in cases where the accused is a national of a State Party, the alleged crime took place on the territory of a State Party, *or* if the U.N. Security Council referred the situation to the ICC.

---

14. *See generally* Sergey Sayapin, *The Definition of Crime of Aggression for the Purpose of the International Criminal court: Problems and Perspectives*, 13 J. CONFLICT & SECURITY L. 333, 346–47 (2008) (proposing a definition for the crime of aggression).

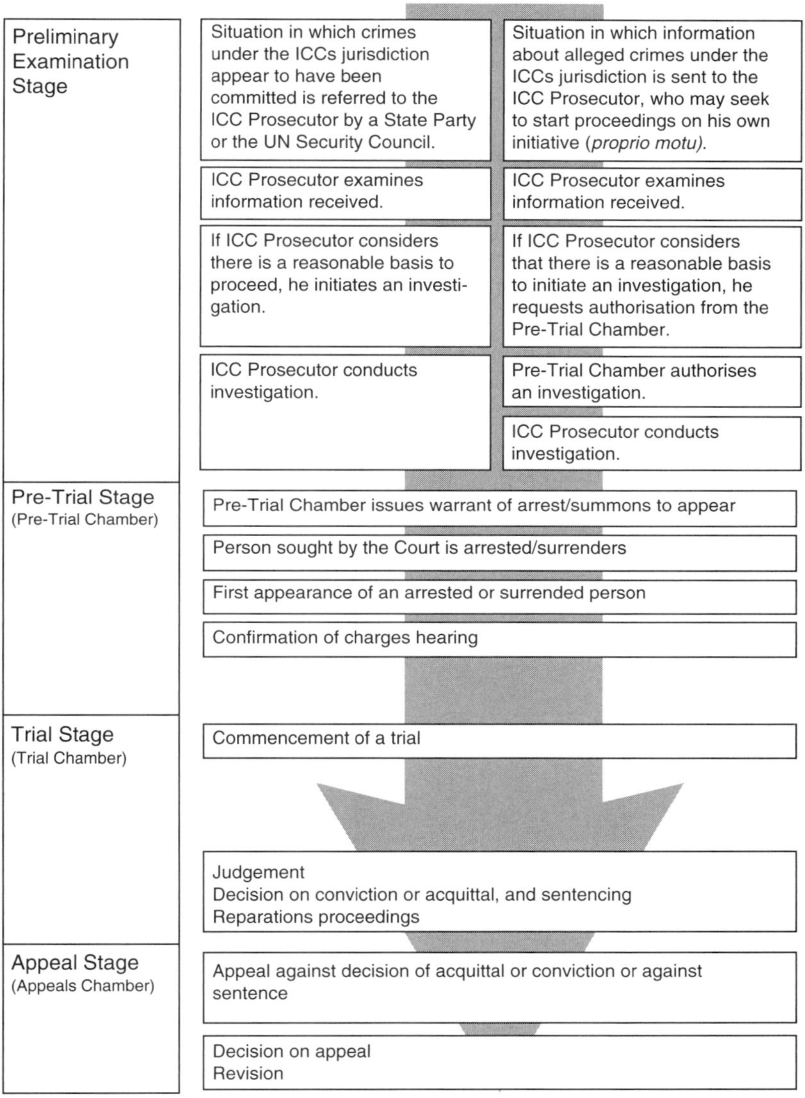

Case Progression Chart

'Victims Before the International Criminal Court. A Guide for the Participation of Victims in the Proceedings of the Court.' Copyright© International Criminal Court 2006.

During the negotiations over the Rome Statute there was substantial disagreement over whether the ICC should be granted universal jurisdiction.[15]

---

15. *See* Henry Kissinger, *The Pitfalls of Universal Jurisdiction*, FOREIGN AFF. (July/August 2001), at 86, 92–93.

The United States, together with other states, ultimately defeated the universalist position. Negotiators, however, reached a compromise permitting the ICC to exercise jurisdiction under the following limited circumstances, as set forth in Articles 12 and 13:

1. The accused is a *national* of a State Party (or, in some cases, where the accused's state has accepted the ICC's jurisdiction);[16]

2. The alleged crime was *committed* on the territory of a State Party (or, in some cases, where the state on whose territory the crime was committed has accepted ICC jurisdiction);

3. The U.N. Security Council *referred* the situation to the ICC (in which case the above-preconditions do not apply; a national of a Non-Party State can be prosecuted, and there is no requirement that the accused commit the alleged crime on the territory of a State Party); *or*

4. A Non-State Party files a declaration with the ICC, inviting the ICC to investigate a crime alleged to have occurred within its territory, or to have been committed by one of its nationals.[17]

E. The ICC's Limited Temporal Jurisdiction

Pursuant to Article 11, the ICC's non-retroactive jurisdiction limits the cases it can hear to crimes committed on or after July 1, 2002 (the date on which the Rome Statute entered into force). For a state that acceded to the Rome Statute *after* that date, the ICC can exercise jurisdiction automatically with respect to crimes committed after the effective date for that particular state.

16. Most of the situations within the purview of the ICC will involve complex civil conflicts, with atrocities committed by both sides. The danger with self-referrals is that they will usually come from a government seeking to have the ICC indict members of the opposition rebel forces. Indeed, other than the Security Council's referral of the Darfur situation, the Prosecutor has targeted not state authorities, but rather those who are the state authorities' enemies. *See generally* William A. Schabas, *Prosecutorial Discretion v. Judicial Activism at the International Criminal Court*, 6 J. INT'L CRIM. JUST. 731, 752–53 (2008) ("The attention to non-state actors is closely related to the concept of 'self-referral,' which has the practical consequence of establishing a degree of complicity between the Office of the Prosecutor and the referring state. . . . Indeed, no government anywhere would respond anymore to an invitation to the Prosecutor to, in practice, prosecute themselves. Self-referral will be viewed as a trap, a Trojan horse of the Court.").

17. Note that three of the four situations currently before the ICC are the result of such self-referrals.

F. The ICC's Due Process Guarantees

With the exception of the right to a jury trial, the fundamental due process rights accorded by the ICC's Rome Statute roughly mirror those provided under the United States Constitution.[18] These rights include, but are not limited to, the presumption of innocence (Article 66(1)); the right to confrontation and cross-examination (Article 67(1)(e)); the right to remain silent (Articles 55(2)(b) and 67(1)(g)); the right to a speedy trial (Article 67(1)(c)); the right to assistance of counsel (Article 67(1)(b) and (d)); the right to a written statement outlining the charges against the accused (Article 61(3)); the right of compulsory process to bring in witnesses on the accused's behalf (Article 67(1)(e)); the prohibition against *ex post facto* crimes (Article 22(1)); the protection against double jeopardy (Article 20(3)); the right to be free from warrantless searches and arrests (Articles 57(3)(a) and 58); the right to be present during the trial (Article 63); and the limited right to exclude unreliable evidence obtained illegally (Article 69(7)).[19] This list of rights is one of the more comprehensive codifications of due process guarantees promulgated to date.[20]

G. The "Complementarity" Firewall: Understanding the ICC's Key Admissibility Test

Despite the ICC's generally clear statutory language, in many circles confusion abounds over the scope of the ICC's jurisdiction. Failure to understand the narrow universe of cases triable at the ICC results in victim representatives overlooking fundamental defense strategies calculated to circumvent altogether an ICC prosecution.

---

18. *See generally* Scheffer & Cox, *supra* note 10, at 1047–59 ("[T]here is no fundamental due process right protected by the U.S. Constitution that is not also found in significant form in the Rome Statute.").

19. *See generally* Sasha Markovic, *The Modern Version of the Shot Heard'Round the World: America's Flawed Revolution Against the International Criminal Court and the Rest of the World*, 51 CLEV. ST. L. REV. 263, 291–97 (2004) (comparing constitutional rights of Americans with rights guaranteed in the Rome Statute).

20. For a full analysis of this topic, *see* SALVATORE ZAPPALA, HUMAN RIGHTS IN INTERNATIONAL CRIMINAL PROCEEDINGS (2003) (taking a procedural approach to human rights guarantees in international proceedings, including those at the ICC).

The pivotal point here is that the ICC is purpose-built to *complement*, rather than replace, existing national judicial systems. The ICC is, thus, intended to function as a backstop court of last resort, investigating and prosecuting only where national courts have failed to, or are unable to, bring perpetrators of atrocity crimes to justice. That is, the complementarity principle stands for the proposition that the primary responsibility to investigate and punish crimes remains with the individual states; the "complementarity privilege," accordingly, *extinguishes* ICC jurisdiction.

Both Non-Party States and State Parties are entitled to avail themselves of the complementarity privilege.[21] In this sense, complementarity is a reverse-federalism paradigm, in that the overarching ICC yields to the subsumed states whenever the states are able and willing to adjudicate those cases over which the ICC otherwise would have jurisdiction. More specifically, Article 17(1) of the Statute provides that a case is "inadmissible" (that is, the ICC lacks jurisdiction) if:

1. The state that has domestic jurisdiction over the case is investigating or prosecuting it, unless the state is *unwilling or genuinely unable* to carry out the investigation or prosecution;

2. A state that has jurisdiction over the case has investigated it and decided not to prosecute the person concerned, unless the decision resulted from the unwillingness or inability of the state genuinely to prosecute the matter;

3. The domestic prosecutors have already tried the target of the investigation for conduct which is the subject of the complaint, and a trial at the ICC is therefore not permitted pursuant to Article 20(3); *or*

4. The Prosecutor determines the case to be of insufficient gravity to justify further action by the ICC.

---

21. *See generally* Tom Ginsburg, *The Clash of Commitments at the International Criminal Court*, 9 CHI. J. INT'L L. 499, 501 (2009) ("The complementarity regime virtually assures that the ICC will not hear cases against major international military actors such as the United States because a state can avoid prosecution of its national by initiating a credible investigation or prosecution; the only states likely to have their nationals prosecuted are those that either (1) want the prosecution to go forward (say because of domestic regime change) and with the international community to bear the costs of prosecution, or (2) have too little state capacity to initiate a credible prosecution or investigations. Sudan forms a potential third category: a recalcitrant state that wishes to avoid prosecution.").

As discussed in greater detail in Articles 17(2) and 17(3), the ICC, therefore, exercises its jurisdiction *only* when national courts are (1) *unwilling* or (2) *unable*—due to inadequacies in the domestic legal capabilities, for political reasons, or as the result of some other circumstance—to investigate and prosecute in their domestic courts crimes otherwise within the ICC's jurisdiction. Certain governments and individuals, concerned with the possibility of ICC investigation and prosecution, are as a consequence carefully studying the complementarity firewall in order to use it proactively to frustrate ICC jurisdiction.

By way of example, in the case of Sudan,[22] the Khartoum government appears to be keenly aware of Article 17. The government, even prior to the ICC's indictment of Sudan President Omar al-Bashir on war crimes and crimes against humanity charges, signaled its intent to update and modernize Sudan's criminal justice system. It is not much of a leap to conclude that the Khartoum government did this solely to demonstrate its institutional "readiness" to "genuinely carry out" in its domestic courts the investigation and prosecution of Darfur-related war crimes over which the ICC may otherwise have jurisdiction.

Such ICC-inspired "law reform" may of course bring genuine advances to a country's legal system.[23] It can just as easily, however, represent a thinly veiled ploy to evade ICC jurisdiction and the corresponding international human rights spotlight that accompanies an ICC trial. By invoking the privilege, a state such as Sudan can seek to strip the ICC of its jurisdiction, thereby aiding its alleged war criminals' efforts to avoid prosecution by the Court.

The concern about the Court's potential political bias in evaluating whether a state is "unwilling" to prosecute a matter within its domestic courts has been a substantial stumbling block for Non-Party States, including the United States. ICC sceptics point to this language as amendable to broad, politically motivated construction (and, even worse, application). If a

---

22. For a humanized history of the Darfur conflict, *see* DAVID K. EGGERS, WHAT IS THE WHAT (2008).

23. This is a development that even opponents of the Khartoum government view as positive. Although they may favor full ICC involvement in bringing cases against the government's leadership, they also realize that the present law reforms are a positive externality of the ICC's complementarity firewall. *See generally* William Burke-White, *Proactive Complementarity: The International Criminal Court and National Courts in the Rome System of International Justice*, 49 HARV. INT'L L.J. 53, 92–93 (2008) ("Through a policy of proactive complementarity, the ICC may be able to facilitate domestic judicial reform efforts that can transform a state previously unable to prosecute international crimes into a state both able and willing to undertake domestic investigations and prosecutions. This policy might include the training of officials, the provision of resources, or assistance with investigations.").

nation, such as the United States, becomes a State Party, and thereafter fails to prosecute certain political officials or members of the military leadership for their roles in what some in the international community may regard as atrocity crimes, it would certainly be within the ICC's competence to declare that state "unwilling" to pursue the matter, thus deactivating the complementarity privilege as it relates to the particular case.[24]

Proponents of the United States joining the ICC may, in rebuttal, contend that, given the United States' significant political power and standing in the world, it is a practical impossibility that the Office of the Prosecutor would ever seriously consider charging members of the United States military or United States political leaders, absent unforeseeable and extraordinary circumstances. However, even members of the Office of the Prosecutor will privately concede that such arguably politically-motivated prosecutions are more than a purely hypothetical possibility. By way of example, they will point to the fact that the Office recently came quite close to formally investigating—and perhaps charging—alleged war crimes involving British troops during the Iraq war (specifically, Britain's use of "indiscriminate weapons systems" to attack purported "urban areas").

Britain undoubtedly is a politically powerful nation with a long history of safeguarding human rights, and it certainly has the ability to properly investigate and prosecute such cases in its domestic courts. That the Office of the Prosecutor, in a world chockfull of past and current dictators, militia leaders, and military commanders responsible for mass homicides and gross human rights abuses, would, despite the existence of the complementarity firewall, consider devoting scarce time and resources towards investigating British

---

24. *See generally* Lee A. Casey, *The Case Against the International Criminal Court*, 25 FORDHAM INT'L L.J. 840, 861 (2002); *see also* David B. Rivken Jr. & Lee A. Casey, *That's Why They Call It War*, WASH. POST. (March 16, 2003), at BO4 ("[International human rights] NGOs suggest that United States armed forces, precisely because they have better weapons, should be held to a higher standard than less advanced militaries. This would apply particularly to the question of civilian casualties, or 'collateral damage,' where a rule of near zero tolerance is promoted."); Lee A. Casey & David B. Rivkin, Jr., *Court Dismissed: The ICC Is a Snare and a Monstrosity—with No Standing*, NAT'L REV. (November 11, 2002) (asserting that the United States considers the Rome Statute "an open invitation to abuse by ambitious and/or biased prosecutors and judges"). For an intriguing discussion of the constitutionality of United States participation in the ICC, and of the changes in United States law required prior to the complementarity preempting ICC jurisdiction, *see* Scheffer & Cox, *supra* note 10, at 983 (pointing out that persecution, which encompasses ethnic cleansing, is not criminalized by United States law, and calling for the United States to "modernize its codes, civilian and military, so that the United States has the ability to investigate and prosecute U.S. nationals before U.S. Courts for the full range of atrocity crimes falling within the subject matter jurisdiction of the ICC").

troops at a minimum undercuts the categorical claim that the Court would realistically *never* think of investigating and charging the military or political leaders of rule-of-law driven democracies.

Consider in this regard also the U.N. Economic and Social Council's 2001 decision to vote the United States off of the 53-seat, Geneva-based U.N. Commission on Human Rights, of which the United States in 1947 was a founding member. The fact that the U.N. Commission at the time had among its ranks states with significant, established histories of human rights abuses, such as Libya, China, Cuba, Pakistan, Sudan, Uganda, and Sierra Leone, continues to fuel the fires of ICC sceptics. The sceptics point to this incident as a relatively clear example of international retaliation against, or animosity towards, the United States.

If the United States one day decided not to prosecute a particular political or military leader, there is nothing in the ICC's legal provisions formally stopping the Prosecutor or the Chamber from concluding there from that such a decision is the result of the kind of corrupt, or atrocity-crimes-tolerating, failed-state judicial system for which the ICC was meant to be a substitute. There, moreover, is no system of democratic accountability that would necessarily prevent such arguable overreaching by an unaccountable and unreviewable prosecutor, who has virtually unfettered discretion to charge atrocity crimes all the way up the chain of command.

Weighing the benefits to the United States of joining the ICC against the unpredictable dangers down the road might fortify ICC sceptics' belief that becoming a State Party is not necessarily in the Nation's best interest. It is of course possible, however, that the ICC sceptics are simply overreacting, selectively singling out isolated incidents in an ongoing attempt to discredit the demand that United States, like all member states, give up some level of sovereignty in the pursuit of international justice. Moreover, any sovereign nation has in its arsenal the ability to rely on self-help. The United States, satisfied that it has the capacity and willingness to properly investigate a particular matter in its own courts, or convinced that the ICC breached the complementarity firewall for purely political reasons, could simply refuse to comply with the ICC's requests for assistance in investigating, apprehending, or extraditing individuals within its domestic jurisdiction. But such inaction would represent a clear breach of the United States' treaty obligations.

If such an impasse were reached, the Court, pursuant to Article 87(7), could "make a finding [of non-compliance] and refer the matter to the Assembly of State Parties or, where the [U.N.] Security Council referred the matter to the Court, to the Security Council." Article 112(2)(f), in turn, enables the Assembly of State Parties to "[c]onsider pursuant to article 87, paragraphs 5 and 7, any question relating to non-cooperation." However, Article 112 fatally contains no enforcement mechanisms.

In theory, the Security Council could, pursuant to Article 39 of the Charter of the U.N., make a determination that the United States' act of non-compliance constitutes a "threat to the peace, breach of the peace, or act of aggression," thus permitting the Security Council to take enforcement measures discussed in Charter Articles 40–42 to prompt compliance. Such drastic action against the United States is, however, highly unlikely, particularly given the United States' seat on the Security Council. In the end, then, this issue is more complicated than it may at first appear.

H. Case Initiation

Victims are, by article and rule, formally independent, co-equal "participants" (though not necessarily co-equal "parties," which, pursuant to Article 82(1) and its grant of appeals rights to "[e]ither party," is a term of art referring only to the prosecution and defense). That said, victims are also to a significant extent reliant on the Prosecutor. The victims' interest in the Prosecutor's action reaches its apex when it comes to the Prosecutor's charging decision. Whether a given victim will have any involvement in the Court's litigation, indeed, depends on the threshold question of who the Prosecutor decides to charge, and with what. It is, therefore, important to understand the role prosecutorial discretion plays at the ICC.

The analysis of prosecutorial discretion at the ICC requires a two-stage process, divided into a review of the Prosecutor's discretion in the context of "situations," and the application of this discretion with respect to individual "cases" encompassed within a given situation. The Prosecutor, in short, must obtain jurisdiction over the broad situation prior to indicting specific cases arising out of that situation. Distinguishing situations from cases in this manner is unique to the ICC. Prior *ad hoc* tribunals, including the post World War II tribunals convened at Nuremberg, Tokyo, the ICTY, and the International Criminal Tribunal for Rwanda (ICTR), did not have to select situations, since their enabling legislation was inherently situation-specific.[25]

---

25. *See, e.g.*, Statute of the International Criminal Tribunal for the Former Yugoslavia, U.N. SCOR, 48th Sess., 3217th mtg., Article 3, U.N. Doc. S/RES/827 (1993); Statute of the International Criminal Tribunal for Rwanda, U.N. SCOR, 49th Sess., 3453rd mtg., Article 4, U.N. Doc. S/RES/955 (1994).

Situations can be identified in one of three ways: (1) State Party referral (such as Uganda), pursuant to Article 14; (2) Security Council referral (such as Darfur), pursuant to Article 13(b); or (3) at the initiation of the Prosecutor, pursuant to Article 15. Neither the Court nor the Prosecutor may decline a situation referred by the State Party or U.N. Security Council mechanisms, since referrals under both processes are manifestations of state sovereignty.[26] Cases within the situation, on the other hand, are a different matter.

1. State Party Initiation or Security Council Referral

If the State Party or Security Council referral process activates the Court's jurisdiction, then the Prosecutor, pursuant to Article 53, must decide what particular cases, if any, to charge.

Article 53 provides in relevant part:

> 1. The Prosecutor shall, having evaluated the information made available to him or her, initiate an investigation unless he or she determines that there is no reasonable basis to proceed under this Statute. In deciding whether to initiate an investigation, the Prosecutor shall consider whether:
>
> (a) The information available to the Prosecutor provides a reasonable basis to believe that a crime within the jurisdiction of the Court was or is being committed;
>
> (b) The case is or would be admissible under Article 17;[27] *and*
>
> (c) Taking into account the gravity of the crime and *the interests of victims*, there are nonetheless substantial reasons to believe that an investigation would not serve the interests of justice.[28]

Should the Prosecutor determine there is no reasonable basis to proceed with the prosecution, and that decision is based solely on the subsection 1(c)

---

26. *See generally* Schabas, *supra* note 16, at 734–40 (providing an excellent analysis of the promises and pitfalls of prosecutorial discretion, as exercised at the ICC).

27. Article 17 provides that the Court shall determine a case inadmissible if (1) the complementarity firewall is triggered, or (2) the "case is *not of sufficient gravity* to justify further action by the Court." (Emphasis added).

28. Emphasis added.

"safety-valve,"[29] then the Prosecutor must inform the Pre-Trial Chamber of his decision.[30] If, on the other hand, the Prosecutor bases his declination decision on the other two criteria discussed above, then the Prosecutor must inform (i) the Pre-Trial Chamber, and (ii) either the state making the Article 14 referral, or the Security Council, of this decision.[31] Note, however, that, in addition to the criteria listed in Article 53(1), Article 53(2)(c) permits the Prosecutor to decline prosecution if he determines that the prosecution is "not in the interests of justice, taking into account all the circumstances, including the gravity of the crime, *the interests of the victims* and the age or infirmity of the alleged perpetrator, and his or her role in the alleged crime. . . ."[32]

The referring State Party and the U.N. Security Council have the right to request that the Pre-Trial Chamber review the Prosecutor's finding that there is no sufficient basis for prosecution.[33] The Pre-Trial Chamber, moreover, on its own initiative may review the Prosecutor's decision not to proceed if the Prosecutor based his decision solely on Article 53 subparagraphs 1(c) or 2(c).[34] Of course, if new facts come to light, the Prosecutor can always reconsider his decision to charge, or to decline, a particular case.[35] This statutory framework, as a practical matter, therefore gives the Prosecutor notably broad discretion over case-related charging decisions.

2. The Prosecutor's Initiation of a Case

As touched on above, the Rome Statute authorizes the Prosecutor to initiate investigations on his own accord (*proprio motu*), provided the alleged crimes are within the jurisdiction of the Court.[36] This power is one of the most

29. I employ the term "safety valve" because both Article 53(1)(c)'s "gravity" criteria and the "interests of justice" criteria are extremely broad, giving the Prosecutor significant discretion to decline prosecutions.

30. *See* Article 53(a).

31. *See* Article 53(2).

32. Emphasis added.

33. *See* Article 53(3)(a).

34. *See* Article 53(3)(b).

35. *See* Article 53(4).

36. Article 15(1).

distinctive features of the ICC, not found in previous *ad hoc* and international tribunals. As one might imagine, such power vested in the Prosecutor and the Court also raises considerable concerns, including the above-described fears that such independent power could undermine the credibility of the Court by leading to "frivolous and politicized" prosecutions.[37]

The Rome Statute expects the "seriousness of the information received [from written or oral witness statements, state actors, organs of the U.N., NGOs, intergovernmental organizations, and 'other reliable sources that he or she deems appropriate']" to inform the Prosecutor's charging decision. After the Prosecutor undertakes such an analysis, he may seek the Court's permission to commence an investigation.[38] If, however, the Prosecutor concludes from his investigation that there is no "reasonable basis for an investigation," then the Prosecutor must inform those parties who provided him with information of this decision.[39] Although the drafters clearly included this last "notification" provision in the interest of transparency, the "shall inform" language only requires the Prosecutor to inform the parties of his *decision*, but not of the underlying *reasoning* leading to the Prosecutor reaching the decision.

The charging decision is formally made by the Prosecutor, but at least some victim representatives take the position that they have the legal authority to request that the Chamber expand the indictment to include other charges supported by the trial evidence. For example, on May 22, 2009, victim representatives in the *Lubanga* trial formally requested that the Chamber include sexual slavery and cruel and inhumane treatment charges in the indictment. The prosecution did not appreciate such interference with "its" case, and the defense understandably also complained that such last-minute attempts to expand the charges threatened to deprive the accused of due process. How the ICC will grapple with such unorthodox, but creative, legal maneuvering on the part of the victims remains to be seen, but it is likely that this particular request will ultimately be rejected.

The Pre-Trial Chamber, moreover, can approve or decline any investigations the Prosecutor conducts *proprio motu*. The Pre-Trial Chamber may

---

37. *See* Luis Moreno-Ocampo, *The International Criminal Court: Seeking Global Justice*, 40 CASE W. RES. J. INT'L L. 215, 219 (2007–08).

38. Article 15(2), (3), and (4).

39. Article 15(6).

authorize such an investigation if, having reviewed the Prosecutor's request, together with any collected supporting materials, it concludes that there is a reasonable basis to proceed with the investigation, and the case appears to fall within the jurisdiction of the Court. Of course, the Trial Chamber reviews any *prima facie* determination by the Pre-Trial as to the jurisdiction and the admissibility of a case. If, on the other hand, the Pre-Trial Chamber determines that the case-accepting criterion is not met, the Prosecutor may either decide not to proceed with the investigation, or may opt to re-present a further request involving the same situation, but based on new facts or evidence.[40]

Despite the broad powers possessed by the Prosecutor, to date the Prosecutor has not relied on this Article 15 statutory authority to initiate cases at his own initiative[41] (though reports indicate that the Office of the Prosecutor is actively investigating certain national officials with an eye on possible charges). Therefore, there is no way to prospectively gauge how deferential judges will be in reviewing the Prosecutor's *proprio motu* charging decisions.

3. Prosecutorial Guidelines: Determining the "Gravity" of a Case

Although in most domestic contexts there is a presumption that the Prosecutor will pursue all non-*de minimus* crimes, the ICC Prosecutor, no different from a federal prosecutor in the United States, must select from a fairly vast pool of meritorious cases, isolating those that are most significant and most deserving of prosecution. The Prosecutor's "Prosecutorial Strategy" policy paper reflects this fairly simple and expected accommodation, stating that "the Office adopted a policy of focusing its efforts on the most serious crimes and on those [individuals] who bear the greatest responsibility for these crimes."[42] The Office of the Prosecutor assesses the "gravity" of a

---

40. *See* Article 53(4).

41. One possible explanation for the absence of cases initiated by the Prosecutor is that the very grant of this authority was a highly contentious part of the drafting process.

42. *See* Schabas, *supra* note 16, at 735–36 (quoting the Office of the Prosecutor: "Although any crime falling within the jurisdiction of the Court is a serious matter, the Statute clearly foresees and requires an additional consideration of 'gravity,' whereby the Office must determine that a case is of sufficient gravity to justify further action by the Court. . . .

particular case on the basis of the scale of the crimes, the nature of the crimes, the manner of commission of the crimes, and the impact of the crimes.[43] These criteria seem reasonable, in that they take into account not only the harm caused to the victims, but also the degree of participation and the degree of barbarism of the alleged acts. In the end, however, these words do little (and in reality, little can be done in this regard) to help outsiders identify those cases the Prosecutor is most likely to pursue.[44] Indeed, when one compares recent history's extensive rogues gallery of perpetrators with the few accused brought (or sought to be brought) to account at the ICC, one cannot help but wonder to what extent the ICC is, in fact, effectively pursuing today's most deserving violators of international criminal law and human rights (and human decency) norms.[45]

I. A New Paradigm: The ICC's Hybrid System of Advocacy

The ICC's new forum brings with it unique challenges. Lawyers advocating on behalf of victims must first and foremost gain familiarity with the ICC's idiosyncratic mix of legal principles. In terms of trial practice at the ICC, the Court, like the ICTY and the ICTR before it, incorporates elements of both the common law and civil law legal systems into its "hybrid" system of

---

[F]actors relevant in assessing gravity include: the scale of the crimes; the nature of the crimes; the manner of commission of the crimes and the impact of the crimes.").

43. *Id.; see also* Statements on Communications Concerning Iraq, The Hague (February 9, 2009), at 8–9 (the Prosecutor explains his decision not to proceed on complaints filed concerning alleged crimes committed by British troops in Iraq following the 2003 invasion, concluding that there is no evidence that war crimes, as defined by Article 8, had been committed, and noting that the "4 to 12 [alleged] victims of willful killing and the limited number of victims of [alleged] inhuman treatment . . . was of a different order than the number of victims found in other situations under investigation or analysis by the Office [of the Prosecutor]"; the matter therefore also failed Article 53(1)(b), and by cross-reference Article 17's, gravity requirement).

44. *See generally* Schabas, *supra* note 16, at 743 ("There is no attempt within the ICC Statute itself to rank crimes based on gravity, and it might be claimed, as judges have done at the ICTY, that there is no objective distinction between war crimes, crimes against humanity and genocide in terms of seriousness. In reply, however, there is implicit evidence in the ICC Statute that war crimes are less serious than genocide and crimes against humanity.") (Citations omitted).

45. Though, in fairness to the prosecution, the state of the available evidence against some of the potential accused may make prosecution difficult (though, perhaps, not impossible).

procedural and substantive law.[46] The ICC's brand of justice is, therefore, neither purely adversarial (that is, based on the common law tradition), nor purely inquisitorial (that is, based on the Napoleonic civil law tradition).

Practitioners accustomed to ICTY and ICTR proceedings will, nonetheless, recognize many of the ICC's features, such as the requirement that law enforcement officials instruct the accused of the right to remain silent during questioning, the right to have legal assistance, and the right to the presence of counsel prior to and during questioning by the ICC prosecutor or national authorities.[47] Lawyers versed in the United States and English common-law tradition, on the other hand, will notice that the ICC departs from common-law procedure in many respects.

The most notable difference between practice at the ICC and common-law trial practice is that the accused at the ICC has no right to a trial by jury,[48] which in the United States is constitutionally engraved in the Sixth Amendment. Moreover, rulings at the ICC merely represent persuasive authority, and therefore do not constitute binding precedent (*stare decisis*[49]).[50]

---

46. *See generally* Brianne N. McGonigle, *Bridging the Divides in International Criminal Proceedings: An Examination into the Victim Participation Endeavor of the International Criminal Court*, 21 FLA. J. INT'L L. 93, 106–09 (2009) ("In combining retributive and restorative justice principles the Court has maintained the primary goal of seeking to establish the truth as it pertains to the guilt or innocence of an accused through efficient and fair proceedings. Yet it has also expanded its mandate by incorporating ancillary goals pertaining to, *inter alia*, victim participation in the proceedings."); Alexandra H. Guhr, *Victim Participation During the Pre-Trial Stage at the International Criminal Court*, 8 INT'L CRIM. L. REV. 109 (2008).

47. *See* Article 55 ("Rights of Persons During an Investigation").

48. Not only is the jury system a relative outlier in terms of the global administration of the criminal law (though some civil law countries, such as Belgium, Norway, Spain, and France, permit jury trials), but the very act of using an international tribunal to (in theory, at least) prosecute only the "masterminds" having command responsibility for inherently complex atrocity crimes would present serious challenges for the jury selection process.

49. The term "stare decisis" is derived from the maxim "*stare decisis et non quieta movere*." BLACK'S LAW DICTIONARY 1406 (6th ed. 1990). As Justice Douglas observed, "there will be no equal justice under law if a negligence rule is applied in the morning but not in the afternoon." William O. Douglas, *Stare Decisis*, 49 COLUM. L. REV. 735, 736 (1949).

50. Article 21(2) provides that "[t]he Court *may* apply principles and rules of law as interpreted in *its previous* decisions." (Emphasis added.) Indeed, in terms of the order of priority, earlier decisions of the Chamber take a back seat to the Statute, Elements of Crimes, Rules of Procedure and Evidence, applicable treaties, principles and rules of international law, and general principles of law derived from by the Court from national laws of legal systems of the world (including the laws of the state that would normally exercise jurisdiction over the crime). Judges from civil law countries, where judicial precedents only

Other elements of the civil law system incorporated into ICC procedure include the Court's active Pre-Trial Division, which determines, among other things, whether a case should proceed to trial.[51] The Rome Statute, indeed, authorizes judges to play a much more active role during the course of the main trial than is the norm in adversarial proceedings. The ICC's Office of the Prosecutor, likewise, is more powerful than its counterparts in many common-law jurisdictions. This is because the Office acts as the principal investigator for the prosecution *and* the defense, with the stated goal of impartially "establish[ing] the truth" by investigating "incriminating and exonerating circumstances equally."[52]

Lawyers from civil law countries, on the other hand, will notice aspects of ICC law with which they may not be familiar. For example, an accused at the ICC may plead guilty to charges against him to avoid trial,[53] which is a procedure generally unavailable in civil justice systems. To the extent that the Trial Chamber concludes that the interests of justice, and in particular, the interests of the victims, require a more complete presentation of the facts of the case than is contained in the accused's Article 64 guilty plea *colloqui* or factual basis, Article 65(4) authorizes the Chamber to order the trial continued, and to order that the Prosecutor present specific additional evidence. This additional evidence should complete the factual record by elaborating on the accused's precise role in the offense, or by further detailing the surrounding circumstances leading up to the offense. Victims must pay particular attention to ensuring that such guilty pleas contain admissions as to all relevant facts, including, where possible, those facts demonstrating specific instances of victimization.

Although ICC procedures, therefore, have inquisitorial aspects, the ICC trial process in the main follows the adversarial model, with the accused having the important right to call and cross-examine witnesses.[54] In addition, the ICC's substantive law provides for criminal liability in a manner

---

have persuasive weight, and criminal codes enjoy a decisive legal status, do not see the same binding value common law attorneys attach to prior rulings on the same issue.

51. *See generally* Article 57 ("Functions and Powers of the Pre-Trial Chamber"); *see also* the discussion on the Pre-Trial Chamber's role, *supra*, at Part XII(A).

52. Article 54(1)(a) ("Duties and Powers of the Prosecutor With Respect to Investigations").

53. *See* Articles 64(8)(a) and 65 ("Proceedings on an Admission of Guilt").

54. *See* Article 67 ("Rights of the Accused").

similar to common-law conspiracy and joint criminal enterprise doctrines;[55] these concepts are generally foreign to civil law systems.

Although the discussion to this point has attempted to provide a birds-eye view of the ICC's dual-natured system, it must be said that the relative looseness of the statutory language leaves to the ICC's judiciary the demanding task of fixing the precise balance between the adversarial and inquisitorial elements. As cases are brought before the Court, as the "fear of the unknown" concerning victim participation abates, and as judges issue rulings interpreting the Rome Statute's articles and the ICC's rules, the ICC's jurisprudence will naturally develop and gain in uniformity and predictability. By way of example, the early fights at the ICC revolved around who qualified as a victim (that is, what qualifications victims had to possess to receive permission to participate in the proceedings pursuant to Rule 85). The Chamber has answered this question, leaving the precise contours of Article 68's "victim participation" as the next major battlefield for victim representatives.[56] Faced with unique challenges, and opportunities, flowing from such a new system fairly early in its development, victim representatives will have substantial substantive input, and must make their views known.

J. Reconciling the ICC's Sweeping Promises to Victims with the Realities on the Ground

The ICC, as well as the various *ad hoc* tribunals that preceded it, are said to fulfill a variety of both historic and practical goals, not the least of which are: (1) fostering accountability by bringing the perpetrators of some of the most barbaric criminal acts imaginable to justice and punishing them;[57]

---

55. *See generally* Article 25 ("Individual Criminal Responsibility"); Article 28 ("Responsibility of Commanders and Other Superiors"); Article 30 ("Mental Element"); and Elements of Crime General Introduction 2 and 3.

56. *See, e.g.*, Situation in the Democratic Republic of the Congo, Case No. ICC 01/04-01/06: *Decision on the Manner of Questioning Witnesses by the Legal Representatives of Victims* (September 16, 2009), at 13-14 (holding that "[Article 68] establishes the unequivocal right of victims to present their views and concerns when their interests are affected, provided this is not prejudicial to, or inconsistent with, the rights of the accused and a fair and impartial trial," but recognizing that the ICC's legal framework has failed to provide for any guidance concerning "the manner of questioning").

57. *See* Preamble to the Rome Statute ("Affirming that the most serious crimes of concern to the international community as a whole must not go unpunished. . . .").

(2) stemming the ongoing cycles of violence; (3) removing the perpetrators from power (or at least staving their effectiveness); (4) introducing the rule of law to effectively lawless regions and/or societies; (5) deterring future leaders who might consider engaging in the same, or similar, conduct;[58] (6) planting the seeds of reconciliation between the warring sides; (7) providing closure, and perhaps reparations,[59] for those victimized by the wrongdoer; (8) bringing the charged conduct to public light and scrutiny; and (9) impressing on the rest of the world the moral condemnation such conduct deserves.[60]

Following the Nuremberg trials' imposition of individual accountability on those convicted of committing human rights violations, the international community appropriately no longer considers the brutal treatment of civilians by ruling groups a purely "domestic" affair. Instead, these are now matters subject to international justice. And so the negotiators established the ICTY with the stated goal of "the restoration and maintenance of peace."[61] The Security Council Resolution creating the ICTR similarly listed as one of the Court's primary objectives "the process of national reconciliation and [] the restoration and maintenance of peace."[62] In addition, the Royal Government of Cambodia and the U.N. established the Extraordinary Chambers in Cambodia to try senior members of the Khmer Rouge for crimes against humanity, including genocide, and to ensure "reconciliation

58. *See id.* ("Determined to put an end to impunity for perpetrators of these crimes and thus to contribute to the prevention of such crimes. . . .").

59. Although reparations were originally viewed as being owed to an aggrieved state in order to compensate for international wrongs, under contemporary international human rights law and the law of the ICC, reparations now include procedural rights accorded to victims seeking reparations for harm they personally suffered.

60. *See* Preamble to the Rome Statute ("Conscious that all peoples are united by common bonds, their cultures pieced together in a shared heritage, and concerned that this delicate mosaic may be shattered at any time, [m]indful that during this century millions of children, women, and men have been victims of unimaginable atrocities that deeply shock the conscience of humanity. . . .").

61. S.C. Res. 827 at 1, U.N. Doc. S/RES/827 (May 25, 1993); *see also* The Secretary-General, Report on the International Tribunal for the Prosecution of Persons Responsible for Serious Violations of International Humanitarian Law Committed in the Territory of the Former Yugoslavia Since 1991, at para. 16, delivered to the Security Council and the General Assembly, U.N. Doc. S/1994/1007, A/49/342 (August 29, 1994); M. Cherif Bassiouni, *Searching for Peace and Achieving Justice: The Need for Accountability*, 59 LAW & CONTEMP. PROBS. 9, 13 (1996) ("If peace is not intended to be a brief interlude between conflicts," then it must be accompanied by justice).

62. S.C. Res. 955, at 1, U.N. Doc. S/RES/955 (November 8, 1994).

and stability within the state."[63] The ICC in its Preamble likewise notes that "such grave crimes threaten the peace, security, and well-being of the world. . . ."[64] This renewed period of focus on human dignity, and the near-universal agreement on the inviolability of certain autonomy rights, led to the creation of these courts during a time that some observers have labeled the "Age of Rights."[65]

Despite the ICC's significant resources, and the considerable efforts of talented, hardworking, and dedicated personnel, critics, as touched on above, note that the ICC's practical impact to date, in terms of vindicting atrocity crimes (that is, successfully investigating, prosecuting, and convicting individuals responsible for such crimes), has been underwhelming.[66] As things stand, ICC supporters will likely find themselves hard-pressed to argue that today's ICC, as an institution, successfully deters the world's criminals, who on a day-by-day basis are much more likely to be murdered by rivals or erstwhile supporters than to be arrested, extradited, tried, convicted, and sentenced at the ICC.

This reality goes some way to explaining why some present and former prosecutors at the ICC privately do not describe their primary role as bringing perpetrators to justice. Rather, they view their role as a symbolic one in which they build international consensus concerning certain wrong-doing, expose to the world how certain groups or governments are mistreating their people, and attempt to persuade and cajole domestic courts to do the work that may otherwise fall to the ICC.

This self-perception of prosecutors as one-person, roving hybrid politicians, diplomats, and public educators may well be consistent with the Court's present activities, but will no doubt strike many victims and international observers as worrying and, perhaps, inappropriate. Are ICC prosecutors, they may ask, charged with these general public-service functions, or are they, instead, to simply investigate, charge, and win cases, leaving public relations activities to the diplomats and politicians?

In the end, the drafting of well-intentioned international documents, and the increased emphasis placed on individual/human rights by the international legal community and in international law, has to date sadly done

63. G.A. Res. 57/228 at 1, U.N. Doc. A/RES/57/228 (December 18, 2002).

64. Preamble to the Rome Statute.

65. Louis Henkin, The Age of Rights (1990).

66. *See, e.g.*, Katy Glassborow, *et al.*, *ICC Struggles to Reach Out to Darfuris*, Institute for War & Peace Reporting's AllAfrica.com (October 20, 2007) (noting concern over "the lack of arrests, the slow pace of investigations and the [ICC's] low profile on the ground").

relatively little to curtail human rights abuses. Considering that the twentieth century not only led to the birth of the ICC and its predecessor tribunals, but also represents the all-time high-water-mark for human barbarity and killing, international conventions appear not to have had the hoped-for general preventative/deterrent effect on those intent on committing atrocity crimes. Instead, actual accountability, regrettably, continues to be the exception, rather than the rule.

More specifically, since becoming functional in 2002, the ICC has actively heard cases relating to only two situations—one involving the Democratic Republic of the Congo,[67] and the other the Central African Republic.[68] Although the ICC has received complaints about alleged crimes occurring in some 139 countries, the Office of the Prosecutor as of this writing has only opened investigations into the four already identified "situations," namely, those in Uganda, the Democratic Republic of Congo, the Central African Republic, and Darfur.[69] The Court, moreover, only issued 12 arrest warrants.

---

67. The Democratic Republic of Congo, a State Party, referred that situation to the Court in April 2004.

68. The Central African Republic, a State Party, referred that situation to the ICC in December 2004, with the investigation formally being opened on May 22, 2007.

69. As noted above, cases come before the ICC through the referral of "situations" involving atrocity crimes. Such situations involve large-scale, multiple commissions of crimes within a particular event, such as the alleged ethnic cleansings against African tribes in the Darfur region of Sudan, the mass atrocities in the Ituri region of the Democratic Republic of the Congo ("DRC"), the mass rapes in the Central African Republic, and the conflict between the Lord's Resistance Army ("LRA") and the Ugandan Army.

To date, three State Parties to the Rome Statute—Uganda, the Democratic Republic of the Congo, and the Central African Republic—have referred situations occurring on their territories to the Court. In addition, the Security Council has referred the situation in Darfur, Sudan—a non-State Party (the United Nations Security Council referred the situation in Darfur to the Court in March 2005, with the first two arrest warrants issued the Pre-Trial Chamber I on May 2, 2007).

In the situation in Uganda, the case *The Prosecutor v. Joseph Kony, Vincent Otti, Okot Odhiambo and Dominic Ongwen* is currently being heard before Pre-Trial Chamber II. In that case, the Chamber issued five warrants of arrest against five top members of the Lords Resistance Army. In the situation in the Democratic Republic of the Congo, three cases are being heard before the relevant Chambers: *The Prosecutor v. Thomas Lubanga Dyilo; The Prosecutor v. Bosco Ntaganda*; and *The Prosecutor v. Germain Katanga and Mathieu Ngudjolo Chui.* Two cases are at the pre-trial stage, while the proceedings against Thomas Lubanga Dyilo are at the trial stage. In the situation in Darfur, Sudan, the case of *The Prosecutor v. Ahmad Muhammad Harun and Ali Muhammad Ali Abd-Al-Rahman,* is being heard before Pre-Trial Chamber I. In the situation in the Central African Republic, the case of *The Prosecutor v. Jean-Pierre Bemba Gombo* is at the pre-trial stage of the proceedings, and is currently being heard before Pre-Trial Chamber III.

The ICC, out of respect for national sovereignty, and because it lacks the ability to do so, must, however, rely on states and international organizations to effect the arrests and deliver the accuseds to The Hague.[70]

The bottom line is that, in the first six years of the ICC's existence, the Court held not a single trial. Because of the absence of trials, during this time no victims sat at counsel's table, and victims received not a single cent in court-ordered reparations.[71] Even the most ardent supporter of the ICC will likely agree that this is not a sustainable state of affairs.

In 2009, the ICC finally began its long-awaited first trial, namely, the trial of 48-year-old accused former Democratic Republic of Congo rebel leader Thomas Lubanga Dyilo. International observers accuse rebels under Lubanga's direct command of significant human rights violations, including systematic and strategic mutilation, rape, torture, murder, and ethnic massacres, as well as the killing of peacekeepers. The Office of the Prosecutor, however, only charged Lubanga with enlisting and conscripting children under the age of 15 as soldiers, as well as with using them to participate actively in hostilities. Critics argue that the charges levelled against Lubanga dramatically understated his extensive criminal activities.[72]

In any event, ICC insiders will privately agree that the *Lubanga* case, as charged, is not particularly legally or factually complex. This, of course, may be a good thing, given the relative inexperience of some of the judges and many (though certainly not all) of the prosecutors. When bringing the Court's first accused to trial, carefully selecting a "winnable" case evidences sound thinking.

---

70. *See generally* Rene Blattman & Kirsten Bowman, *Achievements and Problems of the International Criminal Court*, 6 J. INT'L CRIM. JUST. 711, 723 (2008) ("[E]nsuring the necessary cooperation [to affect arrests] is a primary challenge for both the ICC and the State Parties.").

71. The Trust Fund for Victims, however, in 2008 spent some $2,500,000 on 34 different projects in Uganda and the Democratic Republic of Congo. The projects included providing physical rehabilitation and psychological support for men, women, and children who experienced sexual violence, and who were ex-child soldiers and abducted children. The projects tangibly benefitted victims, but they at bottom are simply transfer payments, not Court-ordered reparations.

72. Prosecutors contend that they simply do not have sufficient evidence to convict Lubanga of the sex-related charges many victims and outside observers have called for. Moreover, the Democratic Republic of Congo filed charges against Lubanga in its domestic courts. The prosecution team argues that the complementarity principle discussed in Part IV(G) therefore precludes the prosecution from pursuing similar charges at the ICC. Observers have raised similar arguments in the proceedings against Germain Katanga, who local prosecutors in the Democratic Republic of Congo had charged with crimes against humanity by the time he was surrender to the ICC; in that case, at least, the Prosecutor was clearly not impressed with the accused's complementarity argument.

Although optimism surrounding the ICC's promise and potential in many political, diplomatic, and academic circles continues on undiminished,[73] few representatives of the ICC's 108 current Member States would argue that the ICC has fully lived up to the expectations it has created through its many relatively broad public proclamations and promises to victims. Alas, the proof of the pudding is in the eating, and thus far indictments and trials have been few, delays common, and frustration on the part of victims widespread.[74] Defense counsel consider these delays, which have kept accused such as Lubanga incarcerated for some four years prior to his trial, as violating the accuseds' speedy trial and due process rights. In the words of one ICC expert, "the ICC has shown itself to be the slowest institution of its kind since the beginnings at Nuremberg."[75]

The proclaimed benefits of international justice, such as promoting peace, fostering reconciliation, and deterring similar conduct in the future,[76] although of course laudable, must, therefore, be analyzed realistically. International institutions such as the ICC risk rendering themselves impotent if people begin to regard them as representing "all talk and no action." A promise not delivered is, as the saying goes, often worse than not making the promise at all. Similarly, making exaggerated, and perphaps ultimately unsupportable, claims concerning the ICC's prospective benefits to the world threatens to marginalize the Court's actual work.

---

73. *See, e.g.*, David Scheffer & John Hutson, Strategy for U.S. Engagement With the International Criminal Court (Century Foundation Report, 2008).

74. In this context, it must be noted that the Court's official vacation schedule indicates that the Court is in recess some *62* days a year (not counting weekends and leave time). Suffice it to say that few domestic prosecutors or judges enjoy such a generous vacation schedule. Moreover, the ICC presently only has one full court room at its disposal; the Court is therefore, as a matter of simple logistics, unable to properly accommodate multiple simultaneous trials. Facts such as these may leave the first-time visitor to the Court wondering whether it genuinely views itself as charged with bringing the world's multitude of notorious criminals to justice.

75. Schabas, *supra* note 16, at 758.

76. *See, e.g.*, Michael P. Scharf, *The ICTY at Ten: A Critical Assessment of the Major Rulings of the International Criminal Tribunal Over the Past Decade*, 37 New Eng. L. Rev. 915, 916 (2003) (describing the ambitions of the ICTY as making it "easier for victims to eventually forgive, or at least, reconcile with former neighbors caught up in the institutionalized violence. This would also promote a political catharsis in Serbia, enabling the new leadership to distance themselves from the discredited nationalistic policies of the past. The historic record generated from the trial would educate the Serb people, long subject to Milosevic's propaganda, about what really happened in Kosovo, Croatia, and Bosnia, and help ensure that such horrific acts are not repeated in the future."); *see also* Michael P. Scharf, *Trading Justice for Efficiency*, 2 J. Int'l. Crim. Just. 1070, 1072–73 (2004) (same); M. Cherif Bassiouni, Introduction to International Criminal Law (2003).

At bottom, living up to the Rome Statute's promises of ending the impunity of the atrocity lords, making victims "whole," and deterring the inhumane treatment of civilians will likely require a more efficient, professional, and effective ICC, generally, and more experienced prosecutors and judges, specifically.[77] The admittedly sensitive, and to some extent controversial, topic of how to best improve the ICC's performance must, therefore, be addressed.

The judges and prosecutors of the ICC are routinely given high marks in terms of their earnestness, their enthusiasm for ensuring that justice is done, and their hope that the ICC, as a new institution, is respected. That said, when questioned further on the topic, most ICC insiders with whom the author has spoken privately share the view that the ICC's performance must be improved. More specifically, observers believe the Prosecutor must investigate and indict more cases, the parties must file briefs that are more polished and well-researched, and the judges must become better at moving cases along and delivering rulings that are more timely, consistent, and sound. Without exception, however, both ICC employees and ICC observers who have discussed the matter with the author to varying degrees single out the collective performance of the ICC's judges as the prime institutional weakness, followed by the relative inexperience within the ICC's cadre of ambitious and bright prosecutors. These two key components of the ICC—the Judiciary and the Office of the Prosecutor—will therefore be subjected to closer examination.

1. Understanding ICC Judges' Backgrounds, Habits, and Competence

The discussion up to this point has made repeated note of the vagueness and imprecision characterizing many of the ICC's statutory provisions. Compounding the inherent difficulty in divining the meaning of a given rule

---

77. The Court describes the expectations it sets for itself as follows:

> With the strategic goal being to [e]xcel in achieving the desired results with minimal resources and through streamlined structures and processes, while maintaining flexibility, guaranteeing accountability, and drawing upon sufficient qualified and motivated staff within a caring environment, senior management has made clear its intention to maintain continuous scrutiny of its internal organization in order to achieve state-of-the-art administrative and core processes, putting strong emphasis on efficiency in terms of non-bureaucracy, flexibility and accountability.

See www.icc-cpi.int/iccdocs/asp_docs/ASP8/ICC-ASP-8-10.Proposed%20Programme%20Budget%20for%202010.ADVANCE.17Jul1630.pdf (citation and quotation omitted).

or article in a system that has a mix of adversarial and inquisitorial elements is the reality that the judges at the ICC come from varying legal traditions and backgrounds. It is only natural, then, that these judges will tend to embark on the task of interpreting the statutory provisions—many of which have limited objective content—with a considerable bias towards how the given legal issues are resolved within the particular judge's own legal tradition. It, therefore, is not surprising to encounter the drastically divergent interpretations of elemental legal terms such as "representation," "submission of observations," and "participation."[78] To gain a fuller understanding of the backgrounds and points of view of the ICC's judiciary, however, we must also consider *who* the State Parties have appointed to these pivotal positions.

As it turns out, the judges of the ICC are split into an unexpected mix of experienced jurists, as well as individuals with no real criminal justice backgrounds, no trial experience, no judicial records, and indeed, in at least one case, no law degree or legal training. The somewhat surprising decision to on occasion transform judicial laymen, with backgrounds in diplomacy, at NGOs, or in the academy, into practicing judges in a criminal court of the ICC's stature, and then to pay them some $22,000 a month (tax free), is a difficult one to defend. One does not, after all, usually play one's first concert at Carnegie Hall, and the ICC is arguably the worst place for judicial novices for the first time don their black robes and make their maiden appearances in a criminal courtroom. Yet, this is precisely what has been done at the ICC. If the Court is indeed designed to handle some of the most weighty, difficult legal and moral matters, then one can reasonably expect those at the institution's helm to be fully equipped to perform at the highest level. The reason this may not, as a rule, always be the case requires a frank discussion of the judicial selection process.

Self-selection begins the process, as ICC judges are recommended to the Assembly of State Parties. In other words, the first step is for an aspiring ICC

78. *Compare* the January 17, 2007 Pre-Trial Chamber I Ruling in Situation in the Democratic Republic of Congo, Case No. ICC-01/04–101-tEN-Corr: *Decision on the Application of Participation in the Proceedings* (January 17, 2007) (defining Rule 68(3)'s "personal interests [of victims]" broadly to accord victims significant participatory rights, while creating two-phase process for victims during the investigatory phase and victims once the prosecution of a particular case has been decided) *with* the September 22, 2006 Pre-Trial Chamber I ruling in Situation in the Democratic Republic of Congo, Case No. ICC-01/04–01–06–462: *Decision on the Arrangements for Participation of Victims* (September 22, 2006) (balancing rights of anonymous victims against rights of accused, and according victims only limited participation in the proceedings).

judge to gain the endorsement of his State-Party government. What will—or at least should—be surprising to the uninitiated is that there is *no* requirement that ICC judges have any experience as a domestic judge. Indeed, there in fact is no general requirement that ICC judges have *any* practical in-court experience, or, for that matter, even have attended law school or obtained a law degree.

Receiving the endorsement of one's home country, pursuant to Article 36(4)(b), is of course in itself a highly politicized task. As expected, some of the best and brightest judges may not be all that motivated to leave secure positions in their domestic court for the temporal and substantive vagaries of overseas work at The Hague.

Once the aspiring ICC judge has used his political and professional connections to successfully gain his country's endorsement, the lobbying process starts in earnest. Given the large number of State Parties, and the much more limited universe of judicial vacancies, election to a judicial position at the ICC can be an exhausting exercise in negotiation and diplomacy. By way of example, assume State Party A wishes to receive support for its country's judicial pick. The Ambassador from State Party A, therefore, meets with State Party B's Ambassador, knowing that State Party B needs State Party A's support on some other international/U.N./treaty issue, such as import limitations, technical assistance, sanctions, or tariff issues. If State Party B wishes to receive State Party A's support, then one way to gain it is to endorse State Party A's judicial pick. It is through such a negotiation process, conducted by diplomats typically possessing a highly limited understanding of the merits or demerits of the particular judge, or of what professional background or personal characteristics are most desirable, that applicants assume the prestige and authority of the Court.

The unwritten reality of the ICC, therefore, has been that judicial candidates in the end typically obtain their positions after surviving a gauntlet of negotiations, lobbying, and old-fashioned "horse trading." Although many of the ICC's judges are highly competent and dedicated professionals, appointments are routinely as much a product of politics as they are of professional merit. Article 36(3)(b), indeed, explicitly distinguishes between judicial candidates who have actual criminal law and procedure experience ("List A" judges), and others who either have some unspecified "competence in relevant areas of international law," or "experience in a professional legal capacity" which is relevant to the judicial work of the Court ("List B" judges).

This bifurcation between experienced List A judges and those falling under List B is the loophole through which diplomats, politicians, and others with little or no relevant in-court experience can obtain judicial appointments. Added to this mix, Article 36(8)(b) provides that the State Parties must "take into consideration" the "need" to include judges with "legal expertise on specific issues, including, but not limited to, violence against women and children." This process of judicial selection arguably contributes little to ensuring that the judges are the "best and brightest" of their profession.

Those who deeply care about the institution of the Court may understandably be gravely concerned that it is possible — and has in fact happened — that some of the ICC's judges for the first time participate in a criminal case after they arrive at the Court. Regrettably, there is no realistic way to change this process in the short term, even though it is likely responsible for bringing some judges to the Court who, by most accounts, are professionally, experientially, and temperamentally unsuited for the job. Such deficits predictably prevent cases from efficiently moving through the system, spawn further delays, raise significant speedy trial concerns for the defense, contribute to the creation of additional uneven case law, and institutionalize a lack of judicial predictability. Moreover, they threaten to vest the judges' various young legal officers, who work in a capacity similar to law clerks in the United States, with disproportionately great power to shape the law.

The State Parties should, in the interest of much-needed transparency, moreover, consider abandoning Article 36(6)(a)'s practice of electing judges by "secret ballot." Instead, the international community should strive to hold publicly accountable those State Parties who nominate and elect un- or under-qualified judges, and in so doing risk seriously diminishing the stature, credibility, and performance of the Court.

Setting aside possible reform in the judicial selection process, the reality is, and always will be, that the Court's judges will be draw from vastly different legal cultures and backgrounds. Considering the broad discretion the ICC's legal provisions vest in the Chamber,[79] the victim representative must

79. The Registry in one case has in fact brought to the Chamber's attention that, when it comes to issues such as processing victim applications, dealing with protective measures for victims, and handling the issue of reparations, there was "conflicting jurisprudence and practice among the Court's chambers." *See* Situation in the Democratic Republic of the Congo In the Case of the Prosecutor v. Germain Katanga and Mathieu Ngudjolo Chui, Case No. ICC-01/04–01/07: *Order Instructing the Participants and the Registry to File Additional Documents* (December 10, 2008), at 8. The Chamber, in response, commendably asked the Registry to file a list of the requested directions and a summary of the purported conflicting rulings, as well as "practical proposals for

thus in all cases at the outset gain familiarity with the judges' individual backgrounds and practices in order to customize an appropriate "message" and legal strategy. Lawyers who have practiced before other international tribunals will be familiar with the unwritten rule that the personalities and legal backgrounds of the judges of a particular Chamber are likely to significantly influence the proceedings. And these backgrounds are, indeed, diverse: At the time of this writing, the President of the Court is from the Republic of Korea, the First Vice-President is from Mali, and the Second Vice-President is from Germany; the other judges of the Court hail from Costa Rica, Ghana, Finland, Latvia, the U.K., Brazil, Bulgaria, Uganda, France, Kenya, Botswana, Belgium, Italy, and Bolivia. Recognizing this dynamic, and reacting to it proactively, is the job of each participant in the proceedings.

2. The Office of the Prosecutor

The job of prosecutor at the ICC is prestigious and much sought-after, and the salary of ICC prosecutors is competitive. Although starting salaries are determined by a variety of factors, on average senior trial attorneys begin with a salary of approximately $150,000, and the most junior prosecutors begin with a salary of approximately $45,000. Of the 250 or so employees in the Office of the Prosecutor, roughly 30 have the formal title of "prosecutor."

The complaint on occasion heard about the ICC's prosecutors is not that they are unmotivated, educationally or temperamentally unqualified, or unprofessional. Rather, it is that a number of the prosecutors, having previously occupied non-litigation positions such as researchers, NGO lawyers, and junior legal officers in other tribunals, have little or no actual courtroom experience. Although victim representatives, assistants to counsel, and counsel for the defense face fairly strict minimum qualifications, no such prerequisits exist for the Office of the Prosecutor, which is in charge of its own hiring.

To better understand the inherent recruiting challenges facing the Office of the Prosecutor, it is necessary to understand the impact going to the ICC can have on a prosecutor's career. In most non-U.S. domestic jurisdictions, becoming a prosecutor, like becoming a judge, is a lifetime career-track position. As with judges, prosecutors who are competent and well respected in

---

the improvement of current practices, explaining how the latter should be modified." *Id.* at 8–9.

their home jurisdictions often have their eye on moving up the professional ladder and on handling more important and complex cases. To leave his domestic jurisdiction and begin working at the ICC, the typical prosecutor must resign, thereby all but abandoning his prior prosecutorial career. For example, a German prosecutor who decides to spend some years at the ICC will likely find that, upon his return to Germany, his civil service career prospects have significantly suffered.

The anticipated trade-off for the aspiring ICC prosecutor is a long-term career at the Court, perhaps punctuated by a position teaching international law, or as part of some other international legal venture. Once at the ICC, moreover, these prosecutors, now planning on a full career at the Court, may consider it prudent to conduct themselves in a manner that guarantees their (now necessary) long-term employment. This dynamic, in turn, risks breeding a certain sense of institutional conformity. Recruiting experienced prosecutors who are willing to challenge the Court, to criticize the process, to recommend change, or to otherwise, when necessary, "make waves," may be exactly what the ICC needs.

One way to attract top-flight prosecutors to the ICC is to persuade the prosecutors' home jurisdictions to provide temporary two, three, or four-year waivers so that the prosecutors are guaranteed to receive their civil service positions back upon their return. Although prosecutors going to the ICC may still suffer some professional set-backs because of their absence from the domestic arena, this may at least help alleviate some of their concerns. Moreover, since the prosecutors know they have secure positions back home, they may feel they have more freedom to speak their minds, and to act with greater independence.

Although there is undoubtedly much good to be found in the performance of those working at the ICC, many insiders will in private candidly point out that the Court must improve its performance if the institution is to gain greater legitimacy. Victim participation, it is generally agreed, is not the problem. Rather, it is a relatively inexperienced and, at times, overmatched judiciary, combined with prosecutors who on occasion lack sufficient real-world trial experience, that contribute to keeping the ICC from performing at peak capacity. As the ICC matures, however, one can expect some of these shortfalls to work themselves out, for institutional capacity to increase, and for multiple simultaneous trials to become the rule, rather than the exception. That said, maturity alone, without thoughtful and targeted institutional reform, is not likely to deliver the Court to where it should be.

PART V

The Rome Statute's Groundbreaking (and Expansive) Recognition of Victims' Rights

THE MOST INNOVATIVE FEATURE distinguishing the ICC from other predecessor tribunals and regional courts is that it formally, and comprehensively, enshrines the rights of victims to participate in proceedings,[1] state their views and concerns, and claim reparations, including compensation, rehabilitation, and restitution.[2] The ICC's restorative system of victim rights, indeed, finds no equal in any other tribunal or regional court, with victim-related provisions distributed throughout the ICC's legal framework. Such rights did not exist in predecessor international criminal courts, including the ICTR, the ICTY, or the Special Court for Sierra Leone.

The ICC's forward-thinking treatment of victims is, indeed, part and parcel of the broader restorative trend and emerging consensus in international law described in Part III, namely, that victims' rights extend beyond those possessed by witnesses. By way of example, the ICC describes victims as "participants" at the trial, provides official protection to victims during the proceedings,[3] and accords victims the explicit right to reparations/compensation derived directly from their victimizers,[4] as well as from a partially state-funded victim

---

1. *See, e.g.*, Situation in the Central African Republic In the Case of the Prosecutor v. Jean-Pierre Bemba Gombo, Case No. ICC-10/05–01/08: *Sixth Decision on Victims' Participation Relating to Certain Questions Raised by the Office of Public Counsel for Victims* (January 8, 2009), at 3–9 (noting that victims, as participants to the proceedings, have the right to: Attend public parts of hearings and certain *in camera* hearings, depending on the circumstances; gain access to all public decisions and documents contained in the record; gain access all non-confidential evidence adduced by the parties; and make succinct oral submissions on issues of law and fact if granted by, and subject to any other direction from, the Chamber).

2. *See generally* Situation in the Central African Republic In the Case of the Prosecutor v. Jean-Pierre Bemba Gombo, Case No. ICC-10/05–01/08: *Fourth Decision on Victims' Participation* (December 12, 2008), at 29. The general notion that victims should be awarded damages is of course nothing new—it can be found in ancient Assyrian, Hittite, and Roman law, as well as in the Code of Hammurabi (1750 B.C.), *see* Part III(A).

3. *See* Article 68.

4. Whether reparation proceedings will be separated from the guilt/innocence phase remains to be determined. *See generally* Part XIV(B). In Trial Chamber I, Situation in the Democratic

Trust Fund.[5] Such victim-centric provisions reflect the unique collective restorative ambition that victim representatives have been pressing for decades.

Moving from the general to the specific, the Rome Statute recognizes that victims of atrocity crimes, such as genocide, crimes against humanity, and war crimes, have a variety of legitimate needs that the Court must address in order to break the recurring cycles of violence. Victimized groups, in turn, must feel that the international community recognizes their plight, is taking their situations seriously, remains intent on creating a historic record of their abuse, and will ensure that meaningful justice is done.[6]

Victims' needs encompass, but are not limited to:

— A legitimate and unbiased forum in which the victims can speak, and can be heard.
— Recognition and validation of their victimization.
— Promotion of a sense of social solidarity among the victims.
— Creation of a permanent historic record of the criminal activity generally, as well as a record of how the conduct affected particular victims.
— Closure and truth about the political and social environment which permitted the crimes to take place.
— An explanation of the victimization, and a corresponding answer to the pivotal question of "why me/us."
— An opportunity for victims to regain a sense of control over their lives.

Republic of the Congo, Case No. ICC-01/04–01/06–1191: Prosecutor v. Thomas Lubanga Dyilo, *Decision on the Defence and Prosecution Requests for Leave to Appeal the Decision on Victims' Participation of 18 January 2008* (February 26, 2008), the majority stated that some evidence regarding reparations may be heard during the trial.

5. Article 79(2) provides that the Trust Fund is to be financed through property and/or funds collected through fines and forfeitures, but any reparation orders may only be made against individual offenders (rather than against the State); *see also* Resolution ICC-ASP/4/Res.3 (Regulations of the Trust Fund for victims). Applications for (1) participation and (2) reparations are, however, treated separately. Although both participation and reparations applications may be submitted concurrently, the mere application for participation does not automatically result in an application for reparations being lodged.

   As a matter of strategy, it is, therefore, probably preferable to submit the reparations application early in the process, thereby making it easier to argue that the particular victim has a "personal interest" in the Article 68(3) sense, and that the Chamber, thus, should permit victims to participate at certain stages.

6. For a discussion on the increased focus on victim compensation at the international and national law level, *see* M. Cherif Bassiouni, *International Recognition of Victims' Rights*, 6 Human Rights L. Rev. 203 (2006) ("An individual victim's right to redress has increasingly become an indispensable component of efforts to protect individual human rights.").

— Avoidance of future victimization.
— Financial compensation for the harm the accused caused to the victims and their family members.
— A means of ensuring that those responsible for the criminal activity receive just punishment, and that the victims play some part in determining this punishment.[7]

The ICC, as summarized below, provides a variety of statutory modalities for addressing these needs and aspirations.

A. Victims' Rights Enshrined in the ICC's Rome Statute

The Rome Statute contains broad language guaranteeing victims the right to security, to meaningful participation, and to reparations. Understanding these provisions is the first step to competent victim advocacy. For ease of reference, the key provisions of the founding Rome Statute relating to victims are summarized immediately below:

Key Rome Statute Victims' Rights Provisions	
Article 15(3)	Permits victims to make representations to the Pre-Trial Chamber concerning the Prosecutor's decision to proceed with an investigation.
Article 19(3)	Grants victims permission to submit observations concerning jurisdiction of the ICC and the admissibility of cases.
Article 43(6)	Empowers the Registrar to set up Victims and Witness Unit within the Registry.
Article 53(1)(c)	Requires the Prosecutor to consider the interests of victims when deciding whether to initiate an investigation.

7. *See generally* Situation in the Democratic Republic of Congo, Case No. ICC-01/04–101: *Decision on the Applications for Participation in the Proceedings* (January 17, 2006) (summarizing cases from European Court of Human Rights holding that victims, defense, and prosecutors have different interests in criminal proceedings, as well as decisions from the Inter-American Court on Human Rights, etc.); Mugambi Jouet, *Reconciling the Conflicting Rights of Victims and Defendants at the International Criminal Court*, 26 St. Louis U. Pub. L. Rev. 249 (2007).

Article 57(3)(c)	Grants to the Pre-Trial Chamber the authority to provide for the security and privacy of victims.
Article 64(2)	Requires the Trial Chamber to ensure the trial is conducted with due regard for the protection of victims.
Article 65(4)	Vests the Trial Chamber with discretion to, in the context of plea agreements, require a more complete presentation of the facts of the case if the interests of the victims require it.
Article 68	Governs victim "participation in the proceedings": – Requires the Court to protect the safety, physical and psychological well-being, dignity, and privacy of victims. – Permits *in camera* proceedings, video conferencing, and other modes of evidence presentation, as well as the redaction of discovery, in order to protect victims. – Mandates that victims be given an opportunity to present their "views and concerns" when their "personal interests" are affected. Such views and concerns are to be "presented and considered at stages of the proceedings determined to be appropriate by the Court and in a manner which is not prejudicial to or inconsistent with the rights of the accused and a fair and impartial trial."
Article 75	Provides for reparations to victims.
Article 79	Sets up Trust Fund for Victims.
Article 82(4)	Accords to victims the right to appeal reparations orders.

B. Summary of the ICC's Victim-Related Rules of Procedure and Evidence

Understanding the strategic choices impacting when and how, as a matter of procedure, to secure victims' rights is as important as understanding the above-described substantive victim rights. The ICC's most relevant Rules, summarized for ease of reference, follow:

Key ICC Rules of Procedure and Rules of Evidence	
Rule16	Describes the responsibilities of the Registrar as they relate to victims. These responsibilities include: – Assisting victims in obtaining legal advice and organizing their legal representation. – Providing victims' legal representatives with adequate support, assistance, and information at all stages of the proceedings. – Ensuring that victims are kept updated on the Court's decisions that may have an impact on their interests.

Rules 17 and 18	Outlines the functions and responsibilities of the Victim and Witness Unit, which include: – Providing victims with adequate long and short-term protective and security measures. – Assisting victims in obtaining medical, psychological, and other appropriate assistance. – Making training on issues involving trauma, sexual violence, security, and confidentiality available to the Court and the parties.
Rule 43	Requires the Court to ensure that all published documents comply with the relevant rules governing the confidentiality of the proceedings, as well as witness security.
Rule 50	Mandates that the Prosecutor notify victims of his intent to initiate an investigation. Such notice is not, however, required if the Prosecutor believes it may pose a danger to the integrity of the investigation, or to the life or well-being of victims and witnesses. Rule 50 also permits victims to make written representations concerning the Prosecutor's decision to initiate a particular investigation. If the Pre-Trial Chamber concludes that it needs more information prior to issuing its decision on whether to authorize the commencement of the requested investigation, it may seek such information from the victims.
Rule 59	Requires the Registrar to inform victims who have communicated with the Court of any questions concerning, or challenges to, jurisdiction or admissibility.
Rule 69	Allows the Chamber to consider the interests of the victims when deciding whether to accept certain stipulated facts.
Rules 70 and 72	Addresses issues relating to a victim's "consent" in cases of sexual violence.
Rule 81(3)	Restricts, for security reasons, disclosure of confidential information relating to victims.
Rule 85	Defines Victims: "'Victims' means natural persons who have suffered harm as a result of the commission of any crime within the jurisdiction of the Court."
Rules 87 and 88	Provides protective and other special measures for victims.
Rule 89	Grants the Chamber broad discretion to consider victims' applications to participate, and to determine the nature and scope of such participation during any phase of the proceedings: "[T]he Chamber shall . . . specify the proceedings and manner in which participation is considered appropriate, which may include making opening and closing statements."

Rules 90 and 91	Provides legal representation to victims. – "Where there are a number of victims, the Chamber may, for the purposes of ensuring the effectiveness of the proceedings, request the victims or particular groups of victims, if necessary with the assistance of the Registry, to choose a common legal representative or representatives." Rule 90(2) – "A legal representative of a victim shall be entitled to attend and participate in the proceedings in accordance with the terms of the ruling of the Chamber and any modification thereof given under rules 89 and 90. This shall include participation in hearings unless, in the circumstances of the case, the Chamber concerned is of the view that the representative's intervention should be confined to written observations or submissions." Rule 91(2)
Rule 92	Sets forth the victim-notification requirements.
Rule 93	"A Chamber may seek the views of [participating] victims or their legal representatives [on any issue]. In addition, a Chamber may seek the views of other victims, as appropriate."
Rule 94	Describes the information required of a victim who wishes to submit a formal reparations request.
Rule 95	Sets forth the notification requirements in those cases in which the Court proceeds *sua sponte* on reparations.
Rule 96	Requires the Registrar to notify victims of upcoming reparations proceedings.
Rule 97	Authorizes the Court to appoint an expert to assist in determining the scope of reparations, and provides that victims may request such an expert be appointed.
Rule 98	Provides that reparations awards be deposited in the Trust Fund For Victims.
Rule 119(3)	Requires the Court, in possible conditional release cases, to consult with victims who the Chamber deems to be at potential risk.
Rule 121(10)	Provides victims and their representatives with the right to access the record of the proceedings prior to the confirmation hearing.
Rule 131(2)	Permits victim access to the record of proceedings transmitted by the Pre-Trial Chamber.
Rule 144(1)	Instructs the Trial Chamber that, when possible, it must deliver rulings concerning admissibility of the case, jurisdiction of the Court, criminal responsibility of the accused, sentence to be imposed, and reparations publicly and in the presence of the victims or their representatives.

Rule 145	Governs sentencing, and mandates that the Court consider the harm caused to the victims and their families, whether the victim was defenseless, whether there were multiple victims, the nature of and motivation for the offense, any efforts made by the convicted person to compensate victims, and any cooperation offered by the convicted person when determining an appropriate sentence.
Rule 221	Allows victims to express their views concerning the disposition of the convicted person's assets.
Rule 224	Requires Appeals Chamber to invite victim input whenever a convicted person submits a sentencing reduction request.

C. Exploring the Role of Victims as "Participants" in ICC Proceedings

Article 68(3) is the key provision of the Rome Statute with regard to victims' participatory rights. It provides:

> Where the *personal interests* of the victims are affected, the Court *shall* permit their *views and concerns* to be presented and considered at stages of the proceedings determined to be appropriate by the Court *and* in a manner which is not prejudicial to or inconsistent with the rights of the accused and a fair and impartial trial. Such views and concerns may be presented by the legal representatives of the victims where the Court considers it appropriate, in accordance with the Rules of Procedure and Evidence.[8]

This broad language vests the ICC judges with significant discretion over when and how victims may participate in the criminal proceedings. As discussed above, the ICC judiciary's differing interpretations of this language demonstrate the inherent statutory ambiguity the drafters intended, and

8. Emphasis added. *See also* Situation in the Democratic Republic of the Congo in the Case of The Prosecutor v. Thomas Lubanga Dyilo, Case No. ICC-01/04–01/06: *Redacted Version of "Decision on 'Indirect Victims'"* (April 8, 2009), at 15, 19–22 (holding that applicants who were alleged to have been victims of crimes committed by children who were conscripted into the army when under 15 years of age, or who were used to participate in the hostilities, did not qualify as either "direct" or "indirect" victims of the crimes confirmed against the accused).

built into, the legal framework in order to overcome political/drafting impasses.

Article 68, nevertheless, reflects an unmistakable concern that the rights of the victims be limited, and that the Court at all times carefully balance them against the rights of the accused. The prepared victim representative must bear in mind that, regardless of what persuasive statutory arguments he might develop, and despite certain "pro-victim" rulings, the judges working in the ICC, to some extent fearful of the unknown, can, during these formative years of the ICC's existence, be expected to be inherently resistant to an expansive role for victim representatives, or aggressive victim representation, once cases reach the trial stage.

Those familiar with staffing at the ICC understand that few of the experienced judges view the Rome Statute as having opened the proverbial floodgates for victims. And, as borne out by the case law to date, fewer yet will permit conduct on the part of victim representatives potentially impinging on the prerogatives and authority of the prosecution, or leading to the presentation of evidence by victim representatives that is systematically at odds with the prosecution's theory of the case.

Understanding the context of this somewhat ingrained reluctance to permit "full" victim participation requires a brief historical detour. The very inclusion of victim rights in the Rome Statute was a matter of some controversy, with advocates of many governments arguing for a very *limited* role for victims. Their concern was, in part, that victim participation could threaten the accused's due process rights by lowering the prosecution's burden of proof, shifting the burden to the defense, undermining the presumption of innocence, interfering with the Prosecutor's strategic decisions, and impeding the Chamber's ability to effectively manage the proceedings.

Many of today's ICC judges will be aware of this contentious history, and may well frown on victim representatives who view the Rome Statute as an open invitation to demand an aggressive, quasi-prosecutorial role for victims in the proceedings. The victim representative must, therefore, remain mindful of the careful case-by-case balancing act the Chamber will conduct, and of his burden to persuade the Chamber (and the prosecution) that the victim representative (1) understands the limited nature of his involvement, and, having that understanding, (2) presents little danger of impinging upon, or undermining, the Prosecutor's role under the Rome Statute and Rules or the fairness of the proceedings.

The Office of the Prosecutor has also consistently expressed concern that the participation of a large number of putative victims not adversely impact the Prosecutor's independence and efficiency, particularly during the investigative phase.[9] Specifically, the prosecutors (and, for that matter, defense counsel) are concerned that victims may attempt to improperly influence the outcome of the investigation or the charging decisions. Although this should not typically concern prosecutors, given that victims lobbying for a particular outcome is a common phenomenon, it is true that, for victims in a case to prevail, they must establish certain central facts, and that the legal elements essential to the victims will typically overlap substantially with those the prosecution must prove. To the extent that the evidence important to victims differs from that necessary to establish the elements of the charged crime(s), victim representatives should either bring this to the prosecution's attention, or should convince the Chamber that it should grant the victims an opportunity to present this evidence.

Fears that victim participation in the prosecution of a case can jeopardize the appearance, integrity, and objectivity of proceedings,[10] while understandable, are largely over-emphasized. Although prosecutorial independence and objectivity are frequently challenged by those who disagree with a given prosecutor's decision to charge, or to decline charging, a particular crime, the true mark of a prosecutor's integrity is whether he objectively evaluates the existing evidence. Those familiar with both domestic and international criminal cases understand that victims (and, for that matter, many witnesses, as well as a host of third parties) will have significant interests—whether financial, personal, or otherwise—in the outcome of particular prosecutions. An experienced prosecutor will be vigilant in ensuring that such potential interests do not adversely impact the fairness of the proceedings, or improperly influence the prosecutor's independence.[11]

---

9. *See generally* Matthew R. Brubacher, *Prosecutorial Discretion Within the International Criminal Court*, 2 J. INT'L CRIM. JUST. 71, 84–85 (2004) ("Prosecutorial independence is a fundamental component of fulfilling the human rights norm of receiving a fair trial and is a crucial element in determining the long-term legitimacy of the ICC.").

10. *See* Article 42(1) (mandating prosecutorial independence and impartiality).

11. Such fairness could, for example, be impacted if the victim provided biased, fabricated, or otherwise unreliable information or evidence in order to further the victim's personal agenda. *See* Timothy Kuhner, *The Status of Victims in the Enforcement of International Criminal Law*, 6 OR. REV. INT'L L. 95 (2004) (critical of victim-involvement in ICC proceedings, and contending, *inter alia*, that such participation threatens fairness of the proceedings).

D. The Modality and Extent of Victim Participation Remain Unsettled

The parties for some time have hotly debated whether the Rome Statute permits victim representatives to independently present witnesses and introduce evidence. In fact, this issue has in recent years supplanted, as the current legal battlefield, the debate over the requisite qualifications for victim participation in proceedings. The ICC's Articles and Rules of course further confuse the matter by using, interchangeably, the term "participant" (implying more limited procedural rights),[12] and "party" (implying more substantial involvement at trial and broader procedural rights, including the victims' right to present evidence and witnesses).[13]

In 2006,[14] and again in 2007,[15] the Pre-Trial Chamber granted victims broad participatory rights, including the right to take part during the investigative phase of the proceedings. Many familiar with the back-room workings of the Court interpret these early "pro-victim" rulings as the real-world result of the judges making a statement and standing their ground against the Office of the Prosecutor for initially adopting a very hard-line position that there must be *no* victim participation. This reported quasi-absolutist position may have resulted from prosecutors being somewhat new to the job, still unfamiliar with the full contours of the ICC's provisions relating to victim participation. The ICC judges, who clearly did not appreciate this apparent inflexibility and non-adherence to the plain language and spirit of the Rome Statute, responded by permitting *full* participation, including during the investigative stages.

Such rulings, understandably, created great frustration and anxiety within the Office of the Prosecutor, as well as in the defense bar. Prosecutors feared that the Chamber had irrevocably opened the floodgates. In direct and calculated response, the prosecutors began commenting on—and indeed

---

12. *See, e.g.*, Rule 87(3)(b).

13. *See, e.g.*, Rule 87(2)(c); *see also* M. Cherif Bassiouni, *International Recognition of Victims' Rights*, 6 HUMAN RIGHTS L. REV. 244 (2006) (recognizing the discrepancy, but concluding that "there is nothing in the legislative history of the ICC Statute to assume that the victim was to be anything more than a participant").

14. Situation in the Democratic Republic of Congo, Case No. ICC-01/04-101: *Decision on the Applications for Participation in the Proceedings* (January 17, 2006).

15. Situation in Uganda, Case No. ICC-02/04-101: *Decision on Victims' Applications for Participation* (August 10, 2007).

challenging—virtually all newly filed victim applications to participate in the proceedings. Prosecutors apparently intended this tactic to slow the proceedings, and to signal to all involved the Office's frustration with the Chamber's ruling. This tactical nit-picking approach, by which the Prosecutor threatened to challenge all applications, may have, in fact, been the reason the Chamber subsequently dramatically reversed course.

In 2008, the Appeals Chamber in *Lubanga* confirmed victims' participatory rights.[16] The Chamber, however, held in relevant part that:

> [T]he Trial Chamber did not create an unfettered right for victims to lead or challenge evidence, instead victims are required to demonstrate why their interests are affected by the evidence or issue, upon which the Chamber will decide, on a case-by-case basis whether or not to allow such participation. For example, should a victim demonstrate that his personal interests would be negatively affected if a particular witness (who could attest to the harm suffered by the victim) was not called to testify or if a piece of evidence (which would have ramifications on the safety and security of the victim) were to be declared admissible, then the victim would be able to move the Chamber to exercise its powers under Article 69(3) to present the evidence or challenge the admissibility of the evidence, respectively.[17]

With these safeguards in place, the Appeals Chamber viewed participatory rights of victims—including submission of evidence pertaining to the guilt of the accused and challenges to the admissibility or relevance of evidence—to be in keeping with the Prosecutor's burden of proving the accused's guilt, as well as with the accused's right to a fair trial.[18]

---

16. Interim appeals are governed by Article 82. *See generally* Situation in Darfur, Sudan, in the Case of the Prosecutor v. Omar Hassan Ahmad Al Bashir ("Omar Al Bashir"), Case No. ICC-02/05-01/09: *Decision on the Prosecutor's Application for Leave to Appeal the "Decision on the Prosecution's Application for a Warrant of Arrest Against Omar Hassan Ahmad Al Bashir"* (June 24, 2009), at 4.

17. Appeals Chamber, Situation in the Democratic Republic of the Congo In the Case of the Prosecutor v. Thomas Lubanga Dyilo, Case No. ICC-01/04-01/06: *Judgment on the Appeals of The Prosecutor and The Defence against Trial Chamber I's Decision on Victims' Participation of 18 January 2008* (July 11, 2008), at 33.

18. *Id., cited in* Situation in the Democratic Republic of the Congo, Case No. ICC 01/04-01/06: *Decision on the Manner of Questioning Witnesses by the Legal Representatives of Victims* (September 16, 2009), at 15–16 ("[D]epending on the circumstances, the alleged guilt of the accused may be a subject that substantively affects the personal interests of

This pronouncement from the Court has (for now at least) answered the question of whether the Chamber will grant victims full and co-equal participation. No such blanket right exists, the Chamber concluded. Rather, the Trial Chamber will evaluate victim requests to participate during the trial on a "case-by-case" basis. It must be noted, however, that some prosecutors at the ICC interpret this ruling, although on its face fairly neutral and non-definitive, as signalling that the Chamber will not *ever* permit victims to present evidence (though, given the non-binding/non-precedential nature of ICC rulings,[19] no such conclusion can really be drawn).

In terms of the precise modality of victim participation, the ICC Rules do not explicitly vest in victim representatives the right to personally question witnesses, as opposed to having the Chamber or Prosecutor pose the questions.[20] However, Article 68(3) provides the groundwork for victim participation, and Article 69(3), in addition to granting "parties" permission to submit evidence, also grants the Court the broad "authority to request the submission of *all evidence* that it considers necessary for the determination of the truth."[21] Thus, even under the stingiest reading of Article 68(3), Article 69(3) continues to explicitly permit the Court to consider victims' submissions of evidence for possible admission at trial.

Victim representatives must rely on the rules and rulings to date to argue that unduly limiting victim participation is fundamentally at odds with the ICC's victim-centric framework discussed herein. If the Chamber does not permit victims, as defined in Rule 85, to, for example, present evidence, then, as a practical matter, it will be virtually impossible for victims to prevail and receive reparations unless they have the full cooperation of the Prosecutor.[22] For example, although the Prosecutor can prove his case by establishing, say,

---

the victims, and the Appeals Chamber has determined that the Trial Chamber may authorize the victims' legal representative to question witnesses on subjects related to this issue. . . . It follows that victims' legal representatives may, for instance, question witnesses on areas relevant to the interests of the victims in order to clarify details of their evidence and to elicit additional facts, notwithstanding its relevance to the guilt or innocence of the accused.").

19. *See* Article 21(2).

20. *See generally* Rule 89(1) (Chamber may specify manner of victim participation as the Chamber deems "appropriate").

21. Article 69(3) (emphasis added).

22. And if the Prosecutor were deemed bound to do as the victim representatives wish, this would risk bringing an improper influence to bear on the prosecutorial function, which is inconsistent with Articles 42 and 51, as well as Articles 5 and 6 of the ICC Code of Professional Conduct.

that the accused committed particular charged atrocities in a given village, the victim must *additionally* establish that a particular accused, or group of persons under the accused's control, harmed the victim (or perhaps a relative, depending on how Rule 85(a) is construed) on a particular day, and in a particular manner.

The most sensible, and legally supportable, solution to any such prosecutor/victim conflict is to ask the Chamber to rule early in the proceedings on victim requests to present supplemental evidence and witnesses, and to limit such participatory rights in a manner that ensures the smooth and efficient presentation of the evidence. It is, consequently, incumbent on victim representatives to focus on those issues that matter most to their clients, so as to assure the Chamber and the Office of the Prosecutor that the victims' proposed participation will not interfere with the effective and proper administration of justice. Victim representatives must, therefore, carefully prepare narrowly tailored, and persuasive, arguments for why the Chamber should permit them to participate at specifically outlined stages in the proceedings, and in the manner proposed.

PART VI

Qualifying as Legal Counsel for Victims

MANY CASUAL OBSERVERS of the ICC misunderstand a lawyer's ability to participate in the Court's proceedings. For example, many believe that attorneys from war-torn areas, such as Sudan's Darfur region, who are well placed to represent victims at the ICC, given their intimate familiarity with the tragic events that took place (and are taking place) in that region, will be regularly involved in the ICC's work.[1] Often overlooked, however, are the surprisingly demanding barriers to entry for attorneys. These barriers assure that many aspiring victim representatives will in reality never appear before the ICC. In an unfortunate twist of irony, the very conflict and devastation in their home countries effectively precludes most of these attorneys from obtaining the requisite below-described legal and linguistic background demanded of a registered ICC victim representative. Understanding these threshold requirements is, therefore, the first step on the long road to a lawyer's substantive in-court victim advocacy.

A. Becoming a Formally Recognized ICC "Victim Representative"

The process of becoming formally qualified as an "ICC Victim Representative" is quite involved. To qualify, the applicant must demonstrate sufficient

1. The importance of having attorneys with some "local knowledge" has in fact been emphasized by Trial Chamber II. *See generally* Situation in the Democratic Republic of the Congo In the Case of the Prosecutor v. Germain Katanga and Mathieu Ngudjolo Chui, ICC-01/04–01/07: *Order on the Organisation of Common Legal Representation of Victims* (July 22, 2009), at 10 ("[T]he Chamber considers that it would be desirable if the common legal representative (or at least one member of his or her team) has a strong connection with the local situation of the victims and the region in general. This will assist the common legal representative in presenting the genuine perspective of the victims, as is his or her primary role.").

relevant legal experience, knowledge of international or criminal law, and the requisite language skills.[2]

According to Rule 90(6), the legal representative of victims "shall have the same qualifications" as a counsel for the defense. The qualifications for counsel for the defense are, in turn, set out in Rule 22(1). Rule 22(1) requires counsel to furnish proof of the following:

1. Established competence in international or criminal law and procedure;

2. Ten years of relevant experience in criminal proceedings, whether as a judge, prosecutor, advocate, or in another similar capacity;

3. "Excellent knowledge" of, and "fluency" in, at least one of the "working languages" of the ICC;[3] *and*

4. A record free of convictions for "serious" criminal or disciplinary offences considered incompatible with the nature of the office of counsel before the Chamber.[4]

The aspiring legal representative must submit a Candidate Application Form, including the following documentation establishing his ability to meet the above criteria:[5]

— A Certificate of Good Standing from the applicant's home bar or licensing association.
— A valid practicing certificate.
— A certificate issued by the relevant authority of each state of which the applicant is a national, or where the applicant is domiciled, stating the existence, if any, or the absence, of criminal convictions.

---

2. *See also* Appendix VI.

3. The "working languages" of the Court are English and French, as well as any other authorized language, as determined on a case-by-case basis. *See* Article 50(2); *see also* Rule 41 (authorizing use of official language of the Court as working language when majority involved in case and participants request it, or if it otherwise would "facilitate the efficiency of the proceedings"). The "official languages" of the Court, on the other hand, are Arabic, Chinese, English, French, Russian, and Spanish. *See* Article 50(1).

4. *See* Regulation of the Court 67.

5. *See generally* Regulation of the Court 67 (criteria to be met by counsel); Regulation of the Court 68 (assistants to counsel); Regulation of the Court 69 (proof and control of criteria to be met by counsel); and Regulation of the Court 70 ("Inclusion in the List of Counsel").

— A detailed *curriculum vitae* allowing for the appraisal of the applicant's competence and experience.
— A valid copy of the applicant's professional insurance policy.
— A legible copy of the applicant's birth certificate.
— A legible copy of the applicant's identity card.
— A legible copy of the applicant's passport/travel document.
— Two passport-size photographs of the applicant.

Lawyers who successfully submit their applications and are assigned victims should immediately contact the Office of Public Counsel for Victims (OPCV). The OPCV has the greatest institutional and legal familiarity with the Court's written and unwritten rules governing victims. Moreover, the OPCV may have advised, or represented, these victims prior to the victim receiving assigned legal representation,[6] and victim representatives must of course gather all possible information relating to any such prior contacts.

B. An Alternative Mode of Legal Representation: "Assistant to Counsel"

Although the Rules may preclude many aspiring victim representatives from becoming qualified ICC counsel, oft-overlooked ICC Registry Regulations 124 and 125[7] allow lawyers with more limited experience to formally register as "Assistants to Counsel." This fall-back option, while still requiring the applicant to demonstrate knowledge of international or criminal law, constitutes the most promising avenue of ICC participation for many lawyers hailing from regions where relevant courtroom experience, and the necessary language skills, are difficult to come by.[8]

6. *See generally* Situation in the Democratic Republic of Congo, Case No. ICC-01/04–01/06: *Decision on the Role of the Office of Public Counsel for Victims and Its Request for Access to Documents* (March 6, 2008), at 13–17 (limiting OPCV's legal representation of victims to the point in time that "the Chamber issues a decision on [the victims'] application to participate").

7. By reference to Rule 22(1) and Regulation of the Court 68.

8. Of particular significance to potential Assistants to Counsel is that they are not required to have Rule 22(1)'s "excellent knowledge of," and fluency in, at least one of the working languages of the Court.

To become an Assistant to Counsel, the applicant must have either (1) five years of relevant experience in criminal proceedings, *or* (2) "specific competence" in international or criminal law and procedure. Lawyers with five years of criminal law experience, therefore, can qualify, as can members of the legal academy or lawyers working for non-governmental organizations who have "specific competence" (a term that remains undefined) in international law or criminal law and procedure. This wording, moreover, is notably vague, leaving significant room for argument that a given lawyer is qualified to be an ICC Assistant to Counsel.

PART VII

Steps to Formal Recognition as a "Victim"

RULE 85(a) defines the term "victims." Full participation at the ICC requires victims to first obtain official ICC registration. The task of becoming a registered victim, however, is, like many of the ICC's procedural hurdles, more challenging than it at first blush might appear.

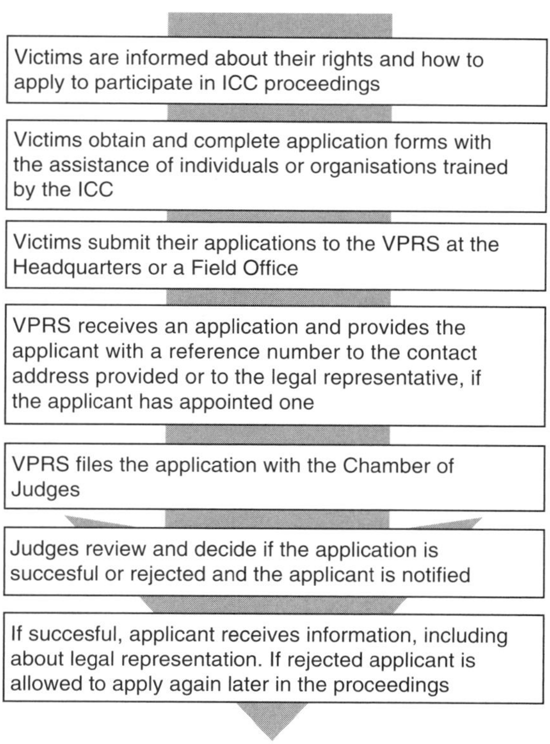

'Victims Before the International Criminal Court. A Guide for the Participation of Victims in the Proceedings of the Court.' Copyright© International Criminal Court 2006.

A. The Long Road to Formal Recognition as a "Victim"

In order to qualify for victim status in ICC proceedings under Rule 85, the Chamber must first determine whether, based on the putative victim's application, there are "grounds to believe"[1] the putative victim meets the following criteria:

1. The putative victim is a natural (or legal) person;
2. The putative victim has suffered cognizable harm;
3. The alleged crime from which the harm resulted falls within the jurisdiction of the ICC; *and*
4. The alleged crime and the harm are causally linked.[2]

In the past, applications prepared by NGOs have contained errors, prompting the Court to dismiss them. Victim representatives must therefore take great care that information, such as a prospective victim's age, be accurate and verified, and that the time, date, nature, and location of the alleged harm carefully correspond with the criminal conduct alleged in the charging document. If the Court deems a victim's application incomplete, Rule 89(2) permits the applicant later in the proceeding to file a new application containing the missing or incomplete information.[3]

In the *Lubanga* Trial Chamber's January 18, 2008 ruling, the Chamber summarized and condensed Rule 85(a)'s requirements for victim participation at trial. The Chamber required a showing that (1) there exists a "real evidential link" between the (likely) proffered evidence at trial and the victim, and that (2) the trial could impact the victim's personal interests because those interests "are in a real sense engaged" by "an issue arising" during the trial.[4]

1. Note, also, that this "pre-judging" of these criteria by necessity also requires the Chamber to, in a sense, provide at least its preliminary judgment on the underlying case.
2. *See* Rule 85(a); *see also* Situation in the Democratic Republic of the Congo in the Case of The Prosecutor v. Thomas Lubanga Dyilo, Case No. ICC-01/04–01/06: *Redacted Version of "Decision on 'Indirect Victims'"* (April 8, 2009), at 15, 19–22 (pursuant to Rule 85, victims must have suffered either direct or indirect harm; "indirect victims" suffered harm as a result of the harm suffered by direct victims).
3. *See, e.g.*, Situation in the Democratic Republic of the Congo In the Case of the Prosecutor v. Thomas Lubanga Dyilo, Case No. ICC-01/04–01/06: *Decision on the Applications for Participation* (November 4, 2008), at 13.
4. *See* Situation in the Democratic Republic of the Congo, Case No. II-01/04–01/06–1119: *Decision on Victims' Participation* (January 18, 2008), at 32–34.

The second element of having a personal interest impacted by the proceedings appears to particularly favor victims who may also be witnesses at trial, because it focuses on a connection between the proposed participation and the evidence (or issues) likely to arise during the trial.[5]

In order to maximize the chances of securing participatory rights, then, it is advisable that the victim representative go beyond the minimum statutory requirements by (1) identifying for the Chamber the victim's *personal* interests (as opposed to common interests shared by all victims) impacted by the charged conduct, and (2) demonstrating, with some specificity, why the vindication of the victim's personal interests will not outweigh or negatively impact the fairness or efficiency of the proceedings.[6]

Grounds resulting in the rejection of a victim's application have included that (1) the applicant was a minor, and the person who submitted the application on his behalf had not yet attained the age of majority;[7] (2) the applicant failed to sufficiently identify the date and location of the alleged crimes; (3) the proof of the victim's identity was insufficient; (4) the applicant merely submitted a legal conclusion of harm (torture), rather than specific facts which, *prima facie*, constitute harm within the meaning of the Statute; (5) no reports or similar external sources confirm the alleged attacks in the area of residence of the applicant; (6) the emotional harm described by the applicant resulted from information the applicant received from others, as opposed to having witnessed the harmful conduct first-hand; and (7) that the person

---

5. *See id.* at 37. Note, however, that Judge Pikis in his separate opinion criticized the majority view that the victim need only show a link between the victim and a crime within the Court's jurisdiction, and, instead, argued in favor of a requirement that the victim's involvement be linked to the facts or circumstances of the *charged* conduct. *See id.* at 8. Judge Pikis further criticized the majority opinion as requiring an overly burdensome case-by-case evaluation of each victim's involvement "for every procedural action." *Id.* at 60.

6. *See generally* Situation in the Democratic Republic of the Congo in the Case of The Prosecutor v. Thomas Lubanga Dyilo, Case No. ICC-01/04–01/06: *Decision on the Defence Application For Disclosure of Victims' Applications* (January 21, 2009), at 7 ("The critical tension revealed by this application [for disclosure of dual victim-witnesses' unredacted applications for participation and reparations] is between the rights of victims to appropriate protective measures and the right of the accused to a fair trial, and, in the particular context of this application, to the exculpatory material in the possession of the prosecution and the VPRS.").

7. Note, however, that under certain circumstances the Court may permit children to apply to participate without an intermediary. *See* Situation in the Democratic Republic of the Congo In the Case of the Prosecutor v. Thomas Lubanga Dyilo, Case No. ICC-01/04–01/06: *Decision on the Applications by Victims to Participate in the Proceedings* (December 15, 2008) (permitting, on a case-by-case basis, child conscripts who were separated from their parents and other adult relatives at a relatively young age to apply on their own behalf).

acting on behalf of the applicant suffered the harm alleged, rather than the applicant himself.[8] A review of the cases, and Rule 85's language, leads to the conclusion that the Chamber will grant a victim's application if it meets the following specific requirements:[9]

1. The applicant has reached majority,[10] or a person who has reached majority submits the Application on behalf of a minor;[11]

2. The applicant submitted sufficient proof of identity (such proof includes voting cards);[12]

3. The Application includes the necessary date and location of the alleged crimes;

4. The applicant sufficiently describes the alleged "harm" suffered within the meaning of Rule 85.

Such "harm" includes:

Moral Harm: Emotional harm suffered, for example, as a result of the militia killing a family member, or making death threats; witnessing events "of an exceedingly violent and shocking nature," such as a militia person's sexual abuse and torture of an applicant's mother or the

---

8. *See generally id.*

9. The victim representative must be sure to include the actual proof—such as the applicant's voting card—as part of the application. Moreover, the standard of proof is proof "to a level which might be considered satisfactory for the limited purposes of rule 85(a)." Situation in Uganda, Case No. ICC-02/04: *Decision on Victims' Applications for Participation* (November 17, 2008), at 7.

10. Under certain circumstances, the Chamber may permit children to apply to participate without an intermediary. *See* Situation in the Democratic Republic of the Congo In the Case of the Prosecutor v. Thomas Lubanga Dyilo, Case No. ICC-01/04–01/06: *Decision on the Applications by Victims to Participate in the Proceedings* (December 15, 2008) (permitting, on a case-by-case basis, child conscripts who were separated from their parents and other adult relatives at a relatively young age to apply on their own behalf).

11. In the case of a deceased person, the primary applicant may be the person acting on behalf of the deceased person.

12. *See generally* Situation in the Central African Republic In the Case of the Prosecutor v. Jean-Pierre Bemba Gombo, Case No. ICC-10/05–01/08: *Fourth Decision on Victims' Participation* (December 12, 2008), at 14–17 (deeming, in instances where victims are unable to obtain standard identification documents, a "statement signed by two witnesses attesting to the identity of the victim applicant and including, where applicable, the relationship between the victim applicant and the person acting on his or her behalf" to be sufficient).

mutilation of a child; or abducting a victim's child and forcing that child to participate in armed fighting.[13]

Material Harm: Economic loss, for example, as a result of the pillaging of the victims' personal belongings, destruction of household items, cattle, goats, and sheep, or the destruction of the victim's home.

Physical Harm: Rape, sexual enslavement, assaults and battery, and other similar acts.

5. The alleged crimes within the jurisdiction of the ICC (*ratione materiae*) appear, *prima facie*, to have caused the alleged harm;

6. The harm caused by the alleged crimes within the ICC's jurisdiction occurred within the Court's temporal jurisdiction (*ratione temporis*). As a general rule, this means the crime(s) were alleged to have occurred after the Rome Statute entered into force, or after the State Party joined the ICC;

7. The harm caused by the alleged crimes within the ICC's jurisdiction occurred within the Court's territorial jurisdiction (*ratione loci*); *and*

8. The applicant signed, or placed his thumbprint on, the application.[14]

To illustrate how in practice the Pre-Trial Chamber analyzes such applications, consider the terse ruling on the fairly routine application of "Applicant a/0031/08":

> Applicant a/0031/08 appears *prima facie* to have suffered moral harm (emotional suffering) as a result of the killing of members of his family and

---

13. *See generally* Situation in the Democratic Republic of the Congo in the Case of The Prosecutor v. Thomas Lubanga Dyilo, Case No. ICC-01/04–01/06: *Redacted Version of "Decision on 'Indirect Victims'"* (April 8, 2009), at 19–22 (distinguishing "direct" from "indirect" victims, noting that a "close personal relationship, such as those between parents and children, are a precondition of participation by indirect victims," and emphasizing that a "causal link must exist between the crimes charged and the victims' harm. . . .").

14. *See generally* Situation in Uganda, Case No. ICC-02/04: *Decision on Victims' Applications for Participation* (November 21, 2008), at 6–7 (setting out requirements for victim participation, and noting that "[e]ach statement by Applicant victims will . . . be assessed both on the merits of its intrinsic coherence and on the basis of information otherwise available to the Chamber. . . . [F]ailure by applicants to submit certificates relating to the injuries allegedly sustained in the incidents does not hinder the holding that the alleged harm is proved to a satisfactory degree for the purposes of the present proceedings."); Situation in Darfur, Sudan, Case No. ICC-02/05: *Corrigendum to Decision on the Applications for Participation in the Proceedings* (December 17, 2007) (discussing requirements of Regulation of the Court 86(2)); *see also* Situation in the Democratic Republic of the Congo, Case No. ICC-01/04: *Decision on the Applications for Participation* (November 4, 2008), at 13–38.

> material harm (economic loss) as a result of the pillaging of his cattle, allegedly by members of a militia. The moral and material harm suffered by Applicant a/0031/08 appears *prima facie* to have been caused by crime(s) within the jurisdiction of the Court, such as, among others, those enumerated in Articles 7(1)(a), 8(2)(a)(i), or 8(2)(c)(i), and 8(2)(b)(xvi), or 8(2)(e)(v). The Applicant alleges that the harm caused by the crime(s) within the jurisdiction of the Court occurred within the Court's temporal and territorial jurisdiction: in February 2003 on the territory of the DRC.[15]

Defense teams may contend that Rule 85(a)'s pre-trial qualification requirement conflicts with Article 68(3), since Rule 85(a) requires the Chamber to "pre-judge" the case. Although it is true that the Chamber will formally acknowledge the connection between the victim and the interests involved at trial before the Chamber has ruled on the guilt of the accused, this is not inconsistent with Article 68. Put simply, the standard of proof for victim qualification ("grounds to believe") is substantially lower than the standard required for conviction ("the Court must be convinced of the guilt of the accused beyond a reasonable doubt"[16]). Indeed, the "grounds to believe" standard also governs detention rulings, whether the Chamber provides a witness with counsel, and whether an individual has a right to be warned against the possibility of self-incrimination. None of these preliminary conclusions require the Chamber to make any final determinations concerning the guilt or innocence of the accused, and they certainly do not place any doubt on the fairness of the proceedings. Victim representatives should, therefore, resist defense claims that a finding of "victimization" somehow as a general matter undermines the accused's right to a fair and impartial trial.

In addition to the Chamber's formal recognition of individuals as "victims," Rule 50(1) requires the Office of the Prosecutor to inform potential victims and the Victim and Witness Unit of any decision to seek Pre-Trial Chamber authorization to initiate an investigation in accordance with Article 15(3). Such an informal decision by the Prosecutor to consider a person a "victim" necessarily precedes any formal victim-status determination by the

15. Situation in the Democratic Republic of the Congo, Case No. ICC-01/04: *Decision on the Applications for Participation* (November 4, 2008), at 21.

16. Article 66(3).

Pre-Trail Chamber pursuant to Article 69(3) and Rule 85. Victim representatives should, therefore, also be on guard against attempts by the defense to argue that such an informal and preliminary determination of victimhood is inconsistent with the Prosecutor's duty to remain "neutral" during the investigation of the case.

B. Victims as Witnesses

Experienced criminal law practitioners realize that, in many cases, victims may also be witnesses.[17] This dynamic of course also holds true at the ICC. Although certain rules relating to pre-trial contact between parties in the proceedings and witnesses differ from the rules relating to victims, there is nothing inherently inconsistent about being both a victim and a witness (indeed, in practice, victim representatives may suggest to the prosecution certain victims—perhaps not already be known to the prosecution—who may serve as particularly effective witnesses).

Victim as a participant	Victim as a witness
Participation is voluntary	Called by the defence, the prosecution, other victims participating in the proceedings or the Chamber
Communicating to the Court their own interests and concerns	Serve the interests of the Court and the party that calls them
It is up to the victims to decide what they want to say	Give evidence in testifying and answering related questions
Participation is possible at all stages of proceedings when considered appropriate by the Judges	Called to testify at a specific time
Always entitled to be represented before the ICC by a legal representative	Does not normally have a legal representative
Normally participates via a legal representative, and need not appear in person	Always testifies in person

17. *See generally* Situation in the Democratic Republic of the Congo In the Case of the Prosecutor v. Thomas Lubanga Dyilo, Case No. ICC-01/04-01/06: *Public Decision On Certain Practicalities Regarding Individuals Who Have the Dual Status of Witness and Victim* (June 5, 2008) (regulating contact and disclosure obligations of victims who are expected to testify as witnesses).

That said, the Chamber has demonstrated some vacillation concerning the proper treatment of such "dual" victim/witnesses. What is clear, however, is that legal representative must provide the prosecution with the names and identifying details of victims who the legal representative believes may also be witnesses *as soon as* the legal representative becomes aware of this possibility.[18] The prosecution, which must treat this information confidentially, then makes a determination of whether the victim has such dual status, and informs the legal representative of its conclusion.[19] Similarly, the legal representative of a victim must also furnish such information to the defense, which in turn must inform the victim if the defense intends to call the victim in its case.[20] Notice to the legal representative, therefore, must precede all contacts between prosecution, defense, and a victim with dual status.[21]

---

18. *Id.* at 22.
19. *Id.* at 22–23.
20. *Id.* at 24.
21. *Id.* at 24–27.

PART VIII

Preparing for Complex Group Representation

THE COMPLEXITY OF ATROCITY CRIMES CASES is one of the chief explanations advanced for the cumbersome, and at-times halting, progress of ICC investigations and prosecutions.[1] Such complexity presents challenges not only to the Prosecutor and the Chamber, but also to victim representatives. Complicating matters, in light of the professional backgrounds of the lawyers and judges at the ICC discussed above in Part IV(J), a number of ICC practitioners will likely not have previously dealt with large, multi-defendant criminal cases. Given the sheer number of potential victims in ICC cases, as well as the practical problems presented by having, say, 200 victims represented in court by 200 separate victim representatives, group representation will probably (and, indeed, should) emerge as the norm.

A. Promises and Potential Pitfalls of Group Representation—The Class Action Model

For a graphic illustration of how unfeasible individual representation is, consider the situation involving the Democratic Republic of Congo, where the individual victim can seem, and be made to feel, like a firefly in a canyon. With literally millions of potential victims, the Chamber, the Office of the Prosecutor, and defense counsel would not be able to address individual *en masse* pre-trial filings submitted by hundreds, or thousands, of lawyers representing individual victims. Likewise, the Victim and Witness Unit and the Registry would be unable to meet the needs of, and to provide notice to,

1. *See generally* Rene Blattman & Kirsten Bowman, *Achievements and Problems of the International Criminal Court*, 6 J. INT'L CRIM. JUST. 724 (2008) ("[B]oth the complexity and the magnitude of international crimes are exceptional circumstances that influence the pace of conducting and concluding such trials."). As discussed above, however, the cases the ICC is currently processing are not necessarily exceptionally complex.

such a far-flung group.[2] Moreover, pursuant to Rule 90(5), the Court covers the costs if a "victim or group of victims ... lack the necessary means to pay for a common legal representative chosen by the Court. ..." The financial and logistical burdens—which already at times appear to buckle the ICC's capacity—occasioned by individual or small-group representation of victims would bring to an almost certain grinding halt the criminal proceedings, thereby prejudicing all participants.[3]

As a result of these time, space, capacity, and financial constraints,[4] the Court has repeatedly signaled its intention to assign a common legal representative to groups of victims who have suffered "mainly similar crimes [occurring in the same geographic region] and ... allegedly committed by the same group of perpetrators."[5] The Chamber in the *Lubanga* case in fact noted that "there is likely to be joint representation of, and joint presentation of common issues by, participating victims. . . ."[6] Nevertheless, at least one

---

2. Consider, for example, the basic resource and capacity problems that would be posed by Rule 90(5), which requires the Registry to provide financial and logistical assistance to a victim, or group of victims, who do not have the necessary means of paying for legal representation. Moreover, there is an open question concerning from what point in time protective measures must be taken, and who must pay for them.

3. *See generally* Prosecution's Application for Leave to Appeal PTC I's Decision in the Situation in the Democratic Republic of Congo, Case No. ICC-01/04–103: *Applications for Participation in the Proceedings* (January 23, 2006), at 14 (arguing that Court's limited resources would be stretched beyond capacity if virtually unlimited victim participation were permitted); *see also id.* at 14–15 (warning of flood of petitions to Court and detrimental impact on efficiency of pre-trial proceedings, and expressing concern about Registrar's ability to provide notice, legal advice, etc., as provided for by Rules 16, 90, 92, and Regulation of the Court 86).

4. Even the relatively modestly sized main courtroom at the ICC (there are two smaller courtrooms as well) can barely accommodate the participants in the one-defendant *Lubanga* case. The main courtroom, moreover, is the only full-sized courtroom in the cavernous building housing the Court. The time will soon come when the Court will have to accommodate two (or more) trials in the same room. Multiple trials, something that should be the rule, rather than the exception, will undoubtedly further delay the proceedings unless necessary changes are made.

5. Situation in the Central African Republic In the Case of the Prosecutor v. Jean-Pierre Bemba Gombo, Case No. ICC-10/05–01/08: *Fifth Decision on Victims' Issues Concerning Common Legal Representation of Victims* (December 16, 2008), at 5–8 ("In case the victims participating in the present case are unable to choose a common legal representative, the Single Judge requests, pursuant to rule 90(3) of the Rules, the Registrar to choose one common legal representative from the CAR"; in the case of victims objecting to the common legal representative, or a the presence of a possible conflict of interest, the OPCV is to be appointed as interim victim representative, "if need be").

6. Trial Chamber I, Situation in the Democratic Republic of the Congo, Case No. ICC-01/04–01/06–1191: *The Prosecutor v. Thomas Lubanga Dyilo, Decision on the Defence and Prosecution Requests for Leave to Appeal the Decision on Victims' Participation of 18 January 2008* (February 26, 2008), at 10–11; *see also* Situation in Uganda, Case No. ICC-02/04:

Chamber has, in the context of arranging group representation for victims, emphasized that it "attaches the greatest importance to the requirement that the participation of victims, through their legal representatives . . . be as meaningful as possible as opposed to being purely symbolic."[7] If the Chamber chooses to order group representation, it can do so pursuant to Rule 90 and Regulation of the Court 79(2).[8]

Rule 90 starts out broadly permissive, stating that "[a] victim shall be free to choose a legal representative."[9] However, Rule 90(2) quickly adds:

> Where there are a number of victims, the Chamber may, for the purpose of ensuring the effectiveness of the proceedings, request the victims or particular groups of victims, if necessary with the assistance of the Registry, to choose a common legal representative or representatives. In facilitating the coordination of victim representation, the Registry may

Decision on Legal Representation of Victims (February 9, 2009), at 5–6 (ordering joint representation in light of the "similarity of [the victims'] respective experiences and with a view to preserving the efficiency of the proceedings"); Situation in the Democratic Republic of the Congo in the Case of the Prosecutor v. Thomas Lubanga Dyilo, Case No. ICC-01/04–01/06: *Decision on the Applications for Participation* (November 4, 2008) (ordering the Registrar to assist persons to whom the Chamber granted the procedural status of victims so that they "may choose one or more common legal representatives," and directing the prosecution and defense to abstain from any direct contact with such persons without their legal representatives' approval).

7. Situation in the Democratic Republic of the Congo In the Case of the Prosecutor v. Germain Katanga and Mathieu Ngudjolo Chui, ICC-01/04–01/07: *Order on the Organisation of Common Legal Representation of Victims* (July 22, 2009), at 7 ("[T]he Chamber considers it of utmost importance that there be a steady and reliable flow of information about the proceedings to the victims and that there is real involvement by the victims in terms of instructing the legal representatives on how their interests should be presented.").

8. Regulation of the Court 79, and, by reference, Rule 90(3), govern the criteria for common legal representation. *See generally* Situation in the Democratic Republic of the Congo In the Case of the Prosecutor v. Thomas Lubanga Dyilo, Case No. ICC-01/04–01/06: *Decision on the Applications by Victims to Participate in the Proceedings* (December 15, 2008), at 34 (noting that the Chamber granted 91 applicants the right to participate in the trial, and finding that, "[g]iven that the views and concerns of many victims will coincide or overlap, the opportunity in this case for joint representation must be carefully explored"); Situation in Uganda, Case No. ICC-02/04: *Decision on Victims' Applications for Participation* (November 21, 2008), at 65 ("As regards applicants granted the status of victims in the Case, in light of the similarity of their experiences and statements, the Single Judge is of the view that they also should be jointly represented by one common legal representative."); Situation in Uganda, Case No. ICC-02/04: *Decision on Victims' Applications for Participation* (November 17, 2008), at 18 (appointing Office of Public Counsel for Victims' attorney Adesola Adeboyejo to represent all victims of the situation).

9. Rule 90(1).

provide assistance, *inter alia*, by referring the victims to a list of counsel, maintained by the Registry, or suggesting one or more common legal representatives.

This language gives the Chamber broad discretion to appoint counsel of its choosing to the victims, and to subdivide the representation in whatever manner it deems appropriate under the circumstances of the case.

It is, therefore, likely that the Chamber will rely on Rule 90(2) to appoint a small group of attorneys to represent the many victims expected in any atrocity crimes case of the type likely to be brought before the ICC. Rule 90(4) provides that the Chamber and Registry "shall take all reasonable steps to ensure that in the selection of common legal representatives, the distinct interests of the victims . . . are represented and that any conflict of interest is avoided." Regulation of the Court 79 goes on to state that the Chamber may combine the decision to permit victims, or groups of victims, to participate in the proceedings with the decision to appoint them a common legal representative.

Although the Chamber may aggregate victims in a number of ways, victim representatives should assume that they will represent the victims on a group basis—whether as individual attorneys working alone, or as teams of attorneys who coordinating among themselves. In the *Lubanga* trial, for example, there were three teams of victim representatives: Paolina Massidda, the Principal Counsel of the Office of Public Counsel for Victims, headed one team, and "external" (that is, non-ICC) legal representatives headed the other two.

The initial question, then, is how will the Chamber handle the inevitability of group representation? The options are two-fold: (1) The Chamber may call upon a single lawyer (or team of lawyers) to represent a large number of victims, or (2) the Chamber could call on multiple lawyers, each representing sub-groups of similarly situated clients, to work together and aggregate their efforts on behalf of the victims as a whole. In either case, there exists the danger that victims will enter the case with a belief that the lawyer will represent them individually in the classic sense, in that they will have at least some meaningful control over their attorney's conduct and decisions. In reality, however, victims will be involved in collective litigation.

Regardless of the aggregation method settled on by the Chamber, group representation will encompass preparing pleadings for the group, handling collective discovery issues, and preparing for pre-trial hearings and the main trial. Depending on the number of victims assigned to a particular attorney, or group of attorneys, and where the victims are situated, it is unlikely that the attorney will have significant personal involvement with each victim, or will have the level of personal interaction and discussion that would be the norm if the attorney only represented a small number of victims. The fact that, in most cases, the Chamber will have appointed the attorneys to represent victims, as opposed to the victims seeking out the representative themselves, compounds this problem.

There are certainly significant challenges posed by the group representation mechanism, but there are also real, notable advantages. For example, victim representatives can collaborate in their efforts to produce high-quality legal briefs, thereby avoiding the need to inundate the Chamber with duplicative submissions and time-consuming appeals from individually filed matters. Moreover, given the enormity of the stakes for the victims, and considering the suffering they have already endured, the Chamber can be expected to be more sensitive to the victims' needs, and to permit greater victim involvement, if the victims' issues are collectively addressed by one lead victim representative, who speaks on behalf of all victims or groups of victims, and who keeps the litigation moving.

Of course, it is also conceivable that the Chamber will employ formal aggregation processes in order to handle larger numbers of victims. Under such a scenario, it is likely that a number of trial teams will be assembled, and that a "hub" or "lead" victim representative will bear responsibility for addressing the Chamber and filing all submissions. Even without such formal aggregation, to the extent that groups of lawyers represent individual groups of victims, careful coordination and a decision on who will be the lead attorney is required.

Considering the somewhat politicized nature of the ICC, and the need to know the written and unwritten ins and outs of handling a case at the Court, victims will ideally be represented by a "mixed" team of victim representatives, namely, one or more ICC "insiders" with knowledge of the politics and the rules of the ICC, and one or more experienced trial attorneys from the victims' domestic jurisdiction ("external representatives") who can best relate to the victims and help the victims feel comfortable. By following this approach, the ICC insiders, who know the written and unwritten rules and practices of the ICC, will be in a position to augment the "on-the-ground" knowledge of the lawyers from the victims' home jurisdiction, thereby improving the victims' comfort and quality of representation.

That resources for victims are not limitless is not only a practical truism.[10] Regulation of the Court 83(1) and (2) make it clear that, although the Court

10. *See generally* Situation in the Democratic Republic of the Congo In the Case of the Prosecutor v. Germain Katanga and Mathieu Ngudjolo Chui, ICC-01/04–01/07: *Order on*

will cover all "reasonably necessary" defense costs, providing legal assistance to indigent victims is subject to a determination by the "Registrar in consultation with the Chamber, where appropriate." Thus, under virtually all scenarios, the victim representatives will have to select a lead attorney, and set up logistical mechanisms, in order to effectively and efficiently coordinate efforts and develop a sound trial strategy. The pooling of resources in such a manner permits the victim representatives to reap the benefits of economies of scale by dividing up investigative and research efforts among the attorneys, and by spreading the limited financial and intellectual resources, know-how, and contacts among many victims. Not only will the victim representatives be able to focus more directly on those issues impacting the victims as a group, but they will also be able to expend resources on investigators and research in a manner that maximizes utility.

In terms of strategy, victim representatives must tailor their approach very much like a class action lawyer approaches representing the interests of a large number of individuals in a class action lawsuit. Counsel must be prepared to address the complex questions of how to frame the case and how to present persuasive evidence of harm to a large group of similarly-situated victims, frequently in the context of a "leadership crime." In this sense, ICC litigation involving victims resembles what Professor Abram Chayes in 1976 described as "public law litigation," that is, litigation relating to matters such as union governance, school desegregation, employment discrimination, environmental management, and securities fraud. In those classes of cases, the putative victims are aggregated, and counsel, through litigation, seeks to achieve certain collectively-held group ambitions.

Addressing such complexity requires creative thinking. Although group representation may have some of the above-described upsides (it, for example, may be easier to demonstrate harm to a group of victims as a result of the accused's systematic planning of, say, the ethnic cleansing of the village in

---

the Organisation of Common Legal Representation of Victims (July 22, 2009), at 8 ("[A]lthough victims are free to choose a legal representative, this right is subject to the important practical, financial, infrastructural and logistical constraints faced by the Court. Common legal representation is the primary procedural mechanism for reconciling the conflicting requirements of having fair and expeditious proceedings, whilst at the same time ensuring meaningful participation by potentially thousands of victims, all within the bounds of what is practically possible. The Chamber considers, therefore, that the freedom to choose a personal legal representative, set out in rule 90(1) is qualified by rule 90(2) and subject to the inherent and express powers of the Chamber to take all measures necessary if the interests of justice so require.") (Citations omitted).

which they all resided), the corollary downside is that the victim representative will have to formulate a more complex strategy to successfully advocate the victims' collective position.[11]

Since the ICC's legal provisions make group representation the likely default position for qualified victims, victim representatives must turn to analogous non-ICC group litigation situations for guidance on how to proceed, both ethically and strategically. The class action attorney's ethical and practical challenges are probably the closest analogy the victim representative can draw on, whether the Chamber has asked him to represent five, fifty, or five hundred victims.[12]

In federal court in the United States, where class action lawsuits are not unusual, Federal Rule of Civil Procedure 23 sets forth the four prerequisites to any class action: (1) numerosity, (2) commonality, (3) typicality, and (4) adequacy of representation. Federal Rule 23's requirement of numerosity is, to some extent, analogous to ICC Rule 90(1)'s requirement that the Chamber must determine a grouping that ensures the "effectiveness of the proceedings"[13] by, for example, limiting duplicative filings and allowing the victims to benefit from the efficiencies and focus provided by litigation economies of scale.

---

11. *See also* Appeals Chamber, Situation in the Democratic Republic of the Congo In the Case of the Prosecutor v. Thomas Lubanga Dyilo, Case No. ICC-01/04–01/06–1432: *Judgment on the Appeals of The Prosecutor and The Defence against Trial Chamber I's Decision on Victims' Participation of 18 January 2008* (July 11, 2008), at 42 ("The burden of proof of the guilt of the accused lies squarely with the Prosecutor (Article 66 (2) of the Statute).").

12. Class action litigation is commonly viewed as being one of a group of "entrepreneurial" legal practices (along with contingency-fee financing of litigation, reliance on juries as fact-finders, costly pre-trial discovery, rejection of "loser-pays" rules dictating who must pay for the litigation on the basis of who loses the litigation, and the availability of punitive tort damages and the like) popular in the United States—and unpopular among European lawyers. Such a view is a bit antiquated, however, given that class action litigation is making significant gains in Europe. Consider, for example, that class action-style litigation is permitted, and increasingly popular, in Germany (in the securities litigation context, *see Kapitalanleger-Musterverfahrensgesetz*), England (in the group litigation orders context, *see* Civil Procedure Rules 1998, S.I. 1998/3123, Part 19, Section III), Holland (in the collective settlements context, *see Burgerlijk Wetboek* Articles 3:305a-b), Italy (in the class action context, *see Codice di consume,* Article 140), and in other Continental jurisdictions.

13. Federal Rule 23, in contrast, requires that the Court initially find that naming each individual member of the class as a separate party in the lawsuit would be logistically inconvenient or otherwise impractical; in ICC proceedings, however, the qualified victims are all named participants in the proceedings and, therefore, do not constitute a "class" in the Federal Rule 23 sense, but rather operate as a group.

Turning next to the commonality and typicality of claims, the Chamber at the victim qualification stage, likewise, must conclude that there are questions of law and/or fact common to the group. Federal Rule 23's requirement that the proposed class members have adequate representation, moreover, mirrors ICC Rule 90(4)'s mandate that the Chamber select counsel for victims based on the "distinct interests of the victims," while striving to ensure that "any conflict of interest is avoided." It is, however, as discussed below, virtually impossible for an attorney representing a large number of victims to avoid "any" conflict of interest among the victims, as is required by Rule 90(4). Rather, the attorney must attempt to avoid conflicts of interests between the attorney's interests and the *group's* objectives, as well as conflicts among the victims within the group.

B. The Victim Representative's Duty of Loyalty to Clients

The attorney's duty of loyalty traditionally runs to each individual client. In the context of group representation, however, lawyers exercise their duty of loyalty by properly representing the interests of the group in a diligent, transparent, and conflict-free manner. Most victims of atrocity crimes, given their likely cultural, socio-economic, and educational backgrounds, as well as the ICC's relative novelty, will not truly understand what they can expect from their attorney.

The need to explain to victims the potential conflicts inherent in group representation is critical. The ICC's Code of Professional Conduct in fact takes the position that the attorney has created a representation agreement once he accepts the Chamber's assignment.[14] Although the rational victim may, *ex ante*, prefer group representation, and wish the attorney to advance collective, rather than individual, interests, this does not absolve counsel from the requirement to, at the outset, inform all victims of the scope, nature, and limitations of the representation, as well as of potential conflicts of interest that inhere in collective representation. Prior to discussing these potential conflicts, however, we must distinguish between class action and collective representation litigation.

The ICC's Code of Professional Conduct for Counsel, which claims primacy over any inconsistent ethics code which may bind the victim

14. *See* Code Article 11.

representative in his home jurisdiction,[15] reflects the drafters' foresight by appropriately recognizing the ethical difficulties involved in group litigation. The Code starts out by requiring all counsel, including counsel for victims, to perform their duties with "integrity and diligence, honourably, freely, independently, expeditiously and conscientiously. . . ."[16] Article 12 of the Code prevents counsel, absent consent,[17] from representing a client in any case in which that client's interests are incompatible with the interests of another client counsel has or had.[18] Article 14, in turn, mandates that counsel act with candor, fairness, and integrity towards each client, and that counsel also "[a]bide by the client's decisions concerning the objectives of his or her representation . . ." and "[c]onsult the client on the means by which the objectives of his or her representation are to be pursued."[19] Moreover, Article 16(1) requires counsel to "put the client's interest before counsel's own interests or those of any other person. . . ." These ethical provisions seem to operate against large-group representation of victims.

The Code, fortunately, anticipates some of the above-described ethical problems, which are part and parcel of group representation. Article 16(2), for example, provides:

> Where counsel has been retained or appointed as a common legal representative for victims or particular groups of victims, he or she shall advise his or her clients at the outset of the nature of the representation and the potential conflicting interests within the group. Counsel shall exercise all care to ensure a fair representation of the different yet consistent positions of his or her clients.

---

15. Code of Professional Conduct for Counsel, Article 4.

16. *Id.* at Code Article 5.

17. *Id.* at Code Article 12(2).

18. *See generally* Situation in the Democratic Republic of the Congo In the Case of the Prosecutor v. Germain Katanga and Mathieu Ngudjolo Chui, Case No. ICC-01/04–01/07: *Decision on the Apparent Conflict of Interest in Relation to Legal Representative of Victims* (July 16, 2008), at 8–11 (finding that victim representative's prior legal contacts with an accused did not provide the requisite indicia of the existence of a conflict of interest).

19. It must be noted that the ICC's Victims booklet states that the Court will, except in undefined "exceptional circumstances," not cover the cost of travel and lodging for victims who wish to personally appear before the Court. *See* VICTIMS BEFORE THE INTERNATIONAL COURT 27.

In terms of what action to take when a conflict of interest arises, Code Article 16(3) instructs counsel to inform all "potentially affected clients of the existence of the conflict," and to thereafter either seek Chamber's consent to withdraw from representing one or more clients, or to obtain the "full and informed consent—in writing—of all potentially affected clients to continue representation." Although the Code, therefore, goes a long way towards recognizing that conflicts may arise in group representation, it surprisingly does not define what actually constitutes a conflict of interest, or what qualifies as Article 16(2)'s "different yet consistent positions" among clients.

In any event, the attorney's duty of loyalty encompasses not only the avoidance of conflicts of interest, but also requires diligence in the individual case, and imposes a duty to inform and advise clients of case-related developments. In aggregate litigation, the client usually retains two critical phases where he can traditionally exercise his autonomy, namely, at the outset by opting into (or, more commonly, opting out of) the litigation, and again at the settlement phase. One could argue that this arrangement still provides the client insufficient autonomy. However, in ICC proceedings, even these limited instances of autonomy may be absent; the Court at the "opt-in" stage provides the oft-impoverished victim living in fear of retribution, and generally located thousands of miles from the courtroom in remote communities, with an attorney who will represent him. The victim has little control at this initial stage. Additionally, outside of the Prosecutor's guilty-plea negotiations and the reparations stage, there is nothing approximating a "settlement phase."

Victim representatives, in the end, must ensure themselves that their clients understand the nature of the proceedings, as well as the above-described inherent potential conflicts of interest, so that they can provide informed consent going forward. Victim representatives, therefore, at a minimum must explain to their clients (1) the nature of the litigation, (2) the number and nature of the other victims the attorney represents, (3) the advantages provided to victims by a collective and coordinated group effort, (4) the trade-offs involved in such litigation, such as more limited contacts with counsel and diminished ability to enforce individual objectives if those objectives are deemed by counsel to be at odds with the group's interests, and (5) the reality that, in cases of conflicts between the individual and the group's interests, the attorney must engage in priority-setting, resolving such client-client conflicts in favor of pursuing the group's interests. Once victims have this basic information, they will be in a better position to accept the representation, reject the representation and opt out, or reject the representation and petition the Chamber pursuant to Regulation 79(3) to grant them alternative counsel.[20]

To understand why the likelihood of having alternative or additional counsel appointed is low, consider that Regulation 79(3) provides that "[v]ictims may request the relevant Chamber to review the Registrar's choice of a common legal representative . . . within 30 days of the Registrar's decision." The Regulation's restrictive 30-day window to raise objections makes it highly unlikely that the attorney and victims will have had substantive interactions or discussions relating to trial strategy or to the conflicts that will necessarily inhere in group representation situations. Without such interactions, a victim will generally be unable to ground a claim of extraordinary circumstances warranting an alternative appointment. The 30-day window for objections raised by a victim (who necessarily will be appearing *pro se*) to the Chamber's choice of counsel, therefore, is likely to ensure that most victims will not be in a position to timely raise the necessary objections (or, for that matter, to even form a basis for such an objection) to the appointment of counsel.

Opting out of the litigation altogether after the 30 days have passed due to dissatisfaction with appointed counsel will be a drastic decision that leaves the victim with no alternative methods of participation. Victims are, therefore, as a practical matter assigned counsel, and they can either take it or leave it. In establishing this procedural reality, the ICC arguably fails to live up to its own promise of treating each victim as a true "participant" in the proceedings who, as such, is entitled to qualified counsel (per Rule 90).

---

20. The ICC's Victims booklet discusses this topic in a slightly more optimistic (or, at least, victim-centric) fashion:

> Where there are many victims, the judge may contact a victim and ask him or her to join with other victims to become part of a group of victims that will be represented by the same legal representative or team of representatives. This is called common legal representation, and the purpose is to help to make the proceedings more efficient. Their own interests will *always* be protected even through common legal representation.
>
> If for any reason the victims are unable to organize themselves in this way and to choose a common legal representative, the judges may ask the Registrar of the ICC to do so. If the victims are not happy with the Registrar's choice, they may ask the judges to review it. Victims who prefer not to be joined with other victims in the same groups, for instance because they believe that their interests need to be represented separately due to a conflict of interest, can also ask the judges to review this decision.

VICTIMS BEFORE THE INTERNATIONAL COURT 22 (emphasis added).

In light of these many uncertainties, as well as the power imbalance between the victim and his attorney, best practices counsel victim representatives to summarize the terms of representation in a form document (either a standard terms-of-representation contract, or a power-of-attorney contract[21]). Each victim must review, understand, and sign the form document if the victim consents to the group representation. Such a procedure is not contemplated in the ICC's present rules and regulations. However, the virtual minefield of conflicts, necessary priority-setting, and aggregation focus inherent in group representation, combined with the likely lack of familiarity victims will have with legal proceedings, speaks to the wisdom of making such a formal informed-consent document part of the victim representative's routine practice.

Some traditionalists will no doubt consider even this proposed method of ensuring (or, at least, promoting) informed consent insufficient. They may argue that the victim, in actuality, has no realistic alternative but to accept the Chamber's appointment decision, as well as the victim representative's aggregate litigation strategy. Such *de facto* compelled group representation, the argument might go, dilutes the duty of loyalty the attorney owes each individual client. If the victim does not like this arrangement, the victim is simply out of luck because the Chamber will not permit dozens or hundreds of attorneys, each representing one or a small group of similarly situated victims, to participate in the proceedings. The traditionalist may sum up his position by re-emphasizing that such compulsory, take-it-or-leave-it group representation deprives the individual victim of the dignity conferred by pursuing his own litigation strategy, and prevents the victim from truly participating in the trial of his former tormentors.

A candid response to the traditionalist's complaint requires the concession that there is some force to the argument that compulsory large-group representation is, indeed, inconsistent with "participation" in the truest sense of the term. However, under the current system, the Chamber in the final analysis dictates that Attorney X will be responsible for representing victims A–Y. This is the current state of the law, and there is no indication that this will change. The other alternative, which is for victims to simply bypass participation in the ICC, is not much of an option, and in the end some participation will be better than no participation at all. Despite the current

21. *See generally* Regulation of the Court 123 ("Acknowledgment of Appointment").

system's shortcomings, victim representatives advance their clients' individual autonomy by being sensitive to the potential conflicts between clients, as well as conflicts between clients and their attorneys, by explaining these conflicts to the victims, and by seeking the victims' informed authorization to proceed.

PART IX

Understanding Victims' Interests and Recognizing the Importance of Managing and Guiding Expectations

AS INTERNATIONAL LAW PRACTITIONERS and interested observers appreciate, the drafting of aspirational legislation containing sweeping, optimistic preambles is a far more simple and straightforward undertaking than lending substantive meaning to those codified ambitions. As with many things in life, reality can be an enemy. The ICC's articles and rules, on their face, may lead to the reasonable belief that victim participation will be both substantive and widespread. In truth, however, the ICC to date has not lived up to the high expectations it has set for itself in this regard.

A. Promises Collide With Reality

Once again, the numbers tell the tale. Consider, for example, the number of potential victims in the Democratic Republic of the Congo, where ethnic cleansing, systematic rape, forced labor, torture, killing, maiming, and looting by government troops and rebel fighters spread terror throughout the countryside.[1] Between August 1998 and April 2004, the war resulted in the deaths of over three million people from murder, starvation, and disease.[2] Millions more were displaced. Even given these mass atrocities, as well as those committed in Darfur, northern Uganda, and the Central African Republic, the ICC in the first seven years of its existence received fewer than 1,000 victim applications to participate in proceedings. This number obviously represents only a tiny sliver of the literally millions of potential victims from these conflicts. Moreover, only a small fraction of these putative victims

---

1. *See generally* Human Rights Watch, *Seeking Justice: Prosecution of Sexual Violence in the Congo War* (March 7, 2005).

2. *See* Karl Vick, *Death Toll in Congo May Approach 3 Million: Conflict Leaves Trail of Starvation, Disease and Carnage*, WASHINGTON POST (April 30, 2001), at AO1.

have actually obtained the "status of victim" in the Democratic Republic of Congo, Uganda, and Darfur proceedings.

By most estimates, applicants on average wait in excess of a year for a determination on their "status as a victim," which itself is merely a preliminary finding signifying nothing more than that the individual in principle *may* participate in the specific proceedings. Those to whom the Court accords such participatory rights represent only the tiniest subset of the universe of actual victims. And even this small number of applications has resulted in logistical burdens the ICC has been hard-pressed to effectively tackle.

Those lucky few who are given actual participatory rights will be additionally put upon in ways not immediately obvious. One side-effect of the ICC's slow handling of victim applications is that the few "official" victims will become the *de facto* spokespersons for the sea of individuals who suffered at the hands of their alleged victimizers. The simple act of the Court adjudicating their applications as meeting the requisite criteria, thus, saddles this sub-group of victims, who never sought such status, with this daunting responsibility.

The mounting delays resulting from the processing of relatively few applications are emblematic of the ICC's ongoing struggle with how to reconcile the Rome Statute's broad invitation for victim participation with the practical realities of running a functioning Court. Unfortunately, this is a struggle the ICC is presently losing. Indeed, members of the Office of the Prosecutor fear that the actual involvement of thousands of victims, or even hundreds of victims, is a logistical impossibility, and that the realities of daily ICC practice cannot be reconciled with the broad language of the ICC's Preamble and the equally broad language of Article 68. Compounding the frustration resulting from such inefficiencies, the ICC has publicly given victims explicit guarantees of substantively meaningful participation in the proceedings, the vindication of their interests, the timely resolution of the underlying cases, and the creation of a historical record.

Subtle messages delivered during the victim-application process can trigger unjustified expectations. For example, the 17-page standard form to participate in ICC proceedings for "Individual Victims and Persons Acting on Their Behalf" provides as follows:

> Please complete this Application Form if you believe you have suffered harm as a result of a crime under the jurisdiction of the [ICC] and wish to participate in the proceedings before the ICC by putting forward your

observations, views or concerns, or if you are acting on behalf of such a person.[3]

The Form goes on to state that the "ICC can help victims find a legal representative by providing a list of qualified counsel."[4] (The ICC's Standard Application Form for Reparations' language almost verbatim tracks that of the Victim Application Form).[5] Nothing in these materials, however, gives applicants an honest sense of how exceedingly unlikely it is that the Chamber will grant a given application, or that, if granted, the Chamber will accord the victim an opportunity to substantively participate in the proceedings. These applications, therefore, run the risk of fostering false hopes on the part of victims who will often have little, if any, education, and who have already endured tremendous pain and suffering.

Delays, and the unwitting creation of potentially false expectations, can of course, in part, be attributed to the reality that the ICC is a new system that is still establishing itself, and to the fact that the drafters may not have given sufficient consideration to the sheer numbers of victims and the resulting flood of applications that threaten to block all organs of the ICC. It, nonetheless, remains important that victim representatives appropriately manage victim expectations, guarding against any unrealistic promises of a timely "day in court."

Stated plainly, to date, there is a want of meaningful outlets for victim involvement of a type that would justify promising victims that they will play an active role in the process of ensuring that justice is done. The victims of atrocity crimes have endured unspeakable and dehumanizing degradation and pain. Re-victimizing these vulnerable individuals by giving them false hopes of recompense and personal participation in the process of delivering justice is the last thing the international community, or for that matter, victim representatives, should be doing. Realism must, therefore, supplant bald hope and optimism in all dealings with victims.

---

3. *See* Appendix VII.

4. *Id.*

5. *See* Appendix VIII.

B. Managing Expectations

In light of the aforementioned, victim representatives must take great care to prepare victims for the real possibility that they will receive no reparations or substantive in-court involvement in their alleged victimizers' criminal proceedings. As with any group dynamic, there will be some members of the victim-group who will accept a given outcome, while others will not. The key for the victim representative is to determine what the victims, as a group, wish to accomplish, to personally explain clearly to the victims the realistic range of outcomes, and to instill in the victims an understanding that the lawyer is committed to their case and will do his best to most effectively represent the victims' interests.

In this regard, the Principal of the Office of Public Counsel for Victims reports that her office in 95 percent of all cases personally meets the victims well in advance of trial. This, of course, takes time and costs money. Depending on the security limitations, moreover, the victim representative may face difficulty arranging such in-person meetings for each and every client. But the OPCV appropriately has concluded that such meetings are necessary in order to build trust between the lawyer and the client, and to assure the victims that their hopes and concerns are of the utmost interest to the victim representative.

Of course, even the prospect of meeting with lawyers may overwhelm and scare many victims involved in ICC proceedings. Victims can further be expected to feel varying levels of discomfort when it comes to discussing their alleged victimizers and the very personal details of their victimization. Differing cultural mores will impact on such communication patterns; the self-perception of the victim, and the victims' understanding of the purpose of the questioning, are matters the victim representative must expect, and prepare for. Conducting the necessary background investigation, and becoming attuned to the likely challenges posed by different groups of victims from a particular region, is, therefore, compulsory.

In this regard, the Office of the Prosecutor has recently adopted a commendable approach towards giving victims an early sense that the "system" takes their views seriously. The Office of the Prosecutor conducts victim outreach by holding "town hall" meetings in the impacted regions (that is, in the "field"). These village-based field meetings help the prosecution team identify the best witnesses to call at trial, but they also permit the victims to, in a cathartic group setting, express their views and concerns, and to tell their stories.

The Office of the Prosecutor considers these meetings extremely valuable to both the Office, as well as to the victims. Such early involvement of victims is, indeed, laudable. Whether such airings of grievances with a branch of the ICC amount, as some prosecutors believe, to substantive victim "participation," however, remains open to debate.

In the final analysis, the practical toll of administrative burdens foisted on this court of limited jurisdiction, with finite resources and at times limited practical experience to draw on, will undoubtedly dissuade many potential victims from joining the process. Other victims, to date all hailing from war-torn countries in Africa, may be left feeling that the largely Western international community—flush with good intentions and promises often unmatched by observable real-world results—is merely paying lip service to the victims' understandable thirst for justice. It is up to the victim representative to not exacerbate these very real concerns; instead, the victim representative, in the course of engaging in a frank discussion of the realities of victim participation, must seek to provide victims with his honest and plainly-worded assessment of what to expect.

C. Ensuring Victims' Safety

> *By the terms of Article 68 (1) of the Statute, the Prosecutor is bound to take measures protective of the safety and well-being of victims. The Prosecutor is equally under obligation to take measures or request that measures be taken for the protection of any person including no doubt victims.*[6]

Most victims have good reason to fear reprisals resulting from their involvement with the Court. The perpetrators, or their criminal associates and followers, may direct such reprisals against the victims and their property, or, alternatively, against the victims' families and friends. The role of the competent victim representative, therefore, includes ensuring that the

---

6. Situation in the Democratic Republic of the Congo, Case No. ICC 01/04: *Judgment On Victim Participation in the Investigation State of the Proceedings* (December 19, 2008), at 23–24 (citations omitted).

Chamber and the Prosecutor[7] are aware of any security issues relating to the victims.[8]

Rule 89(1) requires that the Victim Witness Unit provide both the accused and the Prosecutor with copies of the victims' applications. The Rule further mandates that the Chamber provide both the accused and the prosecution an opportunity to "comment" on all such applications. This, of course, is a ripe opportunity for the accused (or other, uncharged, perpetrators and their allies) interested in silencing victims to learn who will be involved in the proceedings, where they live, and how to locate them and their families. To the extent that victims have a grounded fear of reprisals, their representatives have a duty to submit requests for protective measures (in this regard, note that Article 68(1) requires the Chamber to ensure the victims' protection).[9] As the Chamber ruled in *Lubanga*, "[p]articipation by an individual as a victim in the proceedings shall not compromise his or her security. . . ."[10]

At the application stage, protecting the victims may simply involve a request to ensure that the necessary redactions to protect the victims'

7. *See generally* Situation in the Democratic Republic of the Congo In the Case of the Prosecutor v. Germain Katanga and Mathieu Ngudjolo Chui, Case No. ICC-01/04-01/07: *On the Appeal of the Prosecutor Against the "Decision on Evidentiary Scope of the Confirmation Hearing, Preventative Relocation and Disclosure under Article 67(2) of the Statute and Rule 77 of the Rules" of Pre-Trial Chamber I* (November 26, 2008), at 52–54 (dissenting opinion of Judge Pikis arguing that Article 68(1) and (4) "confer and acknowledge power on the Prosecutor to take protective measures for victims and witnesses, including, no doubt, relocation whenever their safety to requires. . . . The provision of protection and support to victims and witnesses is a cause common to the Victims and Witness Unit and the Prosecutor.").

8. *See generally* Situation in the Democratic Republic of the Congo In the Case of the Prosecutor v. Thomas Lubanga Dyilo, Case No. ICC 01/04-01/06: *Decision on the Defense Application For Disclosure of Victims' Applications* (January 21, 2009) (Trial Chamber ruling that victims who hold dual status as both victims and witnesses are entitled to notice through their legal representatives when the prosecution intends to turn over information relevant to them; victims must be given an opportunity to raise security-related objections to such planned disclosures).

9. *See also* Situation in the Democratic Republic of the Congo In the Case of the Prosecutor v. Thomas Lubanga Dyilo, Case No. ICC-01/04-01/06: *Decision on the Applications by Victims to Participate in the Proceedings* (December 15, 2008), at 36 ("Depending on the facts, it may be acceptable for the victim to remain anonymous as regards the public, whilst revealing his or her identity to the accused.").

10. Situation in the Democratic Republic of the Congo In the Case of the Prosecutor v. Thomas Lubanga Dyilo, Case No. ICC-01/04-01/06: *Public Decision On Certain Practicalities Regarding Individuals Who Have the Dual Status of Witness and Victim* (June 5, 2008), at 20.

identities are made to the applications prior to the accused receiving them.[11] At subsequent stages of the proceedings, however, victim representatives, pursuant to Rule 17, may have to request more extensive protective measures from the Victim and Witness Unit, such as temporary, or even permanent, relocation.[12] Rule 16(4), in fact, provides that "[a]greements on relocation and provision of support services [for traumatized and/or threatened victims, witnesses, and others] may be negotiated with the States by the Registrar on behalf of the Court. Such agreements may remain confidential." Moreover, in the context of witnesses, the Chamber has ruled that, on balance, "putting in place arrangements to enable [certain witnesses'] voices and faces to be distorted does not jeopardize the interests of the accused persons any more than it is prejudicial to or inconsistent with the rights of the accused and a fair and impartial trial."[13] Victim representatives, starting well before the trial, must therefore think of the best way to ensure the safety of their clients.

---

11. *See generally* Article 43(6) (creating a Victims and Witnesses Unit within the Registry of the Court responsible for protecting victims and witnesses); Article 68(2) (allowing for evidence to be presented *in camera* when safety of witness, victim, or accused may be endangered); Article 68(5) (allowing Prosecutor to submit evidence in summary form in pre-trial proceedings when disclosure of witness identity could cause grave threat to witness' safety).

12. *See* Rene Blattman & Kirsten Bowman, *Achievements and Problems of the International Criminal Court*, 6 J. INT'L CRIM. JUST. 723 (2008) (discussing seven agreements between the ICC and State Parties governing the protection of witnesses and relocation arrangements, with Austria in October 2005 being the first State Party to sign such an agreement). Moreover, the majority of the Appeals Chamber, over a powerful dissenting opinion written by Judge Pikis, has barred the Prosecutor, except in extraordinary circumstances where the victim or witness is facing "a serious threat of imminent harm that requires and immediate response," from "preventatively relocating" witnesses (or, by logical extension, victims) either before the Registrar has decided whether the relocation of a particular witness was required, or after the Registrar has concluded that the individual should not be relocated. *See* Situation in the Democratic Republic of the Congo In the Case of the Prosecutor v. Germain Katanga and Mathieu Ngudjolo Chui, Case No. ICC-01/04-01/07: *On the Appeal of the Prosecutor Against the "Decision on Evidentiary Scope of the Confirmation Hearing, Preventative Relocation and Disclosure under Article 67(2) of the Statute and Rule 77 of the Rules" of Pre-Trial Chamber I* (November 26, 2008), at 26–39.

13. Situation in the Democratic Republic of the Congo In the Case of the Prosecutor v. Germain Katanga and Mathieu Ngudjolo Chu, Case No. ICC-01/04-01/07: *Decision on the Prosecutor's Application for Protective Measures Pursuant to Article 54(3)(f) of the Statute and Rule 81(4) of the Rules* (March 25, 2009), at 5–6.

PART X

Holding a Pre-Trial Evidentiary Hearing to Establish the Historic Record

WHATEVER ONE MAY SAY about the present impact of international justice and international trials when it comes to deterring future perpetrators of atrocity crimes, one of the clear benefits of such proceedings is the possibility of creating a (relatively) neutral, and reliable, historic record. There, indeed, is a considerable consensus among victims that making such a record available to future generations is a prime motivator of victim participation, since it will help memorialize, and perhaps explain, the atrocities.[1]

A. Litigation Aimed at Creating Present and Future Individual (and Group) Accountability

Survivors of atrocity crimes, as well as the families and loved ones of those who were injured or murdered, want to know first and foremost what happened, who committed the crimes, and why the crimes were committed. Put another way, victims seek the truth because the truth, to some extent at least, alleviates their anguish, vindicates their status, encourages individual accountability, and has the potential of removing the perpetrators and their allies from power.

Such a record, moreover, makes it more difficult for those accused to create fictionalized, self-serving accounts of what occurred. A proper understanding of the historic events, and even public outrage over the conduct that often took place in the public's name, can replace the twin dangers of complacency and resentment towards victims.

Substitutes for trial, such as truth commissions, are largely reliant on state cooperation, and, therefore, frequently avoid naming individual perpetrators

1. *See, e.g.*, MARTHA MINOW, BETWEEN VENGEANCE AND FORGIVENESS: FACING HISTORY AFTER GENOCIDE AND MASS VIOLENCE 123–28 (1998).

or imposing any sanctions (no court of law, after all, has formally found these persons guilty of anything). Although amnesty-based truth commissions and state-sponsored panels, as alternatives to prosecution, may well help address some of the concerns born by victims, they also permit the state to potentially whitewash inconvenient episodes, and fail to affix blame, create accountability, or punish the perpetrators.

Nuremberg Chief Prosecutor Robert J. Jackson famously remarked that he felt entrusted with the duty to "establish incredible events by credible evidence."[2] Justice Jackson, reporting to United States President Harry Truman, noted that the true legacy of the Nuremberg prosecutions was that they carefully documented the scope of the Nazi atrocities "with such authenticity and in such detail that there can be no responsible denial of these crimes in the future and no tradition of martyrdom of the Nazi leaders can arise among informed people."[3]

Some 50 years later it would be the trial of Dusko Tadic at the ICTY which similarly created a comprehensive historic record of the abuses in the Balkans, including what happened to individual victims, a description of the planning and execution of the crimes, and who it was that bore command responsibility for the offenses. Both the Nuremberg trials and the *Tadic* case

---

2. *Report to the President from Justice Robert H. Jackson, Chief of Counsel for the United States in the Prosecution of Axis War Criminals* (June 7, 1945), *in* 39 AM. J. INT'L L. 178, 184 (Supp. 1945); *see also* HANNAH ARENDT, EICHMAN IN JERUSALEM: A REPORT ON THE BANALITY OF EVIL 19 (1963) ("For it was history that, as far as the prosecution was concerned, stood in the center of the [Adolf Eichmann] trial."); GIDEON HAUSNER, JUSTICE IN JERUSALEM (1966) (former Israel Attorney General recalling that Prime Minister David Ben-Gurion told Hausner his (Hausner's) job was to create a permanent record of what occurred during the Holocaust); STEPHAN LANDSMAN, CRIMES OF THE HOLOCAUST: THE LAW CONFRONTS HARD CASES (2005) (describing "successor trials" as demonstrating the inherent tensions in proceedings that have the dual mission of determining guilt and innocence, while attempting to establish a detailed historical record of atrocities). Of course, criminal cases involving individuals (or small groups of individuals) will, by necessity, lead to the creation of a more limited historical record. That said, the prosecutors in Nuremberg, in the Adolf Eichmann trial, at the ICTR, and at the ICTY clearly endeavored to show how the criminal episodes fit within the broader historic context.

3. Jackson, *supra* note 2, at 184. For a concise, and very interesting, first-hand account from a member of Justice Jackson's prosecution team during the Nuremberg trials, *see* Whitney R. Harris, *A World of Peace and Justice Under the Rule of Law: From Nuremberg to the International Criminal Court*, 6 WASH. U. GLOBAL STUD. L. REV. 689 (2007) (discussing the work of the Nuremberg Tribunal and how the argument that trials would commend maximum public support, receive the respect of history, and create a permanent and authentic record of the Nazi crimes won the day over the proposed alternative of summary executions).

demonstrate that there is no more authoritative rendering of the historic record than that created in the crucible of a fair trial. During such a proceeding both sides have subpoena power, are represented by competent and experienced counsel, deal with witnesses subject to perjury prosecutions, and have the evidence tested by a court prior to its admission.[4]

Trial, moreover, provides the most likely mechanism for meaningful institutional reform, and sets the stage for a committed and honest confrontation with the state's dark pasts. Even grappling with emotionally difficult issues such as exhumations, confirmation of death through forensic exams, and proper burials can be crucial in the process of permitting the survivors to grieve. These processes also allow survivors to come to grips with their anger and desires for revenge, and, in the end, achieve some sense of closure. It is, therefore, crucial that there be a process of learning *why* a loved one was murdered or otherwise brutalized. The historic record also serves as a moral educator, preventing the perpetrators from wrongfully accusing the victims of wrongdoing or misconduct, such as subversion or spying, or from otherwise justifying their own criminal acts.

Some argue that the creation of a neutral judicial record will not contribute significantly towards long-term reconciliation,[5] or to the creation of a

---

4. Some argue that truth commissions are useful alternatives to courts. *See generally* Christopher D. Totten & Nicholas Tyler, *Arguing for an Integrated Approach to Resolving the Crisis in Darfur: The Challenge of Complementarity, Enforcement, and Related Issues in the International Criminal Court*, 98 J. CRIM. L. & CRIMINOLOGY 1069, 1107 (2008) ("A Sudanese truth commission, unlike a court or tribunal, does not necessarily have to engage in the tasks of assigning blame on particular individuals for past conduct and punish those individuals as a result of that conduct. As a result, Sudanese actors themselves will be more likely to participate in a truth commission and be more willing to include individuals from diverse backgrounds in the work of the commission."). However, for the reasons set forth above, truth commissions are a significantly inferior method of establishing an accurate factual record of events.

5. Indeed, the term "reconciliation" is inherently ambiguous, meaning drastically different things to different people. The meaning of the term can range from a minimalist interpretation, in which to be "reconciled" means to no longer kill each other, to a truth-commission-style maximalist interpretation, according to which being reconciled encompasses mutual healing, forgiveness, repentance, redemption, and ultimately solidarity between former foes/victimizers. *See generally* Sheri P. Rosenberg, *What's Law Got to Do With It: The Bosnia v. Serbia Decision's Impact on Reconciliation*, 61 RUTGERS L. REV. 131, 139 (2008) ("Commentators have suggested that the idea of societal repentance and forgiveness is a utopian dream and, in fact, illiberal and undemocratic, as it expects an entire society to prescribe to a single comprehensive moral idea about the past. The moderate understanding of reconciliation lies between simple coexistence and complete repentance and forgiveness.... Reconciliation is so vague that some authors prefer to jettison the term for

future national consensus.[6] The sceptic's core contention is that locally held versions of the truth are not amendable to being shifted by findings or proclamations coming from an international tribunal, and that the creation of such a historic record, therefore, is of only limited utility.

The weakness of this reasoning is that it assumes the paramount objective of the historic record to be the creation of a shift in the thinking of those individuals who were actually *involved* in the crimes (or those who sympathize with them). Although it indeed may be true that no historic record will, for example, convince some contemporary Serbians that the Serbian government did anything wrong in Bosnia, Croatia, or Kosovo, it is entirely unclear that *anything* will shift such deeply entrenched views.

Following the Nuremberg trials, after all, there was also no immediate universal recognition of the extent of the German state's responsibility for the atrocities that occurred under the Nazi regime. Nor was the German population necessarily convinced that the trials were fair and even-handed, rather than simple "victor's justice."[7] The full measure of benefits flowing from the Nuremberg Trials' detailed and neutrally created historic record, however, is the impact it has had on subsequent generations who were not hands-on participants in the crimes, and who, therefore, had less reason

---

other terms, such as coexistence or social reconstruction. That said, reconciliation is a concept often employed by public policymakers, academics, and the NGO community.") (Citations omitted). The "civic view" of reconciliation is, arguably, the most realistic. In this view, a society is "reconciled" when citizens who were former foes trust each other as citizens, meaning that they are committed to shared bedrock norms and democratic values.

6. *See id.* at 156 ("The impact of the BiH v. Serbia decision belies the claim that the 'authoritative' power of the law will dismantle locally held versions of the truth about what happened during the conflict and lead to reconciliation. Locally held versions of the 'truth' remain strong in BiH, entrenched as they are in a very particular sense of ethnic identification. It is a fallacy to think that abstracted, arguably western notions of the value of the 'rule of law' will displace these deep feelings."); *see also* Ruti Teitel, *Bringing the Messiah Through the Law, in* HUMAN RIGHTS IN POLITICAL TRANSITION: GETTYSBURG TO BOSNIA 177, 181–83 (1999) ("It has almost become dogma in contemporary foreign policy that establishing the 'truth' about a state's repressive past can lay the foundation for national reconciliation."); Christopher D. Totten, *The International Criminal Court and Truth Commissions: A Framework for Cross-Interaction in Sudan and Beyond*, 7 NW. U. J. INT'L. HUM. RTS. L. 1 (2009) (examining ICC's likely future interactions with truth commissions).

7. *See generally* Rosenberg, *supra* note 5, at 158 ("It was only a generation later where the lessons [of the Nuremberg trial] apparently took place. It is common sense that psychologically it may be that only the next generation, which is not directly implicated in the crimes, can absorb these facts."); TELFORD TAYLOR, THE ANATOMY OF THE NUREMBERG TRIALS 334–37 (1993) (describing as a modern myth the notion that the majority of the German people at the time of the Nuremberg Trials accepted the trials' legitimacy and fairness).

to rationalize or justify them. Few contemporary Germans born after the 1940s, for example, are not intimately familiar with their country's wrongdoing during World War II, including the identities of the chief perpetrators. Today's Germans revile Nazi henchmen such as Joseph Goebbels, Heinrich Himmler, Hermann Goering, and Adolf Eichmann. Virtually every German, moreover, has seen the extensive footage of the Nuremberg trials, as well as the graphic images of the carnage and atrocities committed by, or at the direction of, the Nazis, that the prosecution introduced into evidence during the proceedings.

Of course, this is not to say that everyone will necessarily accept as neutral, complete, or accurate the historic trial record—whether beamed live into the world's living rooms, or summarized in written form. As any experienced prosecutor can attest, there will always be those sympathetic to a defendant who, despite the admission of mountains of compelling evidence at trial, will steadfastly claim that the prosecutor or the court conducted a "sham trial" during which the "cards were stacked" against the (morally, factually, or legally "innocent") accused.

It is not difficult, as a matter of psychology, to trace the origins of such intransigence. But whether *everyone* accepts the historic record should not be outcome determinative. Instead, the purpose of the prosecution must be to create a record that will, in Justice Jackson's words, persuade "informed people" (that is, people with knowledge of, and reasonably open minds about, the given historic events). Moreover, consider the ICC Preamble's, perhaps slightly overstated, observation that the common bonds and shared heritage of all people form a "delicate mosaic [which] may be shattered at any time."[8] The drafters went to some lengths to send the message that geography and culture do not immunize any group from the possibility of similar atrocities taking place where they live. The prosecutors in Nuremberg, in the Adolf Eichmann trial, at the ICTR, and at the ICTY clearly saw as part of their mission the creation of trial records which vividly demonstrated to future generations precisely how the charged criminal episodes fit within the broader historic context. The discussion below examines some methods victim representatives should consider in pursuit of this fundamental objective.

---

8. Rome Statute Preamble.

B. Convening a Pre-Trial Evidentiary Hearing to Develop the Common Factual Backdrop of the Case

One problem with using individual "successor" criminal cases as vehicles for creating the historic record is that the piecemeal record (historic or otherwise) developed through criminal cases involving individuals, or small groups of individuals, is, by necessity, limited. In each case, the prosecutor charges the accused, or group of accuseds, with specific misconduct. The prosecutor, therefore, must investigate and establish that the accused, with a specific state of mind, committed specific alleged criminal acts. In addition to these very case-specific criminal acts, however, the prosecution teams at the ICC must also establish certain more general "chapeau elements."

Chapeau elements are the common elements conferring international jurisdiction over the offense. An example of such a chapeau element is proof that the alleged crime was part of, or connected to, a widespread or systematic attack against a civilian population.[9] Proving chapeau elements typically requires evidence establishing the broader context of the violence, and of the organized activity leading to it. For example, the chapeau elements may include (a) whether there were manifest patterns of the specified charged conduct (or similar conduct) directed against a national, ethnic, racial, or religious group that had the effect of destroying those groups (if the prosecution charged genocide, pursuant to Elements of Crime Article 6); (b) whether there at the time existed a pattern of widespread or systematic attack directed against a civilian population (if the prosecution charged crimes against humanity, pursuant to Article 7); or (c) whether there existed either an international armed conflict, or an armed conflict not of an international character (if the prosecution charged war crimes, pursuant to Article 8).

Thus, to convict an accused of genocide by killing, the Prosecutor must establish that the charged conduct took place "in the context of a manifest pattern of similar conduct directed against [a national, ethnic, racial, or religious group the accused intended to 'destroy'] or was conduct that could itself affect such destruction."[10] Similarly, to prove an accused guilty of

---

9. *See, e.g.*, Elements of Crime Article 7 (Crimes Against Humanity).

10. ICC Elements of Crime, Article 6(a) (Genocide by Killing); *see similarly* Article 6(b)(4) (Genocide by Causing Bodily or Mental Harm); Article 6(c)(5) (Genocide by Deliberately Inflicting Conditions of Life Calculated to Bring About Physical Destruction); Article 6(d)(5) (Genocide by Imposing Measures Intended to Prevent Births); and Article 6(e)(7) (Genocide by Forcibly Transferring Children).

engaging in any of the enumerated crimes against humanity, there must be evidence that the accused's conduct was "part of a widespread or systematic attack directed against a civilian population."[11] Finally, "war crimes" also contain a shared element that the charged conduct "took place in the context of and was associated with" either an "international armed conflict,"[12] or an "armed conflict not of an international character."[13]

In all cases of genocide, crimes against humanity, and war crimes, there are, therefore, certain "macro" or "background" elements that must be proved in each individual case, but that do not necessarily bear on the particular accused's conduct or state of mind. Given the nature of such elements, virtually all cases charged as part of a situation will involve these chapeau elements, and the findings will not likely change much from case to case.

Experience teaches that proving these background facts takes up a very significant amount of time and resources. Compounding this problem is that the Prosecutor must re-establish these historic/situational elements at each individual trial. At the ICTY, for example, the prosecution had to prove breaches of the Geneva Conventions. To do so, the prosecution used the same group of expert witnesses in each trial to testify that the conflict was not a civil war, but, rather, was an international armed conflict. This practice necessarily consumed considerable resources, resulting in unnecessary delays, duplication, and inefficiencies.

---

11. *See, e.g.*, Elements of Crime Article 7(1)(a)(2) (Crime Against Humanity of Murder); Article 7(1)(b)(3) (Crime Against Humanity of Extermination); Article 7(1)(c)(2) (Crime Against Humanity of Enslavement); Article 7(1)(d)(4) (Crime Against Humanity of Deportation or Forcible Transfer of Population); Article 7(1)(e)(4) (Crime Against Humanity of Imprisonment or Other Severe Deprivation of Physical Liberty); Article 7(1)(f)(4) (Crime Against Humanity of Torture); Article 7(1)(g)-1(3) (Crime Against Humanity of Rape); Article 7(1)(g)-2(3) (Crime Against Humanity of Sexual Slavery); Article 7(1)(g)-(3) (Crime Against Humanity of Enforced Prostitution); Article 7(1)(j)(4) (Crime Against Humanity of Apartheid); and Article 7(i)(k)(4) (Crime Against Humanity of Other Inhumane Acts).

12. *See, e.g.*, Article 8(2)(a)(i)(4) (War Crime of Willful Killing); Article 8(2)(a)(ii)-1(5) (War Crime of Torture); Article 8(2)(a)(ii)-2(4) (War Crime of Inhumane Treatment); Article 8(2)(a)(v)(4) (War Crime of Compelling Service in Hostile Forces); Article 8(2)(a)(vii)-1(4) (War Crime of Unlawful Deportation and Transfer); Article 8(2)(b)(i)(4)(War Crimes of Attacking Civilians); Article 8(2)(b)(iv)(4) (War Crime of Excessive Incidental Death, Injury, or Damage); Article 8(2)(b)(x)-1(5) (War Crime of Mutilation); Article 8(2)(b)(xvii)(3) (War Crime of Employing Poison or Poisoned Weapons); and Article 8(2)(b)(xxii)-1(3) (War Crime of Rape).

13. *See, e.g.*, Article 8(2)((c)(i)-1(4) (War Crime of Murder); Article 8(2)(c)(i)-4(5) (War Crime of Torture); Article 8(2)(e)(vi)-5(3) (War Crime of Enforced Sterilization); and Article 8(2)(e)(vi)-1(3) (War Crime of Rape).

One way to assemble the complete historic record of the situation, while at the same time remaining efficient and guaranteeing the accused procedural fairness, is for the Chamber to convene a pre-trial evidentiary hearing prior to the main trial of the first case within the situation to determine the chapeau elements of the various cases that are part of that situation. All parties would have a right to participate and present evidence and argument at the hearing. At the conclusion of the hearing, which the victim representatives should of course petition to participate in, the Chamber delivers its comprehensive factual findings. Those judicial findings will most likely be based on the "grounds to believe" standard of proof employed for factual findings other than the ultimate guilt of the accused (which, pursuant to Article 66(3), is of course guilt beyond a reasonable doubt). These macro findings, moreover, will be binding on all Participants in all cases.

The Chamber could take judicial notice of this record during subsequent trials of cases within the situation. In order to preserve an accused's right to due process, however, the Chamber must of course permit those accused added after the date of the preliminary hearing to present evidence to the Court challenging the Court's record and earlier conclusions. Likewise, accused would be permitted to present newly-discovered evidence bearing on the earlier finding. Such a proceeding, however, would be far less time-consuming and cumbersome than re-litigating the full historic backdrop of the case over and over again. Moreover, the record will likely be more comprehensive and carefully prepared since more participants will be involved in its creation, and the defense, prosecution, and victims know they will get only one opportunity to provide their input and focus their efforts.

Alternatively, the Pre-Trial Chamber handling the first case within a situation could notify all participants of its intent to conduct a full evidentiary hearing to establish the chapeau elements. The Chamber would permit all participants—including accuseds that have been charged as part of other cases—to participate and present evidence during these discrete proceedings. The Trial Chamber in subsequent trials could then take judicial notice of the first Pre-Trial Chamber's written findings, subject, again, to the Trial Chamber granting the participants permission to present supplemental evidence or argument.

Such a comprehensive record would educate the target population specifically, and the world community generally, help counteract propaganda and systemic regional biases and claims of right, and streamline the proceedings by preventing a re-hash of the same factual and legal arguments. This proposed procedure would also conserve time and resources, promote more orderly and focused litigation, and provide future generations with one central source summarizing the macro events occurring at the time of the charged offenses.

The ICC already has procedures in place to maintain, and make publicly available, such findings. Rule 137, for example, gives the Registrar the responsibility of ensuring the proper maintenance a "full and accurate record of all proceedings," and the Chamber, in turn, may order that the entire record be made public following the close of the case. Moreover, the Chamber can authorize persons other than the Registrar to capture "the sound or image of the trial." The Registrar, pursuant to Article 138, is also to maintain the evidence and other materials offered during the trial.

Those on the "losing" side of the record will always complain that there is nothing "neutral" about the proceedings taking place in international tribunals, and nothing "irrefutable" about the historic record produced in the course of such proceedings. A more promising alternative, however, is not available. Indeed, of all the claimed benefits of international justice, the creation of a historical record, tested in court and subject to adversarial examination, stands out as most unambiguously invaluable.

PART XI

Compiling a "Victimization Dossier" as a Permanent Historic Record of Abuse

ALTHOUGH HOLDING A PRE-TRIAL HEARING to establish the historic background and chapeau elements is one method of establishing the record of abuse, there is another, perhaps additional, way for victims to tell their particular side of the story. The discussion to this point has shown that a victim representative's involvement in ICC proceedings is never guaranteed, and even if achieved, will to some extent likely be limited. Actual conflicts, such as in the Democratic Republic of Congo, moreover, involve mass murders, rapes, forced labor, torture, looting, displacement, and maiming. In that example alone, the total number of victims is in the millions.[1] It is, therefore, entirely unrealistic to expect a victim representative, or the independent prosecutors, to act on behalf of, and take into account in a meaningful sense, the disparate views of such a large number of victims. Given the significant hurdles that potential victims must overcome prior to the Chamber certifying them in a given case, actual victim participation in ICC litigating will be the rare exception, not the rule. And even if the Chamber permits a victim's participation, such participation will in all likelihood be many years removed from the crimes. Victim representatives must, therefore, be creative and consider all available alternatives to full in-court participation.

A. The Carefully Tailored Dossier as a Useful Tool for Victim Representatives

In order to make a meaningful contribution to the ICC proceedings, and to advance the victims' concrete interests, victim representatives should consider compiling a dossier summarizing, in a professional manner, the victims'

1. *See* Alexandra H. Guhr, *Victim Participation During the Pre-Trial Stage at the International Criminal Court*, 8 INT'L CRIM. L. REV. 13 (2008).

experiences and evidence. Such a dossier can provide an extremely valuable tool for future prosecutions, can be used as a persuasive means of influencing the Prosecutor, government officials, or the media, and can be relied on by the Chamber when it rules on the chapeau elements.[2] A victimization dossier, moreover, represents an accessible method of creating a permanent, historic record from the victims' perspective, identifying how, where, when, why, and who took part in the alleged abuses. Victim representatives, moreover, can compile these dossiers well in advance of the Office of the Prosecutor formally charging a specific case.

A factually accurate dossier, compiled as close as possible to the time of the incident(s) at issue,[3] and put together in a manner that, if possible, does not undermine, or work at cross-purposes with, the Prosecutors' efforts, will go far in creating a permanent account of the facts of history. Such a record, moreover, serves to secure testimony that may not be available in future years, and will provide investigators and prosecutors with important investigative leads to later follow up on.[4]

Victim representatives can submit dossiers in advance of any formal Rule 85 determination addressing the question of who is a "victim." Where and how to submit the dossier, however, deserves careful attention, for there are a number of potential alternative legal bases for incorporating it into the ICC's permanent record.[5] A carefully prepared, accurate, and professional dossier, submitted to the Prosecutor and Chamber pursuant to stated legal authority, will significantly assist the Prosecutor in conducting the investigation and framing possible charges. Such a dossier will also aid the Chamber in assessing the merits of the case.

---

2. For more on establishing the chapeau elements, *see* Part X.

3. In light of the slow pace of ICC investigations and proceedings, it is, indeed, quite possible that such dossiers will serve as one of the best—and in some cases perhaps the only—sources of evidence against particular identified perpetrators.

4. The Kosovo experience with such investigative files/dossiers gives reason to believe that, when properly compiled, such documents can be of great value to investigators and prosecutors. The Kosovo files, compiled in Pristina shortly after the cessation of hostilities in 1999, were not acted upon for many years; now—over a decade later—prosecutors and investigators are finally examining them, as they are the only evidentiary links to many of the atrocities committed in and around Kosovo. Although the collection of the materials contained in these files did not always live up to the highest standards of investigative professionalism, they today to a large extent constitute the only investigative option.

5. Note that the ICC, like most Continental legal systems and the various *ad hoc* tribunals, permits "hearsay" evidence; dossiers can therefore be considered by the Court even if they contain such evidence.

B. Devising Standard Procedures for Compiling Evidence

Creating a sound dossier begins with devising reliable standard procedures for collecting evidence. In the context of investigating atrocity crimes, forensic experts help determine the "forensic truth."[6] Legal experts, in turn, translate this forensic truth into the "procedural truth" used in the legal arena to establish a factual account of the events integrated into the legal narrative. This interplay between lawyers and forensic experts can occur during the pre-forensic investigative phase, during the actual forensic investigation, and in preparation for the forensic experts' testimony. The types of forensic documentation and evidence potentially of value in the dossier include, but are not limited to: Reports on exhumations/victimization; laboratory analysis; photographic evidence; material artifacts; expert witness testimony; and evidence of adherence to relevant scientific protocols. Victim representatives should always include in the dossier expert reports, the expert's *curriculum vitae*, methodology employed, and similar supporting documentation establishing the use of standard procedures.

C. Developing Interview Protocols

In addition to this forensic evidence, victim representatives must also develop standard interview protocols those who interview potential witnesses and victims must adhere to.[7] Such interview protocols must be specifically tailored to each investigation, and must focus on the key elements the victim representative wishes to establish. That said, the protocols must allow for sufficient flexibility to adjust to the answers provided by the interviewees in the field.

---

6. The construction of the "forensic truth" may involve experts from the fields of forensic anthropology (specialists in the analysis of skeletal and dental remains, as well as taphonomic alterations), pathology (specialists in post-mortem examinations of bodies and human remains, with a focus on establishing cause of death and identity of the victim), and archaeology (specialists in site-surveying and excavation, with particular experience in identifying, excavating, and recording complex features).

7. Note, however, that victim representatives, like all parties, must be careful to keep up-to-date on the ICC's latest case law relating to the appropriateness of witness interviews. *See generally* Situation in the Democratic Republic of the Congo, Case No. II-01/04–01/06: *Decision Regarding the Protocol on the Practices To Be Used to Prepare Witnesses for Trial* (May 23, 2008), at 15–16 and 19–20 ("The party calling the witness is not to hold discussions with the latter about the topics that are to be dealt with in court during their evidence or the exhibits which may be produced."). More on this in Part XII(E).

D. Submitting the Dossier to the Court

As touched on above, the dossier may, in many cases, be the victim representative's best—and perhaps only—opportunity to comprehensively summarize the victims' case for future generations, and to explain to the Chamber why the victims are legally (and morally) entitled to be heard. The mechanics of such a submission, however, will depend on a number of contingencies. The victim representative should, therefore, consider all available alternative procedures for making the submission.

1. The Most Promising Submission Options

Rule 103(1) allows the Chamber to, at any stage in the proceedings, grant leave to "persons" to submit, in writing or orally, "*any* observation on any issue that the Chamber deems appropriate."[8] Pursuant to Article 103(3), the victim representative must file any such written observations with the Registrar, who in turn provides copies to the Prosecutor and the defense. Such an "observation" can of course include a dossier, to which either party may respond. Rule 145(1), moreover, permits the Chamber to consider "all" relevant mitigating and aggravating factors. The dossier, properly constructed, contains relevant evidence bearing on such aggravating, and perhaps even mitigating, factors.

2. Other Submission Alternatives

— Article 19(3) permits victims to "submit observations" on the issues of jurisdiction and admissibility of a case.

— Article 56(2)(f) permits the Pre-Trial Chamber to "[t]ak[e] such other action as may be necessary to collect or preserve evidence." Dossiers, the factual contents of which the victim representatives can often compile

8. Emphasis added. *See, e.g.*, Situation in the Central African Republic In the Case of the Prosecutor v. Jean-Pierre Bemba Gombo, Case No. ICC-10/05-01/08: *Amicus Curiae Observations on Superior Responsibility Submitted Pursuant to Rule 103 of the Rules of Procedure and Evidence* (April 20, 2009) (30-page report submitted by Amnesty International).

well in advance of any formal ICC investigation, can help preserve such evidence for the Pre-Trial Chamber.

— Article 68(3) permits victims who have "personal interests" affected during the proceedings to present their "views and concerns . . . at stages of the proceedings determined to be appropriate by the Court . . . ."[9] Although "victims" are formally defined in Rule 85, and although Rule 89 requires official registration and limits the participation of victims in formal "proceedings," the statutory scheme does not prevent "other" victims from simply submitting dossiers pursuant to Article 68(3). Whether such submissions, if they occur in bulk and require individual examination, negatively impact the accused's due process and speedy trial rights will depend on the specifics of the particular case.

— Article 69(3) vests the Chamber with the authority to "request the submission of all evidence that it considers necessary for the determination of the truth." The victim representative can include the dossier made on the victims' behalf.

— Article 75(3), dealing with victim reparations, allows "other interested persons" to make representations to the Chamber prior to the Chamber issuing reparations orders. Victims, including those not formally so recognized, are undoubtedly such "interested persons."

— Article 76(2) permits the Trial Chamber to consider "any additional evidence or submissions relevant to the sentence . . . ." The dossier will likely contain such additional evidence bearing on sentencing.

— Pursuant to Rule 89(1)'s "views and concerns" clause, a victim who is formally recognized as such under Rule 89 may submit a dossier prepared by a non-registered victim, provided the Rule 89 victim can show that the contents of the dossier are relevant to his case.

E. Submitting the Dossier to the Office of the Prosecutor

In addition to the Chamber, the Office of the Prosecutor may also find victim dossiers useful. Recall that Article 15(1) permits the Prosecutor to

---

9. *See generally* Situation in the Central African Republic In the Case of the Prosecutor v. Jean-Pierre Bemba Gombo, Case No. ICC-10/05–01/08: *Fourth Decision on Victims' Participation* (December 12, 2008), at 27–39 ("Under the regime of the Statute, victims are not assigned the role of mere observers. To the contrary, pursuant to article 68(3) of the Statute, they may participate in the proceedings before the Court by expressing their views and concerns.") (Quotation omitted).

initiate investigations on his own accord ("*proprio motu*"). Neither Article 15 nor Article 53, however, limit the sources of evidence and information the Prosecutor may rely on when initiating an action, thereby making the dossier a potentially fertile predecessor component of case-initiation.

— Article 15(3) provides that the Prosecutor, if he concludes there is a reasonable basis to proceed on an investigation, must submit "any supporting material collected," along with the Prosecutor's request for authorization of an investigation, to the Pre-Trial Chamber; "[v]ictims may make representations to the Pre-Trial Chamber, in accordance with the Rules of Procedure and Evidence."
— Article 53(1)(c) requires the Prosecutor to take into account the "interests of victims" when deciding whether to initiate an investigation.
— Article 54(1)(a) requires the Prosecutor to "extend the investigation to cover *all* facts and evidence relevant to an assessment of whether there is criminal responsibility . . . ." [10]
— Article 54(1)(b) directs prosecutors to respect the interests and circumstances of not only witnesses, but also of victims.[11] A properly prepared dossier will contain facts and evidence bearing on these issues.

Rule 10, moreover, vests in the Prosecutor the responsibility for the retention, storage, and security of "information and physical evidence obtained in the course of the investigations. . . ." There is no restriction on what types of information the Prosecutor must retain. Rule 104(2), furthermore, allows the Prosecutor to "seek additional information from . . . other reliable sources that he or she deems appropriate. . . ." The format of this "additional information" is not specified; Rule 104(2), therefore, does not exclude dossiers.

In 2009, the Appeals Chamber provided additional support for the idea of submitting dossiers to the Prosecutor. The Appeals Chamber, although it rejected the Pre-Trial Chamber's decision that Article 68(3) gave victims a

10. Emphasis added.

11. *See also* THE OFFICE OF THE PROSECUTOR, REPORT ON PROSECUTORIAL STRATEGY 8 (September 14, 2006).

right to participate in the investigative phase of the proceedings, ruled that victims are permitted to provide information to the Prosecutor:

> [T]here is ample scope within the statutory scheme of the Statute for victims and anyone else with relevant information to pass it on to the Prosecutor without first being formally accorded 'a general right to participate.' For example under Article 15(2) the Prosecutor is authorized to receive information from, *inter alia*, any 'reliable source'—including victims. He is similarly authorized under Article 42(1) to receive and consider 'any substantiated information on crimes within the jurisdiction of the Court.' Victims may thus make representations to the Prosecutor on any matter pertaining to the investigations and to their interests. They are also specifically granted the right to make representations under Articles 15(3) and 19(3) of the Statute.[12]

The Appeals Chamber went on to emphasize the Prosecutor's duty to consider victims' interests:

> [V]ictims should be reminded that their protection and the sustenance of their interests is a recurring theme of the Statute. Article 54(1)(b) of the Statute lays down that in carrying out his investigations, the Prosecutor must 'respect the interests and personal circumstances of victims and witnesses. . . . Article 53(1)(c) of the Statute makes the interests of victims one of the factors to which the Prosecutor should attach due importance in deciding whether to start an investigation into a particular crime. The interests of victims are likewise a factor to be taken into account by the Prosecutor in deciding whether to mount a prosecution. . . . *Information that victims can provide to the Prosecutor about the scope of his investigations cannot but be welcome as it could provide nothing other than assistance.*[13]

---

12. Situation in the Democratic Republic of the Congo, Case No. ICC 01/04: *Judgment on Victim Participation In the Investigation State of the Proceedings* (February 2, 2009), at 14.

13. *Id.* at 14–15 (emphasis added).

For those harmed as a result of atrocity crimes, the dossier creates a permanent chronicle of their victimization. This public record will help ensure that the Prosecutor, the Chamber, the defense, the public, and the writers and students of history do not forget, or overlook, the victims' experiences. And the dossier—as well as the process through which it was created—will demonstrate to the victims that their experiences matter to the international community. In short, even if full formal participation in trial proceedings is not likely to become a reality for many groups of victims and aspiring victim representatives, the alternative modality of "participating" through the submission of a dossier furthers justice within the parameters of the ICC's statutory scheme, while at the same time advancing the victims' litigative, as well as psychological/emotional, interests.

PART XII

Pre-Trial Proceedings

TO THIS POINT THE BOOK has examined the history and the operation of the ICC, as well as various statutory provisions relating to victims. The discussion can therefore now turn to some more "practical" issues. This section draws on the earlier discussion of the promises and pitfalls of the ICC's legal provisions, as well as the realities of practice at the ICC, to sketch out trial strategies and trial skills necessary for effective victim representation.

A. Functions of the Pre-Trial Chamber

The Pre-Trial Division is composed of no less than six judges serving three-year terms (or until the completion of any cases they are hearing).[1] Regulation of the Court 14 demands that the judges of the Pre-Trial Division elect a President of the Division from among their members.[2] Pursuant to Article 38, the President oversees the administration of the Division.

Article 57 summarizes the functions and powers of the Pre-Trial Chamber. In accord with Article 36(3)(b), the Pre-Trial judges elected under "List A" must have criminal law and international law experience, regardless of whether that experience is gained as a judge, prosecutor, advocate, or in a similar capacity. "List B" judges, on the other hand, need not have any legal experience of the kind traditionally deemed necessary even for "novice" domestic judges.

The Pre-Trial Chamber, in turn, carries out the Pre-Trial Division's judicial functions. Regulation 46(1) gives the Presidency the authority to set up the Pre-Trial Chambers. A single judge, or three judges, make up the Pre-Trial

1. *See* Article 39(1) and (3)(a).

2. The President of the Division is elected to a one-year term. *See* Regulation 14.

Chamber.[3] At present, Pre-Trial Chamber I handles the situations in the Democratic Republic of the Congo, as well as in Darfur, Sudan. Pre-Trial Chamber II has been assigned to the Situations in Uganda and the Central African Republic.

In terms of the Pre-Trial Chambers' functions, they essentially are responsible for all judicial proceedings prior to, and including, the confirmation of the Prosecutor's charges.[4] Thus, the Pre-Trial Chamber is, in the end, tasked with overseeing the overall integrity and fairness of the proceedings during the investigation phase of cases.

Article 57(3)(c) also charges the Pre-Trial Chamber during the entire pretrial phase with safeguarding the security and other interests of victims, including the victims' physical and psychological well-being, as well as their dignity and privacy. For this purpose, the Pre-Trial Chamber may issue such orders as are necessary, and commence any other measure as may be required, taking into account the rights of the accused. The Pre-Trial Chamber may also seek the cooperation of states to take protective measures once it issues a warrant of arrest or summons to appear.

In cases in which a state refers the situation for investigation, in accord with Article 14, the Prosecutor may ask the Pre-Trial Chamber for permission to authorize the continued investigation of a particular case that one or more states have asked the Court to defer.[5] The Pre-Trial Chamber must also deal with any Article 19 jurisdictional challenges, or a state's challenge to the admissibility of a case, as well as such challenges lodged by an accused for whom the Chamber has issued an arrest warrant or summons to appear.

The Rome Statute also vests the Pre-Trial Chamber with authority to review the Prosecutor's decision not to proceed with an investigation.[6] Such a review can occur on the Pre-Trial Chamber's own motion, following the request of a state that had made an Article 14 referral, or after the Security Council refers the case pursuant to Article 13(b).

---

3. *See* Article 57(2) and Rule 7.

4. *See generally* Article 61 (setting out the Pre-Trial Chamber's duty to, within a reasonable time of the person's surrender or voluntary appearance before the Court, hold a hearing to confirm the Prosecutor's charges, and outlining the procedures to be followed during such a hearing); Rules 121–26 (detailing the procedures to be followed prior to, and during, the confirmation hearing).

5. *See* Article 18(2).

6. *See* Article 53(2) and (3).

After the prosecution has initiated an investigation, the Prosecutor may apply to the Pre-Trial Chamber for the issuance of a warrant of arrest or a summons to appear.[7] The Pre-Trial Chamber must issue a warrant of arrest or a summons to appear once it has satisfied itself that there are indeed reasonable grounds to believe that the person has committed a crime within the jurisdiction of the Court.

In the event law enforcement or the military arrest the accused, or he appears pursuant to a summons, the Pre-Trial Chamber may issue orders or seek the cooperation of states as may be necessary to assist the accused in the preparation of his defense. The Pre-Trial Chamber must also ensure that the accused is not subjected to unreasonable pre-trial detention.[8]

Following the surrender or voluntary appearance of an accused, the Pre-Trial Chamber is required to hold a hearing in the presence of the Prosecutor, the accused, and the accused's counsel to determine whether to confirm the charges. At the confirmation hearing, the Prosecutor must support the charges with sufficient evidence to establish substantial grounds to believe that the person committed the charged crime(s). The accused has the right to object to the charges, to challenge the evidence presented by the Prosecutor, or to present his own evidence. The Pre-Trial Chamber can either confirm the charges, decline to confirm the charges, or adjourn the hearing to give the Prosecutor additional time to provide certain missing evidence, conduct additional investigation, or amend the charges to bring them into conformity with the Pre-Trial Chamber's requirements.

Once the Chamber confirms the charges, the formal written confirmation decision, the committal of the accused to the Trial Chamber, and the record of the proceedings are transmitted to the Presidency.[9] The Presidency, thereafter, must constitute a Trial Chamber[10] and transmit to the Trial Chamber the records received from the Pre-Trial Chamber.[11] However, Article 64(4) provides that the Trial Chamber may, at its discretion, refer preliminary issues either back to the Pre-Trial Chamber, or to an available judge of the Pre-Trial Division, for resolution. Once the case is in the Trial Chamber, moreover, Regulation of the Court 55 provides that the Chamber may modify the

7. *See* Article 18.

8. *See* Article 60(1)-(4) and Rule 119.

9. *See* Rules 129–30.

10. *See* Article 61(11).

11. *See* Rule 130.

charges, provided that it does not exceed the charged facts and circumstances—which is a procedure the victims in *Lubanga*, over the heavy opposition by the prosecution and the defense, attempted to avail themselves of.

B. The Office of Public Counsel for the Defense

Like the Office of Public Counsel for Victims,[12] the Office of Public Counsel for Defense is an independent office inside the Court[13] that is, for administrative purposes, linked to the Registry.[14] The core function of the Office is to protect the rights of the accused by providing technical and legal assistance to defense counsel. Notably, the five attorneys in the Office do not involve themselves in the facts of the case or in trial strategy, concerning themselves solely with assisting external defense counsel, as well as with reviewing, and at times challenging under their own name, the perceived legal sufficiency of victim participation applications.

Although the Rules require external counsel to have competence in international or criminal law, as well as necessary relevant experience,[15] the ICC's legal provisions and practical realities are such that the Registry has set up both the Office of Public Counsel for Victims and the Office of Public Counsel for the Defense in order to provide ICC-internal expertise to the external victim representatives and defense attorneys, respectively. The paramount objective, therefore, is to assure the equality of arms between the parties.

Although the Office of Public Counsel for Victims provides both technical and legal assistance to external victim representatives, it has gone beyond this original mandate in the *Lubanga* case, and now represents registered victims in the proceedings. This expansion of its initial mission—and particularly the Office's request on behalf of victims in the *Lubanga* case to expand

12. The Office of Public Counsel for Victims was established on September 19, 2005, pursuant to Regulation 81. The explicit mandate of the Office of Public Counsel for Victims is to provide to victim representatives, who often will be unfamiliar with the ICC's legal framework and practical realities, legal support and advice. Moreover, Regulation 80 allows that members of the Office of Public Counsel for Victims may be appointed as *pro bono* victim representatives.

13. *See* Regulation 77.

14. *See generally* Rule 20 (requiring the Registry to provide technical assistance to the defense); Regulation 77 (governing the operation of the Office of Public Counsel for Defense).

15. *See generally* Rules 22 and 90(6).

the charges pursuant to Regulation 55[16]—has been of some concern to the Office of the Prosecutor, as well as to defense counsel. The Office of Public Counsel for the Defence, for example, is in particular worried that victim representatives not become back-up prosecutors, or be treated like parties to the trial, rather than simply as participants.[17] The Office considers the present balance between the prosecution and the defense extremely fragile, and views the grant of broader rights to victims, and expansive collaboration between victims and the prosecution, as serious threats to this tenuous balance.

That said, from the defense perspective, the interests between the prosecution and the victims are not necessarily aligned. This, the defense believes, will prevent victims and prosecutors from being overly collaborative. The Office of Public Counsel for Defense can in any event be expected to continue filing objections to greater victim involvement, premised, in part, on speedy trial and due process grounds; the defense will likely specifically note the additional work required of the defense if and when victim participation is expanded. These defense arguments must be taken seriously. However, as the Office of Public Counsel for Victims has demonstrated, meaningful victim participation is not necessarily accompanied by this feared parade of horribles. Victim involvement in the proceedings, furthermore, is explicitly provided for by the ICC's legal framework.

C. Victim Participation in Pre-Trial Investigative Activities

One of the most contentious and uncertain issues for victim representatives involves the nature and extent of the representatives' involvement in pre-trial investigation. Some victim representatives will want to seek authority to fully participate in the investigative phase of the proceedings. It can, however, also be argued that such participation threatens to undermine the actual, and perceived, integrity and independence of the Prosecutor's function, and threatens to make the proceedings inefficient and slow. The net result, it may be contended, is that these negative impacts have a tendency to bias the outcome of the proceeding in contravention of Article 68(3)'s

---

16. *See generally* Situation in the Democratic Republic of the Congo, Case No. ICC 01/04-01/06: *Decision on the Prosecution and the Defence Applications for Leave to Appeal the 'Decision Giving Notice to the Parties and Participants that the Legal Characterization of the Facts May be Subject to Change in Accordance with Regulation 55(2) of the Regulations of the Court* (September 3, 2009) (this ruling has since been reversed).

17. *See generally id.* at 21 (distinguishing between the "parties [defense and prosecution]" and the "legal representatives," but using the term "participants" to describe both).

admonition that victim participation not be "prejudicial or inconsistent with the rights of the accused and a fair and impartial trial." Although some of these concerns may be slightly exaggerated, they cannot be dismissed out of hand as meritless.

Pursuant to Rules 47–50 and 104–106, the Pre-Trial Chamber may, following the Prosecutor's request, take such measures as may be necessary to ensure the efficiency and integrity of the investigatory proceedings. In particular, the Chamber can appoint an attorney or a judge from the Pre-Trial Chamber to be present during the taking of witness testimony in order to protect the rights of the defense in those cases where there exists a serious risk that the defense may not be able to subsequently take such testimony.

The Pre-Trial Chamber's role in safeguarding the defense's rights may also come into play when the Prosecutor informs the Pre-Trial Chamber of a unique investigative opportunity. For example, the Chamber may opt to recommend, or order, that certain procedures be followed, appoint an expert, authorize appointment of counsel to arrested persons, or order that certain actions necessary for the collection or preservation of evidence be taken.[18] The Pre-Trial Chamber may additionally authorize the Prosecutor to take specific investigative steps within the territory of a State Party, without having first secured the state's cooperation. This process, it must be noted, would only take place in those rare cases in which the state is unable to comply with the request because it possesses no authority competent to execute the request for cooperation.

There are, in summary, three statutory regimes regulating victim involvement in the pre-trial investigative phase:

1. Rule 93's "seeking the views of victims" by the Chamber;
2. Submission of "observations" or "representations" under Articles 15(3)[19] and 19(3)[20]; and
3. Victim participation in accordance with Articles 53(3), 61, and 69(3), and Rules 89–92. (Article 54(1)(b), moreover, directs the Prosecutor

18. *See* Article 56.

19. Permitting victim to make "representations" to the Pre-Trial Chamber at the time the Prosecutor concludes that there exists a reasonable basis to proceed with the investigation.

20. Allowing victim to "submit observations" concerning the jurisdiction of the Court or the admissibility of the case.

investigating and prosecuting crimes to respect the interests and circumstances of not only witnesses, but also victims.[21])

It is incumbent upon victim representatives to reference these statutory provisions when addressing whether, and to what extent, the Chamber should sanction victim participation in the pre-trial investigative phase. Victim representatives must also remember that the Prosecutor is charged with ensuring the integrity, independence, and efficiency of the investigation,[22] and, as such, the Prosecutor must be equally interested in obtaining and examining incriminating, as well as *exculpatory*, evidence. The prosecution, therefore, may have strong feelings concerning who is a (likely) victim, and at what stage of the proceedings victim involvement will be most helpful.[23] In fact, the Appeals Chamber has held:

> Manifestly, authority for the conduct of investigation vests in the Prosecutor. Acknowledgement by the Pre-Trial Chamber of a right to victims to participate in the investigation would necessarily contravene the Statute [Article 42] by reading into it power outside its ambit and remit.... [The position that Rule 68(3) confers participatory rights to victims during investigative proceedings] can find no justification under the Statute, the Rules of Procedure and Evidence or the Regulations of the Court.[24]

D. Pre-Trial Preparation With a Clear Focus on the Main Trial

The prepared victim representative strives to present the case in a clear, logical, and orderly manner consistent with the applicable law and facts, and

21. *See also* THE OFFICE OF THE PROSECUTOR, REPORT ON PROSECUTORIAL STRATEGY 8 (14 September 2006).

22. The Rome Statute in fact requires that the Prosecutor act as an independent and separate organ of the Court, and, in furtherance of this objective, warns that no member of the Office of the Prosecutor shall act on, or seek instructions from, any external sources. *See* Article 42(1).

23. Though perhaps not formally a "stage" of the proceedings, consider also Rule 89(1), which permits the Prosecutor and the defense to submit observations on applications. This has been done both for "general" case applications, but also in regard to specific instances, *i.e.*, applications to participate in the interlocutory appeals processes.

24. Situation in the Democratic Republic of the Congo, Case No. ICC 01/04: *Judgment on Victim Participation in the Investigation State of the Proceedings* (December 19, 2008), at 22–29.

must distill the victims' case for the Chamber. The victim representative at all stages of the proceedings—from the confirmation hearing until the final verdicts—should be organized, in control, well-prepared, and familiar with all aspects of the case.[25] A polished presentation, however, is possible only if the victim representative early in the litigation process establishes a sound organizational framework. Although this advice may seem obvious, even experienced lawyers frequently fail to develop, or adhere to, a consistent, efficient method of trial preparation. Those lawyers, as a consequence, can find themselves in the unenviable position of trying to put things into place at the last moment.

1. Developing the Theory of the Case

Despite the maze of legal jargon, lawyers' mysterious tactics, and obscure court procedures, any criminal case can be reduced to the simple form of a story.[26]

As this discussion has shown, most actual atrocity crimes victims will not have the opportunity to participate in the ICC's proceedings. In the first instance, most potential victims are, to a large extent, randomly "selected" by members of humanitarian and other NGOs working in, or near, the country or region in question. Experience teaches that the NGOs usually have their own internal set of criteria concerning what makes a "good" victim (wealthier victims, for example, are, for sympathy reasons, routinely passed over in favor of poorer victims). The Chamber, thereafter, will likely only qualify a small subset of the hand-selected group of victims the NGOs have brought to the Court's and the prosecution's attention. And even once the victims are so qualified, substantive involvement in the proceedings will likely be strictly limited. That said, regardless of whether the victim wishes to participate during the pre-indictment phase, seeks qualification to participate at the trial, or elects to file a dossier, the victim representative must first develop a theory of the case framed by the available facts, and accounting for the victims' often-divergent interests.

---

25. Organization will be aided by keeping an up-to-date case chronology, or "case tag."

26. W.L. Bennett & M.S. Feldman, Reconstructing Reality in the Courtroom 4 (1981).

The success of the victims' case is, indeed, largely determined long before the prosecution ever calls its first witness. As most experienced lawyers will attest, the preliminary stages frequently determine the outcome of a case. This is equally true in ICC proceedings, where the victim representative at the outset must establish that the accused victimized his clients, thereby justifying the victims' seat at the table.[27] Without a sound theory of the case to build on, such hands-on involvement is unlikely to come to fruition.

The victims' theory of the case must, therefore, clearly identify the elements of the crimes within the situation that the prosecution has—or should have—charged. This analysis, in turn, will lead to a theory of responsibility under which the accused is liable for certain discrete crimes. The theory of the case needs to identify how the crimes affected the victims, and answer the question of how the personal interests of the victims are potentially impacted at various stages in the proceedings. The objective is to crystallize for the Court and the Prosecutor the victims' position and/or to demonstrate to them why they should consider taking certain additional actions on the victims' behalf.

The theory of the case for the victim representative is, therefore, likely to be a specific version of the facts showing that: (1) the accused is guilty of the charged conduct; (2) the accused's alleged criminal conduct harmed the victims; and (3) the victims are, therefore, entitled to participate in the proceedings and are entitled to various remedies, including reparations.[28] The execution of this proposed three-phase approach to theme-driven case presentation depends on whether the victim representative is at the trial stage, is advocating for his client in the media, or is simply supplementing the permanent historical record by filing a dossier with the Prosecutor or the Chamber.

---

27. *See generally* Rule 89(1) (granting the Chamber broad discretion to determine the nature and scope of victim participation in all phases of the proceedings, including during opening and closing statements); Rule 91 (same); and Rule 92 (victim-notification requirements); *see also* Gerard J. Mekjian & Matthew C. Varughese, *Hearing the Victim's Voice: Analysis of Victims' Advocate Participation in the Trial Proceedings of the International Criminal Court*, 17 PACE INT'L L. REV. 1, 8 (2006) (summarizing victims' right of participation).

28. Reparations for victims are explicitly provided for by the ICC. *See, e.g.*, Article 75 (setting forth rules relating to reparations); Article 79 (setting up Trust Fund for purpose of paying reparations, signalling an effort to impose collective responsibility to compensate victims); Article 82(4) and Rule 153 (permitting, *inter alia*, victim representative to appeal reparations decision); Rules 94–99 (dealing with various aspects of reparations); Rule 143 (noting that the Chamber may set hearing date for issues dealing with reparations); Rule 147 (providing for forfeiture of proceeds, property, and assets); and Rules 217–19 (allowing for enforcement of reparation orders).

Consider, for example, a hypothetical case involving coordinated rapes of women in a particular village by a government militia. In such a case, the victim representative's theory of the case might be that the accused, a high-ranking government official not present during the commission of the alleged crimes, knew about, condoned, or coordinated the rapes as part of an organized attempt to terrorize those the government believed tacitly or actively supported rebel factions. The theory in such a case will focus on establishing the accused's command responsibility, in addition to demonstrating how the available facts fit within the legal framework, and must carefully explain how and why these facts compel a pro-conviction outcome.

In terms of organization, it may be helpful to think of the case theory as a newspaper or magazine headline which provides, in summary form, the essence of "what happened." For example, a possible headline in a case in which the ICC Prosecutor charged a battalion commander with permitting the torture and killing of captured combatants might read:

Victims tortured and murdered by battalion members–

> Commander Holguin, who knew his troops would follow him to their deaths, and who, therefore, was certain that his soldiers would strictly adhere to his wishes, condoned, and at times even directly encouraged, the acts of his foot soldiers.

Such a simple, straightforward summary of the theory is the headline of the story that gives everyone the same picture, and that conveys what happened in a form that the Chamber (and the public) can readily understand.

The theory of the case also serves as a guide to what additional investigation needs to be undertaken. In the above example, the victim representative may, for instance, want to locate relatively contemporaneous photographs taken of the accused and his battalion members for in-Chamber examination by witnesses and/or for submission to the Chamber, if permitted. The victim-witnesses may help the Prosecutor determine that the accused shaved or otherwise changed his appearance since being charged; perhaps the accused altered his appearance to make positive in-Chamber identification more difficult. Alternatively, a group photograph may reveal the accused's relative position among his fellow soldiers. For example, is the accused in the middle of the group, or is he sitting when everyone else is standing?

The theory of the case also involves psychological/emotional aspects. Contemplating what was in the minds of those involved in the charged crimes may suggest a different, or opposing, version of the prosecution's case. Therefore, consider the following questions: What would be going through the minds of those involved if the events occurred the way the prosecution or accused say they did? What was the accused's likely perspective and access to information at the time of the alleged crimes? Consider how the parties reacted at various times; were they confused, angry, or gleeful? What if the victim was in an area typically occupied by hostile and armed combatants? What if the victim threatened the battalion members, or was known or believed to be an active combatant? What if the victim was drunk or had a history of violence? Might a self-defense argument be available to the accused?

To be fully prepared, the victim representative must also evaluate whether two different "stories" or "scenarios" can co-exist. The investigation must gather additional information to explain the events from the victims' perspective. The victim representative's job is to understand the *whole* picture, including actions occurring prior to the event that may give meaning to the alleged criminal acts. Developing a complete theory of the case is of course not possible until the investigation is finished, but the victim representative's preliminary theory—which always remains subject to revision—will help identify particular focal areas for forensic and other investigation.

Even when the investigation is complete, the theory of the case will dictate what evidence to seek and present at trial, as well as which legal arguments to advance. A well-thought-out theory of the case will ultimately increase the victims' chances of success by focusing the victim representative's and the Chamber's thinking, thereby conserving scarce time and resources.

2. Framing the Elements of the Crime(s)

During the pre-trial stage, the victim representative must understand the elements of the crime charged by the prosecution, and gain an appreciation for how the crime affected the victims. Obviously, the prosecution's case is based on proving all elements of the charged crimes.[29] In some cases, there

29. The crimes chargeable in the ICC are discussed in Part IV(C), and are set forth in Elements of Crimes 5–8. During the pre-trial phase, victim representatives must also consider the-

may be only one element of the crime that is in dispute, and the investigation and preparation may focus on that crucial element. For example, if the accused is charged with Element of Crimes Article 7(1)(f)'s crime against humanity of torture, the element of the crime in dispute may be whether the accused *knew* that the conduct (torture) was "part of a widespread or systematic attack directed against civilian populations,"[30] rather than a one-off or otherwise isolated incident.

The elements of the crimes that are most crucial to the Prosecutor will likely substantially overlap with the points the victim representative wishes to make. However, the Prosecutor's objectives may not encompass other areas, such as establishing that the accused harmed a *particular* victim, or group of victims, in a particular manner or on a particular date. The Prosecutor's goal, after all, is simply to present evidence proving the accused's overall culpability as to the charged crimes. The victim representative's goal may be far more discrete and detailed.

Compounding the challenge of potentially divergent litigation objectives, institutionally mandated prosecutorial independence may to some extent limit victim representatives' abilities to urge prosecutors to introduce certain evidence, or call certain witnesses, to help establish the victims' legal case. The victim representative, therefore, must engage in an independent review of the available evidence, must evaluate the probative quality of the evidence, and must argue persuasively to the Chamber that his clients were victims of the charged crimes, and that the Chamber should, accordingly, permit the victims to augment the record in order to pursue their litigation strategy. The victim representative, bearing in mind the limitations of his role, should request permission to present certain evidence to ensure that the trial covers all of the elements required for a successful outcome from the *victims'* perspective. Depending on whether or not the Chamber determines that reparations proceedings are bifurcated, the scope and timing for victim submissions may differ.

As touched on above, it is crucial for the Chamber to trust the victim representative's capability and professionalism. The Chamber will use its extremely broad discretionary powers to determine the victim representative's

---

ories of liability, such as joint-enterprise, aider/abettor, and co-conspirator liability. *See* Articles 25 and 30 (*mens rea* elements); and Articles 31 and 32 (mistakes and other defenses).

30. Elements of Crimes Article 7(1)(f)(5).

appropriate level of participation in the proceedings, taking into account factors such as the interests of the victim in the witness, the interests of the witness and the accused, and the need for a fair and efficient trial.[31] If the representative demonstrates from the outset that his questions and submissions are well thought-out, advance the victims' concrete interests without unfairly prejudicing the accused's right to a fair trial, and thus add net value to the proceedings, the Chamber is more likely to grant broader permission to participate.[32]

3. Identifying and Developing the Critical Facts

Once the victim representative has developed a persuasive and comprehensive theory of the case, and has gained a firm grasp of the legal elements he needs to prove in order to prevail, he can begin to focus on the critical facts the Prosecutor and he must prove at trial. Some questions to consider when thinking about the relevance of potential evidence include:

- What happened just before the alleged crime(s)?
- Why was this crime committed?
- Who would have a motive to commit this crime; who benefitted from the crime?
- What are the agendas of the different parties involved?
- What are the relationships among the parties involved?
- What are the personal backgrounds of the parties (age, education, familial background, military rank, mental state, social status, economic circumstances, etc.)?
- Are there aspects of this case that just do not seem to fit together?

---

31. *See generally* Situation in the Democratic Republic of the Congo In the Case of the Prosecutor v. Germain Katanga and Mathieu Ngudjolo Chui, Case No. ICC-01/04–01/07: *Order Instructing the Participants and the Registry to Respond to Questions of Trial Chamber II for the Purpose of the Status Conference (Article 64(3)(a) of the Statute)* (November 13, 2008), at 10 (inviting the victim representatives to inform the Chamber of their intention to "lead evidence pertaining to the guilt or innocence of the accused," to "apply for protective measures," and to "call witnesses and lead evidence pertaining to the issue of reparations at the same time as for the purpose of trial").

32. *See also* Mekjian & Varughese, *supra* note 27, at 27 (noting "presumption" in favor of participation during hearings).

— Is this an unusual way to commit this type of crime?
— Who else could have committed or authorized this crime?

To develop a full set of potentially relevant facts, it may help to organize the facts into categories such as "situational/tangible issues" and "state of mind/psychological issues."

Regarding the former, the victim representative should consider whether the events could have physically occurred in the way the prosecution or defense claim. An investigator's report may say that "X, and then Y, occurred," but photographs taken of the scene may make that particular sequence of events either impossible or highly unlikely. Further analysis or information-gathering may be required.

Visiting the place where the crimes in question took place can be crucial in this regard. The victim representative may feel that something in an official report does not make sense, and upon visiting the scene of the crime it becomes clear that the report author's recorded recollection of the witness is likely not the whole story. Similarly, a certain claim made by the accused or a witness during an interview, or at trial, may be inconsistent with the physical realities of the location where the alleged crime took place. Physically visiting the locations and acting out or imaging the events may well provide additional valuable clues. The victim representative has, therefore, not fully prepared the victims' case without at least considering a visit to the scene of the alleged crime(s).[33]

4. Constructing an "Order of Proof"

To understand the interplay between the elements of the charged offense, the evidence tending to prove each of these elements, what portion of the universe of potential evidence relates most directly to the victims' case, and the best way to structure the presentation of this evidence, victim representatives should create an "order of proof" for their case. An order of proof is nothing more than a detailed, chronological list of the evidence arranged to support the victim representative's theory of the case. Examples of types of

33. Note, however, that the victim representative, as a practical matter, prior to the travel will have to determine precisely who will cover these costs (put another way, do not simply assume that the costs will be borne by the ICC).

evidence to consider are witness testimony, documents, photographs, expert reports, and forensic evidence.

The order of proof must clearly identify the elements of the charged offense that each piece of evidence tends to establish. In addition, a complete order of proof delineates evidence tending to prove the nexus between the crime and the harms the victim suffered. The victim representative should consider the evidence element-by-element, but must also be mindful not to improperly impinge upon, or interfere with, the role of the Prosecutor. Failure to keep this in mind will likely result in drawing the ire of both the Chamber and the prosecution, and that will obviously not advance the victims' long-term objectives.

Although the order of proof outline must be detailed, it should also be flexible enough for the victim representative to revise it as evidence and arguments develop. An integrated method of case preparation permits the victim representative to identify areas where additional evidence may be needed and to avoid overlooking important documents or facts, provides a solid sense of how the case will unfold during the main trial, and allows the victim representative to present the case in an orderly, concise, and strategically sound fashion.

5. Outlining Direct and "Adverse" Examination

The victim representative should dedicate one section of his order of proof to identifying each witness the prosecution, defense, and the victim representative (pending Chamber approval) will likely call. For each witness, moreover, the victim representative must explicitly delineate what elements of the crime the witness' testimony will support, and outline areas to be covered during the questioning. Prior to asking any questions in court, a direct examination outline should be prepared for each witness. Complete examination outlines will contain questions designed to elicit evidence establishing elements of the crimes, and information showing how the alleged crime harmed the victims. Such preparation will make it easier to persuade the Chamber that a given witness should be called, convince the prosecution that the presentation is not inconsistent with their litigation strategy, and assure all participants that the proposed questions are probative.

Victim representatives must of course also be prepared for the possibility that the Chamber will not permit the representative to independently call a witness, but instead will call the witness on the representative's behalf.

The victim representative must plan for such a situation, having all the questions ready to give to the Chamber (note, however, that, per ICC practice, the victim representative will in any event likely be required to have all questions ready to give to the Chamber for *in camera* review, regardless of who calls the witness).

Victim representatives should also outline potential cross, or "adverse," examination questions for each witness.[34] Cross-examination questions can be designed to highlight areas tending to further the victim representative's specific theory of the case, or they can be designed to attack the credibility of the witness's testimony. That said, victim representatives must resist the urge to cross-examine all witnesses, since the Chamber will likely only grant limited permission to pose cross-examination questions. Put simply, the victim representative must choose his cross-examination targets carefully.

As the Chamber has announced, "a victim who wishes to participate in relation to any identified stage of the proceedings should set out in a discrete written application the nature and the detail of the proposed intervention (e.g., by providing the questions that he or she seeks to put)."[35] A sound order of proof, combined with thought-out examinations, will significantly increase the odds that the Chamber will grant the victims' written application to participate.

6. Preparing the Exhibit List

In terms of practical preparatory steps, another key element is the drafting of an exhibit list delineating the evidence expected at trial, and identifying what element(s) of the charged crime the particular pieces of evidence/testimony support. For each piece of evidence, the victim representative should understand, and be prepared to articulate, why it is relevant to the case and is admissible under the ICC rules. Some exhibits will be entered by the Prosecutor, and some by the defense. If there is additional evidence the victim representative would like to have admitted at trial, he must identify

34. For each anticipated witness, the victim representative should create a separate witness file, and place in this file direct and cross-examination questions and any exhibits or evidence the representative wants to have the witness examine.

35. Situation in the Democratic Republic of the Congo In the Case of the Prosecutor v. Thomas Lubanga Dyilo, Case No. ICC-01/04–01/06: *Decision on the Applications by Victims to Participate in the Proceedings* (December 15, 2008), at 37 (citation and quotation omitted).

which witness will establish the admissibility of that evidence.[36] The exhibit list should, accordingly, clearly identify the witnesses through whom each piece of evidence will be presented and admitted.

The victim representative should also list any arguably exculpatory evidence potentially rebutting elements of the crimes charged, such as evidence that the accused had no meaningful control over his troops, evidence that the accused acted in self-defense or defense of others, etc. Of course, the disclosure obligations on the defense are not as exacting as those on the Prosecutor, and this will make it more difficult to determine with precision the defense's trial strategy.

7. Honest Evaluation Required: Critical Examination of the Victims' Case

Although looking at the obvious aspects of a case, such as how the accused's alleged conduct harmed the victims, is of course important, it is also critical to equally consider facts beyond the obvious. To be successful at trial, the victim representative must understand fully any and all weaknesses of the victims' and Prosecutor's case.

Too often, inexperienced lawyers forge ahead with their case, blinded by their purely positive view of it, only to be surprised at trial by damaging evidence they are unable to counter or explain. To avoid this pitfall, prepared victim representatives must hold their case up to the light, examine it from all sides, and honestly identify not only the case's strengths, but also the parts of the case that are weak and most likely to be successfully attacked by the other parties or the Chamber. This can be a difficult process, as trial lawyers typically convince themselves of the merits of their case, and somewhat instinctively do not want to pay attention to any weaknesses in their evidence. However, the

---

36. It is noteworthy that the July 11, 2008, Appeals Chamber ruling in *Lubanga* specified that, if the victim representatives are permitted to independently submit evidence, then the appropriate disclosure obligations have to be fulfilled. *See* Appeals Chamber, Situation in the Democratic Republic of the Congo, Case No. ICC-01/04–01/06: *The Prosecutor v. Thomas Lubanga Dyilo, Judgment on the Appeals of The Prosecutor and The Defence against Trial Chamber I's Decision on Victims' Participation of 18 January 2008* (July 11, 2008), at 43–44. This ruling is of course intended to safeguard the rights of the accused. Nevertheless, at present there are no explicit disclosure obligations for victim representatives (the disclosure obligations for defense and the prosecution, in contrast, are quite detailed). The victim representative must be aware of this apparent gap in the existing rules, as it will likely need to be addressed.

victim representative must put aside personal feelings about the case and examine it from every angle to avoid being caught unprepared at trial, or confronted with unanticipated arguments or lines of questioning. Such a full and honest evaluation of the evidence will assist in the competent development of a viable theory of the case, and will focus the victims' presentation.

8. Preparing a Preliminary Trial Checklist

To avoid the problems stemming from a poorly organized trial system, the victim representative should consider compiling a brief pre-trial checklist of issues to cover, including the following:

— Understand the victims' case, as well as their desires, and discuss with them the aim of their participation (that is, getting a voice, setting the historical record straight, receiving reparations, punishing the perpetrators, etc.).
— Once the victim representative understands the victims' litigation goals, determine whether large or small group representation makes the most sense (or, alternatively, decide how the victim groups should best be split up).
— Obtain a signed acknowledgement or power of attorney from the victims signifying their knowing and voluntary assent to the representation, as well as their understanding of potential conflicts of interest inherent in group representation.
— To the extent that the victim representative has access to discovery,[37] carefully review all physical and documentary evidence.
— Review elements of the offense and the order of proof, and amend as necessary.
— Identify all potential witnesses, including experts.
— Develop a sound theory of the case.
— Draft a preliminary order of proof.
— Match the witnesses to the evidence by interviewing and confirming the witness' familiarity with the exhibits, subject to the limitations on witness "proofing" discussed in Part XII(E), below.

---

37. Persons granted victim status by the ICC do not necessarily have access to non-public documents registered in the record of the investigation. *See, e.g.*, Situation in the Democratic Republic of the Congo In the Case of the Prosecutor v. Thomas Lubanga Dyilo, Case No. ICC-01/04–01/06: *Decision on the Applications for Participation* (November 4, 2008).

— Create a "Contacts" and "To-Do" list containing all important telephone numbers, names, and tasks the victim representative must complete by particular dates.
— Gather and categorize all relevant documents and reports, including interview reports and notes, witness and accused background information, lab reports, and forensic analysis.
— Listen to any audio tapes, and watch any videotapes, prepared as part of the investigation.
— Prepare accurate transcripts.
— Develop appropriate arguments relating to victim security.
— If appropriate, compile information to present to the Chamber and/or the Prosecutor in favor of detaining the accused,[38] or of imposing other

38. Article 59(3)–(6), Rule 118, and Rule 119 authorize detention when there are *reasonable grounds to believe* that (1) the accused *committed* a crime within the jurisdiction of the ICC, and (2) detention is *necessary to ensure the accused's appearance* at trial, that the accused does not obstruct or endanger the investigation or proceedings, or to prevent the continued commission of the subject offense or related offenses within the ICC's jurisdiction. *See* Rule 119(3) (requiring that Pre-Trial Chamber seek view of relevant victims potentially at risk if accused is released); *see also* Situation in the Democratic Republic of the Congo In the Case of the Prosecutor v. Germain Katanga and Mathieu Ngudjolo Chui, Case No. ICC-01/04–01/07: *Review of the "Decision on the Conditions of the Pre-Trial Detention of Germain Katanga"* (August 18, 2008), at 11 (ruling that the accused's detention should continue, in part, because release may "lead to the grave endangerment of the security of victims and witnesses and that therefore continued detention is necessary to ensure that the suspect does not obstruct or endanger the court proceedings"); Situation in the Democratic Republic of the Congo In the Case of the Prosecutor v. Germain Katanga and Mathieu Ngudjolo Chu, Case No. ICC-01/04–01/07: *Third Review of the Decision on the Application for Interim Release of Mathieu Ngudjolo* (March 17, 2009), at 5–8 (reviewing, pursuant to Article 60(3) and Rule 118(2), the Chamber's earlier decision on interim release, and concluding that continued detention was required in light of, *inter alia*, the seriousness of the charges, the length of the potential sentence, the short time to the hearing on the merits, and the threat the accused would pose to "victims and witnesses whose identity had been disclosed").

The victims may have information not in the Prosecutor's possession bearing on these flight and danger-related issues. If so, such material should generally be provided to the Chamber or the Office of the Prosecutor to help in assuring the accused is appropriately detained pending trial. *See generally* Situation in the Democratic Republic of the Congo In the Case of the Prosecutor v. Germain Katanga and Mathieu Ngudjolo Chui, Case No. ICC-01/04–01/07: *Decision Inviting Observations from the Participants Concerning the Detention of Mathieu Ngudjolo Chui (rule 118(2))* (October 30, 2008), at 4 (providing the legal representatives of anonymous and non-anonymous victims with the opportunity to "file their observations on the detention of [the accused]"). Note that Rule 118(3) requires a hearing on interim release or continued detention be held at least once a year. *See generally* Situation in the Central African Republic In the Case of the Prosecutor v. Jean-Pierre Bemba Gombo, Case No. ICC-01/05–01/08: *Decision to Hold a Hearing Pursuant to Rule 118(3) of the Rules of Procedure and Evidence* (June 16, 2009), at 4.

restrictive measures to assure the safety of the community and the accused's presence at future proceedings.

9. Creating a Trial Notebook

A common and simple organizational method is to maintain a comprehensive trial notebook containing the most important information about the case, as summarized above. The trial notebook, therefore, includes everything from the contacts and to-do list, order of poof, and the "document containing the charges" (in the parlance of the ICC; more commonly known as the indictment), to the victim representative's preliminary thoughts on how to argue certain issues which may arise at trial.[39] The trial notebook should also contain the victim representative's legal research; drafted (and filed) pre-trial motions; evidence to be presented; outlines of opening statements, direct examinations, cross-examinations, and draft closing argument; and other similarly important materials. Each section should be separately divided within the trial notebook. This organization method provides the victim representative with one central source to easily locate material and information when needed, and enables the victim representative to separate, outline, and arrange the different aspects of the case. The inability to find a document during trial, after all, is the same as not having the document at all.

10. Complying with Pre-Trial Discovery and Disclosure Obligations

The Pre-Trial Chamber may well order the first round of discovery prior to the Confirmation Hearing.[40] Additional discovery rules and obligations are set forth in Article 64(3)(c) (vesting Trial Chamber with power to require disclosure of documents or information); Article 64(6)(b) (requiring state cooperation in fulfilling discovery requirements); Article 64(6)(d) (providing for general discovery order); Rule 76 (pre-trial disclosure requirements for

---

39. Note that internal documents prepared for purposes or the investigation or trial are generally *not* discoverable. *See* Rule 81(1).

40. *See* Article 61(3).

prosecution witnesses); Rule 77 (requiring the Prosecutor to permit defense to inspect documents and physical evidence the Prosecutor may use at the Confirmation Hearing or at trial, or that may be material to the preparation of the defense); Rule 79 (governing disclosures by the defense); Rule 81(2)-(6) (relating to disclosure of sensitive discovery); Rule 82 (dealing with disclosure of items obtained confidentially, and solely for purpose of generating new evidence); Rule 84 (providing Chamber with authority to fashion discovery deadlines and schedules), and Rule 121 (relating to disclosures prior to the confirmation hearing).[41] Victim representatives, however, must bear in mind that none of these provisions explicitly grant victims the right to receive any non-public information, and that the broadly permissive Rule 84, therefore, may end up being the victims' most promising avenue.

According to the ICC's fairly liberal discovery and admissibility rules, the victim representative should move the Chamber to permit pre-trial inspection of a broad range of documents and evidence. This evidence may include records of examination of the accused, material obtained from, or belonging to, the accused, material concerning investigative actions in which defense counsel would have participated, expert analysis, and all records and physical evidence available after the investigation complete.[42]

The victim representative may well be limited in what discovery the Chamber will permit the representative to receive (consider, in this context, motions practiced under Rule 91, governing victim representative's participation in the proceedings). Indeed, in the *Lubanga* case the prosecution reportedly only provided the legal representative for the victims with the non-redacted discovery one day prior to the commencement of the trial, and did not complete the disclosures until one month into the trial. Thus, once

41. The Chamber, relying on the relative looseness of the statutory language, has gone so far as to require the Prosecutor to submit to all parties, including the victims, a summary table listing the charges confirmed by the Pre-Trial Chamber and the modes of responsibility accompanying the alleged acts, as well as the evidence the Prosecutor intends to rely on at trial. The Prosecutor also has to identify all potentially exculpatory pieces of evidence, and the "modes of responsibility" these potentially exculpatory pieces of evidence *may* be related to. *See* Situation in the Democratic Republic of the Congo In the Case of the Prosecutor v. Germain Katanga and Mathieu Ngudjolo Chui, Case No. ICC-01/04–01/07: *Order Instructing the Participants and the Registry to File Additional Documents* (December 10, 2008), at 5–13. The prosecution objected, reasonably contending that this analysis is "incumbent on the Defence, and not on the Prosecutor . . . ." This approach is a powerful example of the Chamber following procedures in keeping with the inquisitorial model of litigation.

42. *See also* Rule 78.

again, the fate of the victim representative's access to evidence is almost entirely in the hands of the prosecution and the Chamber.

To the extent the Chamber includes the victim representative in the discovery process, the victim representative must keep a careful written record of what materials he tendered to the other participants, as well as when he tendered those materials. This will prevent subsequent questions about (or accusations concerning) alleged failures to turn over documents. The written discovery records can be in the form of a short note, e-mail, or one-page letter to the other participant, and should indicate the date and precise description of the documents or items turned over. The victim representatives should stamp the documents themselves with the case tag and the date of production, and should also consider requiring the other participant to sign an acknowledgement that it received certain discovery. Victim representatives should keep these records in the trial notebook for easy reference.

Relying on Article 68(2), victim representatives should also ask the Chamber to rule on sensitive discovery issues *in camera*. This applies in particular to cases involving conduct of a sexual nature, such as sexual violence.[43] Although the evidence may be in the Prosecutor's possession, the victim representative may have reason early in the proceedings to challenge, on privacy or security grounds, the tendering of certain un-redacted and other discovery to the defense. Moreover, although Rules 76 and 77 admittedly do not grant victims an affirmative right to inspect the discovery or to receive witness names and certain other related statements and documentation,[44] the victim representatives should file discrete motions for the disclosure of particular discovery relating to certain witnesses. This way, the Chamber can better understand what the victim representatives are seeking, why they are seeking these materials, and why turning these materials over to the victims on the eve of trial will unfairly disadvantage them.

The discovery regime's unresolved paradox, however, is that the Chamber requires victim representatives to, by written motion, exceptionally demonstrate that the victims' interests are affected by particular non-public

43. *See* Rules 70–72.

44. In this regard it must be noted that, although Rules 76 and 77 do not define victim applications for participation as "statements," to the extent they contain information inconsistent with other statements made by the victim/witness, or are otherwise impeaching, they must be disclosed.

discovery prior to gaining access to that discovery. Suffice it to say that it is exceedingly difficult in the typical case to demonstrate that a certain category or item of discovery directly affects victims' interests when the victim representative does not even know about the documents and other evidence in the possession of the other parties.

E. Some Observations on Pre-Trial Meetings With (Potential) Witnesses

Nothing in the ICC regulations categorically prohibits victim representatives from meeting, and talking with, potential witnesses prior to, or during, the formal initiation of an investigation.[45] The formal bar on witness contact is not raised until the participants announce that a particular person will be a witness. Once the witness is "official," the Victim Witness Unit takes over, and the other participants may not discuss any substantive matters with the witness. Note, moreover, that a record of the questioning may be required,[46] and that at least one ICC ruling has prohibited prosecutors from, in the context of an ongoing investigation, "proofing" (coaching) a witness. It is therefore permissible—and indeed advisable—for the victim representative, if possible in coordination with the Prosecutor, to interview potential witnesses as soon as they are available (and well before they are officially named as trial witnesses).

Even after a participant has officially identified a specific person as a witness, victim representatives may conduct very basic "field interviews." During these interviews, the victim representative simply reintroduces himself to the victim or witness, and attempts to subtly gain a sense of whether the witness continues to have the right frame of mind and willingness to testify truthfully. Such a non-substantive meeting will not likely raise any eyebrows, but can be extremely valuable in terms of assuring the witness that the victim

---

45. *See generally*, Articles 53–56 (setting out limitations/restrictions on the Prosecutor's ability to conduct pre-trial interviews) and Rule 74 (dealing with self-incrimination by the witness; arguably inapplicable to questioning by victim representatives).

46. *See* Rule 111(1) (requiring that a record be made relating to "formal statements made by any person" who is questioned "in connection" with an investigation or proceeding) and Rule 112 (laying out particular requirements for the recording of questioning in particular cases, including giving the person questioned the right to clarify anything he said, and announcing the requirement that the tape be sealed in the presence of the person questioned or his counsel).

representative has not forgotten him. This approach, moreover, will allow the victim representative to gauge whether anybody has attempted to intimidate the witness, or whether there are any other factors rendering the witness unwilling to truthfully testify.

In the context of pre-trial meetings, it is important for all participants to be aware of the possibility that NGO representatives have early on interviewed the potential victim or witness. In the *Lubanga* case, for example, an NGO set up a program to de-mobilize putative child soldiers. In order to do so, the NGO offered any child who turned in his or her gun a "reintegration kit." Although the thought behind the program was of course noble, it understandably also incentivized lying among youths. In the course of interviewing the children, the NGO created reports of interviews that were factually at odds with subsequent interviews conducted by Prosecutors and the Victim Witness Unit. Even as to issues such as some of the putative child soldiers' ages, the NGO, the prosecution, the Victim Witness Unit, and the Chamber received conflicting information.

Victim representatives must, therefore, be vigilant in seeking out any prior statements, even in those cases in which the NGO refuses to turn them over. Moreover, victim representatives must request any such statements from the prosecution or defense, as they are obviously relevant to the witness' credibility, and because the other participants interested in confronting the witness at trial may wish to use them.

In *Lubanga*,[47] the Chamber considered a Prosecutor's interview of a witness scheduled to testify at a confirmation hearing. In the course of examining defense complaints about this interview, the Chamber distinguished two types of pre-trial contact with witnesses. The Chamber labeled one type of contact "witness familiarization," which the Chamber described as giving the witness an overview of what was likely to happen, how the ICC and the Chamber function, etc.[48] The Chamber described the second type of contact, namely "witness proofing," as having witnesses read their prior statements, refreshing the witness' memory concerning anticipated questions, and putting to the witness the same questions in the same order as the Prosecutor intends to ask them during the trial.[49]

---

47. Situation in the Democratic Republic of the Congo, Case No. ICC-0/04–01/06: *Decision on the Practices of Witness Familiarization and Witness Proofing* (November 8, 2006).

48. *Id.* at 8–12.

49. *Id.* at 19–20.

The *Lubanga* Chamber had little problem with "witness familiarization," provided the Victim and Witnesses Unit conducted the meeting, rather than the Prosecutor.[50] The second type of contact, however, found much more resistance. The Chamber, basing its decision in part on the national law of the Democratic Republic of Congo, and finding the Prosecutor's conduct inconsistent with the Code of Conduct of the Bar Council of England and Wales, declared the practice of more aggressive witness preparation/ "proofing" prohibited.[51]

This "ban on witness proofing," however, arguably only bars the "coaching" of possible trial witnesses, and may not prohibit all contact with potential witnesses made merely to enhance the fairness and efficiency of the proceedings by providing a better understanding of the information in the witness' possession. This latter type of meeting, particularly during early stages of the proceedings, offers the participants an opportunity to learn what information the witness has to offer. Such a meeting also permits the victim representative to gain a sense of whether this information is reliable and probative; interviews of this kind can easily be distinguished from the type of "proofing"—in the sense of "coaching" or "rehearsing"—prohibited by the *Lubanga* Chamber. As practitioners with experience in criminal trials know, such properly-conducted pre-trial meetings enable the participants to determine whether the witness will in fact be able to present relevant evidence at trial.

A 2008 ruling by the Chamber, however, once again placed doubt on whether trial witness interviews are permitted.[52] The Trial Chamber ruled that "parties" (presumably, though not necessarily, including victims) intending to call witnesses may not "hold discussions" with those witnesses about "topics that are to be dealt with in court during their evidence or the exhibits which may be produced."[53] The Chamber went on to state that witnesses,

---

50. *Id.* at 17–20.

51. *Id.* at 17–20; *see also* Case No. IT-05-87-T: *Decision on Ojdanic Motion to Prohibit Witness Proofing* (December 12, 2006), at 18 (ruling that witness proofing "assists (a) in providing a 'detailed review [of relevant and irrelevant facts] in light of the precise charges to be tried'; (b) in aiding 'the process of human recollection'; (c) in 'enabling more accurate, complete, orderly and efficient presentation of the evidence of a witness in the trial'; and (d) in identifying and putting the Defence on notice of differences in recollection thereby preventing undue surprise . . . .").

52. *See* Situation in the Democratic Republic of the Congo, Case No. II-01/04-01/06: *Decision Regarding the Protocol on the Practices to be used to Prepare Witnesses for Trial* (May 23, 2008).

53. *Id.* at 15–16.

however, were entitled to receive copies of any prior statements they made in order to "refresh potentially fallible memories."[54] The Chamber distinguished such permissible reviewing of prior statements from "evidence-checking"—"Any discrepancies [between the statement and the witness' present recollection] should be ventilated in court rather than being discussed and recorded shortly before the witness gives evidence. The Chamber is more likely to identify the truth if the witness explains any reservations about the written account during their oral testimony. . . ."[55] In light of this reasoning, it appears that the Chamber will, at present, rule improper any attempts by victim representatives to "prep" a witness' testimony prior to trial.[56]

It is of course also possible that the Court in the future will reverse course and permit more expansive witness preparation, particularly given that the rulings to date are non-binding and have been subject to heated debate and some controversy. Such a change should be welcomed, since the benefits of such pre-trial encounters are considerable. Proper pre-trial witness interviews permit the victim representative to evaluate the witness' personality, knowledge, and recollection of the relevant facts, and the witness' ability to verbalize those recollections.[57] During such sessions, the victim representatives can also give the witness a sense, from the victim representative's perspective, of what to expect during the trial. Witnesses, after all, are likely to be insecure about appearing in a strange environment with unfamiliar rules, and will therefore typically welcome such a preview.

Of course, as previously noted, the above-described ICC rulings to date only relate to interviewing *identified* witnesses prior to trial. They do not prevent victim representatives from interviewing *potential* witnesses prior to the formal launch of an ICC investigation. Consider also that Articles 3 and

---

54. *Id.* at 19–20.

55. *Id.*

56. *See also* Situation in the Democratic Republic of the Congo, Case No. II-01/04-01/06: *Decision Regarding the Practices Used to Prepare and Familiarise Witnesses for Giving Testimony at Trial* (November 30, 2007), at 22–23 (expressing concern that "preparation of witnesses" may "diminish what would otherwise be helpful spontaneity during the giving of evidence by a witness. The spontaneous nature of testimony can be of paramount importance to the Court's ability to find the truth, and the Trial Chamber is not willing to lose such an important element in the proceedings.").

57. A word of caution on note-taking: If the representative, or one of his colleagues, takes verbatim notes of what the witness says, those notes may be discoverable. If, however, the notes relate only to impressions and legal conclusions, then they will probably not have to be handed over as part of pre-trial discovery. *See generally* Rule 81(1) (providing that internal documents prepared for purposes of the investigation or trial are *not* discoverable).

13 of the European Convention on Human Rights, as interpreted by the European Court of Human Rights, require the government (and therefore Prosecutors) to investigate criminal cases fully.[58] Prosecutors, and perhaps victim representatives attempting to independently uncover relevant information, could thus argue by analogy that, to comply with the affirmative obligation to properly investigate a case, they must assure themselves personally of the veracity and accuracy of the information provided by the various witnesses.

Considering that NGOs are often the first to take victim statements, moreover, and that some of these NGOs have refused to turn these statements over to the prosecution, the defense, or the victim representatives, the importance of gaining a full and unfiltered understanding of the victims' knowledge, and basis for such knowledge, is paramount. Thus, the victim representative should, within the permissible bounds discussed above, pursue an opportunity to speak to potential witnesses in order to enhance the truth-seeking process, and to ensure that the Chamber's time is not wasted with potentially unnecessary questioning.

That said, a word of caution is certainly in order. Victim representatives, even if only meeting potential witnesses or interviewing witnesses prior to the Prosecutor initiating formal proceedings, must proceed carefully and conservatively when conducting any interviews or meetings. The victim representative's adversaries in any future cross-examination will naturally, and appropriately, inquire into the substance and nature of the discussions between the victim representative, the victim representative's investigator, and the witness. The purpose of these inquiries by opposing counsel or the Chamber is to determine whether a victim representative exerted any inappropriate pressure on the witness, or whether the witness changed his version of events as a result of being coached. Such cross-examination is entirely appropriate and justified, and victim representatives should therefore expect in-court inquiry into the nature and circumstances of their interactions with victims.

The most effective, and most ethical, way to commence such a witness meeting is to explicitly instruct the witness that he is only expected to tell the truth, and that the victim representative is not coaching the victim or asking the victim to alter his testimony. In fact, it is sound practice to draft a

---

58. *See generally Tanrikulu v. Turkey*, Case No. 1999-IV EUR. Ct. H.R. 459, 487–88 ("[T]he duty to investigate is not confined to cases where it has been established that the killing was caused by an agent of the state."); *see also* Alastair Mowbray, *Duties of Investigation Under European Convention on Human Rights*, 51 ICLQ 437 (2002).

short, standardized letter, written in the witness' native tongue, summarizing these reciprocal expectations, and to have the witness review, sign, and date the letter prior to commencing the interview. This procedure minimizes subsequent questions concerning the instructions given to, or expectations created in, the witness. If, during a hearing or cross-examination, opposing counsel claims a particular witness met with the victim representative, and that as a result his testimony was improperly influenced, the victim representative need simply ask the witness to repeat the admonitions given at the outset of the meeting to effectively deflect this attack.

Properly interviewing a witness permits the victim representative to understand the evidence, and allows for a more effective streamlining of the case. However, in the final analysis there is still a shortage of reliable guidance on what the Chamber will likely rule permissible in terms of witness contact during the early stages of the investigation. It, therefore, bears repeating that victim representatives must proceed with exceeding caution when it comes to having pre-trial contact with potential witnesses, and must carefully abide by the ICC's restrictions.

The following are some basic witness interview guidelines for victim representatives and their investigators:

— Ensure that any translators facilitating the meeting are properly qualified, and are capable of providing accurate translation.
— Research the latest rulings to verify the contemporary state of the law regarding meetings with witnesses and victims.
— Be sure that the potential witness is meeting with the victim representative freely and voluntarily, and note ("paper") this either in a report, or through a consent or agreement-to-cooperate/meet form.
— At the outset, give the potential witness a sense of the topics to be covered, and probe the extent of his knowledge concerning these topics. The victim representative should *not*, however, coach the victim or witness by, for example, telling him what to say. Continue to emphasize that the only expectation of the potential witness is that he will tell the truth to the Chamber and/or the investigators (depending on the stage of the proceedings).
— Never make any promises of benefits, and always ask a colleague, investigator, or other person to be present as a "prover" when talking to a potential witness. That way, any claims of having threatened, coached, or made promises to the potential witness, or of having engaged in any other misconduct relating to the potential witness, can be rebutted.

- Avoid casual interaction with the potential witness, and never say anything to him that should not be repeated from the witness stand, or in some other formal forum.
- Explain the trial process to the potential witness in simple and lay terms. Put the potential witness in contact with staff of the Victim and Witness Unit, as appropriate.
- Be mindful of the difficult task faced by the potential witness, and of the risk that the mere fact of the questioning may inherently be re-traumatizing.
- Go over the key sequences of events in a logical and easily followable manner that works for the victim representative and for the potential witness.
- Show the potential witness the relevant exhibits.
- Make sure the potential witness understands that he must answer all questions truthfully. And because "the truth" may mean different things to different people, also ask whether the potential witness personally perceived the events at issue; this avoids the situation encountered, for example, in Rwanda in which witnesses at trial described events they had learned about from others.
- Ensure that the potential witness knows that it is acceptable to admit he has spoken with the victim representative.
- Maintain any records of interviews, and be prepared to turn them over to the Chamber or to the other participants. Consider, also, video or audio taping the interviews (or at least the statement portion of the interview), provided this process will not distract the interviewee, or otherwise be counter-productive.

F. Self-Representation and the Corresponding Threat to the Historic Record

One issue that is the subject of considerable ongoing controversy is whether an accused has, or should have, a right to represent himself (that is, proceed *pro se*) when charged in an international tribunal. Victim representatives must be familiar with the ICC provisions relating to self-representation, as well as the potential problems occurring when a defendant elects to represent himself. As discussed below, vivid examples of how self-representation can undermine the dignity of the proceedings and the creation of a neutral historic record abound. Victim representatives must therefore remain alert to the dangers of this procedure, and must be prepared to step in and voice their objections to an accused's continued self-representation if that accused is abusing the privilege, and, in so doing, threatens to undermine the victims' interests.

By way of some background, Article 14(3)(d) of the International Covenant on Civil and Political Rights ("ICCPR"), as well as the articles and rules of the *ad hoc* international tribunals, accord an accused the right to defend himself in person *or* through legal assistance of his own choosing. Although international judges at various tribunals have accepted this as the general state of the law, the position is not universally endorsed.[59] There is, indeed, some weight to the argument that self-representation is *not* a fundamental right enshrined in international law (though, as discussed below, for better or worse it is a limited right accorded to all accused during ICC proceedings).

When observers raise the topic of self-representation in the international justice context, the discussion invariably turns to the now-infamous ICTY trial of Serbian strongman Slobodan Milosevic. During Milosevic's proceedings, the accused, himself a highly-educated lawyer, attempted to make a mockery of the process. Milosevic's almost daily outbursts, stream-of-consciousness speeches, intemperate challenges to the Court's jurisdiction, highly aggressive, threatening, and improper cross-examinations of witnesses, and overall lack of respect and compliance with Presiding Judge Richard May's orders made for at-times entertaining viewing, but also served to embolden Milosevic's supporters. Milosevic's efforts, in the end, to a significant extent succeeded at distorting the trial record and undermining the legitimacy and solemnity of the proceedings.

Milosevic's conduct turned what should have been a historic trial of the facts into a political stage, and in so doing caused excessive, and unnecessary,

---

59. Michael Scharf, *Self-Representation Versus Assignment of Defence Counsel before International Criminal Tribunals*, 4 J. INT'L CRIM. JUST. 31, 32 (2006) (questioning whether the ICCPR, customary international law, and the statutes of international tribunals can be "read as permitting an international criminal tribunal to appoint counsel over the objections of the defendant, as the [ICTR] held in the Barayagwiza case? How international tribunals answer this question in the future will have a significant effect on their ability to contribute to peace, reconciliation and the rule of law by establishing an historic record of atrocities committed by the former regime that is accepted by the target population.").

delays.[60] The victims' interest in creating a complete and impartial historic record of events in the end to a significant extent lost out because the Court did not control Milosevic.

Judicial failure to keep order, ensure that all participants exhibit the proper decorum, adhere to the rules of evidence and procedures, and strictly comply with the Court's orders can be highly disruptive in domestic trials.[61] However, in atrocity crimes cases, such shortfalls can have devastating effects. Not only are the stakes higher for the international community and for the credibility of institutions of international justice, but an accused who engages in theatrics and similar improper conduct threatens to cloud the entire trial record.[62]

Professor Michael Scharf, using the Milosevic example to describe the dangers of self-representation, made the following apt observations:

> In the case of Slobodan Milosevic . . . the tactic of self-representation enabled the former Serb leader to: (1) generate the illusion that he was a solitary individual pitted against an army of foreign lawyers and investigators, when in fact he had a squadron of legal counsel assisting him from behind the scenes; (2) make unfettered caustic speeches throughout the trial which were not restricted by the rules of relevance or subject to cross-examination by the prosecution; (3) repeatedly challenge the legitimacy of the proceedings and treat the witnesses, Prosecutors, and judges in a manner that would earn ordinary Defence Counsel expulsion from the courtroom. [O]pinion polls in Serbia indicate that [this conduct has] had the effect of convincing the majority of the Serb people that this trial was unfair and that [Milosevic] was not guilty of the charges.[63]

---

60. Of course, the length and somewhat disjointed structure of the 108-paragraph 1999 Second Amended Indictment against Milosevic and his four top aides did not help matters in this regard. *See generally* www.icty.org/x/cases/slobodan_milosevic/ind/en/mil-2ai011029e.htm. The indictment charged the defendants with deportation (a crime against humanity), two counts of murder (a crime against humanity and a violation of the customs of war, respectively), and one count of persecution (a crime against humanity). The theories of liability were command responsibility and personal responsibility. Absent from the indictment, however, was a charge of genocide. *Id.*

61. *See, e.g., United States v. Mannie*, 509 F.3d 851 (7th Cir. 2007) (describing case in which accused's conduct "spiraled out of control" to such an extent that the co-defendant was granted a new trial).

62. *See* Scharf, *supra* note 59, at 33.

63. *Id.* at 32.

Critics of the right to self-representation contend that the Court should compel the accused in war crimes trials to work through counsel. They reason that such representation will reduce the likelihood that an accused will act in a manner that disrupts the proceedings. These critics also argue that the nature of the required investigative efforts, and the inherent complexity of international atrocity crimes litigation—demanding a fluid knowledge not only of the specific hybrid substantive and procedural rules governing the Court, but also of international humanitarian law, comparative law, and oral and written advocacy skills—markedly distinguish such trials from ordinary domestic criminal cases. Permitting an accused to represent himself in such an international forum makes it more likely that he will engage in dilatory tactics, attempt to undermine the legitimacy of the proceedings, and otherwise seek to prevent an orderly trial.[64] Moreover, in almost all cases where an accused represents himself, the Chamber will be forced to proactively participate in the proceedings in order to ensure a fair trial, thereby arguably involving itself more than is desirable, or appropriate, in the actual litigation of the adversarial proceeding.[65]

The ICTY's Trial Chamber in the trial of Serbian ultra-nationalist paramilitary leader Vojislav Seselj echoed these concerns when it ruled that the accused was to receive appointed counsel over his objections:

> [T]he complex legal, evidential, and procedural issues that arise in a case of this magnitude may fall outside the competence even of legally qualified accused, especially where that accused is in detention without access to all the facilities he may need. Moreover, the Tribunal has a

64. *Id.* at 33–40 ("[T]he underlying purpose of the defendant's right to defend himself in person or through legal assistance of his own choosing; is to ensure a fair trial—an objective that can best be met in cases of former leaders accused of international crimes by assigning the defendant a highly qualified attorney who is vigilantly committed to representing his client's interests."), *citing* M. Cherif Bassiouni, *Human Rights in the Context of Criminal Justice: Identifying International Procedural Protections and Equivalent Protections in National Constitutions*, 3 DUKE J. COMPARATIVE & INT'L LAW 283 (1993) ("[T]he right to self-representation complements the right to counsel and is not meant as a substitute thereof. . . . [R]epresentation of counsel is not only a matter of interest to the accused, but it is also paramount to due process of the law and to the integrity of the judicial process.").

65. *See generally* Decision on the Application of Samuel Hinga Norman for Self-Representation Under Article 17(4)(d) of the Statute of the Special Court, Sam Hinga Norman (SCSL-10-14-T), Trial Chamber (June 8, 2004), at § 26.

legitimate interest in ensuring that the trial proceeds in a timely manner without interruptions, adjournments or disruptions.[66]

The argument that self-representation is an absolute and universal right is itself a weak one. For one, civil law countries such as Germany and France do not permit defendants to represent themselves. Moreover, the European Court of Human Rights has ruled that, in the administration of justice, states are permitted to assign counsel over the defendant's objections.[67] In addition, even in common law jurisdictions, the right to self-representation is certainly not absolute.[68] The ICC and the various *ad hoc* tribunals of the past are, moreover, *sui generis* institutions not bound by rules and rulings made in predecessor tribunals. These institutions are armed with their own substantive and procedural rules, which include significant civil-law elements (the right to self-representation generally being a characteristic of common-law jurisdictions).[69]

Although self-representation, thus, may not be a right under international law, or be particularly popular among court observers, a plain-language reading[70] of the ICC's statutory language, specifically Article 67, nevertheless

---

66. Decision on Prosecution's Motion for Order Appointing Counsel to Assist Vojislav Seselj with His Defence, Seselj (IT-03–67-PT), Trial Chamber (May 9, 2003), at §21. Incidentally, the ICTY subsequently convicted Seselj of contempt, and sentenced him to 15 months incarceration, for in a book revealing the identities of three officially protected witnesses.

67. *See generally* MANFRED NOWAK, UN COVENANT ON CIVIL AND POLITICAL RIGHTS: CCPR COMMENTARY 259 (1993); *see also* Reasons for Decision on Assignment of Defence Counsel, Milosevic (IT-02–54-T), Trial Chamber (September 22, 2004), at § 33 ("If at any stage of a trial there is a real prospect that it will be disrupted and the integrity of the trial undermined with the risk that it will not be conducted fairly, then the Trial Chamber has a duty to put in place a regime which will avoid that. Should self-representation have that impact, we conclude that it is open to the Trial Chamber to assign counsel to conduct the defence case, if the Accused will not appoint his own counsel.").

68. *See generally Faretta v. California*, 422 U.S. 806, 834 n. 46 (1975) (holding that there is no absolute right to self-representation, and certainly no right "to abuse the dignity of the courtroom").

69. Scharf, *supra* note 59, at 36, *citing* Sean Murphy, *Progress and Jurisprudence in the International Criminal Tribunal for the Former Yugoslavia*, 93 AMERICAN J. OF INT'L LAW 80 (1999) ("The International Tribunal is, in fact, a *sui generis* institution with its own rules of procedure which do not merely constitute a transposition of national legal systems. The same holds for the conduct of the trial which, contrary to Defence arguments, is not similar to an adversarial trial, but is moving towards a more hybrid system.").

70. On the issues of statutory interpretation, the ICC follows the principal rule of interpretation set forth in Article 31(1) of the Vienna Convention on the Law of Treaties, which provides that "[a] treaty shall be interpreted in good faith in accordance with the ordinary meaning to be given to the terms of the treaty in their context and in the light of its object and purpose." The Court thus follows the textualist model, under which recourse

compels the conclusion that self-representation *is* a right the ICC grants to all accused. The Article states, in relevant part, that the accused has a right to a "public hearing conducted impartially, and to the following minimum guarantees, in full equality":

> [T]o conduct the defence *in person or* through legal assistance of the accused's choosing, to be informed, if the accused does not have legal assistance, of this right and to have legal assistance assigned by the Court in any case where the interests of justice so require, and without payment if the accused lacks sufficient means to pay for it....[71]

Regulation of the Registry 119(2), moreover, provides that the Registrar shall "provide appropriate assistance to a person *who has chosen to represent himself or herself.*"[72]

Article 67, thus, clearly grants the accused the right to self-representation,[73] but the right, like all rights, is subject to reasonable restrictions. The cross-reference to Article 63(2), for example, addresses disruptive behavior on the part of the accused:

> If the accused, being present before the Court, continues to disrupt the trial, the Trial Chamber may remove the accused and shall make provision for him or her to observe the trial *and instruct counsel* from outside the courtroom, through the use of communications technology, if required. Such measures shall be taken only in exceptional circumstances

---

to supplementary means of interpretation, including the *travaux preparatoires*, is only appropriate if the statutory language is ambiguous or obscure, or "leads to a result which is manifestly absurd or unreasonable." Situation in the Democratic Republic of the Congo In the Case of the Prosecutor v. Germain Katanga and Mathieu Ngudjolo Chui, Case No. ICC-01/04-01/07: *On the Appeal of the Prosecutor Against the "Decision on Evidentiary Scope of the Confirmation Hearing, Preventative Relocation and Disclosure under Article 67(2) of the Statute and Rule 77 of the Rules" of Pre-Trial Chamber I* (November 26, 2008), at 49.

71. Article 67(1)(d) (emphasis added).

72. Emphasis added.

73. There is one cannon of statutory interpretation that, at we know, rises above all others: If the text of a statute is unambiguous, then judicial inquiry is complete and the need to consult the statute's legislative history extinguishes. Here, Article 67 unambiguously accords the accused the right to represent himself. The text, therefore, settles the dispute definitively.

> after other reasonable alternatives have proved inadequate, and only for such duration as is strictly required.[74]

Article 63(2), therefore, provides the Chamber with some clear guidance on how to deal with an obstructive accused, permitting it to, as a last resort, remove the accused from the courtroom and limit the accused's participation to remotely observing the trial through a television. The accused can use communications technology, such as computers, to maintain contact with counsel as the trial proceeds.

Article 63(2), however, unfortunately fails to address removal of an accused who is proceeding *pro se*. Despite this oversight, it is certainly consistent with due process, and the ICC's statutory framework, to require an otherwise self-represented accused to communicate through in-court counsel in the manner envisioned by Article 63(2) if the accused's conduct forces the Chamber to remove him from the courtroom. These are, after all, circumstances created by the accused, and in such a case the accused's right to self-representation is forfeited, yielding to the institutional interests in a fair, balanced, and orderly trial.[75] In such a case, then, the Chamber must appoint stand-by counsel to represent the accused's in-court interests.

Another noteworthy quirk in the ICC's provisions is that an accused can only plead guilty after "sufficient consultation with defense counsel."[76] Although Article 65(1)(b) does not mention self-represented accused who want to plead guilty, this appears to simply be a drafting oversight. Including "if the accused is represented" at the end of Article 65(1)(b) would easily correct this issue. Provided the judges during the plea colloquy satisfy themselves that the accused understands the proceedings and his rights, and that his waiver of his trial rights is knowing and voluntary, accepting the self-represented accused's plea under Article 65, even as currently drafted, does not improperly deprive the accused of any rights or privileges.

---

74. Article 63(2) (emphasis added).

75. *See generally* Case of Barayagwiza, Decision on Defense Counsel Motion to Withdraw (ICTR-97–19-T) (November 2, 2000) (the court ruled that the statutory right to self-representation, pursuant to both international and certain domestic law, was not absolute, and noted that the purpose of assigned counsel is to "ensure that the Accused receives a fair trial").

76. Article 65(1)(b).

The danger a disruptive defendant poses to the creation of a credible historic record, and to the legitimacy of both his trial and the institution, is undeniable. Victim representatives, like the prosecutors, must therefore keep a close eye on the conduct of the self-represented accused. They must not hesitate to demand that the Chamber use its considerable discretion to enforce Article 63(2) in order to maintain the dignity of the institution, ensure the overall fairness of the trial, and prevent an obstructive defendant from derailing the proceedings and creating a muddled historic record of the events, or, even worse, making a mockery of the judicial system.

G. The Benefits of Guilty Pleas

Whether international tribunals and courts should grant the accused in atrocity-crimes cases the option of pleading guilty is a topic which has generated a surprising amount of controversy. On the upside, guilty pleas permit the accused to accept responsibility and avoid trial, while saving the prosecution and the court valuable time and resources. For these reasons, guilty pleas are routine for attorneys working in common law counties. (Indeed, approximately 97 percent of United States federal convictions taking place within one year of arrest are the result of defendants pleading guilty).[77]

International tribunals, however, have historically been leery of plea bargains, considering them to be inherently at odds with the symbolic purposes of international justice.[78] Plea agreements, the argument goes, permit the accused to take the "easy way out," allowing him to avoid being held to account in the public forum of a trial. As the caseloads of these international courts increased over the years, however, they have started to give accuseds the opportunity to plead guilty, and in some cases imposed reduced sentences in return for such guilty pleas.[79]

---

77. United States Dept. of Justice, Criminal Case Processing Statistics, www.ojp.usdoj.gov/bjs/cases.htm (2008).

78. *See, e.g.*, Statement by the President [of the ICTY] Made at a Briefing to Members of Diplomatic Missions 649, 652, IT/29 (February 11, 1994), *reprinted in* VIRGINIA MORRIS & MICHAEL SCHARF, AN INSIDER'S GUIDE TO THE INTERNATIONAL CRIMINAL TRIBUNAL FOR THE FORMER YUGOSLAVIA, Vol. 2 (1995) (ICTY President Antonio Cassese stating view that plea bargaining would be inappropriate in a Tribunal "charged with the task of trying persons accused of the gravest possible of all crimes").

79. *See, e.g.*, Sentencing Judgment, Plavsic (IT-00-39 & 40/1S), Trial Chamber III (February 27, 2003), at § 132 (in the prosecution of "Serbian Iron Lady" accused of, *inter alia*, committing

Article 65, titled "Proceedings on admission of guilt," has resolved this dispute by following the modern trend of permitting guilty pleas. Prior to accepting the accused's guilty plea, however, the Chamber must assure itself that the accused understands the nature and consequences of his admission of guilt,[80] that the accused voluntarily made the admission after sufficient consultation with defense counsel,[81] and that an adequate factual basis tracking the charging document supports the plea of guilty.[82] To the extent the Chamber determines that the interests of justice (or, critically, the interests of the victims) require a more complete presentation of the facts, the Chamber may ask the Prosecutor to present additional evidence, or can simply reject the accused's request and continue the trial in the ordinary course.[83]

Unlike in the United States, however, accused at the ICC cannot enter into "cooperation agreements" with the prosecution guaranteeing them reduced sentences. That said, the Chamber nevertheless can (and in most cases surely will) take an accused's contrition, acceptance of responsibility reflected by a plea of guilty, as well as any cooperation, into account when fashioning an appropriate sentence.

The statutorily mandated timing of ICC guilty pleas contains an unfortunate oversight, however. Article 65 cross-references Article 64(8)(a), but that Article only provides an accused the opportunity to plead guilty "[a]t the commencement of the trial." Whether the Chamber will permit an accused to plead guilty later in the litigation—once the accused has had more time to review the discovery and other evidence amassed against him, or otherwise realizes the strength of the prosecution's case or the futility of continuing his denials—is therefore unclear.

Permitting an accused to plead guilty, and to even receive a reduced sentence in return for his contrition or cooperation, although undoubtedly unpalatable to some victims, is a practice victim representative should, as a general matter, embrace. An accused's plea of guilty to the charged crimes permits the victim representatives and the Prosecutor to focus their

---

genocide, the accused was permitted to plead guilty in exchange for prosecution dropping charges; after admitting responsibility for the killing of tens of thousands of civilians, the accused, who refused to cooperate with the prosecution, was sentenced to a relatively paltry 11 years imprisonment).

80. Article 65(1)(b).

81. Article 65(1)(b).

82. Article 65(a)(c)(i)-(iii).

83. Article 65(4)(a) and (b).

limited resources on those accused who refuse to accept responsibility for their conduct (consider, in terms of this resource reallocation argument, that the typical ICTY and ICTR trial lasted over a year, and cost well over $50 million[84]). Guilty pleas also allow the prosecution to concentrate on investigating and charging new cases, rather than on proving a particular accused's guilt during a lengthy and costly trial, and reduce the administrative burdens on the Court. To the extent that the victims view the accused's factual admissions as overly narrow, incomplete, inaccurate, or otherwise insufficient, the victim representative, relying on Article 65(4), must petition the Court to either reject the plea,[85] or to request that the Prosecutor present (and the accused admit to) a more complete and accurate picture of the accused's factual guilt.[86] A guilty plea supported by such an adequate factual basis, therefore, should be welcomed as providing victims with a valuable piece of historic information that, to a significant extent, will erase doubts over the nature and extent of the accused's criminal conduct.

---

84. Scharf, *supra* note 59, at 1067. Note, however, that the calculations set forth in Part II, above, reveal that the cost of achieving even a *single* final conviction for a *single* defendant at the ICTY hovers in the neighborhood of $25 million.

85. As provided for in Article 65(4)(b).

86. *See* Article 65(4)(a).

PART XIII

The Main Trial

BY THE TIME OF THE ICC'S "MAIN TRIAL," the prepared victim representative will have a thorough understanding of his theory of the case, as well as of the full spectrum of relevant facts. The representative will have dealt with any outstanding discovery issues, compiled an order of proof, put together his trial notebook, drafted the appropriate motions to assure substantive participation, and addressed any remaining witness issues. Having laid this significant groundwork, the victim representative is now prepared to take on the challenges of actually litigating the case in the Trial Chamber.

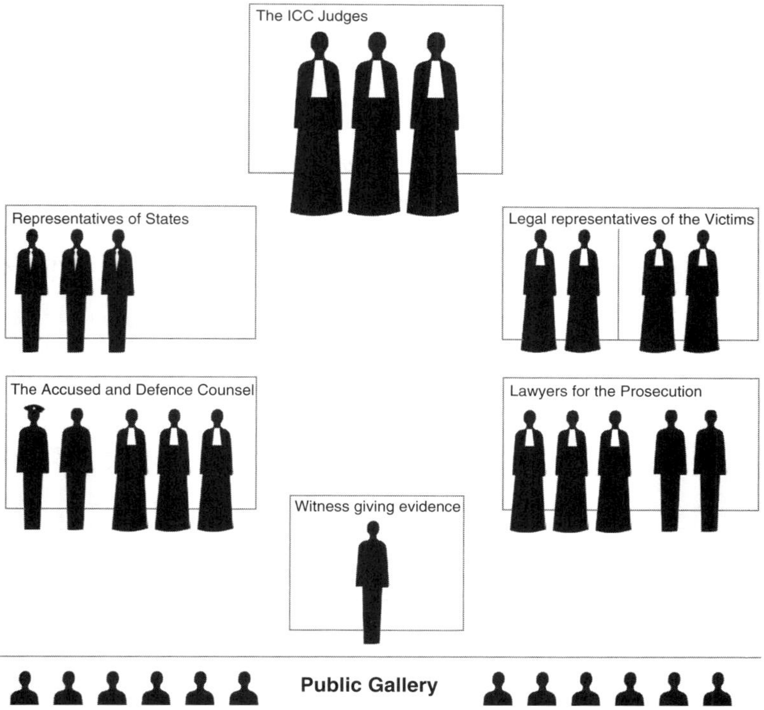

Layout of ICC Trial Chamber

'Victims Before the International Criminal Court. A Guide for the Participation of Victims in the Proceedings of the Court.' Copyright© International Criminal Court 2006.

A. Opening Statement

The opening statement formally begins the trial. In terms of substance and format, victim representatives can think of the opening as the first scene in a play. The opening, in that sense, paves the way to successful advocacy of the victims' interests. Victim representatives must carefully lay out their factual and legal positions during the opening, and demonstrate to the Chamber how the Prosecutor's evidence will establish both the accused's guilt, as well as the legitimacy of the victims' claims.

During the opening, the victim representative must describe for the Chamber his theory of the case in a manner that is "alive," well organized, and persuasive. The theory of the case should be clear and concise, highlighting the anticipated witnesses that are most important to the victims. The victim representative must never risk losing credibility in the eyes of the Chamber by overstating the evidence; first impressions count for much in the law, as well as in life.

The goal during this early stage of the proceedings is to gain the Chamber's attention, and to generate an appreciation for the aspects of the case most crucial to the victims. The Prosecutor's opening statement, after all, is unlikely to identify for the Chamber the specific evidence the victims believe is most critical, how that evidence fits within the elements of the charges, what evidence and theories have emerged since the Prosecutor's drafting of the charging documents, and the nuances of the victims' theory of the case. Opening statements, in short, are beneficial to both the Chamber and the participants, and victim representatives must, therefore, make separate applications for permission to deliver them.[1]

During the *Lubanga* case's confirmation hearing, the Pre-Trial Chamber gave victim representatives the opportunity to provide the Chamber with an opening statement.[2] Moreover, the Trial Chamber has confirmed that there is in fact a "presumption" that victims will receive the opportunity to deliver

1. Whether the Chamber will require the various teams of victim representatives to work together to present one comprehensive opening statement, or will instead permit each team to present their own discrete opening statement, will likely be decided on a case-by-case basis.

2. *See* Situation in the Democratic Republic of the Congo, Case No. ICC-01/04–01/06: *The Prosecutor v. Thomas Lubanga Dyilo, Confirmation of Charges Hearing* (November 9, 2006) (allowing 90 minutes each for the confirmation hearing opening statements of the prosecution and the legal representatives of the victims, and 135 minutes for the opening statement of the defense).

opening statements during the main trial.[3] That said, if the victims are permitted to deliver opening statements, the Chamber will likely also require them to provide it and the other participants with written outlines of their openings in advance.[4] How precise and inclusive these outlines must be will be determined on a case-by-case basis, but the Chamber at a minimum will likely expect the outlines to contain the victim representatives' main legal and factual points. Although one can certainly question the wisdom of the Chamber's decision to require the advance exchange of written opening outlines,[5] the rulings to date at a minimum reflect the Chamber's shared agreement that judges benefit from a concise, thought out, non-theatrical, and earnest opening statement.[6]

When organizing the opening statement, victim representatives must remember that judges tend to recall best what they hear first and last. This is called the rule of primacy and recency.[7] Victim representatives should therefore draft opening statements which are book-ended by the victims' strongest arguments. The victim representative should, in contrast, introduce the weakest portions of their case somewhere in the middle. "Fronting" the case's weakness in this manner, and placing the defensive aspect of the opening in the middle, takes the wind out of the defense's sails.

---

3. *See* Situation in the Democratic Republic of the Congo In the Case of Prosecutor v. Thomas Lubanga Dyilo, Case No. ICC-01/04–01/06: *Decision on Opening and Closing Statements* (May 22, 2008), at 7 (noting permissive nature of ICC provisions' language, such as Rule 89(1)'s permission to victims to make opening and closing statements).

4. *See generally* Situation in the Democratic Republic of the Congo In the Case of the Prosecutor v. Thomas Lubanga Dyilo, Case No. ICC-01/04–01/06: *Decision on the Applications by Victims to Participate in the Proceedings* (December 15, 2008), at 38 (requiring victim representatives to inform the Chamber of their intent to deliver opening and closing statements, and to provide the Chamber and the other participants with outlines seven days in advance of the commencement of trial).

5. *See* Judge Rene Blattman's dissent in Situation in the Democratic Republic of the Congo In the Case of Prosecutor v. Thomas Lubanga Dyilo, Case No. ICC-01/04–01/06: *Decision on Opening and Closing Statements* (May 22, 2008), at 10 ("I do not believe that the disclosure of these statements in advance is necessary in order for the Chamber to manage the case effectively and I am concerned that this requirement of disclosure takes away an important element of spontaneity which may undermine the goal of the trial to search for truth.").

6. *See* Rule 89(1) (vesting in the Chamber the discretion to permit victim representative to give opening statement).

7. "Both social scientists and lawyers have long debated how the order in which information is delivered influences the listener. Researchers suggest that we are more likely to believe the presentation or message we hear first (primacy) and remember the presentation or message we hear last (recency)." RICHARD LUKAS & K. BYRON MCCOY, THE WINNING EDGE: EFFECTIVE COMMUNICATION AND PERSUASION TECHNIQUES FOR LAWYERS 114 (1993), *citing* RONALD J. MATLON, COMMUNICATION IN THE LEGAL PROCESS (1988).

As one of the most critical aspects of the main trial, the opening statement must be fully developed and carefully prepared. Although the Chamber will, as noted above, likely require a written outline of the opening statement, the victim representative should not simply read, or rush through, the opening, but instead must speak in a manner that is relaxed, easy to understand, and persuasive. Victim representatives must also avoid acting as if they are the Prosecutor, or as if they intend to overly aggressively litigate the case; such an approach will immediately alienate the defense (concerned with maintaining the equality of arms and the fragile balance between the prosecution and the defense) and the prosecution (concerned with non-interference in its prosecutorial strategy). The Chamber is unlikely to appreciate any attempt by the victim representatives to go beyond the role the Chamber deems appropriate.

The opening statement, no matter how sound, will of course not by itself guarantee a positive outcome for the victim. However, a properly crafted opening will set the stage for such an outcome, providing the Chamber with a clear roadmap of the case by previewing how the anticipated evidence matches up with the elements of the charge and the victim representative's position.

Victim representatives should consider the following general guidelines for a persuasive opening statement:

- Present a clear and concise explanation of the most important facts proving the accused violated the law, as well as the victims' rights.
- As a default position, be deferential towards the Prosecutor, while emphasizing that there were actual living and breathing victims who suffered harm as a result of the crimes listed in the formal charging document.
- Carefully and strategically choose the subject and timing of divergence from the Prosecutor's position, and, if possible, seek to informally resolve any conflicts, or to come up with a compromise.
- Be humble, and accept the victim representative's more limited role in the proceedings.
- Remain aware that the defense and the Chamber will be concerned that the victim representative's participation not negatively impact the fairness of the proceedings by, for example, placing undue litigation burdens on the defense.
- Do not discuss in granular detail the content of every witness' anticipated testimony. The opening is not the time to argue the case. Rather, it is the first time for the Chamber to hear about the case.

— Provide a roadmap of the case, and refer to what will be established through the "evidence" or the "facts," i.e., "the evidence will show/prove" or "the facts will show/prove."
— Answer the six crucial questions: "Who, what, why, when, where, and how?"
— In most cases, explain the facts chronologically.
— Practice and rehearse the opening before a relative, friend, or colleague who will honestly critique the statement.
— Recognize that the opening is a prologue or synopsis of what the victim representative expects to follow.
— Understate the case rather than overstating it. The defense, whether at the guilt phase or at the sentencing, may well point out things that the victim representative promised in the opening, but did not establish at trial.
— Admit weaknesses to enhance credibility. The victim representative must explain, without vouching for the credibility of any witness, what the victim representative expects the evidence to show.
— Explain for the Chamber's benefit how non-tainted testimony and exhibits will corroborate the key witnesses.

The victim representative can structure an effective opening as follows:

1. "If the Chamber please . . . ."
2. Acceptance or rejection of the issues as defined by the defense and the Prosecutor, plus a summary of any additional issues the victim representative anticipates raising, including particularly how the accused harmed the victims.[8]
3. A cohesive, succinct, confident, and non-argumentative reference to anticipated deficiencies of the defense case, plus a summary of the anticipated evidence. If appropriate, include reference to weaknesses in the victims' case, and touch on how the victim representative will overcome these weaknesses.

---

8. *See* Appeals Chamber, Situation in the Democratic Republic of the Congo In the Case of the Prosecutor v. Thomas Lubanga Dyilo, Case No. ICC-01/04–01/06: *Judgment on the Appeals of The Prosecutor and The Defence against Trial Chamber I's Decision on Victims' Participation of 18 January 2008* (July 11, 2008) (ruling that, in order to reach the trial stage, victims will have to file written applications demonstrating (1) that they are victims within the meaning of Rule 85; and (2) that, pursuant to Article 68(3), they have personal interests that are affected by the trial).

4. A brief statement focusing on why the victims deem their participation necessary. The drafters of the Rome Statute, after all, included victim participation not only for the sake of reparations, but also to advance more general restorative goals in the context of post-conflict justice, such as to help victims break cycles of violence by giving them a voice, and to rehabilitate and empower them, allowing them to regain some sense of normalcy in their lives. Victim representatives must not forget these goals, and, therefore, must present robust and well-considered opposition to the Prosecutor or defense if they seek to marginalize victims.
5. A conclusion that indicates that at the close of the case the victim representative will ask the Chamber to render a finding in favor of the victims.

A sample condensed outline of a victim representative's opening statement follows:

"This case is about the January 31, 2003, murder of 20 civilians living in village A. The prosecution will establish that the man responsible for these criminal attacks is Mr. Kalady."

* * *

"During the course of this trial you will hear the testimony of. . . ." [summarize the basic facts the witnesses will (or should) establish].

* * *

"There is little question that someone is responsible for the bloody attacks on [victim groups], and we firmly believe the responsible party to be this accused, sitting in this courtroom on this day. Justice requires that this Chamber hold Mr. Kalady accountable for his horrific and base deeds."

* * *

"If this Chamber at the end of the evidence agrees with the facts as we have described them, and concludes that Mr. Kalady is in fact responsible for these atrocities, then we will stand prepared to assist the Chamber's understanding of why the victims, who stand humbly before you, are entitled to a just sentence in this case, as well as to reparations, for the horrible harms they suffered at the hands of Mr. Kalady and his henchmen."

If the Chamber permits it, victim representatives should use demonstrative evidence ("visual aids") during the opening to give the Chamber a more tangible understanding of the case from the victims' perspective.[9] Psychologists have found that people learn much more from seeing and hearing, rather than from hearing alone.[10] The use of demonstrative evidence will help focus the Chamber's attention and maintain its interest, and can be used to explain matters relevant to the trial. Consider, for example, an aerial photograph of the area where the alleged crimes took place, or a chart outlining the hierarchy of a particular military unit and the accused's position within that hierarchy. Demonstrative evidence may also include items such as models, diagrams, sketches, and objects at issue. Applications for permission to use such exhibits must be made to the Chamber at least 14 days, and to the other parties at least 7 days, prior to the intended use.[11]

B. Direct Examination of Witnesses

The purpose of direct examination (also referred to as "examination-in-chief") is to "adduce by the putting of proper questions . . . relevant and admissible evidence which supports the contentions of the party who calls the witness."[12] Direct examination is the first opportunity the examining lawyer has to present testimony and evidence that is most relevant and most likely to help move the case to a positive outcome.

The ICC Rules set out the order of examination for prosecutors and the defense, but (non-binding) developing ICC practice in the *Lubanga* trial has

---

9. *See generally* Situation in the Democratic Republic of the Congo In the Case of the Prosecutor v. Thomas Lubanga Dyilo, Case No. ICC 01/04–01/06: *Public Decision On the Use of Visual Aids* (December 2, 2008) (Trial Chamber ruling that any proposed visual aids must be disclosed to the other side at least 7 days prior to their use at trial, and must be provided to the Registry in electronic format at least 3 days prior to its use at trial; visual aids may be used during opening and closing statements to "enhance[s] the presentation of previously disclosed evidence." Application to use visual aids must be made to Chamber no less than 14 days prior to their intended use at trial).

10. *See generally* Cheryl Riechmann-Hruska, *Differences in Learning*, 24 EQUITY & EXCELLENCE 25–26 (1989).

11. *See generally* Situation in the Democratic Republic of the Congo In the Case of the Prosecutor v. Thomas Lubanga Dyilo, Case No. ICC 01/04–01/06: *Public Decision on the Use of Visual Aids* (December 2, 2008), at 7–8.

12. Situation in the Democratic Republic of the Congo, Case No. ICC 01/04-01/06: *Decision on the Manner of Questioning Witnesses by the Legal Representatives of Victims* (September 16, 2009), at 14 (*quoting* ARCHBOLD, CRIMINAL PLEADING, EVIDENCE AND PRACTICE 1304 (2009)).

been that the victim representatives typically ask limited questions after the prosecution has concluded its examination of a witness, but before the defense has begun its cross-examination. (The ICC's legal framework, although it speaks on certain trial procedures, in fact provides no formal guidance on the manner of questioning.)[13] In each case, however, the victim representative must first file a request outlining the proposed questioning; such a request is ideally filed only *after* consultation with the prosecution. This customary procedure is, of course, consistent with the prevailing view that victim representatives augment the prosecutorial function.

1. Purpose of Direct Examination: Telling the Story of the Case from the Victims' Perspective

The fundamental purpose of any witness examination, of course, is to elicit information. The direct examination is vitally important to both the victim representative and the Prosecutor (who, naturally, at all times has the burden of proof, and must prove each and every element of the charged crimes). The ICC regulations and rulings, as discussed above, provide for court-sanctioned direct and adverse examination of trial witnesses by victim representatives. The ability to examine witnesses in open court is, indeed, the most critical skill of a trial lawyer in any type of adversarial justice system. The testimony must be clear and credible. The evidence is essentially worthless, from an evidentiary standpoint, if the Chamber does not understand or believe it.

The basic format for conducting a direct examination is an interrogative dialogue with the witness. The direct examination tells the story of the case in the manner that will be most persuasive to the Chamber. It is, therefore, important at the outset for the victim representative to candidly evaluate the weaknesses of the testimony he intends to elicit, and to be sure not to offer testimony that is, or will be perceived as, unnecessarily cumulative.

To prepare the direct examination properly, the victim representative must review the law and determine the elements necessary to establish the victim's case. Next, the victim representative must outline the key points

13. *See* Situation in the Democratic Republic of the Congo, Case No. ICC 01/04-01/06: *Decision on the Manner of Questioning Witnesses by the Legal Representatives of Victims* (September 16, 2009), at 13–14 (noting that, although the parties have developed the custom of using the Romano Germanic terms "examination-in-chief," "cross-examination," and "re-examination," those terms do not appear in the Rules or Articles).

sought to be elicited through the testimony of each witness. Such a general outline should provide the solid foundation necessary for additional testimony, or the introduction of exhibits or demonstrative exhibits.

Preparing such an outline permits the victim representative to coordinate with the Prosecutor so that the victim representative does not inadvertently undermine the Prosecutor's strategy without good reason. Although such coordination presently is not a common occurrence, and although the defense perceives the prosecutorial function as generally at odds with the victims' interests, there are indications that the victim representatives are beginning to discuss what questions they intend to ask and to otherwise informally collaborate with the prosecution. This is a very promising and important development that should be encouraged, since there is no profit to either the victim or the prosecution in maintaining the adversarial relationship that marked victim-prosecution interactions during the early years of the Court. If such cooperation requires the victim representative to, in some sense, pull back a bit in terms of the nature and extent of the victim's hoped-for presentation, then this in most cases will prove to be a worthwhile accommodation yielding benefits down the road. The prosecution, after all, must be victim-friendly, or at least victim-tolerant, if the victim is to get the most out of the proceedings.

During the trial, the victim representative should develop the direct examination through the use of conversational—but not overly informal—language. Victim representatives should prepare a separate file for each witness that includes the outline, copies of the exhibits to be used with the witness, the relevant interview record/statement(s), and any working notes relating to the witness. Mechanically reading questions to the witness should be avoided. The outline should be used as a reference, but not as a script. Assuming victim representatives are permitted to present witnesses and to conduct direct examinations, they must remember to guide the witnesses through the testimony so as not to waste the Chamber's and other participants' time.

The questions must be kept short, simple, and straightforward. If working through a translator, the victim representative must be sure to speak slowly and clearly. Obvious advice, perhaps, but even experienced lawyers will attest that it is difficult to conduct examinations through translators.

One method of developing an effective direct examination is to imagine oneself as an investigative reporter at the scene of a breaking story. The victim representative should wipe out his knowledge of the case, and attempt to become educated on the issues through the witnesses on the stand. He should ask the types of questions a reporter or investigator would ask to become fully informed of what happened, bearing in mind that the victim representative's more limited role of filling in the evidentiary gaps and watching over the clients' interests. This technique will allow the victim representative to view the case from the Chamber's perspective. The victim representative may know everything about the case, but the Chamber is hearing the full scope of the testimony for the first time at trial. And it is the Chamber—not the Prosecutor—that needs to decide the lofty matter of guilt or innocence.

The Chamber's focus during direct examination should be on the witness, not on the lawyer. The majority of questions should be open-ended, allowing the witness to provide the answer. If the representative's question is difficult to formulate, he should return to the basics: "Who, what, why, when, where, and how?" The victim representative should stay focused on the testimony to be elicited,[14] listen to the answers, and at all times appear interested and engaged in the testimony the witness provides.

2. Structuring the Direct Examination

The simplest approach to structuring the direct examination is to do so chronologically, starting at the beginning of a series of events that the victim representative hopes to establish through a given witness. The victim representative can then walk the witness and the Chamber through the events leading up to the charged crimes and the arrest of the accused. This approach works particularly well for most "primary" witnesses, such as investigators.

Alternatively, the victim representative should consider starting in the middle of the story, emphasizing only a particular topic or piece of evidence. This works best for corroborating witnesses, evidence custodians, witnesses to the crime, criminal confederates, and the like.

In any event, the victim representative should remember to have his outline handy and to only cover those matters the Prosecutor either neglected, or that are otherwise vital to the clients' interests. The victim representative should make sure that his arguments do not undermine the Prosecutor's

---

14. Although some attorneys write out their questions, an alternative approach is to simply outline the discrete bits of information the victim representative wishes to elicit. This procedure keeps the questioning flexible, and ensures that the victim representative gets the desired *information* from the witness (rather than simply assuring that the victim representative asks all of the *questions* he outlined).

position unless the Prosecutor, or the evidence, forces the victim representative's hand.

To the extent possible, the victim representative should open and close the direct examination with the strongest testimony. As noted previously, psychologists have established that people remember best what they hear first and last. The victim representative must anticipate and localize the most troubling, harmful, or difficult testimony in the middle of the presentation to diffuse his opposition's anticipated cross-examination. Additionally, for consistency's sake the witness order should match the order of events discussed in the opening.

Consider also issues of foundation. Even under the ICC's permissive evidentiary rules, certain facts must be in evidence before other testimony will be ruled admissible. Similarly, certain evidence must be introduced through an investigator or evidence custodian before another witness can comment on it. If possible, the victim representative should put strong witnesses in key spots, and position weaker witnesses between strong witnesses.

3. Conducting the Direct Examination

If a witness gives an unexpected answer, the victim representative should remain professional and calm, never showing frustration or annoyance. Although lawyers who gesticulate, nod when things are going their way, shake their heads when things are not, and raise their voices may feel they are passionately making a point, the reality is that they are more likely to be distracting the Chamber and the witness.

The victim representative should conduct the direct examination with certain guidelines in mind:

— Have prepared witness folders, complete with copies of exhibits and prior statements, ready.
— Think about the questions ahead of time. Write them out, if necessary, but do not read them in a monotone or mechanical voice.
— Ask questions in a natural, conversational tone, and be prepared to deviate from the "script" if the answers given are different than expected. That said, be sure not to go beyond the areas the Chamber has given permission to inquire into.
— Questions should be short, simple, and understandable to the witness and Chamber on both direct and cross-examination. Only ask one clear

question at a time. On direct examination, the witness' inability to understand the questions will only exacerbate his insecurity and anxiety.

— Be mindful of areas that are consistent with the Prosecutor's theory of the case, but that the Prosecutor may have missed or intentionally left out. If possible, coordinate such questioning with the Prosecutor prior to the examination.
— Make sure that witnesses answer key questions.
— Have at hand the order of proof chart that lists the elements, and identifies what each witness is going to say in support of those elements. Do not ask questions of a witness who does not have testimony related to one of the elements of the crime, to the restitution issues, or to a defense.
— Never waste the Chamber's time. Always have enough witnesses ready to fill the day. Be organized. Pre-mark exhibits. Test all equipment ahead of time, and retest it every day.
— Sparingly use a technique called "looping" to emphasize particular parts of the testimony. That is, repeat all or part of a prior answer in the form of the next question. (For example, "You testified that you saw the accused on the outskirts of your village on the day of the attack. How were you able to recognize him?").
— Use transition statements to alert the Chamber of a shift to a new topic (for example, "Now I would like to turn your attention to the morning of January 25").
— Ask general leading questions to establish background (more on this later).
— Elicit enough detail to tell the story and rebut defense theories, but do not go overboard and create inconsistencies.
— Remember always that the Chamber may be hearing some of the information for the very first time, and, in some cases, a given panel will contain judges who are not particularly familiar with criminal litigation. Develop the testimony gradually and with sufficient detail to allow the Chamber time to fully digest it.
— Listen to the answers and remain flexible. Be prepared to change topics if the witness brings up a point deserving, or requiring, follow-up.
— Clarify points brought out by the prosecution, defense, or the Chamber, as needed.
— Control the witness within the parameters permitted by the Court. Interrupt the "runaway witness" who is getting ahead of himself (e.g., "Sir, let me just stop you for a moment to clarify a few points. . . . ").

— Protect the witness: Anticipate cross-examination, and organize the testimony to minimize vulnerabilities.
— Take great care to protect the trial record. Make sure the witness' answers are complete. Do not use shorthand. (For example, a given witness answers: "Yes, it was that one." Follow up with: "When you say 'that one,' are you referring to the village outlined in red depicted in "Aerial Photo 1?"). Think about whether the record would make sense to someone reading the transcription. If the victim makes special references or uses gestures, have the witness explain "for the record" what he is doing or what he is referring to.
— Anticipate objections or evidentiary issues the opposing party may raise.
— Avoid duplicative testimony or other unnecessary testimony resulting in diminished returns.
— Sound and look interested at all times. The Chamber certainly will not listen to the testimony if the lawyer is not listening.
— Keep an eye on the Chamber. Gauge the Chamber's reactions and level of interest, and adjust accordingly.
— Do not rustle papers or move around unnecessarily.
— Keep the attention on the witness. Minimize the use of body language, as the Chamber may be composed of judges who, for cultural reasons, may be unfamiliar or uncomfortable with certain physical gestures.

The basic direct examination of an investigator might begin as follows:

— Please state your name.
— Where are you presently employed?
— How long have you been so employed?
— Are you assigned to investigate the activities that occurred on May 12, 2002, in a particular region?
— What area did that assignment cover?
— Where were you assigned on [date]?
— What did you do/what happened/whom did you interview?

Ask the investigator whether he can identify the accused in the courtroom, and have him describe what the accused is wearing so that the official trial record is clear that the investigator has positively identified the accused. If the investigator provides a positive identification, ask the Chamber to verify on the record that the investigator identified the accused.

The direct examination approach should be varied depending on the subject matter the victim representative elicits. For example:

a. Official Witnesses

Make strategic use of the investigator who can provide a good overview at the start of the proceedings, or who may serve as an excellent summary witness at the end. The investigator may need to testify twice (with the Chamber's permission) to address specific issues. Do not call every possible investigator, as this can lead to unnecessary inconsistencies in the testimony, to say nothing of delay, inefficiency, and distraction. Think about which witnesses will admit the bulk of the evidence, and identify those witnesses who can corroborate important points. Make sure to explain terms of art. Establish experience and expertise when necessary, and always pay attention to the "tone" of the testimony.

b. Third-Party Witnesses

Establish clearly a witness' ability to perceive the events supporting the charge. Anticipate, and deal with, any inconsistencies among witnesses. Highlight witnesses with no personal stake in the outcome, or witnesses who are reluctant to testify. If the witness is also a victim, deal up front with issues of anger and revenge.

c. Cooperating Witnesses

Disclose all information relating to a cooperating witness. Discuss the individual's criminal background, prior inconsistent statements, potential substance abuse, protected status, anger at the accused, potential benefits from cooperating, and other relevant areas worthy of probing. Bring out the fact that the witness is aware of the consequences of testifying falsely. Corroborate the testimony, whenever possible, with pictures, documents, additional testimony from other witnesses, etc.

Try to introduce any tape or video recordings of an earlier witness interview using a law enforcement official or investigator present when the tape or video was made to establish the tape or video's authenticity and probative value.

d. Expert Witnesses

The first objective in presenting expert evidence on direct examination is to establish for the Chamber the expert's experience and expertise in an easily understandable way. The victim representative should, when possible, use approved visual aids or common-sense analogies to explain complex or potentially confusing testimony. The victim representative must explain technical terms and listen for words the witness needs to define as the testimony progresses. The Chamber will likely provide the necessary cues.[15]

4. Leading Questions

Leading questions are based on actual facts in evidence, and the victim representative should take care to use them sparingly to guide the witness' narrative during direct examination. Leading questions can be based on previous statements of witnesses or the accused, or on facts that emerged during the investigation. The primary purpose of leading questions during an examination is to point out or rebut inconsistencies in prior statements, or between the witness' statement and other evidence, in a focused and time-saving manner that limits the witness' ability to avoid or deflect the question posed.

There is nothing inherently improper about using leading questions during direct examination in ICC proceedings, provided that the lawyer is not "testifying" through the questions, and that the Chamber has not registered any concerns. That said, at least one Trial Chamber has ruled that leading questions, unless unopposed, are generally inappropriate during the direct examination of a witness.[16] The Chamber, however, also noted that leading questions can be appropriate during cross-examination, where the objective is to raise pertinent questions concerning relevant issues, or to attack the witness' credibility.[17]

The Trial Chamber in *Lubanga*, however, noted that victim representatives, "[a]s participants in the proceedings, rather than parties, . . . have *a unique and separate role* which calls for a *bespoke approach* to the manner in which they ask questions."[18] "[D]epending on the circumstances, the alleged

---

15. In some cases, the Chamber may invite the victim representative to suggest questions to be asked of the Chamber's expert. *See* Situation in the Democratic Republic of the Congo in the Case of The Prosecutor v. Thomas Lubanga Dyilo, Case No. ICC-01/04–01/06: *Instruction to the Court's Expert on Child Soldiers and Trauma* (February 6, 2009), at 5–7.

16. Situation in the Democratic Republic of the Congo, Case No. ICC 01/04-01/06: *Decision on the Manner of Questioning Witnesses by the Legal Representatives of Victims* (September 16, 2009), at 14.

17. *Id.*

18. *Id.* at 15 (emphasis added).

guilt of the accused may be a subject that substantively affects the personal interests of the victims. . . . [T]he Trial Chamber may authorize the victims' legal representative to question witnesses on subjects related to this issue . . . ."[19] The Chamber reasoned that the victim representative's broad purpose in the proceedings is to assist the Court in its pursuit of the truth, and that victim representatives are, therefore, "less likely than the parties to need to resort to the more combative techniques of 'cross-examination.'"[20]

The Chamber's reasoning, however, is questionable, given (1) that victims in the main *do* come before the Court in an inherently adversarial posture, and (2) that cross-examination is just as–or perhaps even more–supportive of the "pursuit of truth" as is direct examination. On the last point, most experienced litigators would indeed agree with Northwestern University School of Law Dean John Henry Wigmore's famous observation that "cross examination is beyond any doubt the greatest legal engine ever invented for the discovery of truth."[21]

In any event, the Chamber in the final analysis accorded victim representatives an (oddly vague) qualified right to, on a case-by-case basis, use leading questions during examinations:

> In certain circumstances . . . it may be fully consistent with the role of the victims' legal representative to seek to press, challenge or discredit a witness, for example when the views and concerns of a victim conflicts with the evidence given by that witness, or when material evidence has not been forthcoming. Under such circumstances, it may be appropriate for the victims' legal representatives to use closed, leading or challenging questions, if approved by the Chamber.
>
> In conclusion, it follows from the object and purpose of questioning by the victims' legal representatives that there is a presumption in favour of a neutral form of questioning, which may be displaced in favour of a more

---

19. *Id.*

20. *Id.* at 17 ("In the judgment of the Trial Chamber, this link (as approved by the Appeals Chamber) between the questioning of witnesses by the vicims participating in the proceedings and the power of the Chamber to determine the truth tends to support a presumption in favour of a neutral approach to questioning on behalf of victims.").

21. 5 J. WIGMORE, EVIDENCE § 1367 (3d ed. 1940), *quoted in California v. Green*, 399 U.S. 149, 158 (1970) (ruling that to deprive a defendant of the opportunity to cross-examine a witness is to deprive him of "the greatest legal engine ever invented for the discovery of truth").

closed form of questioning, along with the use of leading or challenging questions, depending on the issues raised and the interests affected.[22]

An example of the proper use of leading questions during cross-examination follows:

Question: You said previously that at the time when the executions you witnessed occurred, between 12:00–13:00, you were at Restaurant Rron in Veternik for lunch, correct?
Answer: Yes.

Question: You also testified on direct examination that you saw Mr. Rama on the same day at Dragodan at 12:55, correct?
Answer: I have always had a hard time with times and dates. When I said that I saw Mr. Rama at the same time I was at lunch at a different location, perhaps I was somewhere else.

Question: Please answer the question: Did you testify that you saw Mr. Rama at Dragodan at 12:55? Yes or no?
Answer: Yes.

Conducting the examination in such a leading manner points out for the Chamber inconsistencies in the witness' testimony, thereby directly, and appropriately, challenging witness credibility.

Defense counsel can of course always ask additional questions on re-direct examination, but the use of leading questions formulated on facts in evidence helps guide the witness' testimony, and directs the Chamber's and witness' attention to the specific, and important, inconsistencies. This avoids redundancy and waste of time, while concurrently promoting the search for truth. However, prior to asking such leading questions, the victim representative must be sure to first orally articulate to the bench its reasons for why he should receive permission to do so.[23]

---

22. Situation in the Democratic Republic of the Congo, Case No. ICC 01/04-01/06: *Decision on the Manner of Questioning Witnesses by the Legal Representatives of Victims* (September 16, 2009), at 17.

23. *Id.* at 18.

C. Introducing Exhibits

Inexperienced lawyers often spend too much time focusing on which witnesses to call, how to structure the presentation, and how to argue the case, while devoting insufficient energy to properly introducing into evidence exhibits, testimony, and tangible objects. If the Chamber fails to understand what makes a particular item of evidence probative, collecting and presenting the evidence was pointless. Therefore, the victim representative, once granted permission to participate, should follow the guidelines set forth below to ensure that the Chamber understands why the evidence or testimony the victim representative is presenting is in fact relevant and authentic, and why the Chamber should therefore admit it.[24]

1. The ICC's General Rules of Admissibility

The ICC continues a trend, observed in other international tribunals and civil law systems, of broadly favoring the admissibility of virtually all relevant evidence. Article 21(1) provides that the Statute and the Rules of Procedure and Evidence are the primary authorities on evidentiary and procedural issues, followed by principles and rules of law consistent with international law and internationally recognized norms and standards. Article 64(9), in turn, vests in the Trial Chamber the authority to rule on the admissibility of evidence.[25]

---

24. Consider, in this context, that the defense is also required to make certain disclosures. *See generally* Trial Chamber I, Situation in the Democratic Republic of the Congo, Case No. ICC-01/04–01/06: *Prosecutor v. Thomas Lubanga Dyilo, Decision on the Defence Request for Leave to Appeal the "Decision on Disclosure by the Defence"* (May 8, 2008). The defense must, among other things:

> Furnish the Chamber, the prosecution and the participants [including, presumably, victims] three weeks in advance of the trial with a document setting out in general terms the defences the accused intends to rely on and any substantive factual or legal issues that he intends to raise (and including by way of an alibi or grounds for excluding criminal responsibility under Rule 79 of the Rules).
>
> [I]f the defence decides prior to the commencement of the trial that a particular legal issue will be raised as regards admissibility, relevance or otherwise, pending any further order from the Chamber, as a matter of courtesy and to promote efficiency the Court and the other party and the participants should be informed.

25. *See also* Article 69(4) (Chamber to rule on admissibility of evidence, taking into account probative value and danger of unfair prejudice).

As it happens, the ICC's provisions have surprisingly little to say on the topic of admissibility, and are largely modelled after the porous rules of evidence of the ICTY and the ICTR, which provide for the introduction of virtually all evidence.[26] Consistent with international tribunals since Nuremberg, the ICC, thus, follows permissive European civil law rules on the admissibility of evidence, merely requiring the Court to "take[] into account, *inter alia*, the probative value of the evidence and any prejudice that such evidence may cause to a fair trial or to a fair evaluation of the testimony of a witness . . . ."[27]

To provide a partial answer for why, in contrast to common law systems, international tribunals favor such expansive admissibility standards, readers must bear in mind that civil law systems do not offer the accused the right to trial by a lay jury. Civil law systems in fact operate on a built-in assumption that *professional* judges are most capable of filtering out evidence which is not relevant, not credible, etc. This reliance on the impartiality of professional judges is particularly evident in the context of hearsay (which is permissible in international tribunals). The ICC regulations, accordingly, give extraordinarily broad discretion to the Chamber on decisions relating to what relevance, probative value, and weight the Chamber accords a particular item of evidence or a particular witness' testimony.[28] Whether such broad

26. *See generally Prosecutor v. Delalic*, Case No. IT-96-21-T: *Decision on the Motion of Prosecution for Admissibility of Evidence* (January 19, 1998), at 16 ("The approach adopted by the Rules is clearly one in favour of admissibility as long as the evidence is relevant and is deemed to have probative value . . . ."); *see also Ireland v. United Kingdom*, 25 Eur. Ct. H.R. (ser. A) (1978), at 79 ("The Court is not bound, under the Convention or under the general principles applicable to international tribunals, by strict rules of evidence. In order to satisfy itself, the Court is entitled to rely on evidence of any kind . . . .").

27. *See* Article 69(4).

28. *See generally* Christian DeFrancia, *Due Process in International Criminal Courts: Why Procedure Matters*, 87 VA. L. REV. 1381, 1402 (2001) ("The current Draft Rules of Evidence and Procedure of the proposed ICC reveal little in the way of indicators as to the models for admissibility of evidence . . . . Although the Rome Statute articulates strong norms for the rights of the accused, the wide-ranging discretion afforded judges in their decisions on the admissibility of evidence is worrisome. Without more specific provisions restricting the admission of hearsay evidence, the evidentiary bases upon which convictions are obtained run the risk of being unclear. In the absence of more specific evidentiary provisions, however, the developing jurisprudence at the ad hoc Tribunals is the proper starting point for drawing up rules of thumb for the enhancement of procedural protections in the future court."); *see also* Situation in the Democratic Republic of the Congo In the Case of the Prosecutor v. Thomas Lubanga Dyilo, Case No. ICC-01/04-01/06: *Decision on the Request by Legal Representatives of Victims [] for Admission of the Final Report of the Panel of Experts on the Illegal Exploitation of Natural Resources and Other Forms of Wealth of the Democratic Republic of the Congo as Evidence* (September 22, 2009), at 11–12 ("The Chamber . . . will focus, first, on the *relevance* of the materials (viz. does it relate to the

discretion is equally appropriate in a forum where many of the judges are new to the bench, and in some cases indeed resemble laypersons when it comes to their lack of first-hand experience with criminal trials, is of course open to question.

The ICC's legal provisions, in any event, grant the Chamber broad power to reject requests to admit certain evidence not only on the grounds of irrelevance or repetition, but also if the Chamber deems admission unnecessary because the matter is common knowledge.[29] The Chamber may further reject such requests if the evidence is "inappropriate," that is, if the Chamber determines the request to be motivated by a desire to cause delay or prejudice, or for other reasons provided by the Chamber.

The Chamber, interpreting the provisions, has described its "general approach to the admissibility of documents" as consisting of an analysis of (1) the relevance of the material which the victim representative seeks to admit, (2) whether the material has probative value, and (3) whether the evidence's "[unfairly] prejudicial effect" outweighs its probative value.[30] The ICC provisions, however, lack nuanced rules governing admissibility. As a matter of sound trial practice, then, the victim representative should proceed on the bedrock understanding that, to be admissible, evidence must be:

1. Relevant;
2. Material; *and*
3. Credible.[31]

---

matters that are properly to be considered by the Chamber in its investigation of the charges against the accused and its consideration of the views and concerns of participating victims); second, on whether or not it has *probative value*; and third, on the *probative value of the evidence as against its prejudicial effect*.") (Emphasis in original.)

29. Consider also that the Chamber must support its evidentiary rulings with reasoned opinions, *see* Rule 64(2), and that evidence ruled inadmissible must be ignored, *see* Rule 64(3).

30. Situation in the Democratic Republic of the Congo in the Case of the Prosecutor v. Thomas Lubanga Dyilo, Case No. ICC-01/04-01/06: *Decision on the Admission of Material from the "Bar Table"* (June 24, 2009), at 19; *see also* Situation in the Democratic Republic of the Congo In the Case of the Prosecutor v. Thomas Lubanga Dyilo, Case No. ICC-01/04-01/06: *Decision on the Request by Legal Representatives of Victims [] for Admission of the Final Report of the Panel of Experts on the Illegal Exploitation of Natural Resources and Other Forms of Wealth of the Democratic Republic of the Congo as Evidence* (September 22, 2009), at 11–12.

31. The parties may also stipulate that certain evidence is admissible. *See* Rule 69.

Evidence is *relevant* if it reasonably tends to make the fact that it is offered to prove or disprove either more or less probable. To be relevant, a particular item of evidence need not make certain the fact for which it is offered. The evidence is only required to have *some tendency* to increase the likelihood of the fact for which the party is offering it.

Weighing the probative value of the evidence is a task for the Chamber, and although a particular piece of evidence, standing by itself, may only be minimally probative, the Chamber should admit it as relevant, unless the evidence is otherwise incompetent or inadmissible. For example, if the fact to be proved is that the accused inflicted grave bodily injuries on the victim while he and his cohorts detained the victim, testimony by a witness concerning the witness' presence during the act would clearly be relevant, as would be testimony by a witness who heard the victim and the accused exchange angry words while in a government building.

Evidence is *material* if the participant offers it to prove a fact that is at issue in the case. For example, if the Prosecutor offers the testimony of a witness to prove that it was warm on the day the accused burned a particular inhabited village to the ground, such evidence may be relevant to prove the fact for which it is offered. However, the fact that it was warm on that particularly day is, by itself, probably not material to any of the issues in the case (other than, perhaps, to corroborate the witness' presence on that day).

Evidence is *credible* if it meets certain traditional requirements of reliability. Put another way, the factor used to determine whether evidence is credible is whether there are sufficient indicia that the testimony should be believed, that the evidence is what it purports to be, or that it is authentic.

Note also that, under ICC procedures, the Chamber can rule inadmissible evidence obtained through an illegal search. Article 69(7), read in conjunction with Rule 63, represents a limited species of the common law's "exclusionary rule." More specifically, Article 69(7) provides that the Chamber must deem evidence inadmissible only if it was obtained through a violation of the Rome Statute or "internationally recognized human rights," and (1) the nature and extent of the violation places "substantial doubt on the reliability of the evidence," *or* (2) admitting the evidence would be "antithetical to and would seriously damage the integrity of the proceedings."

Attempting to provide some guidance as to what constitutes "serious damage to the integrity of the proceedings," the Court stated that "a balance must be achieved between the seriousness of the violation and the fairness of the trial as a whole"; furthermore, "only serious violations of human rights should lead to the exclusion of evidence."[32] The common law's exclusionary rule, itself premised on the questionable assumption that exclusion of evidence will deter law enforcement misconduct,[33] thus lives on, albeit in blunted form, at the ICC.

2. Developing the Necessary Foundation to Admit Evidence

To establish the necessary foundation for the admission of evidence, the victim representative must, thus, make a preliminary showing that the evidence is relevant, material, and credible, and that it meets the other prerequisites for admissibility.[34] When an attorney raises an objection, arguing that a question, document, or thing lacks the proper foundation, the objector is asserting that a showing of competence, or of another prerequisite of admissibility, needs to be made.

The victim representative must ensure that the Prosecutor has introduced all useful and relevant documentary and other physical evidence, such as military rosters and maps of the areas where the victims claim they were harmed, as well as letters, diagrams, charts, and photographs. Regardless of

32. Situation in the Democratic Republic of the Congo In the Case of the Prosecutor v. Thomas Lubanga Dyilo, Case No. ICC-01/04-01/06: *Decision on the Admission of Material From the "Bar Table"* (June 24, 2009), at 11–26 (summarizing with approval the Pre-Trial Chamber's ruling concerning an unlawful search and seizure, and finding that, in the context of the specific violations at issue and having received the victim representatives views on the matter, exclusion of the evidence was not appropriate because "(i) the violation was not of a particularly grave kind; (ii) the impact of the violation on the integrity of the proceedings is lessened because the rights violated related to someone other than the accused; and (iii) the illegal acts were committed by the Congolese authorities, albeit in the presence of an investigator from the prosecution.").

33. For criticisms of this public policy foundation for the exclusionary rule, *see* Randy Barnett, *Resolving the Dilemma of the Exclusionary Rule: An Application of Restitutive Principles of Justice*, 32 EMORY L.J. 937, 938–40 (1983) (arguing that the exclusionary rule unnecessarily bars reliable evidence, and that the alternative of providing restitution to victims of police misconduct is, as a matter of public policy, preferable); *Bivens v. Six Unknown Named Agents*, 403 U.S. 388, 411, 422 (1971) (Burger, C.J., dissenting) (advocating as a remedy against the government compensation and restitution to persons whose Fourth Amendment rights were violated); *see also* Steven D. Clymer, *Are the Police Free to Disregard Miranda?*, 112 YALE L.J. 447, 450 (2002) (arguing that the exclusionary rule insufficiently deters law enforcement conduct that is not directed at securing conviction).

34. *See generally* Article 69(4).

the type of evidence, the victim representative, if permitted by the Chamber to supplement the evidence presented by the other participants, must lay the proper foundation before the Chamber will enter the documents into evidence. The Chamber must assure itself that the proposed evidence is relevant, material, and credible, and that it has the above-described probative value. The Chamber, in the context of such victim applications to participate in the proceedings, provided some critical guidance:

> The Trial Chamber has identified the procedure and confined limits within which it will exercise its powers to permit victims to tender and examine evidence: (i) a discrete application, (ii) notice to the participants, (iii) demonstration of personal interests that are affected by the specific proceedings, (iv) compliance with disclosure obligations and protection orders, (v) determination of appropriateness, and (vi) consistency with the rights of the accused and a fair trial. With these safeguards in place, the Appeals Chamber does not consider that the grant of participatory rights to victims to lead evidence pertaining to the guilt or innocence of the accused and to challenge the admissibility or relevance of the evidence is inconsistent with the onus of the Prosecutor to prove the guilt of the accused nor is it inconsistent with the rights of the accused and a fair trial.[35]

Based on the above, then, victim representatives should always abide by the following:

1. Submit discrete applications;
2. Provide notice to all participants;
3. Lay out the personal interests affected by the specific proceedings;
4. Comply with all disclosure obligations and protection orders;

---

35. Situation in the Democratic Republic of the Congo In the Case of the Prosecutor v. Thomas Lubanga Dyilo, ICC-01/04-01/06: *Judgment on the Appeals of The Prosecutor and The Defence against Trial Chamber I's Decision on Victims' Participation of 18 January 2008* (July 11, 2008), at 6–7, *quoted in* Situation in the Democratic Republic of the Congo In the Case of the Prosecutor v. Thomas Lubanga Dyilo, Case No. ICC-01/04-01/06: *Decision on the Request by Legal Representatives of Victims [] for Admission of the Final Report of the Panel of Experts on the Illegal Exploitation of Natural Resources and Other Forms of Wealth of the Democratic Republic of the Congo as Evidence* (September 22, 2009), at 10.

5. Demonstrate to the Chamber the appropriateness of participation at each stage; *and*

6. Show that the victims' participation at all times complies with fair trial and due process guarantees.

The participants may raise issues of admissibility, as can the Chamber on its own motion (*sua sponte*). To the extent possible, victim representatives should deal with such issues prior to the main trial through carefully thought-out motions *in limine*.[36] This saves the Chamber time, and ensures a more careful examination of foreseeable evidentiary disputes. It also allows the victim representative to proceed to trial with a fuller understanding of the evidence the participants are likely to introduce.

The Chamber will reject applications to admit evidence it deems duplicative, superfluous, irrelevant, inappropriate, or unobtainable, or when the Chamber is of the opinion that permission is being sought solely for the purpose of delaying the proceedings. Once the Chamber rules a piece of evidence inadmissible, the Chamber may not rely on, or consider, that evidence in arriving at its verdict.

A victim representative who has developed a sound theory of the case, and has carefully examined the strengths and weaknesses of his client's position, will know exactly what evidence to introduce, and will understand the value and impact each piece of evidence has on the parties' theories and proofs. To present evidence in the most persuasive and logical manner, and to avoid foundational problems, the victim representative should consider the following reliable default approaches:

a. Tape Recordings

The victim representative should ask the following types of questions to establish the foundation for tape recordings:

— Have you previously had the opportunity to hear the voice of Mr. Olorunfemi?
— Tell us how you are familiar with Mr. Olorunfemi's voice?
— How many times have you heard his voice?

---

36. *See* Rule 64(1) (providing that the Chamber may request that evidentiary issues be raised in writing).

- — Have you heard the recording marked for identification as "Victim Exhibit A"?
- — Is that your signature on the recording, indicating that you have reviewed it?
- — Did you recognize the voice on the recordings?
- — To whom does the voice belong?
- — "Your honors, we offer Victim Exhibit A into evidence."

b. Photographs

The victim representative should ask the following types of questions to establish the foundation for photographs:

- — I am showing you what has been marked for identification as "Victim Exhibit A."
- — Do you recognize what this photograph depicts?
- — Are you familiar with the scene [town, person, etc.] portrayed in this photograph?
- — How are you familiar with the scene portrayed in the photograph?
- — Does the scene portrayed in the photograph fairly and accurately represent the scene as you remember it on [date in question]?
- — "Your honors, we offer Victim Exhibit A into evidence."

c. Business Records

The victim representative should ask the following types of questions to establish the foundation for business records:

- — Are you familiar with "Victim Exhibit A" [business records]?
- — Can you identify these documents?
- — Were these documents prepared by you or your colleagues in the ordinary scope of the business of your organization?
- — Where are these documents stored after they are prepared?
- — Where were these documents retrieved from?
- — Is it a regular part of your business to keep and maintain records of this type?
- — Are these documents of the type that would be kept under your custody or control?
- — Based on your previous testimony, is the information contained in the documents correct, and was it correct on [the date of the document's creation]?

— "Your honors, we offer Victim Exhibit A into evidence."

d. Signatures

The victim representative should ask the following types of questions to establish the foundation for signatures:

— Are you familiar with the signature of Mr. Omosanya (the person who signed letter or decree)?
— How are you familiar with Mr. Omosanya's signature?
— I am showing you "Victim Exhibit A."
— Do you recognize the signature at the bottom Vicitim Exhibit A?
— Whose signature is it?
— "Your honors, we offer Victim Exhibit A into evidence."

e. Handwritten Documents

The victim representative should ask the following types of questions to establish the foundation for handwritten documents:

— Are you familiar with the handwriting of Mr. Mallon?
— How are you familiar with Mr. Mallon's handwriting?
— I am showing you "Victim Exhibit A."
— Do you recognize the handwriting in this document?
— To whom does it belong?
— "Your honors, we offer Victim Exhibit A into evidence."

f. Diagrams and Demonstrative Exhibits

Part of the prerequisite foundation for the introduction of diagrams and demonstrative exhibits ("visual aids") is a showing that the exhibits will assist the witness in explaining his testimony. The content of such exhibits is, therefore, limited: "[A]ny visual aids to be used by a party or participant shall explain, and be restricted to, previously disclosed evidence."[37]

---

37. *See generally* Situation in the Democratic Republic of the Congo In the Case of the Prosecutor v. Thomas Lubanga Dyilo, Case No. ICC 01/04-C1/06: *Public Decision on the Use of Visual Aids* (December 2, 2008), at 7.

Visual aids enhance the probative value of the testimony. The victim representative must, however, anticipate relevancy objections, founded on arguments that the exhibit raises unnecessary collateral issues, wastes time, or is unduly prejudicial. The Chamber will address these issues, the resolution of which requires reciprocal disclosure of such exhibits seven days in advance of their use. To allow the Chamber time to deal with such issues, participants must, as noted above, make application for the use of such visual aids no later than 14 days before their intended use at trial.[38]

In ruling on the use of such visual aids, the Chamber will employ the classic relevancy-balancing test, meaning the use of such aids is, at bottom, fully discretionary with the Chamber. That said, most judges will likely be inclined to permit their use as aids to understanding witness testimony.

Victim representatives should ask the following types of questions to establish the foundation for diagrams and other demonstrative exhibits:

— Are you familiar with the warehouses located near the government buildings in your hometown?
— How are you familiar with this area?
— I am handing you what has been marked as "Victim Exhibit A."
— Based on your familiarity with the area, can you tell us whether the scene depicted in Victim Exhibit A fairly and accurately represents the area as you recall it on the date in question?
— "Your honors, we offer Victim Exhibit A into evidence."

When "stuck" attempting to introduce evidence at trial, the victim representative should recall the basic steps to establishing an evidentiary foundation:

— Establish the witness' familiarity with the document the victim representative is seeking to admit into evidence.
— Have the witness authenticate the exhibit.
— Establish that the exhibit is what it purports to be.

---

38. *See generally* Situation in the Democratic Republic of the Congo In the Case of the Prosecutor v. Thomas Lubanga Dyilo, Case No. ICC 01/04-01/06: *Public Decision on the Use of Visual Aids* (December 2, 2008). One would think that the Chamber would want reciprocal exchange of such visual aids *prior* to the consideration of applications concerning their use; such a practical requirement, however, to date has not been announced.

— Demonstrate the exhibit's relevance to the case.
— Move the exhibit into evidence.

Once the victim representative has accomplished these steps, it is likely that he has laid the proper foundation for the Chamber to admit the exhibit into evidence. The victim representative should then simply offer it as the next exhibit in the case, and proceed on the assumption that the Chamber will accept this foundation as adequate.

D. Cross-Examination

Rule 140 governs cross-examination, which at the ICC is sometimes termed "adverse examination."[39] Cross-examination is a vital skill in a victim representative's arsenal, and is the trial skill that generally is most difficult to perfect (and is virtually impossible to conduct skillfully without extensive in-court experience). As with direct examination, the goal of effective cross-examination is to provide factual support for the theory of the case advanced by the participant conducting the cross-examination.

Effective cross-examination can enhance the strength of the victims' case in three general ways:

1. It can reveal factual support for the theory of the case that would otherwise not be available because, for example, the witness refused to speak to investigators during the investigative phase, or the direct examination avoided asking certain specific follow-up questions;

2. It can bring out information supportive of the evidence brought out on direct examination of another witness by, for example, demonstrating that the other witness' recollection on certain important facts is consistent with that of the person being cross-examined; or

3. It can demonstrate that the witness being cross-examined by the victim representative should not be believed because, for example, he has a faulty memory, or is biased against the victims.

39. Rule 140 sets out, *inter alia*, the right to examine a witness on "relevant matters related to the witness' testimony and its reliability, the credibility of the witness and other relevant matters." Rule 140(2)(b). However, the examination must be performed in a respectful and courteous manner. *See* Code of Professional Conduct Article 7; *see also* Rule 88(5) ("[A] Chamber shall be vigilant in controlling the manner of questioning a witness or victim so as to avoid any harassment or intimidation . . . .").

The manner in which the victim representative structures and conducts the cross-examination will, therefore, depend in large part on the type of evidence the victim representative wants to elicit, as well as on the extent to which the Chamber permits victim representative involvement.

1. Cross-Examining on Prior Inconsistent Statements

As previously touched on, one of the most effective ways to impeach a witness at trial is through the use of prior inconsistent statements. Practical experience at the ICTR and ICTY has taught, however, that many perceived inconsistencies in statements are the product of earlier inadequate questioning, rather than the result of faulty, or intentionally false, memory. For example, in many cases a prior statement will be taken in the context of the general investigation of crimes that may have taken place within the situation (rather than with an eye toward a specific case). As a result, the investigator in the field may, through no fault of his own, fail to ask the "right" questions because he does not yet know how the case will develop, and lacks the benefit of understanding the ultimate prosecution strategy. The predictable result is that statements may appear inconsistent, or lacking answers to pertinent questions, because the investigator/questioner, without the benefit of hindsight, failed to ask certain key questions.

In this regard, the Office of the Prosecutor of late has wisely abandoned its earlier practice of sending relatively inexperienced investigators and prosecutors into the field with a largely generic list of questions which they simply read to potential witnesses and victims. Under this routine, follow-up questions were understandably rare. The better practice is to have the Senior Trial Attorneys thoroughly discuss with the team going into the field what they intend to get out of the interviews, what follow-up questions may be appropriate, and how each of the planned interviews fits within the overall prosecutorial strategy.[40] Answering these questions prior to in-the-field meetings with potential witnesses will focus the team's thinking, and maximize the benefits of these resource-intensive trips.

In addition to the inherent difficulty of questioning potential witnesses during early stages of the investigation, such meetings are typically also

---

40. This process, of course, should also be followed by victim representatives conducting field interviews.

fraught with language, and timing, challenges. The language problems are relatively obvious, as most witnesses will have to rely on interpreters relaying the question in the exact way it was asked, and then providing back the answer in the exact way it was given. Of course, the same problem arises if the original statement requires translation. Given limited resources and the difficult circumstances present in post-conflict areas, there also may be a shortage of qualified interpreters/translators. This will only compound the pre-existing challenge of interviewing witnesses who speak a different language, and of having materials properly translated.

In terms of "timing" problems, the rather plodding nature of the typical ICC investigation will frequently result in parties taking statements many years after the events in question occurred. The accuracy of such statements naturally suffers. Conversely, when statements are taken closer in time to the events, the time-lag between the initial questioning and when the witness actual testifies in court will also encompass many years. During such extended time periods, memories will fade, recollections will change, and witnesses can be expected to provide answers that will differ to varying degrees from what they said shortly after the events. These challenges, well known to trial lawyers, are exacerbated by the ICC's general prohibition against pre-trial witness preparation/"proofing," discussed above.[41]

Considering these complicating factors, inconsistencies between a witness' statement and the witness' trial testimony are to be expected. This is particularly so if, as often happens, inexperienced NGO employees or volunteers, who are often the first on the ground, prepare or summarize victim-statements, or assist victims in completing their applications to participate at ICC proceedings, without first ensuring that all of the information supplied by the putative victim is correct, both in form and in substance. Although the participant offering the witness' testimony will, of course, argue that these inconsistencies are a product of the just-discussed time lag, and while the Chamber may have some sympathy with this explanation, these inconsistencies may well present an opportunity for the opposing party to place doubt on the witness' veracity and memory.

When a witness makes a statement at trial that is inconsistent with a prior statement, the victim representative must first highlight the question

---

41. *See generally* Situation in the Democratic Republic of the Congo in the Case of Prosecutor v. Thomas Lubanga Dyilo, Case No ICC-01/04-01/06: *Decision on Practices of Witness Familiarization and Witness Proofing* (Nov. 8, 2006), at 15–16 (Pre-Trial Chamber's rejection of the prosecution's assertion that witness-proofing is a "widely accepted practice in international criminal law").

the witness answered differently. The victim representative must make sure the trial testimony he seeks to impeach is *clearly* inconsistent with the witness' prior statement. Victim representatives should be sure not to place undue emphasis on inconsistencies that are minor, or that can be easily explained. To this end, many experienced trial lawyers find it beneficial to create a chart that sets out the key prior testimony or statements of each witness. This allows the victim representative to easily compare such prior statements with what the particular witness says at trial.

The victim representative should ask the following types of questions:

— Do you remember having given a statement to [name of person or organization] regarding how the incident occurred?
— Who was present when you gave your statement?
— When did you give your statement?
— Where did you give your statement?
— What were the circumstances under which you gave the statement?
— Did you give that statement freely and voluntarily?
— I show you what has been marked as Victim Exhibit A. Is this a copy of your earlier statement?

[The victim representative should then read the relevant portion of the statement directly contradicting the in-court testimony of the witness, or, better yet, ask the witness to read the statement.]

The victim representative must undertake impeachment through the use of documented inconsistent statements in an organized fashion, conducting such impeachment smoothly and directly. The relevant pages and sections of the statement or letter at issue should be marked and highlighted beforehand so that the victim representative does not fumble through pages or lose control of the witness. Seeing a lawyer properly impeach a witness through the use of inconsistent statements is impressive, and will certainly draw the Chamber's attention. Such cross-examination is a relatively straightforward procedure to learn, and, once mastered, will become an invaluable tool.

2. Cross-Examining Expert Witnesses

At trial, the presentation and cross-examination of expert witnesses is likely to be extremely challenging.[42] To cross-examine an expert witness effectively,

42. The calling of experts is provided by Article 48(4): Article 93(2); Rule 91(3)(b); Rule 91(4); and Rule 97(2). Whether the Chamber will permit victim

the victim representative must first understand fully the subject matter testified on by the expert. The victim representative should seriously consider cross-examining any expert whose opinion undermines the victim representative's case. On the other hand, it is likely that forensic or medical experts put on by the Prosecutor to demonstrate how the accused committed the alleged crimes will testify in a manner supportive of the victims' case. Of course, victim representatives should also consult with their own experts to frame possible cross-examination questions, since such victims' experts will often be in the best position to critique the findings or testimony offered by the other side's expert.[43]

If the expert testimony seeks to negate the criminal culpability of the accused, the victim representative should develop cross-examination questions for that witness in case the prosecution team does not cover all of the necessary bases. The Chamber may, in fact, view the failure to cross-examine the expert as signalling acceptance of the expert's opinion. Further, the victim representative should consider, if necessary, identifying and calling his own expert to counter such testimony.

The victim representative who cross-examines an expert witness needs to be very careful and well-prepared. Effective cross-examination of any expert is challenging, because the expert is likely more knowledgeable on the substantive subject matter. Nevertheless, the successful cross-examination of an expert witness is possible by narrowly focusing on the limited qualifications of the expert, or on the weaknesses of the expert's testimony, and exposing them to the Chamber.

In preparing to cross-examine an expert witness, the victim representative as an initial matter must read and summarize the reports or other prior statements of the expert. There will likely be many helpful items in these

---

representatives to call or examine experts is a matter decided on a case-by-case basis, however.

43. Victims likewise have the right to offer such reports in order to more fully explain the context and history of the charges against the accused. *See generally* Situation in the Democratic Republic of the Congo In the Case of the Prosecutor v. Thomas Lubanga Dyilo, Case No. ICC-01/04–01/06: *Decision on the Request by Legal Representatives of Victims [] for Admission of the Final Report of the Panel of Experts on the Illegal Exploitation of Natural Resources and Other Forms of Wealth of the Democratic Republic of the Congo as Evidence* (September 22, 2009), at 11–18 (discussing inadmissibility of an expert report concerning economic exploitation, and the financing of the conflict in the DRC and in Ituri, proffered by the victim representatives).

reports or prior statements or testimony. The victim representative must be thoroughly prepped on the subject area that will form the basis of the cross-examination, though it is in most cases not advisable to directly challenge an expert on an area squarely within his expertise. Of course, if the expert's testimony deviates from accepted norms, the victim representative may be able to expose the expert as a hired mouthpiece, or as an otherwise biased or unreliable advocate.

Additionally, the victim representative must research whether the expert has written any articles, books, or editorials that may contradict his opinion in the case, or demonstrate bias. (Has the expert, for example, authored an opinion piece arguing that there should be no such thing as an atrocity crime, or that the ICC's prosecutions are motivated by political considerations?) Next, the victim representative should determine what schools the expert graduated from, and see if any of the professors who taught the expert have different published opinions the victim representative may want to introduce and compare to the expert's opinion at trial.

An effective way to begin such a cross-examination is to subtly place into doubt the expert witness' credibility by exposing the expert's potential biases. The expert witness may be biased because of political motivations, money, or a relationship with the accused. The victim representative can effectively bring such biases to the Chamber's attention by using succinct and precise (leading) questions.

Once the victim representative explores the expert's bias, he can attack the expert's qualifications. No matter how qualified an expert witness may be in a given field, there are probably levels of achievement or training that the expert has not reached. For example, if the expert witness only has a Master's degree, the victim representative can point out that he lacks a Ph.D. If applicable, the victim representative can point out that the expert witness has not published any articles on the subject area, or has not held any relevant teaching positions in colleges or universities. Obviously, it is necessary to discover this information before the cross-examination. One way to learn this information is to obtain the expert's *curriculum vitae* or detailed résumé in advance of trial, and to conduct an online review focusing on the expert's background.

Another means of cross-examining an adverse expert witness is to turn the expert into the victim representative's witness. If possible, the victim representative should have the opposing expert testify as to general principles that are consistent with the victims' theory of the case. If the expert is honest, and if the questions asked are basic questions that he cannot deny, there is a good chance the expert will have to admit the facts suggested, or risk appearing less than credible.

Although there are many ways to cross-examine an opposing expert, the victim representative at trial should choose only two or three areas of attack. Without such limitations, the cross-examination may become too lengthy or overly confused, and may annoy the Chamber. Moreover, the longer an opposing expert witness is on the stand, the greater the likelihood that the expert will hurt the victims' and/or the prosecution's case. Therefore, when cross-examining an opposing expert, the victim representative should be prepared, be thorough, address two or three areas, expose the expert's weak points, and then, following the less-is-more principle, politely thank the expert, and sit down.

E. Re-Direct Examination

Following cross-examination, the counsel who called the witness may conduct re-direct examination (sometimes referred to by ICC attorneys as "re-examination") to clarify for the Chamber certain testimony the witness provided during the witness' cross-examination. To keep the Chamber focused on relevant information, victim representatives must strive to limit re-direct examination to only those issues or facts, brought out in the cross-examination, requiring additional explanation. It is sometimes more beneficial not to conduct any re-direct examination of a particular witness. Victim representatives should, therefore, pay close attention to what the witness said during the cross-examination so that they can make a calculated decision as to whether it is necessary or advisable to conduct re-direct examination.

If another participant during cross-examination has successfully attacked the credibility or reputation for truthfulness of the witness, the lawyer whose witness has been damaged may wish to "save" or "rehabilitate" the witness. The lawyer's questions should be limited to the weaknesses in the testimony exposed during the cross-examination, and must be designed to enhance the witness' truth-telling appearance in the eyes of the Chamber. If the victim representative's witness is having problems answering questions, or is becoming fatigued or agitated, follow-up questions may only make matters worse. Sometimes it is best to say, "Thank you, nothing further of this witness your Honors."

The following are some parting thoughts on redirect examination:

- The victim representative should be brief and to the point.
- The victim representative should use transitions to alert the Chamber to the specific points being clarified.
- Generally, avoid new topic areas.
- Re-direct examination to rehabilitate a witness is not the time to rehash direct examination testimony.
- The victim representative should *never* ask a question without first having a reasonably good sense of what the answer will be.

The victim representative must bear in mind that it is not routine for the Chamber to permit the victim representative to present witnesses. The victim representative must, therefore, take care not to abuse the privilege by presenting cumulative or irrelevant testimony, lest the Chamber deny the privilege the next time, and the victim representative lose credibility.

PART XIV

Summation and Sentencing

A. Summation: Capturing the Whole Story

The summation, known in common law countries as the "closing argument," is a vital part of trial, and, as such, the victim representative must give it considerable thought. The entire trial, in a sense, leads up to this point.[1] The victim representative must seek permission to give a summation; the summation must be simple and precise, and, to the extent possible, should buttress the summation of the prosecution, while adding those factual and legal arguments of particular importance to the victims. During the summation, the victim representative brings all evidentiary pieces together, presenting them in a strong, robust, and persuasive manner. The victim representative, after all, has the task of bringing into sharp focus all points that help prove the victims' theory of the case. Some of the judges may not have extensive experience in criminal trials, so the victim representative must be particularly thorough, going through the elements of the charges one by one, and explaining how the evidence adduced at trial supports each of the charging elements.

The goal with any summation is, of course, to highlight and tie together the evidence introduced at trial that best and most directly supports the advocate's position. The victim representative's professionalism and control, command of the facts, and ability to convey them without hyperbole or exaggeration will keep the Chamber's attention and leave the adjudicators with a favorable parting impression.

The Chamber, consistent with civil practice, will likely require victim representatives to furnish the judges with written outlines in advance of the summation.[2] To what extent a participant can remain flexible and alter his

---

1. *See* Rule 141(2) (providing that the defense always has right to speak last).

2. At present, this requirement has formally been applied to the Prosecutor and the defense, but all indications are that victims will have to comply as well. *See* Situation in the

summation will likely depend on the proclivities of the judges, and, therefore, be a matter for case-by-case determination. One would hope, however, that the Chamber will accord some latitude to the participants, including to the victim representatives.[3]

The victim representative should consider developing a demonstrative chart that lists the elements of the particular charged crimes relevant to the victims, as well as the key points in favor of a restitution award (if the proceedings are not bifurcated). The below points represent a starting outline of the essential elements the victim representative should seek to cover during the summation:

- Think about, prepare, and modify the summation before trial, leaving sufficient flexibility to meet litigation exigencies; avoid unnecessarily impinging on the prosecution's function. The summation will represent the victims' theory of the case. The earlier the victim representative begins to give thought to the summation, the sounder the trial strategy and analysis of the evidence is likely to be.
- The victim representative must remember that judges also have limited attention spans (and patience), and that some of them may have little in-court experience. The victim representative should, therefore, not read in a monotonous voice from a sheet of paper. By the time of the summation, the victim representative must know the facts well enough that only a rough outline is necessary to keep the presentation dynamic, responsive, and persuasive. This approach is more likely to keep the Chamber interested and engaged.
- The summation must not stray from the key issues, or from the actual evidence presented during the trial, and must highlight the most important evidence from the victims' perspective.

Democratic Republic of the Congo In the Case of Prosecutor v. Thomas Lubanga Dyilo, Case No. ICC-01/04-01/06: *Decision on Opening and Closing Statements* (May 22, 2008) (Trial Chamber requiring that the Prosecutor and defense lawyers provide written outlines of opening statements seven days in advance).

3. Situation in the Democratic Republic of the Congo In the Case of Prosecutor v. Thomas Lubanga Dyilo, Case No. ICC-01/04-01/06: *Decision on Opening and Closing Statements* (May 22, 2008) (persuasive dissent by Judge René Blattmann criticizing the majority decision as undermining the search for truth because it eliminates the critical element of spontaneity).

As a matter of *format*, the victim representative should:

— Formally address the Chamber and the other participants.
— Inform the Chamber of the victims' objectives, summarize the facts, and relate these facts to the issues in the case (regardless of whether the victim representative is at the guilt phase, or at the sentencing/reparations phase of the proceedings).
— Deliver the summation in a short, concise, and appropriately limited fashion.
— Inform the Chamber of what the victims consider a just outcome.

As a matter of *delivery*, the victim representative must:

— Avoid excessive or dramatic affectations or body language.
— Not engage in personal attacks or other sorts of *ad hominems*.
— Not tell the Chamber about his personal beliefs, but instead write, act, and speak with appropriate conviction on the victims' behalf.
— Not repeat in chronological order the testimony of each witness. The Chamber, after all, has heard the witnesses. The victim representative must bind the facts elicited during the direct and cross-examination into a cohesive and persuasive whole.

B. Sentencing: Imposition of Justice

If the proceedings result in a conviction, whether through a trial or plea, the Trial Chamber, pursuant to Article 78(1), must determine an appropriate sentence.

1. Available Categories of Punishment: Imprisonment, Fines, Forfeiture, and Reparations

The sentence can include a term of imprisonment,[4] a fine,[5] or the forfeiture of proceeds, property, or assets the accused derived, directly or indirectly,

4. *See* Article 77(1).

5. *See* Article 77(2)(a).

from his crime.[6] In addition, the Chamber has the option of imposing reparations, which the Rome Statute defines as encompassing "restitution, compensation, and rehabilitation."[7] In terms of fixing a specific sentence, the Rome Statute provides:

> To determine an appropriate sentence, the Chamber must take into account both mitigating and aggravating circumstances.[8] The Court as a general matter may not impose a term of imprisonment greater than 30 years.[9] However, in cases involving extremely grave crimes or extremely aggravated circumstances, as evidenced by the existence of one or more of the enumerated aggravating circumstances, the Court may impose a life sentence.[10]

Mitigating circumstances include, but are not limited to, criminal culpability falling short of grounds for exclusion of criminal responsibility (such as an accused's substantially diminished mental capacity or duress), as well as the convicted person's post-crime conduct (such as an accused's efforts to compensate victims and cooperate with the Court).[11] Aggravating circumstances, on the other hand, include prior criminal convictions, abuse of power or official capacity, vulnerability of the victim(s), and notable cruelty or particular reprehensibility motivating the commission of the crime.[12]

Whether the Chamber holds a separate sentencing hearing to develop additional evidence bearing on the various aggravating and mitigating sentencing factors depends, in part, on whether either the prosecution or the accused requests such a hearing (in which case the Chamber is required to convene it). The Chamber, however, is also empowered to schedule such a hearing *sua sponte*.[13]

In light of the seriousness of the cases the ICC will hear, and the range of criminal matters of over which the ICC has jurisdiction, it is likely that most,

---

6. *See* Article 77(2)(b).
7. Article 75(1).
8. *See* Rule 145; *see also* Article 78.
9. *See* Article 77(1)(a).
10. *See* Article 77(1)(b); *see also* Rule 145(3).
11. Rule 145(2)(a).
12. Rule 145(2)(b).
13. *See* Article 76(2).

if not all, aggravating factors will pertain in virtually every case. It is indeed difficult to review the ICC's Elements of Crimes and identify any offenses that, by their very nature, do not involve either military, government, or militia leaders abusing their power or official capacity, harming victims who are particularly vulnerable, or committing offenses notably cruel or motivated by reprehensible reasons. In most cases, then, the Prosecutor will have ample justification for requesting the highest available sentence, and the victim representative will have little reason to take a divergent position in this regard.

However, Article 77, which also governs sentencing, inexplicably is worded permissively, providing that "the Court *may* impose one of the following penalties [namely, imprisonment, fine, forfeiture, or restitution] on a person convicted of a crime . . . ."[14] Thus, in theory, a person convicted of atrocity crimes under the ICC's present provisions can escape even a fine, regardless of the fact that the ICC's offenses are drafted with the purpose of punishing crimes so gross that they are condemned by the world as being outside the boundaries of civilized life.

Considering the serious nature of the available offenses, the rigorous screening process undertaken by the prosecution prior to initiating an investigation, bringing charges, and obtaining a conviction, and the considerable resources involved in bringing a case to trial and achieving a conviction, the Assembly of States Parties should consider modifying the statutory language to require mandatory minimum sentences in the case of conviction, or at least in cases involving Rule 145(2)(b) aggravating factors. Such mandatory minimum sentences are consistent with the Rome Statute Preamble's promise to punish the "most serious crimes of concern to the international community as a whole."

And, in the context of sentencing, the Assembly of States Parties should also consider amending the Rules to provide for a system of sentencing guidelines that give the judges some guidance as to what types of cases and conduct deserve what levels of punishment and condemnation. Such sentencing guidelines would also provide the parties some semblance of sentencing predictability, and offer the opportunity for a transparent discussion

---

14. Emphasis added. Article 75 is also worded permissively, stating that the Chamber "may" order restitution. It is, therefore, the victim representative's responsibility to demonstrate to the Chamber why the Chamber should exercise its discretion in favor of a particular reparations award. Any reparations award can be collected either directly from the accused, or can be awarded through the Trust Fund for Victims.

of what makes (or should make) some crimes "worse" than others. Beyond the basic Rule 145 aggravating factors (prior convictions, abuse of power, defenseless victims, etc.), characteristics of the crime of conviction, such as the number of victims, the number of perpetrators under the convicted person's control, use of minors to commit the crimes, and evidence of attempts to tamper with witnesses, or otherwise obstruct justice in the proceedings, should be enumerated, along with any mitigating factors, and should result in explicit increases or decreases in the guideline sentence. Judges, of course, could remain free to deviate above or below a particular guideline sentence, but, in all cases, the judges should be required to address all aggravating and mitigating factors, and to explain their sentencing decisions in a written ruling.

2. Reparations

Of particular relevance to victims, the Chamber may impose reparations and issue forfeiture orders.[15] Article 75 provides:

> 1. The Court shall establish principles relating to reparations to, or in respect of, victims, including restitution, compensation, and rehabilitation. On this basis, in its decision the Court *may*, either upon request or on its own motion in exceptional circumstances, determine the scope and extent of any damage, loss, and injury to, or in respect of, victims and will state the principles on which it is acting.
> 2. The Court *may* make an order directly against a convicted person specifying appropriate reparations to, or in respect of, victims, including restitution, compensation, and rehabilitation. Where appropriate, the Court *may* order that the award for reparations be made through the Trust Fund provided for in article 79.
> 3. Before making an order under this article, the Court *may* invite and shall take account of representations from or on behalf of the convicted person, victims, other interested persons or interested States.
> 4. In exercising its power under this article, the Court *may*, after a person is convicted of a crime within the jurisdiction of the Court, determine

15. *See* Rule 146 (governing imposition of fines) and Rule 147 (governing orders of forfeiture).

whether, in order to give effect to an order which it may make under this article, it is necessary to seek measures under article 93, paragraph 1.
5. A State Party shall give effect to a decision under this article as if the provisions of article 109 [governing enforcement of fines and forfeiture measures] were applicable to this article.
6. Nothing in this article shall be interpreted as prejudicing the rights of victims under national or international law.[16]

Article 75, therefore, explicitly allows victims to participate at the reparations phase, placing victims at the center of the proceedings.

3. Bifurcating the Guilt Phase from the Reparations Phase

In the earliest days of the ICC's existence, victim representatives thought it a good strategy to request permission to present reparations and sentencing-related evidence at the same time participants introduced evidence of an accused's guilt. The thinking behind this combined approach, contemplated by Regulation of the Court 56,[17] was that it would maximize the victims' chance to introduce evidence and participate at trial, since victims have the most obvious stake in determining what, if any, reparations are or should be awarded. Moreover, given the limited resources available to victims, the victim representatives reasoned that combining these phases of the proceedings would save time and money. This was a bit of a gamble, however, since the victim representatives did not yet know how the Chamber would treat their requests for participation. Combining the proceedings, moreover, had the potential of leading to confusion, thereby generating additional resistance to victim participation.

Although the Chamber has yet to settle on a uniform approach, bifurcating the proceedings allows a cleaner logical and evidentiary separation between the guilt phase and the sentencing/reparations phase. Such bifurcation focuses the proceedings, and prevents extraneous information relating to

16. Emphasis added.

17. Regulation 56 provides that "the Trial Chamber may hear the witnesses and examine the evidence for the purposes of a decision on reparations in accordance with article 75, paragraph 2 [the provisions dealing with reparations for victims], at the same time as for the purposes of trial."

physical, pecuniary, and moral harm suffered by the victims from potentially tainting the fairness of the accused's trial. As a matter of best practices, therefore, the Chamber as a general rule should bifurcate the trial into a guilt phase, with the Chamber, in the event of a conviction, moving on to a sentencing/reparations/forfeiture phase.

Well in advance of the Chamber's verdict, then, the victim representative should move the Court to bifurcate the proceedings. The accused is likely to agree to, and join in, such a motion. Assuming the Chamber grants the request for bifurcation, following a conviction the victim representatives must be ready to immediately switch hats and proceed to the next phase. The convicted person, of course, retains the right to appeal both the conviction, as well as the sentence (including any reparations orders).[18]

4. Preparing the Victims' Sentencing Memorandum

Considering the central role victims play during sentencing proceedings, the different types of sentences the Chamber has at its disposal (namely, imprisonment, fines, forfeiture, and reparations), the various identified mitigating and aggravating sentencing factors, the breadth of information the Chamber may consider in fixing the sentence, and the potential vastness of facts relevant to the Chamber's determination of an appropriate sentence, victim representatives should in all cases prepare a sentencing memorandum for submission to the Chamber. The sentencing memorandum, made part of the Court record, and provided to the other parties with sufficient notice, should contain a concise summary of those facts the victim representative considers most relevant to the above-described sentencing factors. The sentencing memorandum should additionally explain clearly how the accused's criminal conduct resulted in direct harm to the victims' interests, and carefully lay out the nature and impact of that harm. Moreover, the sentencing memorandum should impress on the Chamber how these facts serve to aggravate the accused's case, and why they call out for a particular sentence, fine, forfeiture, or reparations award.

A sensible way to organize such a sentencing memorandum is to include the following sections: An introduction; a factual summary of the charges, and the established (as well as the disputed) criminal conduct resulting in

18. *See generally* Rules 149–61.

the conviction; a summary of the harm suffered by the victim, and the linkage between that harm and the convicted person's criminal conduct; a victim impact statement; a discussion of reparations, fine, and forfeiture issues; and a detailed analysis of *all* applicable Rule 145 aggravating and mitigating sentencing factors.

The appropriate legal basis for submitting such a victims' sentencing memorandum is Article 75(3), which requires the Chamber to "take account of representation from" victims prior to imposing reparations, as well as Article 76(1), directing the Chamber to consider "submissions made during the trial that are relevant to the sentence." (To determine an appropriate sentence, moreover, the Chamber must also weigh the "gravity of the crime," a topic victims are arguably in the best position to comment on.) Finally, the applicability of Article 68(3)'s catchall, requiring the Chamber to permit the presentation and consideration of the victims' "views and concerns" when the victims' personal interests are affected, is at its zenith at the sentencing phase of the proceedings. Depending on how the Chamber decides to structure the sentencing hearing, the victim representative should consider requesting, based on the legal arguments laid out above, that some of the victims personally address the Court. Such an in-person presentation will put a human face on the inhumane acts of the convicted perpetrator(s).

PART XV

Conclusion

MEANINGFUL VICTIM PARTICIPATION at the ICC is a significant step forward in the international community's continuing pursuit of its collective restorative ambitions. Changes in the ICC's jurisprudence and rules reflect an emerging sense of how best to accommodate the victims' interests within the existing legal framework, but they also point to the ICC's developing institutional needs. Ensuring that this laudable, and potentially cathartic, process translates into substantive, constructive participation is the victim representatives' most fundamental obligation.

Whether the ICC will accord victims of atrocity crimes the full promised measure of substantive rights, or whether "victims' rights" instead will translate into little more than notional aspirations showing the international community's good will, remains to be seen. But what is clear is that the ICC, despite its ongoing struggle to deliver to the world community its promised impact, has the long-term potential to transcend cultural, geographic, and geopolitical constraints, and to render justice on the world's most prominent legal stage. In this regard, motivated victim representatives who understand the law, and know their way around a courtroom, can do a great deal to assist the ICC in reaching its full capacity, and, in the process, can help victims regain some sense of control over their shattered lives.

There indeed should be no doubt that victim representatives will continue to help guide the ICC's developing jurisprudence during the Court's formative years. Robust victim participation, when properly conducted, represents sound public policy, and confirms to the world a genuine institutional desire to create a complete historic record of victim abuse, while not diminishing the fairness or efficiency of the proceedings. Future generations will envy the present time, when attorneys at the ICC spend their days shaping the law during its foundational stages. Although the areas crying out for institutional reform, as identified herein, are many, today's ICC lawyers and advocates have the power to clear the path towards just, compassionate, and effective handling of victims' cases. The history books will one day judge whether the international legal establishment enhanced—and lived up to—the ICC's noble mission. The international legal and political community's handling of this opportunity will, indeed, stand as a profound testament to the authenticity of the world's concern for accountability and for those exposed to the worst of humanity.

Selected Articles from the Rome Statute [Articles: 5, 11–21, 42, 51, 53–57, 63–69, 74–79, 81, 82, 103, 106, 109, and 110]

Article 5
Crimes within the jurisdiction of the Court

1. The jurisdiction of the Court shall be limited to the most serious crimes of concern to the international community as a whole. The Court has jurisdiction in accordance with this Statute with respect to the following crimes:

(a) The crime of genocide;

(b) Crimes against humanity;

(c) War crimes;

(d) The crime of aggression.

2. The Court shall exercise jurisdiction over the crime of aggression once a provision is adopted in accordance with articles 121 and 123 defining the crime and setting out the conditions under which the Court shall exercise jurisdiction with respect to this crime. Such a provision shall be consistent with the relevant provisions of the Charter of the United Nations.

Article 11
Jurisdiction ratione temporis

1. The Court has jurisdiction only with respect to crimes committed after the entry into force of this Statute.

2. If a State becomes a Party to this Statute after its entry into force, the Court may exercise its jurisdiction only with respect to crimes committed after the entry into force of this Statute for that State, unless that State has made a declaration under article 12, paragraph 3.

Article 12
Preconditions to the exercise of jurisdiction

1. A State which becomes a Party to this Statute thereby accepts the jurisdiction of the Court with respect to the crimes referred to in article 5.

2. In the case of article 13, paragraph (a) or (c), the Court may exercise its jurisdiction if one or more of the following States are Parties to this Statute or have accepted the jurisdiction of the Court in accordance with paragraph 3:

(a) The State on the territory of which the conduct in question occurred or, if the crime was committed on board a vessel or aircraft, the State of registration of that vessel or aircraft;

(b) The State of which the person accused of the crime is a national.

3. If the acceptance of a State which is not a Party to this Statute is required under paragraph 2, that State may, by declaration lodged with the Registrar, accept the exercise of jurisdiction by the Court with respect to the crime in question. The accepting State shall cooperate with the Court without any delay or exception in accordance with Part 9.

Article 13
Exercise of jurisdiction

The Court may exercise its jurisdiction with respect to a crime referred to in article 5 in accordance with the provisions of this Statute if:

(a) A situation in which one or more of such crimes appears to have been committed is referred to the Prosecutor by a State Party in accordance with article 14;

(b) A situation in which one or more of such crimes appears to have been committed is referred to the Prosecutor by the Security Council acting under Chapter VII of the Charter of the United Nations; or

(c) The Prosecutor has initiated an investigation in respect of such a crime in accordance with article 15.

Article 14
Referral of a situation by a State Party

1. A State Party may refer to the Prosecutor a situation in which one or more crimes within the jurisdiction of the Court appear to have been committed

requesting the Prosecutor to investigate the situation for the purpose of determining whether one or more specific persons should be charged with the commission of such crimes.

2. As far as possible, a referral shall specify the relevant circumstances and be accompanied by such supporting documentation as is available to the State referring the situation.

Article 15
Prosecutor

1. The Prosecutor may initiate investigations *proprio motu* on the basis of information on crimes within the jurisdiction of the Court.

2. The Prosecutor shall analyse the seriousness of the information received. For this purpose, he or she may seek additional information from States, organs of the United Nations, intergovernmental or non-governmental organizations, or other reliable sources that he or she deems appropriate, and may receive written or oral testimony at the seat of the Court.

3. If the Prosecutor concludes that there is a reasonable basis to proceed with an investigation, he or she shall submit to the Pre-Trial Chamber a request for authorization of an investigation, together with any supporting material collected. Victims may make representations to the Pre-Trial Chamber, in accordance with the Rules of Procedure and Evidence.

4. If the Pre-Trial Chamber, upon examination of the request and the supporting material, considers that there is a reasonable basis to proceed with an investigation, and that the case appears to fall within the jurisdiction of the Court, it shall authorize the commencement of the investigation, without prejudice to subsequent determinations by the Court with regard to the jurisdiction and admissibility of a case.

5. The refusal of the Pre-Trial Chamber to authorize the investigation shall not preclude the presentation of a subsequent request by the Prosecutor based on new facts or evidence regarding the same situation.

6. If, after the preliminary examination referred to in paragraphs 1 and 2, the Prosecutor concludes that the information provided does not constitute a reasonable basis for an investigation, he or she shall inform those who provided the information. This shall not preclude the Prosecutor from considering further information submitted to him or her regarding the same situation in the light of new facts or evidence.

Article 16
Deferral of investigation or prosecution

No investigation or prosecution may be commenced or proceeded with under this Statute for a period of 12 months after the Security Council, in a resolution adopted under Chapter VII of the Charter of the United Nations, has requested the Court to that effect; that request may be renewed by the Council under the same conditions.

Article 17
Issues of admissibility

1. Having regard to paragraph 10 of the Preamble and article 1, the Court shall determine that a case is inadmissible where:

(a) The case is being investigated or prosecuted by a State which has jurisdiction over it, unless the State is unwilling or unable genuinely to carry out the investigation or prosecution;

(b) The case has been investigated by a State which has jurisdiction over it and the State has decided not to prosecute the person concerned, unless the decision resulted from the unwillingness or inability of the State genuinely to prosecute;

(c) The person concerned has already been tried for conduct which is the subject of the complaint, and a trial by the Court is not permitted under article 20, paragraph 3;

(d) The case is not of sufficient gravity to justify further action by the Court.

2. In order to determine unwillingness in a particular case, the Court shall consider, having regard to the principles of due process recognized by international law, whether one or more of the following exist, as applicable:

(a) The proceedings were or are being undertaken or the national decision was made for the purpose of shielding the person concerned from criminal responsibility for crimes within the jurisdiction of the Court referred to in article 5;

(b) There has been an unjustified delay in the proceedings which in the circumstances is inconsistent with an intent to bring the person concerned to justice;

(c) The proceedings were not or are not being conducted independently or impartially, and they were or are being conducted in a manner which, in the circumstances, is inconsistent with an intent to bring the person concerned to justice.

3. In order to determine inability in a particular case, the Court shall consider whether, due to a total or substantial collapse or unavailability of its national judicial system, the State is unable to obtain the accused or the necessary evidence and testimony or otherwise unable to carry out its proceedings.

Article 18
Preliminary rulings regarding admissibility

1. When a situation has been referred to the Court pursuant to article 13 (a) and the Prosecutor has determined that there would be a reasonable basis to commence an investigation, or the Prosecutor initiates an investigation pursuant to articles 13 (c) and 15, the Prosecutor shall notify all States Parties and those States which, taking into account the information available, would normally exercise jurisdiction over the crimes concerned. The Prosecutor may notify such States on a confidential basis and, where the Prosecutor believes it necessary to protect persons, prevent destruction of evidence or prevent the absconding of persons, may limit the scope of the information provided to States.

2. Within one month of receipt of that notification, a State may inform the Court that it is investigating or has investigated its nationals or others within its jurisdiction with respect to criminal acts which may constitute crimes referred to in article 5 and which relate to the information provided in the notification to States. At the request of that State, the Prosecutor shall defer to the State's investigation of those persons unless the Pre-Trial Chamber, on the application of the Prosecutor, decides to authorize the investigation.

3. The Prosecutor's deferral to a State's investigation shall be open to review by the Prosecutor six months after the date of deferral or at any time when there has been a significant change of circumstances based on the State's unwillingness or inability genuinely to carry out the investigation.

4. The State concerned or the Prosecutor may appeal to the Appeals Chamber against a ruling of the Pre-Trial Chamber, in accordance with article 82. The appeal may be heard on an expedited basis.

5. When the Prosecutor has deferred an investigation in accordance with paragraph 2, the Prosecutor may request that the State concerned periodically inform the Prosecutor of the progress of its investigations and any subsequent prosecutions. States Parties shall respond to such requests without undue delay.

6. Pending a ruling by the Pre-Trial Chamber, or at any time when the Prosecutor has deferred an investigation under this article, the Prosecutor may, on an exceptional basis, seek authority from the Pre-Trial Chamber to pursue necessary investigative steps for the purpose of preserving evidence where there is a unique opportunity to obtain important evidence or there is a significant risk that such evidence may not be subsequently available.

7. A State which has challenged a ruling of the Pre-Trial Chamber under this article may challenge the admissibility of a case under article 19 on the grounds of additional significant facts or significant change of circumstances.

Article 19
Challenges to the jurisdiction of the Court or the admissibility of a case

1. The Court shall satisfy itself that it has jurisdiction in any case brought before it. The Court may, on its own motion, determine the admissibility of a case in accordance with article 17.

2. Challenges to the admissibility of a case on the grounds referred to in article 17 or challenges to the jurisdiction of the Court may be made by:

(a) An accused or a person for whom a warrant of arrest or a summons to appear has been issued under article 58;

(b) A State which has jurisdiction over a case, on the ground that it is investigating or prosecuting the case or has investigated or prosecuted; or

(c) A State from which acceptance of jurisdiction is required under article 12.

3. The Prosecutor may seek a ruling from the Court regarding a question of jurisdiction or admissibility. In proceedings with respect to jurisdiction or admissibility, those who have referred the situation under article 13, as well as victims, may also submit observations to the Court.

4. The admissibility of a case or the jurisdiction of the Court may be challenged only once by any person or State referred to in paragraph 2. The challenge shall take place prior to or at the commencement of the trial. In exceptional circumstances, the Court may grant leave for a challenge to be brought more than once or at a time later than the commencement of the trial. Challenges to the admissibility of a case, at the commencement of a trial, or subsequently with the leave of the Court, may be based only on article 17, paragraph 1 (c).

5. A State referred to in paragraph 2 (b) and (c) shall make a challenge at the earliest opportunity.

6. Prior to the confirmation of the charges, challenges to the admissibility of a case or challenges to the jurisdiction of the Court shall be referred to the Pre-Trial Chamber. After confirmation of the charges, they shall be referred to the Trial Chamber. Decisions with respect to jurisdiction or admissibility may be appealed to the Appeals Chamber in accordance with article 82.

7. If a challenge is made by a State referred to in paragraph 2 (b) or (c), the Prosecutor shall suspend the investigation until such time as the Court makes a determination in accordance with article 17.

8. Pending a ruling by the Court, the Prosecutor may seek authority from the Court:

(a) To pursue necessary investigative steps of the kind referred to in article 18, paragraph 6;

(b) To take a statement or testimony from a witness or complete the collection and examination of evidence which had begun prior to the making of the challenge; and

(c) In cooperation with the relevant States, to prevent the absconding of persons in respect of whom the Prosecutor has already requested a warrant of arrest under article 58.

9. The making of a challenge shall not affect the validity of any act performed by the Prosecutor or any order or warrant issued by the Court prior to the making of the challenge.

10. If the Court has decided that a case is inadmissible under article 17, the Prosecutor may submit a request for a review of the decision when he or she is fully satisfied that new facts have arisen which negate the basis on which the case had previously been found inadmissible under article 17.

11. If the Prosecutor, having regard to the matters referred to in article 17, defers an investigation, the Prosecutor may request that the relevant State make available to the Prosecutor information on the proceedings. That information shall, at the request of the State concerned, be confidential. If the Prosecutor thereafter decides to proceed with an investigation, he or she shall notify the State to which deferral of the proceedings has taken place.

Article 20
Ne bis in idem

1. Except as provided in this Statute, no person shall be tried before the Court with respect to conduct which formed the basis of crimes for which the person has been convicted or acquitted by the Court.

2. No person shall be tried by another court for a crime referred to in article 5 for which that person has already been convicted or acquitted by the Court.

3. No person who has been tried by another court for conduct also proscribed under article 6, 7 or 8 shall be tried by the Court with respect to the same conduct unless the proceedings in the other court:

(a) Were for the purpose of shielding the person concerned from criminal responsibility for crimes within the jurisdiction of the Court; or

(b) Otherwise were not conducted independently or impartially in accordance with the norms of due process recognized by international law and were conducted in a manner which, in the circumstances, was inconsistent with an intent to bring the person concerned to justice.

Article 21
Applicable law

1. The Court shall apply:

(a) In the first place, this Statute, Elements of Crimes and its Rules of Procedure and Evidence;

(b) In the second place, where appropriate, applicable treaties and the principles and rules of international law, including the established principles of the international law of armed conflict;

(c) Failing that, general principles of law derived by the Court from national laws of legal systems of the world including, as appropriate, the national laws of States that would normally exercise jurisdiction over the crime, provided that those principles are not inconsistent with this Statute and with international law and internationally recognized norms and standards.

2. The Court may apply principles and rules of law as interpreted in its previous decisions.

3. The application and interpretation of law pursuant to this article must be consistent with internationally recognized human rights, and be without any adverse distinction founded on grounds such as gender as defined in article 7, paragraph 3, age, race, colour, language, religion or belief, political or other opinion, national, ethnic or social origin, wealth, birth or other status.

Article 42
The Office of the Prosecutor

1. The Office of the Prosecutor shall act independently as a separate organ of the Court. It shall be responsible for receiving referrals and any substantiated information on crimes within the jurisdiction of the Court, for examining them and for conducting investigations and prosecutions before the Court. A member of the Office shall not seek or act on instructions from any external source.

2. The Office shall be headed by the Prosecutor. The Prosecutor shall have full authority over the management and administration of the Office, including the staff, facilities and other resources thereof. The Prosecutor shall be assisted by one or more Deputy Prosecutors, who shall be entitled to carry out any of the acts required of the Prosecutor under this Statute. The Prosecutor and the Deputy Prosecutors shall be of different nationalities. They shall serve on a full-time basis.

3. The Prosecutor and the Deputy Prosecutors shall be persons of high moral character, be highly competent in and have extensive practical experience in the prosecution or trial of criminal cases. They shall have an excellent knowledge of and be fluent in at least one of the working languages of the Court.

4. The Prosecutor shall be elected by secret ballot by an absolute majority of the members of the Assembly of States Parties. The Deputy Prosecutors shall be elected in the same way from a list of candidates provided by the Prosecutor. The Prosecutor shall nominate three candidates for each position of Deputy Prosecutor to be filled. Unless a shorter term is decided upon at the time of their election, the Prosecutor and the Deputy Prosecutors shall hold office for a term of nine years and shall not be eligible for re-election.

5. Neither the Prosecutor nor a Deputy Prosecutor shall engage in any activity which is likely to interfere with his or her prosecutorial functions or to affect confidence in his or her independence. They shall not engage in any other occupation of a professional nature.

6. The Presidency may excuse the Prosecutor or a Deputy Prosecutor, at his or her request, from acting in a particular case.

7. Neither the Prosecutor nor a Deputy Prosecutor shall participate in any matter in which their impartiality might reasonably be doubted on any ground. They shall be disqualified from a case in accordance with this paragraph if, *inter alia*, they have previously been involved in any capacity in that case before the Court or in a related criminal case at the national level involving the person being investigated or prosecuted.

8. Any question as to the disqualification of the Prosecutor or a Deputy Prosecutor shall be decided by the Appeals Chamber.

(a) The person being investigated or prosecuted may at any time request the disqualification of the Prosecutor or a Deputy Prosecutor on the grounds set out in this article;

(b) The Prosecutor or the Deputy Prosecutor, as appropriate, shall be entitled to present his or her comments on the matter.

9. The Prosecutor shall appoint advisers with legal expertise on specific issues, including, but not limited to, sexual and gender violence and violence against children.

Article 51
Rules of Procedure and Evidence

1. The Rules of Procedure and Evidence shall enter into force upon adoption by a two-thirds majority of the members of the Assembly of States Parties.

2. Amendments to the Rules of Procedure and Evidence may be proposed by:

(a) Any State Party;

(b) The judges acting by an absolute majority; or

(c) The Prosecutor.

Such amendments shall enter into force upon adoption by a two-thirds majority of the members of the Assembly of States Parties.

3. After the adoption of the Rules of Procedure and Evidence, in urgent cases where the Rules do not provide for a specific situation before the Court, the judges may, by a two-thirds majority, draw up provisional Rules to be applied until adopted, amended or rejected at the next ordinary or special session of the Assembly of States Parties.

4. The Rules of Procedure and Evidence, amendments thereto and any provisional Rule shall be consistent with this Statute. Amendments to the Rules of Procedure and Evidence as well as provisional Rules shall not be applied retroactively to the detriment of the person who is being investigated or prosecuted or who has been convicted.

5. In the event of conflict between the Statute and the Rules of Procedure and Evidence, the Statute shall prevail.

Article 53
Initiation of an investigation

1. The Prosecutor shall, having evaluated the information made available to him or her, initiate an investigation unless he or she determines that there is no reasonable basis to proceed under this Statute. In deciding whether to initiate an investigation, the Prosecutor shall consider whether:

(a) The information available to the Prosecutor provides a reasonable basis to believe that a crime within the jurisdiction of the Court has been or is being committed;

(b) The case is or would be admissible under article 17; and

(c) Taking into account the gravity of the crime and the interests of victims, there are nonetheless substantial reasons to believe that an investigation would not serve the interests of justice.

If the Prosecutor determines that there is no reasonable basis to proceed and his or her determination is based solely on subparagraph (c) above, he or she shall inform the Pre-Trial Chamber.

2. If, upon investigation, the Prosecutor concludes that there is not a sufficient basis for a prosecution because:

(a) There is not a sufficient legal or factual basis to seek a warrant or summons under article 58;

(b) The case is inadmissible under article 17; or

(c) A prosecution is not in the interests of justice, taking into account all the circumstances, including the gravity of the crime, the interests of victims and the age or infirmity of the alleged perpetrator, and his or her role in the alleged crime; the Prosecutor shall inform the Pre-Trial Chamber and the State making a referral under article 14 or the Security Council in a case under article 13, paragraph (b), of his or her conclusion and the reasons for the conclusion.

3. (a) At the request of the State making a referral under article 14 or the Security Council under article 13, paragraph (b), the Pre-Trial Chamber may review a decision of the Prosecutor under paragraph 1 or 2 not to proceed and may request the Prosecutor to reconsider that decision.

(b) In addition, the Pre-Trial Chamber may, on its own initiative, review a decision of the Prosecutor not to proceed if it is based solely on paragraph 1 (c) or 2 (c). In such a case, the decision of the Prosecutor shall be effective only if confirmed by the Pre-Trial Chamber.

4. The Prosecutor may, at any time, reconsider a decision whether to initiate an investigation or prosecution based on new facts or information.

Article 54
Duties and powers of the Prosecutor with respect to investigations

1. The Prosecutor shall:

(a) In order to establish the truth, extend the investigation to cover all facts and evidence relevant to an assessment of whether there is criminal responsibility under this Statute, and, in doing so, investigate incriminating and exonerating circumstances equally;

(b) Take appropriate measures to ensure the effective investigation and prosecution of crimes within the jurisdiction of the Court, and in doing so, respect the interests and personal circumstances of victims and witnesses, including age, gender as defined in article 7, paragraph 3, and health, and take into account the nature of the crime, in particular where it involves sexual violence, gender violence or violence against children; and

(c) Fully respect the rights of persons arising under this Statute.

2. The Prosecutor may conduct investigations on the territory of a State:

(a) In accordance with the provisions of Part 9; or

(b) As authorized by the Pre-Trial Chamber under article 57, paragraph 3 (d).

3. The Prosecutor may:

(a) Collect and examine evidence;

(b) Request the presence of and question persons being investigated, victims and witnesses;

(c) Seek the cooperation of any State or intergovernmental organization or arrangement in accordance with its respective competence and/or mandate;

(d) Enter into such arrangements or agreements, not inconsistent with this Statute, as may be necessary to facilitate the cooperation of a State, intergovernmental organization or person;

(e) Agree not to disclose, at any stage of the proceedings, documents or information that the Prosecutor obtains on the condition of confidentiality and solely for the purpose of generating new evidence, unless the provider of the information consents; and

(f) Take necessary measures, or request that necessary measures be taken, to ensure the confidentiality of information, the protection of any person or the preservation of evidence.

Article 55
Rights of persons during an investigation

1. In respect of an investigation under this Statute, a person:

(a) Shall not be compelled to incriminate himself or herself or to confess guilt;

(b) Shall not be subjected to any form of coercion, duress or threat, to torture or to any other form of cruel, inhuman or degrading treatment or punishment;

(c) Shall, if questioned in a language other than a language the person fully understands and speaks, have, free of any cost, the assistance of a competent interpreter and such translations as are necessary to meet the requirements of fairness; and

(d) Shall not be subjected to arbitrary arrest or detention, and shall not be deprived of his or her liberty except on such grounds and in accordance with such procedures as are established in this Statute.

2. Where there are grounds to believe that a person has committed a crime within the jurisdiction of the Court and that person is about to be questioned either by the Prosecutor, or by national authorities pursuant to a request made under Part 9, that person shall also have the following rights of which he or she shall be informed prior to being questioned:

(a) To be informed, prior to being questioned, that there are grounds to believe that he or she has committed a crime within the jurisdiction of the Court;

(b) To remain silent, without such silence being a consideration in the determination of guilt or innocence;

(c) To have legal assistance of the person's choosing, or, if the person does not have legal assistance, to have legal assistance assigned to him or her, in any case where the interests of justice so require, and without payment by the person in any such case if the person does not have sufficient means to pay for it; and

(d) To be questioned in the presence of counsel unless the person has voluntarily waived his or her right to counsel.

Article 56
Role of the Pre-Trial Chamber in relation to a unique investigative opportunity

1. (a) Where the Prosecutor considers an investigation to present a unique opportunity to take testimony or a statement from a witness or to examine, collect or test evidence, which may not be available subsequently for the purposes of a trial, the Prosecutor shall so inform the Pre-Trial Chamber.

(b) In that case, the Pre-Trial Chamber may, upon request of the Prosecutor, take such measures as may be necessary to ensure the efficiency and integrity of the proceedings and, in particular, to protect the rights of the defence.

(c) Unless the Pre-Trial Chamber orders otherwise, the Prosecutor shall provide the relevant information to the person who has been arrested or appeared in response to a summons in connection with the investigation referred to in subparagraph (a), in order that he or she may be heard on the matter.

2. The measures referred to in paragraph 1 (b) may include:

(a) Making recommendations or orders regarding procedures to be followed;

(b) Directing that a record be made of the proceedings;

(c) Appointing an expert to assist;

(d) Authorizing counsel for a person who has been arrested, or appeared before the Court in response to a summons, to participate, or where there has not yet been such an arrest or appearance or counsel has not been designated, appointing another counsel to attend and represent the interests of the defence;

(e) Naming one of its members or, if necessary, another available judge of the Pre-Trial or Trial Division to observe and make recommendations or orders regarding the collection and preservation of evidence and the questioning of persons;

(f) Taking such other action as may be necessary to collect or preserve evidence.

3. (a) Where the Prosecutor has not sought measures pursuant to this article but the Pre-Trial Chamber considers that such measures are required to preserve evidence that it deems would be essential for the defence at trial, it shall consult with the Prosecutor as to whether there is good reason for the Prosecutor's failure to request the measures. If upon consultation, the Pre-Trial Chamber concludes that the Prosecutor's failure to request such measures is unjustified, the Pre-Trial Chamber may take such measures on its own initiative.

(b) A decision of the Pre-Trial Chamber to act on its own initiative under this paragraph may be appealed by the Prosecutor. The appeal shall be heard on an expedited basis.

4. The admissibility of evidence preserved or collected for trial pursuant to this article, or the record thereof, shall be governed at trial by article 69, and given such weight as determined by the Trial Chamber.

Article 57
Functions and powers of the Pre-Trial Chamber

1. Unless otherwise provided in this Statute, the Pre-Trial Chamber shall exercise its functions in accordance with the provisions of this article.

2. (a) Orders or rulings of the Pre-Trial Chamber issued under articles 15, 18, 19, 54, paragraph 2, 61, paragraph 7, and 72 must be concurred in by a majority of its judges.

(b) In all other cases, a single judge of the Pre-Trial Chamber may exercise the functions provided for in this Statute, unless otherwise provided for in the Rules of Procedure and Evidence or by a majority of the Pre-Trial Chamber.

3. In addition to its other functions under this Statute, the Pre-Trial Chamber may:

(a) At the request of the Prosecutor, issue such orders and warrants as may be required for the purposes of an investigation;

(b) Upon the request of a person who has been arrested or has appeared pursuant to a summons under article 58, issue such orders, including measures such as those described in article 56, or seek such cooperation pursuant to Part 9 as may be necessary to assist the person in the preparation of his or her defence;

(c) Where necessary, provide for the protection and privacy of victims and witnesses, the preservation of evidence, the protection of persons who have been arrested or appeared in response to a summons, and the protection of national security information;

(d) Authorize the Prosecutor to take specific investigative steps within the territory of a State Party without having secured the cooperation of that State under Part 9 if, whenever possible having regard to the views of the State concerned, the Pre-Trial Chamber has determined in that case that the State is clearly unable to execute a request for cooperation due to the unavailability of any authority or any component of its judicial system competent to execute the request for cooperation under Part 9;

(e) Where a warrant of arrest or a summons has been issued under article 58, and having due regard to the strength of the evidence and the rights of the parties concerned, as provided for in this Statute and the Rules of Procedure and Evidence, seek the cooperation of States pursuant to article 93, paragraph 1 (k), to take protective measures for the purpose of forfeiture, in particular for the ultimate benefit of victims.

Article 63
Trial in the presence of the accused

1. The accused shall be present during the trial.

2. If the accused, being present before the Court, continues to disrupt the trial, the Trial Chamber may remove the accused and shall make provision for him or her to observe the trial and instruct counsel from outside the courtroom, through the use of communications technology, if required. Such measures shall be taken only in exceptional circumstances after other reasonable alternatives have proved inadequate, and only for such duration as is strictly required.

Article 64
Functions and powers of the Trial Chamber

1. The functions and powers of the Trial Chamber set out in this article shall be exercised in accordance with this Statute and the Rules of Procedure and Evidence.

2. The Trial Chamber shall ensure that a trial is fair and expeditious and is conducted with full respect for the rights of the accused and due regard for the protection of victims and witnesses.

3. Upon assignment of a case for trial in accordance with this Statute, the Trial Chamber assigned to deal with the case shall:

(a) Confer with the parties and adopt such procedures as are necessary to facilitate the fair and expeditious conduct of the proceedings;

(b) Determine the language or languages to be used at trial; and

(c) Subject to any other relevant provisions of this Statute, provide for disclosure of documents or information not previously disclosed, sufficiently in advance of the commencement of the trial to enable adequate preparation for trial.

4. The Trial Chamber may, if necessary for its effective and fair functioning, refer preliminary issues to the Pre-Trial Chamber or, if necessary, to another available judge of the Pre-Trial Division.

5. Upon notice to the parties, the Trial Chamber may, as appropriate, direct that there be joinder or severance in respect of charges against more than one accused.

6. In performing its functions prior to trial or during the course of a trial, the Trial Chamber may, as necessary:

(a) Exercise any functions of the Pre-Trial Chamber referred to in article 61, paragraph 11;

(b) Require the attendance and testimony of witnesses and production of documents and other evidence by obtaining, if necessary, the assistance of States as provided in this Statute;

(c) Provide for the protection of confidential information;

(d) Order the production of evidence in addition to that already collected prior to the trial or presented during the trial by the parties;

(e) Provide for the protection of the accused, witnesses and victims; and

(f) Rule on any other relevant matters.

7. The trial shall be held in public. The Trial Chamber may, however, determine that special circumstances require that certain proceedings be in closed session for the purposes set forth in article 68, or to protect confidential or sensitive information to be given in evidence.

8. (a) At the commencement of the trial, the Trial Chamber shall have read to the accused the charges previously confirmed by the Pre-Trial Chamber. The Trial Chamber shall satisfy itself that the accused understands the nature of the charges. It shall afford him or her the opportunity to make an admission of guilt in accordance with article 65 or to plead not guilty.

(b) At the trial, the presiding judge may give directions for the conduct of proceedings, including to ensure that they are conducted in a fair and impartial manner. Subject to any directions of the presiding judge, the parties may submit evidence in accordance with the provisions of this Statute.

9. The Trial Chamber shall have, *inter alia*, the power on application of a party or on its own motion to:

(a) Rule on the admissibility or relevance of evidence; and

(b) Take all necessary steps to maintain order in the course of a hearing.

10. The Trial Chamber shall ensure that a complete record of the trial, which accurately reflects the proceedings, is made and that it is maintained and preserved by the Registrar.

Article 65
Proceedings on an admission of guilt

1. Where the accused makes an admission of guilt pursuant to article 64, paragraph 8 (a), the Trial Chamber shall determine whether:

(a) The accused understands the nature and consequences of the admission of guilt;

(b) The admission is voluntarily made by the accused after sufficient consultation with defence counsel; and

(c) The admission of guilt is supported by the facts of the case that are contained in:

(i) The charges brought by the Prosecutor and admitted by the accused;

(ii) Any materials presented by the Prosecutor which supplement the charges and which the accused accepts; and

(iii) Any other evidence, such as the testimony of witnesses, presented by the Prosecutor or the accused.

2. Where the Trial Chamber is satisfied that the matters referred to in paragraph 1 are established, it shall consider the admission of guilt, together with any additional evidence presented, as establishing all the essential facts that are required to prove the crime to which the admission of guilt relates, and may convict the accused of that crime.

3. Where the Trial Chamber is not satisfied that the matters referred to in paragraph 1 are established, it shall consider the admission of guilt as not having been made, in which case it shall order that the trial be continued under the ordinary trial procedures provided by this Statute and may remit the case to another Trial Chamber.

4. Where the Trial Chamber is of the opinion that a more complete presentation of the facts of the case is required in the interests of justice, in particular the interests of the victims, the Trial Chamber may:

(a) Request the Prosecutor to present additional evidence, including the testimony of witnesses; or

(b) Order that the trial be continued under the ordinary trial procedures provided by this Statute, in which case it shall consider the admission of guilt as not having been made and may remit the case to another Trial Chamber.

5. Any discussions between the Prosecutor and the defence regarding modification of the charges, the admission of guilt or the penalty to be imposed shall not be binding on the Court.

Article 66
Presumption of innocence

1. Everyone shall be presumed innocent until proved guilty before the Court in accordance with the applicable law.

2. The onus is on the Prosecutor to prove the guilt of the accused.

3. In order to convict the accused, the Court must be convinced of the guilt of the accused beyond reasonable doubt.

Article 67
Rights of the accused

1. In the determination of any charge, the accused shall be entitled to a public hearing, having regard to the provisions of this Statute, to a fair hearing conducted impartially, and to the following minimum guarantees, in full equality:

(a) To be informed promptly and in detail of the nature, cause and content of the charge, in a language which the accused fully understands and speaks;

(b) To have adequate time and facilities for the preparation of the defence and to communicate freely with counsel of the accused's choosing in confidence;

(c) To be tried without undue delay;

(d) Subject to article 63, paragraph 2, to be present at the trial, to conduct the defence in person or through legal assistance of the accused's choosing, to be informed, if the accused does not have legal assistance, of this right and to have legal assistance assigned by the Court in any case where the interests of justice so require, and without payment if the accused lacks sufficient means to pay for it;

(e) To examine, or have examined, the witnesses against him or her and to obtain the attendance and examination of witnesses on his or her behalf under the same conditions as witnesses against him or her. The accused shall also be entitled to raise defences and to present other evidence admissible under this Statute;

(f) To have, free of any cost, the assistance of a competent interpreter and such translations as are necessary to meet the requirements of fairness, if any of the proceedings of or documents presented to the Court are not in a language which the accused fully understands and speaks;

(g) Not to be compelled to testify or to confess guilt and to remain silent, without such silence being a consideration in the determination of guilt or innocence;

(h) To make an unsworn oral or written statement in his or her defence; and

(i) Not to have imposed on him or her any reversal of the burden of proof or any onus of rebuttal.

2. In addition to any other disclosure provided for in this Statute, the Prosecutor shall, as soon as practicable, disclose to the defence evidence in the Prosecutor's possession or control which he or she believes shows or tends to show the innocence of the accused, or to mitigate the guilt of the accused, or which may affect the credibility of prosecution evidence. In case of doubt as to the application of this paragraph, the Court shall decide.

Article 68
Protection of the victims and witnesses and their participation in the Proceedings

1. The Court shall take appropriate measures to protect the safety, physical and psychological well-being, dignity and privacy of victims and witnesses. In so doing, the Court shall have regard to all relevant factors, including age, gender as defined in article 7, paragraph 3, and health, and the nature of the

crime, in particular, but not limited to, where the crime involves sexual or gender violence or violence against children. The Prosecutor shall take such measures particularly during the investigation and prosecution of such crimes. These measures shall not be prejudicial to or inconsistent with the rights of the accused and a fair and impartial trial.

2. As an exception to the principle of public hearings provided for in article 67, the Chambers of the Court may, to protect victims and witnesses or an accused, conduct any part of the proceedings *in camera* or allow the presentation of evidence by electronic or other special means. In particular, such measures shall be implemented in the case of a victim of sexual violence or a child who is a victim or a witness, unless otherwise ordered by the Court, having regard to all the circumstances, particularly the views of the victim or witness.

3. Where the personal interests of the victims are affected, the Court shall permit their views and concerns to be presented and considered at stages of the proceedings determined to be appropriate by the Court and in a manner which is not prejudicial to or inconsistent with the rights of the accused and a fair and impartial trial. Such views and concerns may be presented by the legal representatives of the victims where the Court considers it appropriate, in accordance with the Rules of Procedure and Evidence.

4. The Victims and Witnesses Unit may advise the Prosecutor and the Court on appropriate protective measures, security arrangements, counselling and assistance as referred to in article 43, paragraph 6.

5. Where the disclosure of evidence or information pursuant to this Statute may lead to the grave endangerment of the security of a witness or his or her family, the Prosecutor may, for the purposes of any proceedings conducted prior to the commencement of the trial, withhold such evidence or information and instead submit a summary thereof. Such measures shall be exercised in a manner which is not prejudicial to or inconsistent with the rights of the accused and a fair and impartial trial.

6. A State may make an application for necessary measures to be taken in respect of the protection of its servants or agents and the protection of confidential or sensitive information.

Article 69
Evidence

1. Before testifying, each witness shall, in accordance with the Rules of Procedure and Evidence, give an undertaking as to the truthfulness of the evidence to be given by that witness.

2. The testimony of a witness at trial shall be given in person, except to the extent provided by the measures set forth in article 68 or in the Rules of Procedure and Evidence. The Court may also permit the giving of *viva voce* (oral) or recorded testimony of a witness by means of video or audio technology, as well as the introduction of documents or written transcripts, subject to this Statute and in accordance with the Rules of Procedure and Evidence. These measures shall not be prejudicial to or inconsistent with the rights of the accused.

3. The parties may submit evidence relevant to the case, in accordance with article 64. The Court shall have the authority to request the submission of all evidence that it considers necessary for the determination of the truth.

4. The Court may rule on the relevance or admissibility of any evidence, taking into account, *inter alia*, the probative value of the evidence and any prejudice that such evidence may cause to a fair trial or to a fair evaluation of the testimony of a witness, in accordance with the Rules of Procedure and Evidence.

5. The Court shall respect and observe privileges on confidentiality as provided for in the Rules of Procedure and Evidence.

6. The Court shall not require proof of facts of common knowledge but may take judicial notice of them.

7. Evidence obtained by means of a violation of this Statute or internationally recognized human rights shall not be admissible if:

(a) The violation casts substantial doubt on the reliability of the evidence; or

(b) The admission of the evidence would be antithetical to and would seriously damage the integrity of the proceedings.

8. When deciding on the relevance or admissibility of evidence collected by a State, the Court shall not rule on the application of the State's national law.

Article 74
Requirements for the decision

1. All the judges of the Trial Chamber shall be present at each stage of the trial and throughout their deliberations. The Presidency may, on a case-by-case basis, designate, as available, one or more alternate judges to be present at each stage of the trial and to replace a member of the Trial Chamber if that member is unable to continue attending.

2. The Trial Chamber's decision shall be based on its evaluation of the evidence and the entire proceedings. The decision shall not exceed the facts and circumstances described in the charges and any amendments to the charges. The Court may base its decision only on evidence submitted and discussed before it at the trial.

3. The judges shall attempt to achieve unanimity in their decision, failing which the decision shall be taken by a majority of the judges.

4. The deliberations of the Trial Chamber shall remain secret.

5. The decision shall be in writing and shall contain a full and reasoned statement of the Trial Chamber's findings on the evidence and conclusions. The Trial Chamber shall issue one decision. When there is no unanimity, the Trial Chamber's decision shall contain the views of the majority and the minority. The decision or a summary thereof shall be delivered in open court.

Article 75
Reparations to victims

1. The Court shall establish principles relating to reparations to, or in respect of, victims, including restitution, compensation and rehabilitation. On this basis, in its decision the Court may, either upon request or on its own motion in exceptional circumstances, determine the scope and extent of any damage, loss and injury to, or in respect of, victims and will state the principles on which it is acting.

2. The Court may make an order directly against a convicted person specifying appropriate reparations to, or in respect of, victims, including restitution, compensation and rehabilitation.

Where appropriate, the Court may order that the award for reparations be made through the Trust Fund provided for in article 79.

3. Before making an order under this article, the Court may invite and shall take account of representations from or on behalf of the convicted person, victims, other interested persons or interested States.

4. In exercising its power under this article, the Court may, after a person is convicted of a crime within the jurisdiction of the Court, determine whether, in order to give effect to an order which it may make under this article, it is necessary to seek measures under article 93, paragraph 1.

5. A State Party shall give effect to a decision under this article as if the provisions of article 109 were applicable to this article.

6. Nothing in this article shall be interpreted as prejudicing the rights of victims under national or international law.

Article 76
Sentencing

1. In the event of a conviction, the Trial Chamber shall consider the appropriate sentence to be imposed and shall take into account the evidence presented and submissions made during the trial that are relevant to the sentence.

2. Except where article 65 applies and before the completion of the trial, the Trial Chamber may on its own motion and shall, at the request of the Prosecutor or the accused, hold a further hearing to hear any additional evidence or submissions relevant to the sentence, in accordance with the Rules of Procedure and Evidence.

3. Where paragraph 2 applies, any representations under article 75 shall be heard during the further hearing referred to in paragraph 2 and, if necessary, during any additional hearing.

4. The sentence shall be pronounced in public and, wherever possible, in the presence of the accused.

Article 77
Applicable penalties

1. Subject to article 110, the Court may impose one of the following penalties on a person convicted of a crime referred to in article 5 of this Statute:

(a) Imprisonment for a specified number of years, which may not exceed a maximum of 30 years; or

(b) A term of life imprisonment when justified by the extreme gravity of the crime and the individual circumstances of the convicted person.

2. In addition to imprisonment, the Court may order:

(a) A fine under the criteria provided for in the Rules of Procedure and Evidence;

(b) A forfeiture of proceeds, property and assets derived directly or indirectly from that crime, without prejudice to the rights of bona fide third parties.

Article 78
Determination of the sentence

1. In determining the sentence, the Court shall, in accordance with the Rules of Procedure and Evidence, take into account such factors as the gravity of the crime and the individual circumstances of the convicted person.

2. In imposing a sentence of imprisonment, the Court shall deduct the time, if any, previously spent in detention in accordance with an order of the Court. The Court may deduct any time otherwise spent in detention in connection with conduct underlying the crime.

3. When a person has been convicted of more than one crime, the Court shall pronounce a sentence for each crime and a joint sentence specifying the total period of imprisonment. This period shall be no less than the highest individual sentence pronounced and shall not exceed 30 years imprisonment or a sentence of life imprisonment in conformity with article 77, paragraph 1 (b).

Article 79
Trust Fund

1. A Trust Fund shall be established by decision of the Assembly of States Parties for the benefit of victims of crimes within the jurisdiction of the Court, and of the families of such victims.

2. The Court may order money and other property collected through fines or forfeiture to be transferred, by order of the Court, to the Trust Fund.

3. The Trust Fund shall be managed according to criteria to be determined by the Assembly of States Parties.

Article 81
Appeal against decision of acquittal or conviction or against sentence

1. A decision under article 74 may be appealed in accordance with the Rules of Procedure and Evidence as follows:

(a) The Prosecutor may make an appeal on any of the following grounds:

(i) Procedural error,

(ii) Error of fact, or

(iii) Error of law;

(b) The convicted person, or the Prosecutor on that person's behalf, may make an appeal on any of the following grounds:

(i) Procedural error,

(ii) Error of fact,

(iii) Error of law, or

(iv) Any other ground that affects the fairness or reliability of the proceedings or decision.

2. (a) A sentence may be appealed, in accordance with the Rules of Procedure and Evidence, by the Prosecutor or the convicted person on the ground of disproportion between the crime and the sentence;

(b) If on an appeal against sentence the Court considers that there are grounds on which the conviction might be set aside, wholly or in part, it may invite the Prosecutor and the convicted person to submit grounds under article 81, paragraph 1 (a) or (b), and may render a decision on conviction in accordance with article 83;

(c) The same procedure applies when the Court, on an appeal against conviction only, considers that there are grounds to reduce the sentence under paragraph 2 (a).

3. (a) Unless the Trial Chamber orders otherwise, a convicted person shall remain in custody pending an appeal;

(b) When a convicted person's time in custody exceeds the sentence of imprisonment imposed, that person shall be released, except that if the Prosecutor is also appealing, the release may be subject to the conditions under subparagraph (c) below;

(c) In case of an acquittal, the accused shall be released immediately, subject to the following:

(i) Under exceptional circumstances, and having regard, *inter alia*, to the concrete risk of flight, the seriousness of the offence charged and the probability of success on appeal, the Trial Chamber, at the request of the Prosecutor, may maintain the detention of the person pending appeal;

(ii) A decision by the Trial Chamber under subparagraph (c) (i) may be appealed in accordance with the Rules of Procedure and Evidence.

4. Subject to the provisions of paragraph 3 (a) and (b), execution of the decision or sentence shall be suspended during the period allowed for appeal and for the duration of the appeal proceedings.

Article 82
Appeal against other decisions

1. Either party may appeal any of the following decisions in accordance with the Rules of Procedure and Evidence:

(a) A decision with respect to jurisdiction or admissibility;

(b) A decision granting or denying release of the person being investigated or prosecuted;

(c) A decision of the Pre-Trial Chamber to act on its own initiative under article 56, paragraph 3;

(d) A decision that involves an issue that would significantly affect the fair and expeditious conduct of the proceedings or the outcome of the trial, and for which, in the opinion of the Pre-Trial or Trial Chamber, an immediate resolution by the Appeals Chamber may materially advance the proceedings.

2. A decision of the Pre-Trial Chamber under article 57, paragraph 3 (d), may be appealed against by the State concerned or by the Prosecutor, with the leave of the Pre-Trial Chamber. The appeal shall be heard on an expedited basis.

3. An appeal shall not of itself have suspensive effect unless the Appeals Chamber so orders, upon request, in accordance with the Rules of Procedure and Evidence.

4. A legal representative of the victims, the convicted person or a bona fide owner of property adversely affected by an order under article 75 may appeal against the order for reparations, as provided in the Rules of Procedure and Evidence.

Article 103
Role of States in enforcement of sentences of imprisonment

1. (a) A sentence of imprisonment shall be served in a State designated by the Court from a list of States which have indicated to the Court their willingness to accept sentenced persons.

(b) At the time of declaring its willingness to accept sentenced persons, a State may attach conditions to its acceptance as agreed by the Court and in accordance with this Part.

(c) A State designated in a particular case shall promptly inform the Court whether it accepts the Court's designation.

2. (a) The State of enforcement shall notify the Court of any circumstances, including the exercise of any conditions agreed under paragraph 1, which could materially affect the terms or extent of the imprisonment. The Court shall be given at least 45 days' notice of any such known or foreseeable circumstances. During this period, the State of enforcement shall take no action that might prejudice its obligations under article 110.

(b) Where the Court cannot agree to the circumstances referred to in subparagraph (a), it shall notify the State of enforcement and proceed in accordance with article 104, paragraph 1.

3. In exercising its discretion to make a designation under paragraph 1, the Court shall take into account the following:

(a) The principle that States Parties should share the responsibility for enforcing sentences of imprisonment, in accordance with principles of equitable distribution, as provided in the Rules of Procedure and Evidence;

(b) The application of widely accepted international treaty standards governing the treatment of prisoners;

(c) The views of the sentenced person;

(d) The nationality of the sentenced person;

(e) Such other factors regarding the circumstances of the crime or the person sentenced, or the effective enforcement of the sentence, as may be appropriate in designating the State of enforcement.

4. If no State is designated under paragraph 1, the sentence of imprisonment shall be served in a prison facility made available by the host State, in accordance with the conditions set out in the headquarters agreement referred to in article 3, paragraph 2. In such a case, the costs arising out of the enforcement of a sentence of imprisonment shall be borne by the Court.

Article 106
Supervision of enforcement of sentences and conditions of imprisonment

1. The enforcement of a sentence of imprisonment shall be subject to the supervision of the Court and shall be consistent with widely accepted international treaty standards governing treatment of prisoners.

2. The conditions of imprisonment shall be governed by the law of the State of enforcement and shall be consistent with widely accepted international treaty standards governing treatment of prisoners; in no case shall such conditions be more or less favourable than those available to prisoners convicted of similar offences in the State of enforcement.

3. Communications between a sentenced person and the Court shall be unimpeded and confidential.

Article 109
Enforcement of fines and forfeiture measures

1. States Parties shall give effect to fines or forfeitures ordered by the Court under Part 7, without prejudice to the rights of bona fide third parties, and in accordance with the procedure of their national law.

2. If a State Party is unable to give effect to an order for forfeiture, it shall take measures to recover the value of the proceeds, property or assets ordered by the Court to be forfeited, without prejudice to the rights of bona fide third parties.

3. Property, or the proceeds of the sale of real property or, where appropriate, the sale of other property, which is obtained by a State Party as a result of its enforcement of a judgement of the Court shall be transferred to the Court.

Article 110
Review by the Court concerning reduction of sentence

1. The State of enforcement shall not release the person before expiry of the sentence pronounced by the Court.

2. The Court alone shall have the right to decide any reduction of sentence, and shall rule on the matter after having heard the person.

3. When the person has served two thirds of the sentence, or 25 years in the case of life imprisonment, the Court shall review the sentence to determine whether it should be reduced. Such a review shall not be conducted before that time.

4. In its review under paragraph 3, the Court may reduce the sentence if it finds that one or more of the following factors are present:

(a) The early and continuing willingness of the person to cooperate with the Court in its investigations and prosecutions;

(b) The voluntary assistance of the person in enabling the enforcement of the judgements and orders of the Court in other cases, and in particular providing assistance in locating assets subject to orders of fine, forfeiture or reparation which may be used for the benefit of victims; or

(c) Other factors establishing a clear and significant change of circumstances sufficient to justify the reduction of sentence, as provided in the Rules of Procedure and Evidence.

5. If the Court determines in its initial review under paragraph 3 that it is not appropriate to reduce the sentence, it shall thereafter review the question of reduction of sentence at such intervals and applying such criteria as provided for in the Rules of Procedure and Evidence.

APPENDIX II

Selected Rules of Procedure and Evidence [Rules 10, 16–18, 21, 22, 47–64, 67–69, 76–79, 81–99, 103–06, 118, 119, 121, 137–40, 144–48]

Rule 10
Retention of information and evidence

The Prosecutor shall be responsible for the retention, storage and security of information and physical evidence obtained in the course of the investigations by his or her Office.

Rule 16
Responsibilities of the Registrar relating to victims and witnesses

1. In relation to victims, the Registrar shall be responsible for the performance of the following functions in accordance with the Statute and these Rules:

(a) Providing notice or notification to victims or their legal representatives;

(b) Assisting them in obtaining legal advice and organizing their legal representation, and providing their legal representatives with adequate support, assistance and information, including such facilities as may be necessary for the direct performance of their duty, for the purpose of protecting their rights during all stages of the proceedings in accordance with rules 89 to 91;

(c) Assisting them in participating in the different phases of the proceedings in accordance with rules 89 to 91;

(d) Taking gender-sensitive measures to facilitate the participation of victims of sexual violence at all stages of the proceedings.

2. In relation to victims, witnesses and others who are at risk on account of testimony given by such witnesses, the Registrar shall be responsible for the

performance of the following functions in accordance with the Statute and these Rules:

(a) Informing them of their rights under the Statute and the Rules, and of the existence, functions and availability of the Victims and Witnesses Unit;

(b) Ensuring that they are aware, in a timely manner, of the relevant decisions of the Court that may have an impact on their interests, subject to provisions on confidentiality.

3. For the fulfilment of his or her functions, the Registrar may keep a special register for victims who have expressed their intention to participate in relation to a specific case.

4. Agreements on relocation and provision of support services on the territory of a State of traumatized or threatened victims, witnesses and others who are at risk on account of testimony given by such witnesses may be negotiated with the States by the Registrar on behalf of the Court. Such agreements may remain confidential.

Rule 17
Functions of the Unit

1. The Victims and Witnesses Unit shall exercise its functions in accordance with article 43, paragraph 6.

2. The Victims and Witnesses Unit shall, *inter alia*, perform the following functions, in accordance with the Statute and the Rules, and in consultation with the Chamber, the Prosecutor and the defence, as appropriate:

(a) With respect to all witnesses, victims who appear before the Court, and others who are at risk on account of testimony given by such witnesses, in accordance with their particular needs and circumstances:

(i) Providing them with adequate protective and security measures and formulating long- and short-term plans for their protection;

(ii) Recommending to the organs of the Court the adoption of protection measures and also advising relevant States of such measures;

(iii) Assisting them in obtaining medical, psychological and other appropriate assistance;

(iv) Making available to the Court and the parties training in issues of trauma, sexual violence, security and confidentiality;

(v) Recommending, in consultation with the Office of the Prosecutor, the elaboration of a code of conduct, emphasizing the vital nature of security and confidentiality for investigators of the Court and of the defence and all intergovernmental and non-governmental organizations acting at the request of the Court, as appropriate;

(vi) Cooperating with States, where necessary, in providing any of the measures stipulated in this rule;

(b) With respect to witnesses:

(i) Advising them where to obtain legal advice for the purpose of protecting their rights, in particular in relation to their testimony;

(ii) Assisting them when they are called to testify before the Court;

(iii) Taking gender-sensitive measures to facilitate the testimony of victims of sexual violence at all stages of the proceedings.

3. In performing its functions, the Unit shall give due regard to the particular needs of children, elderly persons and persons with disabilities. In order to facilitate the participation and protection of children as witnesses, the Unit may assign, as appropriate, and with the agreement of the parents or the legal guardian, a child-support person to assist a child through all stages of the proceedings.

Rule 18
Responsibilities of the Unit

For the efficient and effective performance of its work, the Victims and Witnesses Unit shall:

(a) Ensure that the staff in the Unit maintain confidentiality at all times;

(b) While recognizing the specific interests of the Office of the Prosecutor, the defence and the witnesses, respect the interests of the witness, including, where necessary, by maintaining an appropriate separation of the services provided to the prosecution and defence witnesses, and act impartially when cooperating with all parties and in accordance with the rulings and decisions of the Chambers;

(c) Have administrative and technical assistance available for witnesses, victims who appear before the Court, and others who are at risk on account of testimony given by such witnesses, during all stages of the proceedings and thereafter, as reasonably appropriate;

(d) Ensure training of its staff with respect to victims' and witnesses' security, integrity and dignity, including matters related to gender and cultural sensitivity;

(e) Where appropriate, cooperate with intergovernmental and non-governmental organizations.

Rule 21
Assignment of legal assistance

1. Subject to article 55, paragraph 2 (c), and article 67, paragraph 1 (d), criteria and procedures for assignment of legal assistance shall be established in the Regulations, based on a proposal by the Registrar, following consultations with any independent representative body of counsel or legal associations, as referred to in rule 20, sub-rule 3.

2. The Registrar shall create and maintain a list of counsel who meet the criteria set forth in rule 22 and the Regulations. The person shall freely choose his or her counsel from this list or other counsel who meets the required criteria and is willing to be included in the list.

3. A person may seek from the Presidency a review of a decision to refuse a request for assignment of counsel. The decision of the Presidency shall be final. If a request is refused, a further request may be made by a person to the Registrar, upon showing a change in circumstances.

4. A person choosing to represent himself or herself shall so notify the Registrar in writing at the first opportunity.

5. Where a person claims to have insufficient means to pay for legal assistance and this is subsequently found not to be so, the Chamber dealing with the case at that time may make an order of contribution to recover the cost of providing counsel.

Rule 22
Appointment and qualifications of Counsel for the defence

1. A counsel for the defence shall have established competence in international or criminal law and procedure, as well as the necessary relevant experience, whether as judge, prosecutor, advocate or in other similar capacity, in criminal proceedings. A counsel for the defence shall have an excellent knowledge of and be fluent in at least one of the working languages of the

Court. Counsel for the defence may be assisted by other persons, including professors of law, with relevant expertise.

2. Counsel for the defence engaged by a person exercising his or her right under the Statute to retain legal counsel of his or her choosing shall file a power of attorney with the Registrar at the earliest opportunity.

3. In the performance of their duties, Counsel for the defence shall be subject to the Statute, the Rules, the Regulations, the Code of Professional Conduct for Counsel adopted in accordance with rule 8 and any other document adopted by the Court that may be relevant to the performance of their duties.

Rule 47
Testimony under article 15, paragraph 2

1. The provisions of rules 111 and 112 shall apply, *mutatis mutandis*, to testimony received by the Prosecutor pursuant to article 15, paragraph 2.

2. When the Prosecutor considers that there is a serious risk that it might not be possible for the testimony to be taken subsequently, he or she may request the Pre-Trial Chamber to take such measures as may be necessary to ensure the efficiency and integrity of the proceedings and, in particular, to appoint a counsel or a judge from the Pre-Trial Chamber to be present during the taking of the testimony in order to protect the rights of the defence. If the testimony is subsequently presented in the proceedings, its admissibility shall be governed by article 69, paragraph 4, and given such weight as determined by the relevant Chamber.

Rule 48
Determination of reasonable basis to proceed with an investigation under article 15, paragraph 3

In determining whether there is a reasonable basis to proceed with an investigation under article 15, paragraph 3, the Prosecutor shall consider the factors set out in article 53, paragraph 1 (a) to (c).

Rule 49
Decision and notice under article 15, paragraph 6

1. Where a decision under article 15, paragraph 6, is taken, the Prosecutor shall promptly ensure that notice is provided, including reasons for his or her

decision, in a manner that prevents any danger to the safety, well-being and privacy of those who provided information to him or her under article 15, paragraphs 1 and 2, or the integrity of investigations or proceedings.

2. The notice shall also advise of the possibility of submitting further information regarding the same situation in the light of new facts and evidence.

Rule 50
Procedure for authorization by the Pre-Trial Chamber of the commencement of the investigation

1. When the Prosecutor intends to seek authorization from the Pre-Trial Chamber to initiate an investigation pursuant to article 15, paragraph 3, the Prosecutor shall inform victims, known to him or her or to the Victims and Witnesses Unit, or their legal representatives, unless the Prosecutor decides that doing so would pose a danger to the integrity of the investigation or the life or well-being of victims and witnesses. The Prosecutor may also give notice by general means in order to reach groups of victims if he or she determines in the particular circumstances of the case that such notice could not pose a danger to the integrity and effective conduct of the investigation or to the security and well-being of victims and witnesses. In performing these functions, the Prosecutor may seek the assistance of the Victims and Witnesses Unit as appropriate.

2. A request for authorization by the Prosecutor shall be in writing.

3. Following information given in accordance with sub-rule 1, victims may make representations in writing to the Pre-Trial Chamber within such time limit as set forth in the Regulations.

4. The Pre-Trial Chamber, in deciding on the procedure to be followed, may request additional information from the Prosecutor and from any of the victims who have made representations, and, if it considers it appropriate, may hold a hearing.

5. The Pre-Trial Chamber shall issue its decision, including its reasons, as to whether to authorize the commencement of the investigation in accordance with article 15, paragraph 4, with respect to all or any part of the request by the Prosecutor. The Chamber shall give notice of the decision to victims who have made representations.

6. The above procedure shall also apply to a new request to the Pre-Trial Chamber pursuant to article 15, paragraph 5.

Rule 51
Information provided under article 17

In considering the matters referred to in article 17, paragraph 2, and in the context of the circumstances of the case, the Court may consider, *inter alia*, information that the State referred to in article 17, paragraph 1, may choose to bring to the attention of the Court showing that its courts meet internationally recognized norms and standards for the independent and impartial prosecution of similar conduct, or that the State has confirmed in writing to the Prosecutor that the case is being investigated or prosecuted.

Rule 52
Notification provided for in article 18, paragraph 1

1. Subject to the limitations provided for in article 18, paragraph 1, the notification shall contain information about the acts that may constitute crimes referred to in article 5, relevant for the purposes of article 18, paragraph 2.

2. A State may request additional information from the Prosecutor to assist it in the application of article 18, paragraph 2. Such a request shall not affect the onemonth time limit provided for in article 18, paragraph 2, and shall be responded to by the Prosecutor on an expedited basis.

Rule 53
Deferral provided for in article 18, paragraph 2

When a State requests a deferral pursuant to article 18, paragraph 2, that State shall make this request in writing and provide information concerning its investigation, taking into account article 18, paragraph 2. The Prosecutor may request additional information from that State.

Rule 54
Application by the Prosecutor under article 18, paragraph 2

1. An application submitted by the Prosecutor to the Pre-Trial Chamber in accordance with article 18, paragraph 2, shall be in writing and shall contain the basis for the application. The information provided by the State under rule 53 shall be communicated by the Prosecutor to the Pre-Trial Chamber.

2. The Prosecutor shall inform that State in writing when he or she makes an application to the Pre-Trial Chamber under article 18, paragraph 2, and shall include in the notice a summary of the basis of the application.

Rule 55
Proceedings concerning article 18, paragraph 2

1. The Pre-Trial Chamber shall decide on the procedure to be followed and may take appropriate measures for the proper conduct of the proceedings. It may hold a hearing.

2. The Pre-Trial Chamber shall examine the Prosecutor's application and any observations submitted by a State that requested a deferral in accordance with article 18, paragraph 2, and shall consider the factors in article 17 in deciding whether to authorize an investigation.

3. The decision and the basis for the decision of the Pre-Trial Chamber shall be communicated as soon as possible to the Prosecutor and to the State that requested a deferral of an investigation.

Rule 56
Application by the Prosecutor following review under article 18, paragraph 3

1. Following a review by the Prosecutor as set forth in article 18, paragraph 3, the Prosecutor may apply to the Pre-Trial Chamber for authorization in accordance with article 18, paragraph 2. The application to the Pre-Trial Chamber shall be in writing and shall contain the basis for the application.

2. Any further information provided by the State under article 18, paragraph 5, shall be communicated by the Prosecutor to the Pre-Trial Chamber.

3. The proceedings shall be conducted in accordance with rules 54, sub-rule 2, and 55.

Rule 57
Provisional measures under article 18, paragraph 6

An application to the Pre-Trial Chamber by the Prosecutor in the circumstances provided for in article 18, paragraph 6, shall be considered *ex parte* and in camera. The Pre-Trial Chamber shall rule on the application on an expedited basis.

Rule 58
Proceedings under article 19

1. A request or application made under article 19 shall be in writing and contain the basis for it.

2. When a Chamber receives a request or application raising a challenge or question concerning its jurisdiction or the admissibility of a case in accordance with article 19, paragraph 2 or 3, or is acting on its own motion as provided for in article 19, paragraph 1, it shall decide on the procedure to be followed and may take appropriate measures for the proper conduct of the proceedings. It may hold a hearing. It may join the challenge or question to a confirmation or a trial proceeding as long as this does not cause undue delay, and in this circumstance shall hear and decide on the challenge or question first.

3. The Court shall transmit a request or application received under sub-rule 2 to the Prosecutor and to the person referred to in article 19, paragraph 2, who has been surrendered to the Court or who has appeared voluntarily or pursuant to a summons, and shall allow them to submit written observations to the request or application within a period of time determined by the Chamber.

4. The Court shall rule on any challenge or question of jurisdiction first and then on any challenge or question of admissibility.

Rule 59
Participation in proceedings under article 19, paragraph 3

1. For the purpose of article 19, paragraph 3, the Registrar shall inform the following of any question or challenge of jurisdiction or admissibility which has arisen pursuant to article 19, paragraphs 1, 2 and 3:

(a) Those who have referred a situation pursuant to article 13;

(b) The victims who have already communicated with the Court in relation to that case or their legal representatives.

2. The Registrar shall provide those referred to in sub-rule 1, in a manner consistent with the duty of the Court regarding the confidentiality of

information, the protection of any person and the preservation of evidence, with a summary of the grounds on which the jurisdiction of the Court or the admissibility of the case has been challenged.

3. Those receiving the information, as provided for in sub-rule 1, may make representation in writing to the competent Chamber within such time limit as it considers appropriate.

Rule 60
Competent organ to receive challenges

If a challenge to the jurisdiction of the Court or to the admissibility of a case is made after a confirmation of the charges but before the constitution or designation of the Trial Chamber, it shall be addressed to the Presidency, which shall refer it to the Trial Chamber as soon as the latter is constituted or designated in accordance with rule 130.

Rule 61
Provisional measures under article 19, paragraph 8

When the Prosecutor makes application to the competent Chamber in the circumstances provided for in article 19, paragraph 8, rule 57 shall apply.

Rule 62
Proceedings under article 19, paragraph 10

1. If the Prosecutor makes a request under article 19, paragraph 10, he or she shall make the request to the Chamber that made the latest ruling on admissibility. The provisions of rules 58, 59 and 61 shall be applicable.

2. The State or States whose challenge to admissibility under article 19, paragraph 2, provoked the decision of inadmissibility provided for in article 19, paragraph 10, shall be notified of the request of the Prosecutor and shall be given a time limit within which to make representations.

Rule 63
General provisions relating to evidence

1. The rules of evidence set forth in this chapter, together with article 69, shall apply in proceedings before all Chambers.

2. A Chamber shall have the authority, in accordance with the discretion described in article 64, paragraph 9, to assess freely all evidence submitted in order to determine its relevance or admissibility in accordance with article 69.

3. A Chamber shall rule on an application of a party or on its own motion, made under article 64, subparagraph 9 (a), concerning admissibility when it is based on the grounds set out in article 69, paragraph 7.

4. Without prejudice to article 66, paragraph 3, a Chamber shall not impose a legal requirement that corroboration is required in order to prove any crime within the jurisdiction of the Court, in particular, crimes of sexual violence.

5. The Chambers shall not apply national laws governing evidence, other than in accordance with article 21.

Rule 64
Procedure relating to the relevance or admissibility of evidence

1. An issue relating to relevance or admissibility must be raised at the time when the evidence is submitted to a Chamber. Exceptionally, when those issues were not known at the time when the evidence was submitted, it may be raised immediately after the issue has become known. The Chamber may request that the issue be raised in writing. The written motion shall be communicated by the Court to all those who participate in the proceedings, unless otherwise decided by the Court.

2. A Chamber shall give reasons for any rulings it makes on evidentiary matters. These reasons shall be placed in the record of the proceedings if they have not already been incorporated into the record during the course of the proceedings in accordance with article 64, paragraph 10, and rule 137, sub-rule 1.

3. Evidence ruled irrelevant or inadmissible shall not be considered by the Chamber.

Rule 67
Live testimony by means of audio or video-link technology

1. In accordance with article 69, paragraph 2, a Chamber may allow a witness to give viva voce (oral) testimony before the Chamber by means of audio or video technology, provided that such technology permits the witness to be examined by the Prosecutor, the defence, and by the Chamber itself, at the time that the witness so testifies.

2. The examination of a witness under this rule shall be conducted in accordance with the relevant rules of this chapter.

3. The Chamber, with the assistance of the Registry, shall ensure that the venue chosen for the conduct of the audio or video-link testimony is conducive to the giving of truthful and open testimony and to the safety, physical and psychological well-being, dignity and privacy of the witness.

Rule 68
Prior recorded testimony

When the Pre-Trial Chamber has not taken measures under article 56, the Trial Chamber may, in accordance with article 69, paragraph 2, allow the introduction of previously recorded audio or video testimony of a witness, or the transcript or other documented evidence of such testimony, provided that:

(a) If the witness who gave the previously recorded testimony is not present before the Trial Chamber, both the Prosecutor and the defence had the opportunity to examine the witness during the recording; or

(b) If the witness who gave the previously recorded testimony is present before the Trial Chamber, he or she does not object to the submission of the previously recorded testimony and the Prosecutor, the defence and the Chamber have the opportunity to examine the witness during the proceedings.

Rule 69
Agreements as to evidence

The Prosecutor and the defence may agree that an alleged fact, which is contained in the charges, the contents of a document, the expected testimony of a witness or other evidence is not contested and, accordingly, a Chamber may consider such alleged fact as being proven, unless the Chamber is of the opinion that a more complete presentation of the alleged facts is required in the interests of justice, in particular the interests of the victims.

Rule 76
Pre-trial disclosure relating to prosecution witnesses

1. The Prosecutor shall provide the defence with the names of witnesses whom the Prosecutor intends to call to testify and copies of any prior statements made by those witnesses. This shall be done sufficiently in advance to enable the adequate preparation of the defence.

2. The Prosecutor shall subsequently advise the defence of the names of any additional prosecution witnesses and provide copies of their statements when the decision is made to call those witnesses.

3. The statements of prosecution witnesses shall be made available in original and in a language which the accused fully understands and speaks.

4. This rule is subject to the protection and privacy of victims and witnesses and the protection of confidential information as provided for in the Statute and rules 81 and 82.

Rule 77
Inspection of material in possession or control of the Prosecutor

The Prosecutor shall, subject to the restrictions on disclosure as provided for in the Statute and in rules 81 and 82, permit the defence to inspect any books, documents, photographs and other tangible objects in the possession or control of the Prosecutor, which are material to the preparation of the defence or are intended for use by the Prosecutor as evidence for the purposes of the confirmation hearing or at trial, as the case may be, or were obtained from or belonged to the person.

Rule 78
Inspection of material in possession or control of the defence

The defence shall permit the Prosecutor to inspect any books, documents, photographs and other tangible objects in the possession or control of the defence, which are intended for use by the defence as evidence for the purposes of the confirmation hearing or at trial.

Rule 79
Disclosure by the defence

1. The defence shall notify the Prosecutor of its intent to:

(a) Raise the existence of an alibi, in which case the notification shall specify the place or places at which the accused claims to have been present at the time of the alleged crime and the names of witnesses and any other evidence upon which the accused intends to rely to establish the alibi; or

(b) Raise a ground for excluding criminal responsibility provided for in article 31, paragraph 1, in which case the notification shall specify the names of witnesses and any other evidence upon which the accused intends to rely to establish the ground.

2. With due regard to time limits set forth in other rules, notification under sub-rule 1 shall be given sufficiently in advance to enable the Prosecutor to prepare adequately and to respond. The Chamber dealing with the matter may grant the Prosecutor an adjournment to address the issue raised by the defence.

3. Failure of the defence to provide notice under this rule shall not limit its right to raise matters dealt with in sub-rule 1 and to present evidence.

4. This rule does not prevent a Chamber from ordering disclosure of any other evidence.

Rule 81
Restrictions on disclosure

1. Reports, memoranda or other internal documents prepared by a party, its assistants or representatives in connection with the investigation or preparation of the case are not subject to disclosure.

2. Where material or information is in the possession or control of the Prosecutor which must be disclosed in accordance with the Statute, but disclosure may prejudice further or ongoing investigations, the Prosecutor may apply to the Chamber dealing with the matter for a ruling as to whether the material or information must be disclosed to the defence. The matter shall be heard on an exparte basis by the Chamber. However, the Prosecutor may not introduce such material or information into evidence during the confirmation hearing or the trial without adequate prior disclosure to the accused.

3. Where steps have been taken to ensure the confidentiality of information, in accordance with articles 54, 57, 64, 72 and 93, and, in accordance with article 68, to protect the safety of witnesses and victims and members of their families, such information shall not be disclosed, except in accordance with those articles. When the disclosure of such information may create a risk to the safety of the witness, the Court shall take measures to inform the witness in advance.

4. The Chamber dealing with the matter shall, on its own motion or at the request of the Prosecutor, the accused or any State, take the necessary steps to ensure the confidentiality of information, in accordance with articles 54, 72 and 93, and, in accordance with article 68, to protect the safety of witnesses and victims and members of their families, including by authorizing the non-disclosure of their identity prior to the commencement of the trial.

5. Where material or information is in the possession or control of the Prosecutor which is withheld under article 68, paragraph 5, such material and information may not be subsequently introduced into evidence during the confirmation hearing or the trial without adequate prior disclosure to the accused.

6. Where material or information is in the possession or control of the defence which is subject to disclosure, it may be withheld in circumstances similar to those which would allow the Prosecutor to rely on article 68, paragraph 5, and a summary thereof submitted instead. Such material and information may not be subsequently introduced into evidence during the confirmation hearing or the trial without adequate prior disclosure to the Prosecutor.

Rule 82
Restrictions on disclosure of material and information protected under article 54, paragraph 3 (e)

1. Where material or information is in the possession or control of the Prosecutor which is protected under article 54, paragraph 3 (e), the Prosecutor may not subsequently introduce such material or information into evidence without the prior consent of the provider of the material or information and adequate prior disclosure to the accused.

2. If the Prosecutor introduces material or information protected under article 54, paragraph 3 (e), into evidence, a Chamber may not order the production of additional evidence received from the provider of the initial

material or information, nor may a Chamber for the purpose of obtaining such additional evidence itself summon the provider or a representative of the provider as a witness or order their attendance.

3. If the Prosecutor calls a witness to introduce in evidence any material or information which has been protected under article 54, paragraph 3 (e), a Chamber may not compel that witness to answer any question relating to the material or information or its origin, if the witness declines to answer on grounds of confidentiality.

4. The right of the accused to challenge evidence which has been protected under article 54, paragraph 3 (e), shall remain unaffected subject only to the limitations contained in sub-rules 2 and 3.

5. A Chamber dealing with the matter may order, upon application by the defence, that, in the interests of justice, material or information in the possession of the accused, which has been provided to the accused under the same conditions as set forth in article 54, paragraph 3 (e), and which is to be introduced into evidence, shall be subject *mutatis mutandis* to sub-rules 1, 2 and 3.

Rule 83
Ruling on exculpatory evidence under article 67, paragraph 2

The Prosecutor may request as soon as practicable a hearing on an *ex parte* basis before the Chamber dealing with the matter for the purpose of obtaining a ruling under article 67, paragraph 2.

Rule 84
Disclosure and additional evidence for trial

In order to enable the parties to prepare for trial and to facilitate the fair and expeditious conduct of the proceedings, the Trial Chamber shall, in accordance with article 64, paragraphs 3 (c) and 6 (d), and article 67, paragraph (2), and subject to article 68, paragraph 5, make any necessary orders for the disclosure of documents or information not previously disclosed and for the production of additional evidence. To avoid delay and to ensure that the trial commences on the set date, any such orders shall include strict time limits which shall be kept under review by the Trial Chamber.

Rule 85
Definition of victims

For the purposes of the Statute and the Rules of Procedure and Evidence:

(a) 'Victims' means natural persons who have suffered harm as a result of the commission of any crime within the jurisdiction of the Court;

(b) Victims may include organizations or institutions that have sustained direct harm to any of their property which is dedicated to religion, education, art or science or charitable purposes, and to their historic monuments, hospitals and other places and objects for humanitarian purposes.

Rule 86
General principle

A Chamber in making any direction or order, and other organs of the Court in performing their functions under the Statute or the Rules, shall take into account the needs of all victims and witnesses in accordance with article 68, in particular, children, elderly persons, persons with disabilities and victims of sexual or gender violence.

Rule 87
Protective measures

1. Upon the motion of the Prosecutor or the defence or upon the request of a witness or a victim or his or her legal representative, if any, or on its own motion, and after having consulted with the Victims and Witnesses Unit, as appropriate, a Chamber may order measures to protect a victim, a witness or another person at risk on account of testimony given by a witness pursuant to article 68, paragraphs 1 and 2. The Chamber shall seek to obtain, whenever possible, the consent of the person in respect of whom the protective measure is sought prior to ordering the protective measure.

2. A motion or request under sub-rule 1 shall be governed by rule 134, provided that:

(a) Such a motion or request shall not be submitted *ex parte*;

(b) A request by a witness or by a victim or his or her legal representative, if any, shall be served on both the Prosecutor and the defence, each of whom shall have the opportunity to respond;

(c) A motion or request affecting a particular witness or a particular victim shall be served on that witness or victim or his or her legal representative, if any, in addition to the other party, each of whom shall have the opportunity to respond;

(d) When the Chamber proceeds on its own motion, notice and opportunity to respond shall be given to the Prosecutor and the defence, and to any witness or any victim or his or her legal representative, if any, who would be affected by such protective measure; and

(e) A motion or request may be filed under seal, and, if so filed, shall remain sealed until otherwise ordered by a Chamber. Responses to motions or requests filed under seal shall also be filed under seal.

3. A Chamber may, on a motion or request under sub-rule 1, hold a hearing, which shall be conducted in camera, to determine whether to order measures to prevent the release to the public or press and information agencies, of the identity or the location of a victim, a witness or other person at risk on account of testimony given by a witness by ordering, *inter alia*:

(a) That the name of the victim, witness or other person at risk on account of testimony given by a witness or any information which could lead to his or her identification, be expunged from the public records of the Chamber;

(b) That the Prosecutor, the defence or any other participant in the proceedings be prohibited from disclosing such information to a third party;

(c) That testimony be presented by electronic or other special means, including the use of technical means enabling the alteration of pictures or voice, the use of audio-visual technology, in particular videoconferencing and closed-circuit television, and the exclusive use of the sound media;

(d) That a pseudonym be used for a victim, a witness or other person at risk on account of testimony given by a witness; or

(e) That a Chamber conduct part of its proceedings in camera.

Rule 88
Special measures

1. Upon the motion of the Prosecutor or the defence, or upon the request of a witness or a victim or his or her legal representative, if any, or on its own

motion, and after having consulted with the Victims and Witnesses Unit, as appropriate, a Chamber may, taking into account the views of the victim or witness, order special measures such as, but not limited to, measures to facilitate the testimony of a traumatized victim or witness, a child, an elderly person or a victim of sexual violence, pursuant to article 68, paragraphs 1 and 2. The Chamber shall seek to obtain, whenever possible, the consent of the person in respect of whom the special measure is sought prior to ordering that measure.

2. A Chamber may hold a hearing on a motion or a request under sub-rule 1, if necessary in camera or *ex parte*, to determine whether to order any such special measure, including but not limited to an order that a counsel, a legal representative, a psychologist or a family member be permitted to attend during the testimony of the victim or the witness.

3. For *inter partes* motions or requests filed under this rule, the provisions of rule 87, sub-rules 2 (b) to (d), shall apply *mutatis mutandis*.

4. A motion or request filed under this rule may be filed under seal, and if so filed shall remain sealed until otherwise ordered by a Chamber. Any responses to *inter partes* motions or requests filed under seal shall also be filed under seal.

5. Taking into consideration that violations of the privacy of a witness or victim may create risk to his or her security, a Chamber shall be vigilant in controlling the manner of questioning a witness or victim so as to avoid any harassment or intimidation, paying particular attention to attacks on victims of crimes of sexual violence.

Rule 89
Application for participation of victims in the proceedings

1. In order to present their views and concerns, victims shall make written application to the Registrar, who shall transmit the application to the relevant Chamber. Subject to the provisions of the Statute, in particular article 68, paragraph 1, the Registrar shall provide a copy of the application to the Prosecutor and the defence, who shall be entitled to reply within a time limit to be set by the Chamber. Subject to the provisions of sub-rule 2, the Chamber shall then specify the proceedings and manner in which participation is considered appropriate, which may include making opening and closing statements.

2. The Chamber, on its own initiative or on the application of the Prosecutor or the defence, may reject the application if it considers that the person is not a victim or that the criteria set forth in article 68, paragraph 3, are not otherwise fulfilled. A victim whose application has been rejected may file a new application later in the proceedings.

3. An application referred to in this rule may also be made by a person acting with the consent of the victim, or a person acting on behalf of a victim, in the case of a victim who is a child or, when necessary, a victim who is disabled.

4. Where there are a number of applications, the Chamber may consider the applications in such a manner as to ensure the effectiveness of the proceedings and may issue one decision.

Rule 90
Legal representatives of victims

1. A victim shall be free to choose a legal representative.

2. Where there are a number of victims, the Chamber may, for the purposes of ensuring the effectiveness of the proceedings, request the victims or particular groups of victims, if necessary with the assistance of the Registry, to choose a common legal representative or representatives. In facilitating the coordination of victim representation, the Registry may provide assistance, *inter alia*, by referring the victims to a list of counsel, maintained by the Registry, or suggesting one or more common legal representatives.

3. If the victims are unable to choose a common legal representative or representatives within a time limit that the Chamber may decide, the Chamber may request the Registrar to choose one or more common legal representatives.

4. The Chamber and the Registry shall take all reasonable steps to ensure that in the selection of common legal representatives, the distinct interests of the victims, particularly as provided in article 68, paragraph 1, are represented and that any conflict of interest is avoided.

5. A victim or group of victims who lack the necessary means to pay for a common legal representative chosen by the Court may receive assistance from the Registry, including, as appropriate, financial assistance.

6. A legal representative of a victim or victims shall have the qualifications set forth in rule 22, sub-rule 1.

Rule 91
Participation of legal representatives in the proceedings

1. A Chamber may modify a previous ruling under rule 89.

2. A legal representative of a victim shall be entitled to attend and participate in the proceedings in accordance with the terms of the ruling of the Chamber and any modification thereof given under rules 89 and 90. This shall include participation in hearings unless, in the circumstances of the case, the Chamber concerned is of the view that the representative's intervention should be confined to written observations or submissions. The Prosecutor and the defence shall be allowed to reply to any oral or written observation by the legal representative for victims.

3. (a) When a legal representative attends and participates in accordance with this rule, and wishes to question a witness, including questioning under rules 67 and 68, an expert or the accused, the legal representative must make application to the Chamber. The Chamber may require the legal representative to provide a written note of the questions and in that case the questions shall be communicated to the Prosecutor and, if appropriate, the defence, who shall be allowed to make observations within a time limit set by the Chamber.

(b) The Chamber shall then issue a ruling on the request, taking into account the stage of the proceedings, the rights of the accused, the interests of witnesses, the need for a fair, impartial and expeditious trial and in order to give effect to article 68, paragraph 3. The ruling may include directions on the manner and order of the questions and the production of documents in accordance with the powers of the Chamber under article 64. The Chamber may, if it considers it appropriate, put the question to the witness, expert or accused on behalf of the victim's legal representative.

4. For a hearing limited to reparations under article 75, the restrictions on questioning by the legal representative set forth in sub-rule 2 shall not apply. In that case, the legal representative may, with the permission of the Chamber concerned, question witnesses, experts and the person concerned.

Rule 92
Notification to victims and their legal representatives

1. This rule on notification to victims and their legal representatives shall apply to all proceedings before the Court, except in proceedings provided for in Part 2.

2. In order to allow victims to apply for participation in the proceedings in accordance with rule 89, the Court shall notify victims concerning the decision of the Prosecutor not to initiate an investigation or not to prosecute pursuant to article 53. Such a notification shall be given to victims or their legal representatives who have already participated in the proceedings or, as far as possible, to those who have communicated with the Court in respect of the situation or case in question. The Chamber may order the measures outlined in sub-rule 8 if it considers it appropriate in the particular circumstances.

3. In order to allow victims to apply for participation in the proceedings in accordance with rule 89, the Court shall notify victims regarding its decision to hold a hearing to confirm charges pursuant to article 61. Such a notification shall be given to victims or their legal representatives who have already participated in the proceedings or, as far as possible, to those who have communicated with the Court in respect of the case in question.

4. When a notification for participation as provided for in sub-rules 2 and 3 has been given, any subsequent notification as referred to in sub-rules 5 and 6 shall only be provided to victims or their legal representatives who may participate in the proceedings in accordance with a ruling of the Chamber pursuant to rule 89 and any modification thereof.

5. In a manner consistent with the ruling made under rules 89 to 91, victims or their legal representatives participating in proceedings shall, in respect of those proceedings, be notified by the Registrar in a timely manner of:

(a) Proceedings before the Court, including the date of hearings and any postponements thereof, and the date of delivery of the decision;

(b) Requests, submissions, motions and other documents relating to such requests, submissions or motions.

6. Where victims or their legal representatives have participated in a certain stage of the proceedings, the Registrar shall notify them as soon as possible of the decisions of the Court in those proceedings.

7. Notifications as referred to in sub-rules 5 and 6 shall be in writing or, where written notification is not possible, in any other form as appropriate. The Registry shall keep a record of all notifications. Where necessary, the Registrar may seek the cooperation of States Parties in accordance with article 93, paragraph 1 (d) and (l).

8. For notification as referred to in sub-rule 3 and otherwise at the request of a Chamber, the Registrar shall take necessary measures to give adequate publicity to the proceedings. In doing so, the Registrar may seek, in accordance with Part 9, the cooperation of relevant States Parties, and seek the assistance of intergovernmental organizations.

Rule 93
Views of victims or their legal representatives

A Chamber may seek the views of victims or their legal representatives participating pursuant to rules 89 to 91 on any issue, *inter alia*, in relation to issues referred to in rules 107, 109, 125, 128, 136, 139 and 191. In addition, a Chamber may seek the views of other victims, as appropriate.

Rule 94
Procedure upon request

1. A victim's request for reparations under article 75 shall be made in writing and filed with the Registrar. It shall contain the following particulars:

(a) The identity and address of the claimant;

(b) A description of the injury, loss or harm;

(c) The location and date of the incident and, to the extent possible, the identity of the person or persons the victim believes to be responsible for the injury, loss or harm;

(d) Where restitution of assets, property or other tangible items is sought, a description of them;

(e) Claims for compensation;

(f) Claims for rehabilitation and other forms of remedy;

(g) To the extent possible, any relevant supporting documentation, including names and addresses of witnesses.

2. At commencement of the trial and subject to any protective measures, the Court shall ask the Registrar to provide notification of the request to the person or persons named in the request or identified in the charges and, to the extent possible, to any interested persons or any interested States. Those notified shall file with the Registry any representation made under article 75, paragraph 3.

Rule 95
Procedure on the motion of the Court

1. In cases where the Court intends to proceed on its own motion pursuant to article 75, paragraph 1, it shall ask the Registrar to provide notification of its intention to the person or persons against whom the Court is considering making a determination, and, to the extent possible, to victims, interested persons and interested States. Those notified shall file with the Registry any representation made under article 75, paragraph 3.

2. If, as a result of notification under sub-rule 1:

(a) A victim makes a request for reparations, that request will be determined as if it had been brought under rule 94;

(b) A victim requests that the Court does not make an order for reparations, the Court shall not proceed to make an individual order in respect of that victim.

Rule 96
Publication of reparation proceedings

1. Without prejudice to any other rules on notification of proceedings, the Registrar shall, insofar as practicable, notify the victims or their legal representatives and the person or persons concerned. The Registrar shall also, having regard to any information provided by the Prosecutor, take all the necessary measures to give adequate publicity of the reparation proceedings before the Court, to the extent possible, to other victims, interested persons and interested States.

2. In taking the measures described in sub-rule 1, the Court may seek, in accordance with Part 9, the cooperation of relevant States Parties, and seek the assistance of intergovernmental organizations in order to give

publicity, as widely as possible and by all possible means, to the reparation proceedings before the Court.

Rule 97
Assessment of reparations

1. Taking into account the scope and extent of any damage, loss or injury, the Court may award reparations on an individualized basis or, where it deems it appropriate, on a collective basis or both.

2. At the request of victims or their legal representatives, or at the request of the convicted person, or on its own motion, the Court may appoint appropriate experts to assist it in determining the scope, extent of any damage, loss and injury to, or in respect of victims and to suggest various options concerning the appropriate types and modalities of reparations. The Court shall invite, as appropriate, victims or their legal representatives, the convicted person as well as interested persons and interested States to make observations on the reports of the experts.

3. In all cases, the Court shall respect the rights of victims and the convicted person.

Rule 98
Trust Fund

1. Individual awards for reparations shall be made directly against a convicted person.

2. The Court may order that an award for reparations against a convicted person be deposited with the Trust Fund where at the time of making the order it is impossible or impracticable to make individual awards directly to each victim. The award for reparations thus deposited in the Trust Fund shall be separated from other resources of the Trust Fund and shall be forwarded to each victim as soon as possible.

3. The Court may order that an award for reparations against a convicted person be made through the Trust Fund where the number of the victims and the scope, forms and modalities of reparations makes a collective award more appropriate.

4. Following consultations with interested States and the Trust Fund, the Court may order that an award for reparations be made through the Trust

Fund to an intergovernmental, international or national organization approved by the Trust Fund.

5. Other resources of the Trust Fund may be used for the benefit of victims subject to the provisions of article 79.

Rule 99
Cooperation and protective measures for the purpose of forfeiture under articles 57, paragraph 3 (e), and 75, paragraph 4

1. The Pre-Trial Chamber, pursuant to article 57, paragraph 3 (e), or the Trial Chamber, pursuant to article 75, paragraph 4, may, on its own motion or on the application of the Prosecutor or at the request of the victims or their legal representatives who have made a request for reparations or who have given a written undertaking to do so, determine whether measures should be requested.

2. Notice is not required unless the Court determines, in the particular circumstances of the case, that notification could not jeopardize the effectiveness of the measures requested. In the latter case, the Registrar shall provide notification of the proceedings to the person against whom a request is made and so far as is possible to any interested persons or interested States.

3. If an order is made without prior notification, the relevant Chamber shall request the Registrar, as soon as is consistent with the effectiveness of the measures requested, to notify those against whom a request is made and, to the extent possible, to any interested persons or any interested States and invite them to make observations as to whether the order should be revoked or otherwise modified.

4. The Court may make orders as to the timing and conduct of any proceedings necessary to determine these issues.

Rule 103
Amicus curiae and other forms of submission

1. At any stage of the proceedings, a Chamber may, if it considers it desirable for the proper determination of the case, invite or grant leave to a State, organization or person to submit, in writing or orally, any observation on any issue that the Chamber deems appropriate.

2. The Prosecutor and the defence shall have the opportunity to respond to the observations submitted under sub-rule 1.

3. A written observation submitted under sub-rule 1 shall be filed with the Registrar, who shall provide copies to the Prosecutor and the defence. The Chamber shall determine what time limits shall apply to the filing of such observations.

Rule 104
Evaluation of information by the Prosecutor

1. In acting pursuant to article 53, paragraph 1, the Prosecutor shall, in evaluating the information made available to him or her, analyse the seriousness of the information received.

2. For the purposes of sub-rule 1, the Prosecutor may seek additional information from States, organs of the United Nations, intergovernmental and non-governmental organizations, or other reliable sources that he or she deems appropriate, and may receive written or oral testimony at the seat of the Court. The procedure set out in rule 47 shall apply to the receiving of such testimony.

Rule 105
Notification of a decision by the Prosecutor not to initiate an investigation

1. When the Prosecutor decides not to initiate an investigation under article 53, paragraph 1, he or she shall promptly inform in writing the State or States that referred a situation under article 14, or the Security Council in respect of a situation covered by article 13, paragraph (b).

2. When the Prosecutor decides not to submit to the Pre-Trial Chamber a request for authorization of an investigation, rule 49 shall apply.

3. The notification referred to in sub-rule 1 shall contain the conclusion of the Prosecutor and, having regard to article 68, paragraph 1, the reasons for the conclusion.

4. In case the Prosecutor decides not to investigate solely on the basis of article 53, paragraph 1 (c), he or she shall inform in writing the Pre-Trial Chamber promptly after making that decision.

5. The notification shall contain the conclusion of the Prosecutor and the reasons for the conclusion.

Rule 106
Notification of a decision by the Prosecutor not to prosecute

1. When the Prosecutor decides that there is not a sufficient basis for prosecution under article 53, paragraph 2, he or she shall promptly inform in writing the Pre-Trial Chamber, together with the State or States that referred a situation under article 14, or the Security Council in respect of a situation covered by article 13, paragraph (b).

2. The notifications referred to in sub-rule 1 shall contain the conclusion of the Prosecutor and, having regard to article 68, paragraph 1, the reasons for the conclusion.

Rule 118
Pre-trial detention at the seat of the Court

1. If the person surrendered to the Court makes an initial request for interim release pending trial, either upon first appearance in accordance with rule 121 or subsequently, the Pre-Trial Chamber shall decide upon the request without delay, after seeking the views of the Prosecutor.

2. The Pre-Trial Chamber shall review its ruling on the release or detention of a person in accordance with article 60, paragraph 3, at least every 120 days and may do so at any time on the request of the person or the Prosecutor.

3. After the first appearance, a request for interim release must be made in writing. The Prosecutor shall be given notice of such a request. The Pre-Trial Chamber shall decide after having received observations in writing of the Prosecutor and the detained person. The Pre-Trial Chamber may decide to hold a hearing, at the request of the Prosecutor or the detained person or on its own initiative. A hearing must be held at least once every year.

Rule 119
Conditional release

1. The Pre-Trial Chamber may set one or more conditions restricting liberty, including the following:

(a) The person must not travel beyond territorial limits set by the Pre-Trial Chamber without the explicit agreement of the Chamber;

(b) The person must not go to certain places or associate with certain persons as specified by the Pre-Trial Chamber;

(c) The person must not contact directly or indirectly victims or witnesses;

(d) The person must not engage in certain professional activities;

(e) The person must reside at a particular address as specified by the Pre-Trial Chamber;

(f) The person must respond when summoned by an authority or qualified person designated by the Pre-Trial Chamber;

(g) The person must post bond or provide real or personal security or surety, for which the amount and the schedule and mode of payment shall be determined by the Pre-Trial Chamber;

(h) The person must supply the Registrar with all identity documents, particularly his or her passport.

2. At the request of the person concerned or the Prosecutor or on its own initiative, the Pre-Trial Chamber may at any time decide to amend the conditions set pursuant to sub-rule 1.

3. Before imposing or amending any conditions restricting liberty, the Pre-Trial Chamber shall seek the views of the Prosecutor, the person concerned, any relevant State and victims that have communicated with the Court in that case and whom the Chamber considers could be at risk as a result of a release or conditions imposed.

4. If the Pre-Trial Chamber is convinced that the person concerned has failed to comply with one or more of the obligations imposed, it may, on such basis, at the request of the Prosecutor or on its own initiative, issue a warrant of arrest in respect of the person.

5. When the Pre-Trial Chamber issues a summons to appear pursuant to article 58, paragraph 7, and intends to set conditions restricting liberty, it shall ascertain the relevant provisions of the national law of the State receiving the summons. In a manner that is in keeping with the national law of the State receiving the summons, the Pre-Trial Chamber shall proceed in accordance with sub-rules 1, 2 and 3. If the Pre-Trial Chamber receives information that the person concerned has failed to comply with conditions imposed, it shall proceed in accordance with sub-rule 4.

Rule 121
Proceedings before the confirmation hearing

1. A person subject to a warrant of arrest or a summons to appear under article 58 shall appear before the Pre-Trial Chamber, in the presence of the Prosecutor, promptly upon arriving at the Court. Subject to the provisions of articles 60 and 61, the person shall enjoy the rights set forth in article 67. At this first appearance, the Pre-Trial Chamber shall set the date on which it intends to hold a hearing to confirm the charges. It shall ensure that this date, and any postponements under sub-rule 7, are made public.

2. In accordance with article 61, paragraph 3, the Pre-Trial Chamber shall take the necessary decisions regarding disclosure between the Prosecutor and the person in respect of whom a warrant of arrest or a summons to appear has been issued.

During disclosure:

(a) The person concerned may be assisted or represented by the counsel of his or her choice or by a counsel assigned to him or her;

(b) The Pre-Trial Chamber shall hold status conferences to ensure that disclosure takes place under satisfactory conditions. For each case, a judge of the Pre-Trial Chamber shall be appointed to organize such status conferences, on his or her own motion, or at the request of the Prosecutor or the person;

(c) All evidence disclosed between the Prosecutor and the person for the purposes of the confirmation hearing shall be communicated to the Pre-Trial Chamber.

3. The Prosecutor shall provide to the Pre-Trial Chamber and the person, no later than 30 days before the date of the confirmation hearing, a detailed description of the charges together with a list of the evidence which he or she intends to present at the hearing.

4. Where the Prosecutor intends to amend the charges pursuant to article 61, paragraph 4, he or she shall notify the Pre-Trial Chamber and the person no later than 15 days before the date of the hearing of the amended charges together with a list of evidence that the Prosecutor intends to bring in support of those charges at the hearing.

5. Where the Prosecutor intends to present new evidence at the hearing, he or she shall provide the Pre-Trial Chamber and the person with a list of that evidence no later than 15 days before the date of the hearing.

6. If the person intends to present evidence under article 61, paragraph 6, he or she shall provide a list of that evidence to the Pre-Trial Chamber no later than 15 days before the date of the hearing. The Pre-Trial Chamber shall transmit the list to the Prosecutor without delay. The person shall provide a list of evidence that he or she intends to present in response to any amended charges or a new list of evidence provided by the Prosecutor.

7. The Prosecutor or the person may ask the Pre-Trial Chamber to postpone the date of the confirmation hearing. The Pre-Trial Chamber may also, on its own motion, decide to postpone the hearing.

8. The Pre-Trial Chamber shall not take into consideration charges and evidence presented after the time limit, or any extension thereof, has expired.

9. The Prosecutor and the person may lodge written submissions with the Pre-Trial Chamber, on points of fact and on law, including grounds for excluding criminal responsibility set forth in article 31, paragraph 1, no later than three days before the date of the hearing. A copy of these submissions shall be transmitted immediately to the Prosecutor or the person, as the case may be.

10. The Registry shall create and maintain a full and accurate record of all proceedings before the Pre-Trial Chamber, including all documents transmitted to the Chamber pursuant to this rule. Subject to any restrictions concerning confidentiality and the protection of national security information, the record may be consulted by the Prosecutor, the person and victims or their legal representatives participating in the proceedings pursuant to rules 89 to 91.

Rule 137
Record of the trial proceedings

1. In accordance with article 64, paragraph 10, the Registrar shall take measures to make, and preserve, a full and accurate record of all proceedings, including transcripts, audio- and video-recordings and other means of capturing sound or image.

2. A Trial Chamber may order the disclosure of all or part of the record of closed proceedings when the reasons for ordering its non-disclosure no longer exist.

3. The Trial Chamber may authorize persons other than the Registrar to take photographs, audio- and video-recordings and other means of capturing the sound or image of the trial.

Rule 138
Custody of evidence

The Registrar shall retain and preserve, as necessary, all the evidence and other materials offered during the hearing, subject to any order of the Trial Chamber.

Rule 139
Decision on admission of guilt

1. After having proceeded in accordance with article 65, paragraph 1, the Trial Chamber, in order to decide whether to proceed in accordance with article 65, paragraph 4, may invite the views of the Prosecutor and the defence.

2. The Trial Chamber shall then make its decision on the admission of guilt and shall give reasons for this decision, which shall be placed on the record.

Rule 140
Directions for the conduct of the proceedings and testimony

1. If the Presiding Judge does not give directions under article 64, paragraph 8, the Prosecutor and the defence shall agree on the order and manner in which the evidence shall be submitted to the Trial Chamber. If no agreement can be reached, the Presiding Judge shall issue directions.

2. In all cases, subject to article 64, paragraphs 8 (b) and 9, article 69, paragraph 4, and rule 88, sub-rule 5, a witness may be questioned as follows:

(a) A party that submits evidence in accordance with article 69, paragraph 3, by way of a witness, has the right to question that witness;

(b) The prosecution and the defence have the right to question that witness about relevant matters related to the witness's testimony and its reliability, the credibility of the witness and other relevant matters;

(c) The Trial Chamber has the right to question a witness before or after a witness is questioned by a participant referred to in sub-rules 2 (a) or (b);

(d) The defence shall have the right to be the last to examine a witness.

3. Unless otherwise ordered by the Trial Chamber, a witness other than an expert, or an investigator if he or she has not yet testified, shall not be present when the testimony of another witness is given. However, a witness who has

heard the testimony of another witness shall not for that reason alone be disqualified from testifying. When a witness testifies after hearing the testimony of others, this fact shall be noted in the record and considered by the Trial Chamber when evaluating the evidence.

Rule 144
Delivery of the decisions of the Trial Chamber

1. Decisions of the Trial Chamber concerning admissibility of a case, the jurisdiction of the Court, criminal responsibility of the accused, sentence and reparations shall be pronounced in public and, wherever possible, in the presence of the accused, the Prosecutor, the victims or the legal representatives of the victims participating in the proceedings pursuant to rules 89 to 91, and the representatives of the States which have participated in the proceedings.

2. Copies of all the above-mentioned decisions shall be provided as soon as possible to:

(a) All those who participated in the proceedings, in a working language of the Court;

(b) The accused, in a language he or she fully understands or speaks, if necessary to meet the requirements of fairness under article 67, paragraph 1 (f).

Rule 145
Determination of sentence

1. In its determination of the sentence pursuant to article 78, paragraph 1, the Court shall:

(a) Bear in mind that the totality of any sentence of imprisonment and fine, as the case may be, imposed under article 77 must reflect the culpability of the convicted person;

(b) Balance all the relevant factors, including any mitigating and aggravating factors and consider the circumstances both of the convicted person and of the crime;

(c) In addition to the factors mentioned in article 78, paragraph 1, give consideration, *inter alia*, to the extent of the damage caused, in particular the harm caused to the victims and their families, the nature of the unlawful behaviour and the means employed to execute the crime; the degree of participation of the convicted person; the degree of intent; the circumstances of manner, time and location; and the age, education, social and economic condition of the convicted person.

2. In addition to the factors mentioned above, the Court shall take into account, as appropriate:

(a) Mitigating circumstances such as:

(i) The circumstances falling short of constituting grounds for exclusion of criminal responsibility, such as substantially diminished mental capacity or duress;

(ii) The convicted person's conduct after the act, including any efforts by the person to compensate the victims and any cooperation with the Court;

(b) As aggravating circumstances:

(i) Any relevant prior criminal convictions for crimes under the jurisdiction of the Court or of a similar nature;

(ii) Abuse of power or official capacity;

(iii) Commission of the crime where the victim is particularly defenceless;

(iv) Commission of the crime with particular cruelty or where there were multiple victims;

(v) Commission of the crime for any motive involving discrimination on any of the grounds referred to in article 21, paragraph 3;

(vi) Other circumstances which, although not enumerated above, by virtue of their nature are similar to those mentioned.

3. Life imprisonment may be imposed when justified by the extreme gravity of the crime and the individual circumstances of the convicted person, as evidenced by the existence of one or more aggravating circumstances.

Rule 146
Imposition of fines under article 77

1. In determining whether to order a fine under article 77, paragraph 2 (a), and in fixing the amount of the fine, the Court shall determine whether

imprisonment is a sufficient penalty. The Court shall give due consideration to the financial capacity of the convicted person, including any orders for forfeiture in accordance with article 77, paragraph 2 (b), and, as appropriate, any orders for reparation in accordance with article 75. The Court shall take into account, in addition to the factors referred to in rule 145, whether and to what degree the crime was motivated by personal financial gain.

2. A fine imposed under article 77, paragraph 2 (a), shall be set at an appropriate level. To this end, the Court shall, in addition to the factors referred to above, in particular take into consideration the damage and injuries caused as well as the proportionate gains derived from the crime by the perpetrator. Under no circumstances may the total amount exceed 75 per cent of the value of the convicted person's identifiable assets, liquid or realizable, and property, after deduction of an appropriate amount that would satisfy the financial needs of the convicted person and his or her dependants.

3. In imposing a fine, the Court shall allow the convicted person a reasonable period in which to pay the fine. The Court may provide for payment of a lump sum or by way of instalments during that period.

4. In imposing a fine, the Court may, as an option, calculate it according to a system of daily fines. In such cases, the minimum duration shall be 30 days and the maximum duration five years. The Court shall decide the total amount in accordance with sub-rules 1 and 2. It shall determine the amount of daily payment in the light of the individual circumstances of the convicted person, including the financial needs of his or her dependants.

5. If the convicted person does not pay the fine imposed in accordance with the conditions set above, appropriate measures may be taken by the Court pursuant to rules 217 to 222 and in accordance with article 109. Where, in cases of continued wilful non-payment, the Presidency, on its own motion or at the request of the Prosecutor, is satisfied that all available enforcement measures have been exhausted, it may as a last resort extend the term of imprisonment for a period not to exceed a quarter of such term or five years, whichever is less. In the determination of such period of extension, the Presidency shall take into account the amount of the fine, imposed and paid. Any such extension shall not apply in the case of life imprisonment. The extension may not lead to a total period of imprisonment in excess of 30 years.

6. In order to determine whether to order an extension and the period involved, the Presidency shall sit in camera for the purpose of obtaining the views of the sentenced person and the Prosecutor. The sentenced person shall have the right to be assisted by counsel.

7. In imposing a fine, the Court shall warn the convicted person that failure to pay the fine in accordance with the conditions set out above may result in an extension of the period of imprisonment as described in this rule.

Rule 147
Orders of forfeiture

1. In accordance with article 76, paragraphs 2 and 3, and rules 63, sub-rule 1, and 143, at any hearing to consider an order of forfeiture, Chamber shall hear evidence as to the identification and location of specific proceeds, property or assets which have been derived directly or indirectly from the crime.

2. If before or during the hearing, a Chamber becomes aware of any bona fide third party who appears to have an interest in relevant proceeds, property or assets, it shall give notice to that third party.

3. The Prosecutor, the convicted person and any bona fide third party with an interest in the relevant proceeds, property or assets may submit evidence relevant to the issue.

4. After considering any evidence submitted, a Chamber may issue an order of forfeiture in relation to specific proceeds, property or assets if it is satisfied that these have been derived directly or indirectly from the crime.

Rule 148
Orders to transfer fines or forfeitures to the Trust Fund

Before making an order pursuant to article 79, paragraph 2, a Chamber may request the representatives of the Fund to submit written or oral observations to it.

APPENDIX III

Regulations of the Registry [only Chapters 3 & 4]

Chapter 3
Responsibilities of the Registrar Relating to Victims and Witnesses

Section 1
Assistance to Victims and Witnesses

Regulation 79
General provisions

1. Pursuant to article 43, paragraph 6, and rules 16, 17 and 18, the Registrar shall develop and, to the extent possible, implement policies and procedures to enable witnesses to testify in safety, so that the experience of testifying does not result in further harm, suffering or trauma for the witnesses.

2. The Registrar shall exercise his or her functions regarding witnesses, victims who appear before the Court and persons at risk with no distinction of any kind, whether of gender, age, race, colour, language, religion or belief, political or other opinion, national, ethnic or social origin, wealth, birth or other status.

Regulation 80
Services to victims and witnesses

1. In order to receive services provided by the Registry, the Prosecutor and counsel shall complete a form requesting the provision of services. The Registry may request from the Prosecutor and counsel any additional information necessary for the provision of services.

2. Services such as relocation, accompanying support persons, dependent care, extraordinary allowances for lost earnings and clothing allowances shall be provided on a case-by-case basis, in accordance with an assessment made by the Registry.

Regulation 81
Travel

1. The Registry shall arrange transportation for witnesses, victims who appear before the Court and persons at risk who, pursuant to an order of the Chamber, need to travel for testimony or for support or protection-related purposes.

2. The mode of transport shall be determined on a case-by-case basis, having regard to protection, safety and health considerations.

3. Unless otherwise justified for support or protection reasons, travel shall be based on:

(a) An economy class international round trip air ticket by the shortest route, subject to prior authorisation by the Registry; or

(b) The practice of the Court for staff members for all other means of transport.

Regulation 82
Accommodation

1. The Court shall provide appropriate full board and accommodation in locations selected by the Registry for witnesses, victims who appear before the Court and persons at risk where required for the purposes of the Court.

2. Witnesses, victims who appear before the Court and persons at risk who have chosen not to accept full board and accommodation provided by the Court shall only receive an incidental allowance in accordance with regulation 84 and an attendance allowance in accordance with regulation 85.

Regulation 83
Support programme

1. The Registry shall develop a support programme, which shall also apply in the field, in order to provide psychological, social assistance and advice to victims, witnesses and their families, accompanying persons and persons at risk at the earliest stage possible.

2. In addition, the support programme shall provide, where appropriate, and for the duration of their stay at the seat of the Court, or where proceedings are held, round-the-clock assistance to victims who appear before the Court, witnesses and accompanying persons.

Regulation 84
Incidental allowance

1. An incidental allowance for personal expenses may be provided to witnesses, victims who appear before the Court, persons at risk and accompanying support persons who require overnight accommodation at any stage of their journey.

2. The amount of the incidental allowance shall be determined by the Registrar and shall be reviewed annually. The Registrar shall publish the table of the rate of incidental allowance yearly on the website of the Court.

Regulation 85
Attendance allowance

1. Witnesses shall be provided with an attendance allowance as compensation for wages, earnings and time lost as a result of testifying. Witnesses shall not be required to submit a request or any supporting documentation in order to receive the attendance allowance.

2. The daily minimum wage rate shall be determined by dividing:

(a) The annual salary of the staff of the Court at the General Services, step 1 level 1 in the country in which the witness is residing at the time he or she testifies; by

(b) The number of days per year.

3. The attendance allowance shall be calculated by multiplying:

(a) A percentage rate of the daily minimum wage rate applicable for the staff of the Court in the country in which the witness is residing at the time he or she testifies. The percentage shall be determined by the Registrar and shall be reviewed annually. The Registrar shall publish yearly on the website of the Court the table of the rate of attendance allowance; by

(b) The number of days the witness is required at the seat of the Court or where proceedings are held, including travel days. For the purpose of calculating the attendance allowance, a part of a day used in connection with testifying shall be considered a full day.

Regulation 86
Extraordinary allowance for lost earnings

1. The Registrar may provide an extraordinary allowance for lost earnings for witnesses who suffer undue financial hardship as a result of being absent from legal income earning activities for the purposes of the Court.

2. Witnesses shall submit their request accompanied by any supporting documentation.

3. The Registrar shall inform the participants of any payment of such allowance.

Regulation 87
Expert witnesses

Transportation for expert witnesses who travel for testimony or for support or protectionrelated purposes shall be arranged by the Registry, in accordance with regulation 81. A daily subsistence allowance shall also be provided.

Regulation 88
Information management

1. The Registry shall keep information relating to witnesses, victims who appear before the Court and persons at risk, accompanying persons and family members in a secure environment.

2. A secure electronic database shall be maintained for any information relating to persons referred to in sub-regulation 1. This database can only be accessed by designated staff members of the Registry and, where appropriate, by the Chamber and by participants.

Regulation 89
Healthcare and well-being

1. The Registry shall assist witnesses, victims who appear before the Court and persons at risk, by:

(a) Organising medical care and assistance, as appropriate, for the duration of their stay at the seat of the Court or where proceedings are held; and

(b) Providing psychological assistance, as appropriate, particularly for children, the disabled, the elderly and victims of sexual violence.

2. The Registry shall develop local networks to address the healthcare and well-being of witnesses, victims who appear before the Court and persons at risk, especially in the field.

Regulation 90
Dependent care

1. The Registry may provide dependent care to witnesses and victims who appear before the Court.

2. Dependent care is the provision of appropriate assistance to those who have the primary responsibility in caring for another person, the non-provision of which would prevent their attendance at the Court.

3. The type of assistance shall be based on a case-by-case needs assessment.

Regulation 91
Accompanying support persons

1. Witnesses, victims who appear before the Court and persons at risk may be permitted to bring an accompanying support person with them to the Court. The Registry shall cover the costs of the accompanying support person, in accordance with regulations 81, 82 and 84.

2. In order to determine the eligibility of a witness, a victim who appears before the Court or a person at risk to bring an accompanying support person with him or her to the Court, the following criteria, shall be, *inter alia*, taken into account:

(a) The fact that the person has no surviving close family members;

(b) The presence of severe trauma-related symptoms;

(c) The existence of possible suicidal tendencies;

(d) The potential for violence;

(e) The fear or anxiety of the person to the extent that it would prevent him or her from attending the Court;

(f) The age;

(g) The fact that the person is a victim of sexual or gender violence;

(h) The fact that the person suffers from a pre-existing disease of a physical and/or psychological nature; and

(i) The severity of physical or psychological symptoms.

3. The Registry shall assess the suitability of the accompanying person to provide support.

Regulation 92
Security arrangements

1. The Registry shall implement and coordinate appropriate procedures and measures for the protection and security to ensure the safety of witnesses, victims who appear before the Court and persons at risk, including accompanying support persons.

2. Procedures and measures referred to in sub-regulation 1 shall be confidential.

Regulation 93
Local protection measures

1. The Registry shall implement measures for the protection of witnesses, victims who appear before the Court and persons at risk on the territory of the State where an investigation is taking place.

2. Procedures and measures referred to in sub-regulation 1 shall be confidential.

Regulation 94
Protective measures

Measures taken pursuant to an order of a Chamber under rule 87 to protect the identity of witnesses, victims who appear before the Court and persons at risk may include, *inter alia*:

(a) Pseudonyms, where the person is assigned a pseudonym that is used during the proceeding instead of his or her real name;

(b) Facial distortion, where the image of the person is rendered unrecognisable by an electronic mosaic in the audiovisual feed;

(c) Voice distortion, where the voice of the person is rendered unrecognisable by electronic means in the audiovisual feed;

(d) Private sessions, where the hearing is not open to the public and there is no audiovisual stream broadcast outside the Court;

(e) Closed sessions, where the hearing is held *in camera*;

(f) Videoconferences, where the person takes part in the proceeding via a direct video link;

(g) Expunctions from the public record of the proceeding of any information which might lead to the identification of the victim, witness or person at risk; or

(h) Any combination of the protective measures listed above or any modification of a measure ordered by the Chamber which is technically feasible.

Regulation 95
Protection arrangements

The Registry shall provide participants with round-the-clock telephone access for the purpose of initiating an application for protection or for any enquiry relating to the safety of witnesses, victims who appear before the Court or persons at risk of harm or death.

Regulation 96
Protection programme

1. The Registry shall take all necessary measures to maintain a protection programme for witnesses, including accompanying support persons, and others considered to be at risk of harm and/or death on account of a testimony given by such witnesses or as a result of their contact with the Court.

2. An application for inclusion in the protection programme may be filed by the Prosecutor or by counsel.

3. In assessing admission to the protection programme, in addition to the factors set out in article 68, the Registry shall consider, *inter alia,* the following:

(a) The involvement of the person before the Court;

(b) Whether the person himself or herself, or his or her close relatives are endangered because of their involvement with the Court; and

(c) Whether the person agrees to enter the protection programme.

4. Inclusion in the protection programme shall be subject to the decision of the Registrar after the assessment made under sub-regulation 3.

5. Before being included in the protection programme, the person or–where the person is under the age of 18 or otherwise lacks the legal capacity to do so–his or her representative, shall sign an agreement with the Registry.

Section 2
Victims Participation and Reparations

Subsection 1
General provisions

Regulation 97
Confidentiality of communications

1. Where required for reasons of safety and security of the victim, the Registry shall take all necessary measures within its powers to ensure the confidentiality of the following communications: communications within the Court relating to specific victims, including communications within the Registry and between the Registry and other organs of the Court; between the Court and victims who have communicated with the Court; between the Court and victims' legal representatives; between the Court and persons or organisations acting on behalf of victims; and between the Court and persons or organisations serving as intermediaries between the Court and victims.

2. If a victim decides to withdraw an application for participation or reparations at any time, the Registry shall maintain the confidentiality of the communication.

Regulation 98
Protection of information and communications

1. For the purpose of regulation 97, the Registry shall maintain a secure electronic database for the storage and processing of information provided in applications from victims, any documentation or further information supplied by victims or their legal representatives, and any communications received from or in respect of such victims including communications or

other information from or relating to specific victims that have been made available to the Registry by other organs of the Court.

2. The database referred to in sub-regulation 1 may only be accessed by designated staff members of the Registry and, where appropriate, by the Chamber and by participants.

Regulation 99
Assessment of the disclosure of information

1. Upon receipt of an application from a victim and pending any decision by the Chamber, the Registry shall review the application and assess whether the disclosure to the Prosecutor, the defence and/or other participants of any information contained in such application, may jeopardise the safety and security of the victim concerned.

2. Such review shall take into account the factors set out in article 68, paragraph 1, any request for non-disclosure made by the victim and, *inter alia*, the level of security in the area where the victim lives and the feasibility of implementing local measures for their protection and security and/or protective measures where necessary.

3. The Registry shall inform the Chamber of the results of the assessment.

4. If a victim requests that all or part of the information he or she has provided to the Registry not to be disclosed to the Prosecutor, the defence, or other participants, the Registry shall inform the victim that such requests may be granted or rejected by the Chamber. The Registry shall communicate the victim's request, together with the result of the assessment made pursuant to sub-regulations 1 and 2, to the Chamber and to the legal representative of the victim.

Regulation 100
Protection and security of victims

1. Where the Registry is in direct communication with victims, it shall ensure that it does not endanger their safety, physical and psychological well-being, dignity and privacy. The Registry shall also take all possible measures to ensure that groups mentioned in regulation 105, sub-regulation 1, pursue the same objective in their communications with victims.

2. Where a victim wishing to participate in the proceedings or to claim reparations fears that his or her application is putting him or her at risk, or where the assessment undertaken under regulation 99, sub-regulations 1 and 2, concludes that such a risk might exist, the Registry may advise the Chamber on appropriate protective measures and/or security arrangements in order to protect the safety and the physical and psychological well-being of the victim.

3. The Registry may request non-publication of information in accordance with regulation 43, sub-regulation 3.

Regulation 101
Withdrawal of applications

1. If a victim decides to withdraw an application for participation or reparations before the Registry has presented the application to the Chamber, the Registry shall present the application and the withdrawal to that Chamber, together with a report including any reasons given for the withdrawal.

2. If the application has already been presented to the Chamber, the Registry shall present the withdrawal to that Chamber, including any reasons given for the withdrawal.

Subsection 2
Information and notice to victims

Regulation 102
Assistance in providing information under article 15

1. Where the Prosecutor intends to seek authorisation from the Pre-Trial Chamber to initiate an investigation pursuant to article 15, paragraph 3, the Registry may assist in providing information to victims when so requested.

2. Where the Prosecutor has a duty to inform victims who have provided information to him under article 15, paragraph 6, the Registry may, when so requested, assist in providing information to victims.

Regulation 103
Publicity and notice by general means

1. In determining what measures are necessary to give adequate publicity to the proceedings, as referred to in rule 92, sub-rule 8, and in rule 96, sub-rule 1,

the Registry shall ascertain and take into account factors relating to the specific context such as languages or dialects spoken, local customs and traditions, literacy rates and access to the media. In giving such publicity, the Registry shall seek to ensure that victims make their applications before the start of the stage of the proceedings in which they want to participate, in accordance with regulation 86, sub-regulation 3, of the Regulations of the Court.

2. Where the Prosecutor decides to give notice by general means in accordance with rule 50, sub-rule 1, the Registry may assist in informing victims, where requested to do so, and shall consequently inform the Prosecutor for the purpose of regulation 87, sub-regulation 1, of the Regulations of the Court.

Subsection 3
Participation of victims in the proceedings and reparations

Regulation 104
Standard application forms

1. The standard application forms provided for in regulations 86 and 88 of the Regulations of the Court, and the explanatory material shall, to the extent possible, be made available in the language(s) spoken by the victims. The Registry shall endeavour to prepare the standard application forms in a format that is accessible, that can be used by the Court, and that is compatible with the electronic database referred to in regulation 98, sub-regulation 2.

2. The Registry may propose amendments to the standard application forms on the basis of, *inter alia,* experience in using the forms and the context of specific situations. The proposed amendments shall be submitted to the Presidency for approval in accordance with regulation 23, sub-regulation 2, of the Regulations of the Court.

Regulation 105
Dissemination and completion of standard application forms

1. In order to ensure that standard application forms, as referred to in regulation 86, sub-regulation 1, of the Regulations of the Court, are completed as efficiently as possible, the Registry may establish contact and maintain regular relations with the groups mentioned in regulation 86, sub-regulation 1, of the Regulations of the Court, and may, *inter alia*, prepare guidance

booklets and other materials, or provide education and training, in order to guide those assisting victims in completing the standard application forms.

2. The Registry shall, as far as possible, encourage the use of the standard application forms by victims in making applications.

Regulation 106
Receipt of applications

1. Applications for participation or reparations may be submitted either to the seat of the Court or to a field office of the Court.

2. The Registry shall take measures to encourage victims to complete their applications and to provide further information and communications in a working language of the Court. Such steps may include, *inter alia,* seeking the assistance of groups mentioned in regulation 86, sub-regulation 1, of the Regulations of the Court.

3. Documents and material relating to an application and submitted after the initial application shall be dealt with in accordance with regulation 107.

Regulation 107
Review of applications

1. Where an application is received in hard copy, the Registry shall convert it into image file format, ensuring that the application is not altered in any way.

2. The Registry shall take measures to encourage victims to complete their application using the standard form referred to in regulation 86, sub-regulation 1, of the Regulations of the Court.

3. In seeking further information in accordance with regulation 86, sub-regulation 4, or regulation 88, sub-regulation 2, of the Regulations of the Court, the Registry shall consider the interests of the victim and shall take into account, *inter alia*, whether the victim is represented, the security of the victim, and any time limits for the filing of documents with the Court. When contacting victims or their legal representatives to request further information, the Registry shall inform them that their request may be granted or rejected by the Chamber on the basis, *inter alia,* of information provided by

them and that they may submit a new application later in the proceedings if their application is rejected by the Chamber.

4. The Registry shall endeavour wherever possible to obtain further information in writing, but where the victim has expressed a preference for contact by telephone, and taking security considerations into account, it may receive such information by telephone. In so doing, the Registry shall, to the extent possible, verify the identity of the person and record the conversation.

Regulation 108
Access to applications

1. Applications and related documents and material shall be available to the Chambers and the participants through electronic means, in accordance with their level of confidentiality.

2. Consultation of the original form of the applications and related documents and material shall be requested using the approved standard form.

3. Regulation 16 shall apply *mutatis mutandis.*

Regulation 109
Report to the Chamber regarding participation in the proceedings

1. In order to facilitate the decision of the Chamber and to comply with regulation 86, sub-regulations 5 and 6, of the Regulations of the Court, the Registry shall provide the Chamber with access to the record of applications or to the secure room where the originals are stored.

2. Unless otherwise requested by the Chamber, the report to be provided in accordance with regulation 86, sub-regulations 5 and 6, of the Regulations of the Court, may include information relating to, *inter alia*, victims' legal representatives, legal assistance paid by the Court, requests relating to confidentiality and disclosure or security concerns, and any other relevant information received from other sources and from victims or their legal representatives.

3. For the purpose of preparing the report, the Registry may seek additional information in accordance with regulation 86, sub-regulation 4, of the Regulations of the Court, and may consult with the legal representatives, if any.

Regulation 110
Submission of applications for reparations

1. The Registry shall present all applications for reparations to the Chamber, together with a report thereon, where requested.

2. For the purpose of rule 97, at the request of the Chamber, the Registry may present information or recommendations regarding matters such as the types and modalities of reparations, factors relating to the appropriateness of awarding reparations on an individual or a collective basis, the implementation of reparations awards, the use of the Trust Fund for Victims, enforcement measures, and appropriate experts to assist in accordance with rule 97, sub-rule 2.

Regulation 111
Assistance in the enforcement phase

The Registry may, if so requested, provide the Presidency with relevant information, including information received in applications for participation or reparations, to assist it in its decision-making on matters relating to the disposition or allocation of property or assets in accordance with rule 221.

Subsection 4
Legal representation of victims

Regulation 112
Assistance to victims in choosing legal representatives

In order to assist victims in choosing a legal representative or representatives, the Registry may provide victims with the list of counsel provided for in regulation 122 and information regarding counsel or assistants to counsel, including, at the request of a victim, the *curricula vitae* of counsel appearing on that list, and take measures to ensure that the victim understands such information.

Regulation 113
Legal assistance paid by the Court

1. For the purpose of participation in the proceedings, the Registry shall inform victims that they may apply for legal assistance paid by the Court, and shall supply them with the relevant form(s).

2. In determining whether to grant such assistance, the Registrar shall take into account, *inter alia*, the means of the victims, the factors mentioned in article 68, paragraph 1, any special needs of the victims, the complexity of the case, the possibility of asking the Office of Public Counsel for Victims to act, and the availability of *pro bono* legal advice and assistance.

3. Regulations 130–139 shall apply *mutatis mutandis*.

Subsection 5
Office of Public Counsel for Victims

Regulation 114
Appointment of members of the Office

The members of the Office of Public Counsel for Victims are appointed in accordance with the rules and regulations governing the recruitment of the staff of the Court. A representative of the legal profession shall sit on the selection panel.

Regulation 115
Independence of members of the Office

1. The members of the Office shall not receive any instructions from the Registrar in relation to the conduct of the discharge of their tasks as referred to in regulations 80 and 81 of the Regulations of the Court.

2. In discharging their responsibilities under sub-regulation 1, the members of the Office shall be bound by the Code of Professional Conduct for counsel adopted pursuant to rule 8.

3. For issues other than the conduct of the representation of a person entitled to legal assistance under the Statute and the Rules or assistance to legal representatives of victims, members of the Office shall be bound by the provisions applicable to all staff members.

4. Where a member of the Office is representing a victim or a group of victims, regulation 113 shall apply *mutatis mutandis*.

5. The Registry shall ensure that the confidentiality necessary for the performance of the functions of the Office be respected.

Regulation 116
Information provided by the Registrar to the Office

Where members of the Office act as duty counsel or as legal representatives of victims or appear before a Chamber on behalf of a victim or victims in respect of specific issues, the Registrar shall, having regard to confidentiality, provide them with such information received in the applications sent by victims and such further information and documents as are necessary for the fulfilment of those functions.

Regulation 117
Report on administrative issues relating to the Office

The Office shall report on administrative issues related to its activities to the Registrar on a regular basis and submit an annual report of its work to the Registrar having regard to confidentiality.

Subsection 6
Trust Fund for Victims

Regulation 118
Cooperation with the Trust Fund for Victims

1. For the purpose of rule 98, sub-rule 4, rule 148 and rule 221, sub-rule 1, the Registry shall, where requested by the Chamber or by the Presidency, and after consultation with the victims or their legal representatives, provide information received from or in respect of victims to the Secretariat of the Trust Fund for Victims, and shall provide general advice and information of a non-confidential nature relating to victims.

2. Where an order is issued by the Chamber for an award of reparations through the Trust Fund for Victims, the Registrar shall, having regard to confidentiality, provide the Secretariat of the Trust Fund for Victims with such information received in the applications sent by victims and such further information and documents as are necessary for the implementation of the order.

Chapter 4
Counsel issues and legal assistance

Section 1
General provisions

Regulation 119
Duties of the Registrar in relation to the defence

1. In order to give full effect to the rights of the defence, and pursuant to the provisions of rule 20, the Registrar shall, *inter alia*:

(a) Assist counsel and/or his or her assistants in travelling to the seat of the Court, to the place of the proceedings, to the place of custody of the person entitled to legal assistance, or to various locations in the course of an on-site investigation. Such assistance shall encompass securing the protection of the privileges and immunities as laid down in the Agreement on the Privileges and Immunities of the Court and the relevant provisions of the Headquarters Agreement; and

(b) Establish channels of communication and hold consultations with any independent body of counsel or legal association, including any such body the establishment of which may be facilitated by the Assembly of States Parties.

2. The Registrar shall also provide appropriate assistance to a person who has chosen to represent himself or herself.

3. In the event of disputes occurring between the person entitled to legal assistance and his or her counsel, the Registrar may propose mediation. The Registrar may request the Office of Public Counsel for the Defence or another qualified independent person to act as a mediator.

Regulation 120
Principles governing consultations with legal associations

1. In carrying out his or her responsibilities including those in rule 20, sub-rule 3, the Registrar shall, as appropriate, hold consultations with any independent representative body of counsel or legal association, including any such body the establishment of which may be facilitated by the Assembly of States Parties.

2. International associations of bars and counsel, as well as associations offering specific expertise in fields of law that are relevant to the Court, shall in particular be consulted.

3. The Registrar may also consult any expert he or she identifies on specific issues relating to his or her mandate, as appropriate.

Regulation 121
Forms of consultations

1. Consultations shall be carried out periodically through non-institutionalised channels, including written and oral communication, as well as bilateral and multilateral meetings.

2. The Registrar may, as appropriate, organise seminars for the purpose of holding in-depth discussions on the role of the legal profession before the Court. Associations and individual experts, as well as representatives of other international criminal tribunals, may take part in these seminars.

Section 2
Provisions on counsel and assistants to counsel

Regulation 122
List of counsel

1. The Registry shall produce a standard form for counsel seeking inclusion in the list. The form shall be available on the website of the Court, as well as through other appropriate means, and shall also be provided upon request.

2. Unless counsel requests otherwise, the Registry may publish the following data:

(a) Counsel's full name;

(b) The name, place and country of the bar association to which counsel is affiliated or, if counsel is not a barrister or attorney, his or her profession, including the name of the institution for which he or she works;

(c) The language(s) spoken by counsel; and

(d) Whether counsel would prefer to represent the accused, victims, or both.

Regulation 123
Acknowledgment of appointment

The Registrar shall acknowledge the issuance of power of attorney or the appointment of counsel in writing, stating that he or she has been included in the list. The acknowledgment shall be notified to the person who has chosen the counsel, to the counsel, to the Chamber and to the competent authority exercising regulatory and disciplinary powers over counsel in the national order.

Regulation 124
Assistants to counsel

Persons who assist counsel in the presentation of the case before a Chamber, as referred to in regulation 68 of the Regulations of the Court, shall have either five years of relevant experience in criminal proceedings or specific competence in international or criminal law and procedure. The names of these persons are on the list of assistants to counsel created and maintained by the Registry.

Regulation 125
List of assistants to counsel

1. The Registry shall create and maintain a list of persons who may assist counsel in the presentation of the case before a Chamber and who meet the requirements set out in regulation 124.

2. The Registry shall produce a standard form for persons seeking inclusion in the list. The form shall be available on the website of the Court as well as through other appropriate means, and shall be provided upon request.

3. A person seeking to be included in the list shall complete the standard form and provide the following documentation:

(a) A detailed *curriculum vitae*; and

(b) An indication of the relevant experience or specific competence in accordance with regulation 124.

4. The decision as to whether a person shall be included in the list shall be notified to that person. If the application is refused, the Registrar shall provide reasons and information on how to apply to the Presidency for review of that decision within 15 calendar days of its notification.

5. The Registrar may file a response within 15 calendar days of notification of the application for review.

6. The Presidency may ask the Registrar to provide any additional information necessary to decide on the application. The decision of the Presidency shall be final.

7. Persons included in the list shall inform the Registrar immediately of any change in the information provided by them pursuant to this regulation. The Registrar may take measures to verify the information provided by such persons at any time.

Regulation 126
Removal from the list of assistants to counsel

1. The Registrar shall remove a person from the list of assistants to counsel if that person:

(a) No longer meets the requirements set out under regulation 124;

(b) Has been found guilty of an offence against the administration of justice as described in article 70, paragraph 1;

(c) Has been permanently interdicted from exercising his or her functions before the Court in accordance with rule 171, sub-rule 3; or

(d) Has solicited or accepted a bribe from a person entitled to legal assistance paid by the Court.

2. The Registrar shall notify the relevant person of his or her decision under sub-regulation 1 and shall provide the reasons therefor.

3. The Registrar shall inform the person on how to apply to the Presidency for review of that decision within 15 calendar days of notification.

4. The Registrar may file a response within 15 calendar days of notification of the application for review.

5. The Presidency may ask the Registrar to provide any additional information necessary to decide on the application. The decision of the Presidency shall be final.

Regulation 127
Appointment of assistants to counsel

Persons who assist counsel in the presentation of the case before a Chamber shall be appointed by counsel and selected from the list maintained by the Registrar.

Regulation 128
Assistance by the Registry

1. The Registry shall provide a person seeking legal assistance in the framework of proceedings before the Court with the list of counsel, along with the *curricula vitae* of counsel appearing on that list.

2. The Registry shall provide assistance when a person entitled to legal assistance under the Statute and the Rules is to be questioned pursuant to article 55, or in any other case where legal assistance is needed by a person entitled to it.

Regulation 129
Appointment of duty counsel

1. In accordance with regulation 73, sub-regulation 2, of the Regulations of the Court, the Registry shall guarantee the availability of counsel at the place and the time indicated by the Prosecutor or the Chamber.

2. When requested by a person entitled to legal assistance, the Prosecutor or the Chamber, the Registry shall contact the duty counsel and provide him or her with all the information available.

Section 3
Legal assistance paid by the Court

Regulation 130
Management of legal assistance paid by the Court

1. The Registrar shall manage the legal assistance paid by the Court with due respect to confidentiality and the professional independence of counsel.

2. The Registry staff responsible for managing the funds allocated to legal assistance paid by the Court shall treat all information known with the utmost confidentiality. They shall not communicate such information to any person, except to the Registrar, or to the legal aid commissioners where required for the performance of the tasks specified in regulation 136.

3. The Registrar may transmit to the auditors the necessary information to perform their tasks. They are responsible for ensuring the confidentiality of such information.

Regulation 131
Application procedure for legal assistance paid by the Court

1. As soon as the Registry contacts a person entitled to legal assistance under the Statute and the Rules in order to assist him or her in accordance with regulation 128, it shall provide him or her with the relevant form(s) to submit an application for legal assistance paid by the Court.

2. The Registry shall immediately acknowledge receipt of an application for legal assistance paid by the Court as described in sub-regulation 1. The Registrar shall then establish whether or not the applicant has provided the requisite supporting material as described in regulation 132. He or she shall inform the applicant as soon as possible if, and to what extent, such material are incomplete and shall direct him or her to provide the missing material within a specified time period.

Regulation 132
Proof of indigence

1. A person applying for legal assistance paid by the Court must fill out the approved standard forms and provide the information necessaries to support their request.

2. Where there are grounds to believe that an application for legal assistance paid by the Court and the supporting evidence are not accurate, the Registry may carry out an investigation into the matter. In doing so, it may request information and/or documents from any person or body that it deems appropriate.

3. The Registrar should make a decision as to whether legal assistance should be paid in full or in part by the Court within 30 calendar days of the submission by the person concerned of all the documentation required. Legal assistance shall be provisionally paid by the Court during that period.

4. The person shall communicate to the Registry any change in his or her financial situation that might affect eligibility for legal assistance paid by the Court. The Registry may carry out random checks to verify whether any changes have occurred.

5. If legal assistance paid by the Court has been granted provisionally, the Registry may investigate the person's means. The person shall cooperate with the Registry in its investigation.

Regulation 133
Fees paid to counsel

The fees paid to counsel shall consist of a scheme of payment based on a fixed fee system comprising a maximum allocation of funds for each phase of the proceedings, including, where applicable, fees for assistants to counsel as referred to in regulation 68 of the Regulations of the Court, and for professional investigators as referred to in regulation 137.

Regulation 134
Action plan and modalities of payment

1. Before each phase of the proceedings, or every six months, counsel shall establish an action plan. The action plan shall be approved by the Registrar who may consult the legal aid commissioners appointed pursuant to regulation 136, sub-regulation 1.

2. At the end of every month, the Registry shall issue an order for payment in accordance with the action plan referred to in sub-regulation 1.

3. Every six months, or at the end of each phase of the proceedings, the Registry shall review the action plan and the remaining fees, if any, shall be paid to counsel.

4. When a mission has been carried out in accordance with the action plan, the relevant funds shall be paid upon presentation of the appropriate travel request, as approved by the Registry, together with any supporting documentation.

Regulation 135
Disputes relating to fees

1. The Registrar shall take a decision on any dispute concerning the calculation and payment of fees or the reimbursement of expenses at the earliest possible juncture and notify counsel accordingly.

2. Within 15 calendar days of notification, counsel may request the Chamber to review any decision taken under sub-regulation 1.

Regulation 136
Legal aid commissioners

1. The Registrar, after receiving the proposals and having heard the views of any independent representative body of counsel or legal association, including any such body the establishment of which may be facilitated by the Assembly of States Parties, shall appoint three persons to serve as legal aid commissioners for three years. This appointment shall not be renewable.

2. Legal aid commissioners shall provide the Registrar with advice regarding the management of the funds allocated by the Assembly of States Parties to legal assistance paid by the Court.

To that effect, the commissioners shall:

(a) Evaluate the performance of the system put in place regarding legal assistance paid by the Court, and propose amendments to such system; and

(b) At the request of either counsel or the Registrar, assess whether the means requested by legal teams in their action plans are reasonably necessary for the effective and efficient representation of their client(s).

3. Legal aid commissioners shall perform their tasks independently and with due regard to confidentiality.

Regulation 137
List of professional investigators

1. The Registry shall create and maintain a list of professional investigators.

2. A professional investigator shall have established competence in international or criminal law and procedure and at least ten years of relevant experience in investigative work in criminal proceedings at national or international level. A professional investigator shall have an excellent knowledge of and be fluent in at least one of the working languages of the Court.

Subject to exceptional circumstances, he or she shall speak at least one of the languages of the country in which the investigation is being conducted.

3. The Registry shall produce a standard form for professional investigators seeking inclusion in the list. The form shall be available on the website of the Court, as well as through other appropriate means, and shall also be provided upon request.

4. A person seeking to be included in the list of professional investigators shall complete the standard form and provide the following documentation:

(a) A detailed *curriculum vitae*;

(b) An indication of competence in the relevant field in accordance with sub-regulation 2; and

(c) Where applicable, a statement of whether he or she is included in any list of investigators acting before any national court, or whether he or she is registered with any association of investigators.

5. The decision on whether a person shall be included in the list shall be notified to that person. If the application is refused, the Registrar shall provide reasons and information on how to apply to the Presidency for review of that decision within 15 calendar days of notification.

6. The Registrar may file a response within 15 calendar days of notification of the application for review.

7. The Presidency may ask the Registrar to provide any additional information necessary to decide on the application. The decision of the Presidency shall be final.

8. Professional investigators included in the list shall immediately inform the Registrar of any change in the information provided by them in accordance with this regulation. The Registrar may take steps to verify the information provided by a professional investigator included in the list at any time.

Regulation 138
Removal from the list of professional investigators

1. The Registrar shall remove a person from the list of professional investigators if the person:

(a) No longer meets the criteria required in accordance with regulation 137, sub-regulation 2;

(b) Has been found guilty of an offence against the administration of justice as described in article 70, paragraph 1;

(c) Has been permanently interdicted from exercising his or her functions before the Court in accordance with rule 171, sub-rule 3; or

(d) Has solicited or accepted a bribe from a person entitled to legal assistance paid by the Court.

2. The Registrar shall notify the relevant person of his or her decision under sub-regulation 1 and shall provide the reasons therefor.

3. The Registrar shall inform the investigator on how to apply to the Presidency for review of that decision within 15 calendar days of its notification.

4. The Registrar may file a response within 15 calendar days of notification of the application for review.

5. The Presidency may ask the Registrar to provide any additional information necessary to decide on the application. The decision of the Presidency shall be final.

Regulation 139
Selection of professional investigators

1. Where legal assistance is paid by the Court and includes the fee of a professional investigator, counsel shall select the professional investigator from the list referred to in regulation 137.

2. A person not included in the list of investigators but who has relevant experience with regard to investigations in criminal proceedings, is fluent in at least one of the working languages of the Court and speaks at least one of the languages of the country in which the investigation is being conducted, exceptionally and after confirmation by the Registrar that the above criteria have been met, can be selected by counsel as a resource person in a given case. That resource person shall not be related to the person entitled to legal assistance, to the counsel or any person assisting him or her.

Section 4
Training of counsel

Regulation 140
Role of the Registrar

For the purpose of promoting the specialisation and training of lawyers in the law of the Statute and the Rules, and subject to the availability of resources, the Registrar shall, *inter alia*:

(a) Ensure access to a database of the case law of the Court;

(b) Provide comprehensive information on the Court;

(c) Identify and publish the names of persons and organisations carrying out relevant training;

(d) Provide training materials; and

(e) Offer training enabling persons to qualify to train counsel.

Regulation 141
Training programmes

1. The Registry shall develop a standard for training programmes aimed at fostering knowledge of the law of the Statute and the Rules.

2. To this end, the Registry may make a survey of existing training programmes on a regular basis, and consult with any independent body of counsel or legal association, including any such body the establishment of which may be facilitated by the Assembly of States Parties.

3. Where training programmes receive the Registrar's approval, the organisation offering training may expressly refer to it in its promotional material and in any certificates issued.

4. The Registry shall promote the standard programme amongst organisations offering training, and shall, as appropriate, and in consultation with any independent body of counsel or legal association, including any such body the establishment of which may be facilitated by the Assembly of States Parties, review the standard programme in light of the practical experience gained through such training and the performance of counsel before the Court.

Regulation 142
Equal access and geographical distribution

1. The Registrar shall take all necessary steps to encourage an equal geographical and gender distribution of training opportunities. Training should in particular be made available in countries where the infrastructure does not allow for regular training, or where a situation has been brought before the Court.

2. In view of the limited financial capacity of lawyers in certain countries, the Registrar shall support programmes for the training of counsel in such countries. For this purpose, the Registrar may in particular address the relevant

States and their bar associations or ask the relevant organisations to provide the training free of charge.

Section 5
Office of Public Counsel for the defence

Regulation 143
Appointment of members of the Office

The members of the Office of Public Counsel for the Defence are appointed in accordance with the rules and regulations governing the recruitment of the staff of the Court. A representative of the legal profession shall sit on the selection panel.

Regulation 144
Independence of members of the Office

1. The members of the Office shall not receive any instructions from the Registrar in relation to the discharge of their tasks as referred to in regulations 76 and 77 of the Regulations of the Court.

2. In discharging their responsibilities under sub-regulation 1, the members of the Office shall be bound by the Code of Professional Conduct for counsel adopted pursuant to rule 8.

3. For issues other than the conduct of the representation of a person entitled to legal assistance under the Statute and the Rules or assistance to defence counsel, members of the Office shall be bound by the provisions applicable to all staff members.

4. Where a member of the Office is representing a person entitled to legal assistance under the Statute and the Rules, the relevant provisions of section 3 of this chapter shall apply *mutatis mutandis.*

5. The Registry shall ensure that the confidentiality necessary for the performance of the functions of the Office be respected.

Regulation 145
Information provided by the Registrar to the Office

Where members of the Office act as duty counsel or as counsel before a Chamber on behalf of a person entitled to legal assistance in respect of specific issues, the Registrar shall, having regard to confidentiality, provide them with all information and documents as are necessary for the fulfilment of those functions.

Regulation 146
Report on administrative issues relating to the Office

The Office shall report on administrative issues related to its activities to the Registrar on a regular basis and submit an annual report of its work to the Registrar having regard to the obligation of confidentiality.

Section 6
Provisions relating to articles 36 and 44 of the Code of Professional Conduct for counsel

Regulation 147
Election of the members of the Disciplinary Board

The permanent and alternate members of the Disciplinary Board referred to in article 36 of the Code of Professional Conduct for counsel shall be elected as follows:

(a) At an appropriate time before an election is due under article 36 of the Code of Professional Conduct for counsel, the Registrar shall send a letter to national bar associations and, where appropriate, to any independent representative body of counsel or legal association, as well as to all counsel on the list of counsel, informing them that an election will take place and inviting announcements of candidacy. The letter shall, *inter alia*, set out the procedure to be followed for the election and shall state that those standing for election must have established competence in professional ethics and legal matters.

(b) Persons who wish to stand for election shall announce their candidacy to the Registrar by letter, attaching a curriculum vitae and a statement setting out their specific competence in professional ethics and legal matters. Announcements of candidacy shall be sent to the Registrar by postal or courier services and shall be received at the Court within 90 calendar days of the date of the letter of the Registrar referred to in (a). Persons whose announcements of candidacy are received at the Court after the expiration of that 90 day time period shall not be eligible.

(c) If fewer candidates stand for election than the number of members of the Disciplinary Board who must be elected, all counsel on the list of counsel who have indicated on their application form for the list of counsel that they have been a member of a disciplinary body or had specific responsibilities relating to ethics, shall be considered to have announced their candidacy and are eligible, subject to the provisions of article 36, paragraph 6, and article 44, paragraph 7, of the Code of Professional Conduct for counsel. The Registrar shall, by letter, request such counsel to provide their curriculum vitae and a statement setting out their specific competence in professional ethics and legal matters within 30 calendar days of the date of dispatch of the letter.

(d) When the periods referred to in (b) and (c) have expired, the Registrar shall distribute the list of candidates by postal or courier services, together with the curriculum vitae and the statement setting out the specific competence in professional ethics and legal matters of each candidate as well as a confidential voting slip, to all counsel on the list of counsel and request counsel to vote within 45 calendar days of the date of dispatch.

(e) Counsel shall vote for as many candidates as there are members of the Disciplinary Board to be elected.

(f) The vote shall be secret. Counsel shall cast their vote by completing and returning the confidential voting slip to the Registry by postal or courier services within the time limit set out in (d). All correspondence received shall be treated with due regard for confidentiality. Any votes received after the expiry of that time period shall not be counted.

(g) Once the ballot is closed, the Registry shall count the votes and submit the results to the Registrar.

(h) At the first election, pursuant to article 36, paragraph 4, of the Code of Professional Conduct for counsel, the two candidates having obtained the most votes shall be elected as permanent members. The candidate having obtained the next highest number of votes shall be elected as the alternate member. If two or more candidates obtain the same number of votes, lots shall be drawn between them.

(i) At subsequent elections, the candidate having obtained the most votes shall be elected as the permanent member. Where required, the candidate having obtained the next highest number of votes shall be elected as the alternate member. If two or more candidates obtain the same number of votes, lots shall be drawn between them.

(j) The Registrar shall notify the successful candidate or candidates of their election to the Disciplinary Board, inform counsel on the list of counsel of the outcome of the election and have the results published on the Court website.

(k) Within 15 calendar days of the publication of the outcome on the Court website, a candidate who has not been elected may file a complaint with the Registrar concerning any issue relating to the election procedure. After having considered the complaint, the Registrar shall take a decision, of which the candidate concerned shall be notified.

(l) Within 15 calendar days of notification of the decision taken by the Registrar, a candidate whose complaint has been rejected may apply to the Presidency for review.

(m) The Registrar may file a response within 15 calendar days of notification of the application for review.

(n) The Presidency may ask the Registrar to provide any additional information necessary to decide on the application. The decision of the Presidency shall be final.

Regulation 148
Election of the members of the Disciplinary Appeals Board

The election of the members of the Disciplinary Appeals Board referred to in article 44, paragraphs 4 (b) and 5, of the Code of Professional Conduct for counsel shall be governed, *mutatis mutandis*, by the provisions applying to the election of the permanent and alternate members of the Disciplinary Board under regulation 147.

Regulation 149
Appointment of the Commissioner conducting the investigation

At the request of the Presidency, the Registrar shall assist in the appointment of the Commissioner.

APPENDIX IV

Selected Regulations of the Court [Regulations: 20–32, 41–56, and 67–88]

Chapter 3
Proceedings before the Court

Section 1
Provisions relating to all stages of the proceedings

Subsection 1
General provisions

Regulation 20
Public hearings

1. All hearings shall be held in public, unless otherwise provided in the Statute, Rules, these Regulations or ordered by the Chamber.

2. When a Chamber orders that certain hearings be held in closed session, the Chamber shall make public the reasons for such an order.

3. A Chamber may order the disclosure of all or part of the record of closed proceedings when the reasons for ordering its non-disclosure no longer exist.

Regulation 21
Broadcasting, release of transcripts and recordings

1. The publicity of hearings may extend beyond the courtroom and may be through broadcasting by the Registry or release of transcripts or recordings, unless otherwise ordered by the Chamber.

2. In order to protect sensitive information, broadcasts of audio- and videorecordings of all hearings shall, unless otherwise ordered by the Chamber, be delayed by at least 30 minutes.

3. Witnesses and participants shall be informed that the public hearings of the Chamber are broadcast in accordance with this regulation. Any

objection raised shall be ruled on by the Chamber in accordance with sub-regulations 4 and 5.

4. Any objection to the release of transcripts or recordings, or requests that certain testimony be excluded from broadcast, shall be made as soon as possible and, in any event, no later than at the commencement of the session at which the witness or participant is to appear.

5. The Chamber may decide to prohibit the broadcasting of any hearing of an objection until that objection has been ruled on.

6. The Chamber may order the termination of the broadcast of a hearing at any time.

7. All documentary evidence and other evidence introduced by a participant during a public hearing shall be available for broadcast, unless otherwise ordered by the Chamber.

8. At the request of a participant or the Registry, or *proprio motu*, and when possible within the time set out in sub-regulation 2, the Chamber may, in the interests of justice, order that any information likely to present a risk to the security or safety of victims, witnesses or other persons, or likely to be prejudicial to national security interests, shall not be published in any broadcast, audio- or video-recording or transcript of a public hearing.

9. The audio- and video-record of hearings shall be made available to the participants and the public in accordance with the procedures set out in the Regulations of the Registry, unless otherwise ordered by the Chamber.

Regulation 22
Definition of documents

The term "document" shall include any motion, application, request, response, reply, observation, representation and any other submission in a form capable of delivering a written record to the Court.

Regulation 23
Content of documents

1. Unless otherwise provided in the Statute, Rules, these Regulations or ordered by the Chamber, any document filed with the Court shall, as far as practicable, state:

(a) The identity of the person filing the document;

(b) The situation or case number, the name of the person to whom article 55, paragraph 2, or article 58 applies, the accused, convicted or acquitted person, the name of counsel or representative, if any, and the Chamber to which the matter has been assigned;

(c) A brief summary of the reason for filing the document which is not a response or reply and the relief sought, if any;

(d) All relevant legal and factual issues, including details of the articles, rules, regulations or other applicable law relied upon.

2. All standard forms and templates for use during the proceedings before the Court shall be approved by the Presidency. The Presidency may refer any matter relating to the standard forms and templates to the Advisory Committee on Legal Texts for its consideration.

3. Subject to any order of the Chamber, a participant shall file, with each document, copies of any authorities relied upon or, if appropriate, internet links. Participants are not required to file copies of decisions or orders of the Court. Authorities shall be provided in an authorised version together with a translation in at least one of the working languages of the Court if the original is not in one of those languages.

Regulation 24
Responses and replies

1. The Prosecutor and the defence may file a response to any document filed by any participant in the case in accordance with the Statute, Rules, these Regulations and any order of the Chamber.

2. Victims or their legal representatives may file a response to any document when they are permitted to participate in the proceedings in accordance with article 68, paragraph 3, and rule 89, sub-rule 1, subject to any order of the Chamber.

3. States participating in the proceedings may file a response to any document, subject to any order of the Chamber.

4. A response referred to in sub-regulations 1 to 3 may not be filed to any document which is itself a response or reply.

5. Participants may only reply to a response with the leave of the Chamber, unless otherwise provided in these Regulations.

Regulation 25
Communications other than in writing

A person making a communication to the Court under rule 102 shall indicate at the start of the communication:

(a) His or her identity;

(b) The situation or case number, if known;

(c) The Chamber seized of the matter, if known;

(d) The name of the person to whom article 55, paragraph 2, or article 58 applies, the accused, convicted or acquitted person, if known;

(e) The purpose of the communication;

(f) When referring to a specific event, to the extent possible, the location, date and individuals involved.

Regulation 26
Electronic management

1. The Court shall establish a reliable, secure, efficient electronic system which supports its daily judicial and operational management and its proceedings.

2. The Registry shall be responsible for the implementation of the system described in sub-regulation 1, taking into account the specific requirements of the judicial activity of the Court, including the need to ensure authenticity, accuracy, confidentiality and preservation of judicial records and material.

3. Documents, decisions and orders shall, whenever possible, be submitted in electronic version for registration by the Registry. The electronic version of filings shall be authoritative.

4. In proceedings before the Court, evidence other than live testimony shall be presented in electronic form whenever possible. The original form of such evidence shall be authoritative.

Regulation 27
Transcripts

1. Real time transcripts of hearings shall be provided in at least one of the working languages of the Court to the extent technically possible. Transcripts of proceedings other than hearings may be provided upon request.

2. The transcripts constitute an integral part of the record of the proceedings. The electronic version of transcripts shall be authoritative.

Regulation 28
Questions by a Chamber

1. A Chamber may order the participants to clarify or to provide additional details on any document within a time limit specified by the Chamber.

2. A Chamber may order the participants to address specific issues in their written or oral submissions within a time limit specified by the Chamber.

3. These provisions are without prejudice to the inherent powers of the Chamber.

Regulation 29
Non-compliance with these Regulations and with orders of a Chamber

1. In the event of non-compliance by a participant with the provisions of any regulation, or with an order of a Chamber made thereunder, the Chamber may issue any order that is deemed necessary in the interests of justice.

2. This provision is without prejudice to the inherent powers of the Chamber.

Regulation 30
Status conferences

A Chamber may hold status conferences by way of hearings, including by way of audio- or video-link technology or by way of written submissions. The Chamber may require use of standard forms at a status conference as appropriate. Such standard forms shall be approved in accordance with regulation 23, sub-regulation 2.

Subsection 2
Distribution of documents

Regulation 31
Notification

1. Subject to the Statute, Rules, these Regulations or any order of a Chamber, all participants in the relevant proceedings shall be notified of any document

registered by the Registry or any decision or order, unless, with regard to a document, the participant submitting that document requests otherwise. All participants shall provide to the Registry an electronic, facsimile or postal contact address for notification of documents, preferably in The Hague.

2. Unless otherwise provided in the Statute, Rules, these Regulations or ordered by the Chamber, a participant is deemed notified, informed of or to have had communicated to him or her, a document, decision or order on the day it is effectively sent from the Court by the Registry. Such date shall be written on the notification form to be appended to all copies of the document, decision or order, as relevant. If the document, decision or order is not received, a participant may raise the issue and, as appropriate, may ask for a variation of the time limit in accordance with regulation 35. The Registrar shall retain and, if required, produce proof that the document, decision or order was effectively sent.

3. The relevant person shall be notified by way of personal service of the following documents:

(a) Warrants of arrest;

(b) Summonses to appear;

(c) Documents containing the charges; and

(d) Such other documents, decisions or orders ordered by the Chamber to be notified by way of personal service.

4. Notification by way of personal service may be proved in the following manner:

(a) By confirmation in writing on the prescribed form by the person serving the document that notification by way of personal service has been effected; and

(b) By a signed acknowledgement of notification by way of personal service on the prescribed form by the relevant person.

Where the relevant person declines or is unable to sign an acknowledgement of notification by way of personal service, the confirmation in (a) above shall be proof of such notification.

5. In respect of oral decisions or orders, notification shall be deemed effective on the day the decision or order is rendered orally by the Chamber unless:

(a) A participant was not present or represented when the decision or order was pronounced, in which case that participant shall be notified of the oral decision or order in accordance with sub-regulation 2; or

(b) The Chamber has indicated that a written decision or order will follow, in which case participants shall be notified of the written decision or order in accordance with sub-regulation 2.

Regulation 32
Recipients of documents, decisions and orders notified by the Court

1. A State shall be deemed notified when the official representative designated for proceedings before the Court has been notified of a document, decision or order. If a State does not designate such a representative, the State shall be deemed notified of the document, decision or order when it has been notified through the channel designated by that State in accordance with article 87.

2. Intergovernmental organisations and other organisations and institutions shall be deemed notified when the designated representative identified by the Registrar or the appropriate channel referred to in rule 177 has been notified of a document, decision or order.

3. A participant represented by counsel shall be deemed notified when his or her counsel has been notified of a document, decision or order at the electronic, facsimile or postal address which that counsel has indicated to the Registry in accordance with regulation 31, sub-regulation 1, unless otherwise provided in the Statute, Rules, these Regulations or ordered by the Chamber.

4. A person who is not represented by counsel shall be deemed notified when that person or the person, organisation or institution designated by that person has been notified of a document, decision or order.

5. The Prosecutor shall be deemed notified when the Office of the Prosecutor has been notified of a document, decision or order, unless it is explicitly specified that the Prosecutor shall be notified of the document, decision or order in person.

Subsection 5
Protective measures

Regulation 41
Victims and Witnesses Unit

The Victims and Witnesses Unit may, pursuant to article 68, paragraph 4, draw any matter to the attention of a Chamber where protective or special measures under rules 87 and 88 require consideration.

Regulation 42
Application and variation of protective measures

1. Protective measures once ordered in any proceedings in respect of a victim or witness shall continue to have full force and effect in relation to any other proceedings before the Court and shall continue after proceedings have been concluded, subject to revision by a Chamber.

2. When the Prosecutor discharges disclosure obligations in subsequent proceedings, he or she shall respect the protective measures as previously ordered by a Chamber and shall inform the defence to whom the disclosure is being made of the nature of these protective measures.

3. Any application to vary a protective measure shall first be made to the Chamber which issued the order. If that Chamber is no longer seized of the proceedings in which the protective measure was ordered, application may be made to the Chamber before which a variation of the protective measure is being requested. That Chamber shall obtain all relevant information from the proceedings in which the protective measure was first ordered.

4. Before making a determination under sub-regulation 3, the Chamber shall seek to obtain, whenever possible, the consent of the person in respect of whom the application to rescind, vary or augment protective measures has been made.

Subsection 6
Evidence

Regulation 43
Testimony of witnesses

Subject to the Statute and the Rules, the Presiding Judge, in consultation with the other members of the Chamber, shall determine the mode and order of questioning witnesses and presenting evidence so as to:

(a) Make the questioning of witnesses and the presentation of evidence fair and effective for the determination of the truth;

(b) Avoid delays and ensure the effective use of time.

Regulation 44
Experts

1. The Registrar shall create and maintain a list of experts accessible at all times to all organs of the Court and to all participants. Experts shall be

included on such a list following an appropriate indication of expertise in the relevant field. A person may seek review by the Presidency of a negative decision of the Registrar.

2. The Chamber may direct the joint instruction of an expert by the participants.

3. On receipt of the report prepared by an expert jointly instructed, a participant may apply to the Chamber for leave to instruct a further expert.

4. The Chamber may *proprio motu* instruct an expert.

5. The Chamber may issue any order as to the subject of an expert report, the number of experts to be instructed, the mode of their instruction, the manner in which their evidence is to be presented and the time limits for the preparation and notification of their report.

Section 2
Pre-trial

Regulation 45
Information provided by the Prosecutor

The Prosecutor shall inform the Presidency in writing as soon as a situation has been referred to the Prosecutor by a State Party under article 14 or by the Security Council under article 13, sub-paragraph (b); and shall provide the Presidency with any other information that may facilitate the timely assignment of a situation to a Pre-Trial Chamber, including, in particular, the intention of the Prosecutor to submit a request under article 15, paragraph 3.

Regulation 46
Pre-Trial Chamber

1. The Presidency shall constitute permanent Pre-Trial Chambers with fixed compositions.

2. The Presidency shall assign a situation to a Pre-Trial Chamber as soon as the Prosecutor has informed the Presidency in accordance with regulation 45. The Pre-Trial Chamber shall be responsible for any matter, request or information arising out of the situation assigned to it, save that, at the request of a Presiding Judge of a Pre-Trial Chamber, the President of the Pre-Trial Division may decide to assign a matter, request or information arising out of

that situation to another Pre-Trial Chamber in the interests of the administration of justice.

3. Any matter, request or information not arising out of a situation assigned to a Pre-Trial Chamber in accordance with sub-regulation 2, shall be directed by the President of the Pre-Trial Division to a Pre-Trial Chamber according to a roster established by the President of that Division.

Regulation 47
Single judge

1. The designation of a single judge in accordance with article 39, paragraph 2 (b) (iii), and rule 7 shall be based on criteria agreed upon by the Pre-

Trial Chamber, including seniority of age and criminal trial experience. Other criteria may include consideration of the issues involved and the circumstances of the proceedings before the Chamber, as well as the distribution of work within the Chamber and the proper management and efficiency in the handling of cases.

2. The single judge designated by the Pre-Trial Chamber shall, as far as possible, act for the duration of a case. The Pre-Trial Chamber may designate more than one single judge when the efficient management of the workload of the Chamber so requires.

Regulation 48
Information necessary for the Pre-Trial Chamber

1. The Pre-Trial Chamber may request the Prosecutor to provide specific or additional information or documents in his or her possession, or summaries thereof, that the Pre-Trial Chamber considers necessary in order to exercise the functions and responsibilities set forth in article 53, paragraph 3 (b), article 56, paragraph 3 (a), and article 57, paragraph 3 (c).

2. The Pre-Trial Chamber shall take such measures as are necessary under articles 54, 72 and 93 to protect the information and documents referred to in sub-regulation 1 and under article 68, paragraph 5, to protect the safety of witnesses and victims and members of their families.

3. Nothing in this regulation shall prejudice the requirements of confidentiality applicable under article 54, paragraph 3 (e) and (f).

Regulation 49
The request for authorization

1. A request by the Prosecutor to a Pre-Trial Chamber for authorisation of an investigation pursuant to article 15, paragraph 3, shall be in writing and shall contain:

(a) A reference to the crimes which the Prosecutor believes have been or are being committed and a statement of the facts being alleged to provide the reasonable basis to believe that those crimes have been or are being committed;

(b) A declaration of the Prosecutor with reasons that the listed crimes fall within the jurisdiction of the Court.

2. The statement of the facts referred to in sub-regulation 1 (a) shall indicate, as a minimum:

(a) The places of the alleged commission of the crimes, e.g. country, town, as precisely as possible;

(b) The time or time period of the alleged commission of the crimes; and

(c) The persons involved, if identified, or a description of the persons or groups of persons involved.

3. The appendix to the request shall include, if possible:

(a) The chronology of relevant events;

(b) Maps showing relevant information, including the location of the alleged crimes; and

(c) An explanatory glossary of relevant names of persons, locations and institutions.

Regulation 50
Specific time limits

1. The time limit for victims to make representations under article 15, paragraph 3, and rule 50, sub-rule 3, shall be 30 days following information given in accordance with rule 50, sub-rule 1.

2. The time limit for a State Party to express its views on a request by the Prosecutor for authorisation to take certain measures within its territory in accordance with rule 115, sub-rule 2, shall be ten days from notification.

Regulation 51
Decision on interim release

For the purposes of a decision on interim release, the Pre-Trial Chamber shall seek observations from the host State and from the State to which the person seeks to be released.

Regulation 52
Document containing the charges

The document containing the charges referred to in article 61 shall include:

(a) The full name of the person and any other relevant identifying information;

(b) A statement of the facts, including the time and place of the alleged crimes, which provides a sufficient legal and factual basis to bring the person or persons to trial, including relevant facts for the exercise of jurisdiction by the Court;

(c) A legal characterisation of the facts to accord both with the crimes under articles 6, 7 or 8 and the precise form of participation under articles 25 and 28.

Regulation 53
Decision of the Pre-Trial Chamber following the confirmation hearing

The written decision of the Pre-Trial Chamber setting out its findings on each of the charges shall be delivered within 60 days from the date the confirmation hearing ends.

Section 3
Trial

Regulation 54
Status conferences before the Trial Chamber

At a status conference, the Trial Chamber may, in accordance with the Statute and the Rules, issue any order in the interests of justice for the purposes of the proceedings on, *inter alia*, the following issues:

(a) The length and content of legal arguments and the opening and closing statements;

(b) A summary of the evidence the participants intend to rely on;

(c) The length of the evidence to be relied on;

(d) The length of questioning of the witnesses;

(e) The number and identity (including any pseudonym) of the witnesses to be called;

(f) The production and disclosure of the statements of the witnesses on which the participants propose to rely;

(g) The number of documents as referred to in article 69, paragraph 2, or exhibits to be introduced together with their length and size;

(h) The issues the participants propose to raise during the trial;

(i) The extent to which a participant can rely on recorded evidence, including the transcripts and the audio- and video-record of evidence previously given;

(j) The presentation of evidence in summary form;

(k) The extent to which evidence is to be given by an audio- or videolink;

(l) The disclosure of evidence;

(m) The joint or separate instruction by the participants of expert witnesses;

(n) Evidence to be introduced under rule 69 as regards agreed facts;

(o) The conditions under which victims shall participate in the proceedings;

(p) The defences, if any, to be advanced by the accused.

Regulation 55
Authority of the Chamber to modify the legal characterisation of facts

1. In its decision under article 74, the Chamber may change the legal characterisation of facts to accord with the crimes under articles 6, 7 or 8, or to accord with the form of participation of the accused under articles 25 and 28, without exceeding the facts and circumstances described in the charges and any amendments to the charges.

2. If, at any time during the trial, it appears to the Chamber that the legal characterisation of facts may be subject to change, the Chamber shall give notice to the participants of such a possibility and having heard the evidence, shall, at an appropriate stage of the proceedings, give the participants the opportunity to make oral or written submissions. The Chamber may suspend

the hearing to ensure that the participants have adequate time and facilities for effective preparation or, if necessary, it may order a hearing to consider all matters relevant to the proposed change.

3. For the purposes of sub-regulation 2, the Chamber shall, in particular, ensure that the accused shall:

(a) Have adequate time and facilities for the effective preparation of his or her defence in accordance with article 67, paragraph 1 (b); and

(b) If necessary, be given the opportunity to examine again, or have examined again, a previous witness, to call a new witness or to present other evidence admissible under the Statute in accordance with article 67, paragraph 1 (e).

Regulation 56
Evidence under article 75

The Trial Chamber may hear the witnesses and examine the evidence for the purposes of a decision on reparations in accordance with article 75, paragraph 2, at the same time as for the purposes of trial.

Chapter 4
Counsel issues and legal assistance

Section 1
List of counsel and duty counsel

Regulation 67
Criteria to be met by counsel

1. The necessary relevant experience for counsel as described in rule 22 shall be at least ten years.

2. Counsel should not have been convicted of a serious criminal or disciplinary offence considered to be incompatible with the nature of the office of counsel before the Court.

Regulation 68
Assistants to counsel

Persons assisting counsel as described in rule 22, sub-rule 1, may include persons who can assist counsel in the presentation of the case before a Chamber.

The criteria to be met by these persons shall be determined in the Regulations of the Registry.

Regulation 69
Proof and control of criteria to be met by counsel

1. A person seeking to be included in the list of counsel shall complete the forms provided by the Registrar for this purpose.

2. A person referred to in sub-regulation 1 shall also provide:

(a) A detailed *curriculum vitae*;

(b) A certificate issued by each Bar association the person is registered with, and/or each relevant controlling administrative authority confirming his or her qualifications, the right to practise and the existence, if any, of disciplinary sanctions or ongoing disciplinary proceedings; and

(c) A certificate issued by the relevant authority of each State of which the person is a national or where the person is domiciled stating the existence, if any, of criminal convictions.

3. A person referred to in sub-regulation 1 or counsel already included in the list of counsel shall immediately inform the Registrar of any changes to the information he or she has provided that are more than *de minimis*, including the initiation of any criminal or disciplinary proceedings against the person.

4. The Registrar may at any stage take steps to verify the information provided by any person referred to in sub-regulation 1 and by counsel already included in the list of counsel.

Regulation 70
Inclusion in the list of counsel

1. On receipt of an application by a person seeking to be included in the list of counsel, the Registrar shall establish whether the person has provided the information required under regulation 69. Thereafter, the Registrar shall acknowledge receipt of the application and, where relevant, direct the person to submit additional information.

2. The decision as to whether a person shall be included in the list of counsel shall be notified to that person. If the application is refused, the Registrar shall provide reasons and information on how to apply for review of that decision in accordance with regulation 72.

Regulation 71
Removal and suspension from the list of counsel

1. The Registrar shall remove a counsel from the list of counsel where he or she:

(a) No longer meets the criteria required for inclusion in the list of counsel;

(b) Has been permanently banned from practising before the Court as a result of disciplinary proceedings held in accordance with the Code of Professional Conduct for counsel;

(c) Has been found guilty of an offence against the administration of justice as described in article 70, paragraph 1; or

(d) Has been permanently interdicted from exercising his or her functions before the Court in accordance with rule 171, sub-rule 3.

2. The Registrar shall suspend a counsel from the list of counsel where he or she has been:

(a) Temporarily suspended in a disciplinary proceeding according to the Code of Professional Conduct for counsel; or

(b) Temporarily interdicted from exercising his or her functions before the Court for a period exceeding 30 days in accordance with rule 171, sub-rule 3.

3. The Registrar shall notify the relevant counsel of his or her decision under sub-regulations 1 or 2. The Registrar shall provide reasons and information on how to apply for review of that decision in accordance with regulation 72.

Regulation 72
Review of decisions of the Registrar

1. Application may be made to the Presidency for review of:

(a) A decision under regulation 70, sub-regulation 2, refusing to include a person in the list of counsel;

(b) A decision under regulation 71, sub-regulation 1, removing counsel from the list of counsel; or

(c) A decision under regulation 71, sub-regulation 2, suspending counsel from the list of counsel.

2. Applications as described in sub-regulation 1 shall be set out in accordance with regulation 23 and be filed within 15 days of notification of the relevant decision of the Registrar.

3. The Registrar may file a response within 15 days of notification of the application as referred to in sub-regulations 1 and 2.

4. The Presidency may ask the Registrar to provide any additional information necessary to decide on the application. The decision of the Presidency shall be final.

Regulation 73
Duty counsel

1. The Registrar shall establish and maintain a roster of counsel included in the list of counsel who are available at any time to represent any person before the Court or to represent the interests of the defence.

2. If any person requires urgent legal assistance and has not yet secured legal assistance, or where his or her counsel is unavailable, the Registrar may appoint duty counsel, taking into account the wishes of the person, and the geographical proximity of, and the languages spoken by, the counsel.

Section 2
Defence through counsel

Regulation 74
Defence through counsel

1. Defence counsel shall act in proceedings before the Court either when chosen by the person entitled to legal assistance in accordance with rule 21, sub-rule 2, or when the Chamber has appointed counsel in accordance with the Statute, Rules or these Regulations.

2. When represented by defence counsel, the person entitled to legal assistance shall, subject to article 67, paragraph 1 (h), act before the Court through his or her counsel, unless otherwise authorised by the Chamber.

Regulation 75
Choice of defence counsel

1. If the person entitled to legal assistance chooses a counsel included in the list of counsel, the Registrar shall contact that counsel. If the counsel is

willing and ready to represent the person, the Registrar shall facilitate the issuance of a power of attorney for this counsel by the person.

2. If the person entitled to legal assistance chooses a counsel not on the list of counsel who is willing and ready to represent him or her and to be included in the list, the Registrar shall decide on the eligibility of that counsel in accordance with regulation 70 and, upon inclusion in the list, shall facilitate the issuance of a power of attorney. Until the filing of a power of attorney, the person entitled to legal assistance may be represented by duty counsel in accordance with regulation 73.

Regulation 76
Appointment of defence counsel by a Chamber

1. A Chamber, following consultation with the Registrar, may appoint counsel in the circumstances specified in the Statute and the Rules or where the interests of justice so require.

2. Where the Chamber decides to appoint counsel in accordance with sub-regulation 1, and where the counsel considered for appointment is not included in the list of counsel, the Registrar shall first decide on the eligibility of that counsel to be included in the list in accordance with regulation 70. The Chamber may also appoint counsel from the Office of Public Counsel for the defence.

Regulation 77
Office of Public Counsel for the defence

1. The Registrar shall establish and develop an Office of Public Counsel for the defence for the purpose of providing assistance as described in sub-regulations 4 and 5.

2. The Office of Public Counsel for the defence shall fall within the remit of the Registry solely for administrative purposes and otherwise shall function as a wholly independent office. Counsel and assistants within the Office shall act independently.

3. The Office of Public Counsel for the defence may include a counsel who meets the criteria set out in rule 22 and regulation 67. The Office shall include assistants as referred to in regulation 68.

4. The tasks of the Office of Public Counsel for the defence shall include representing and protecting the rights of the defence during the initial stages of

the investigation, in particular for the application of article 56, paragraph 2 (d), and rule 47, sub-rule 2.

5. The Office of Public Counsel for the defence shall also provide support and assistance to defence counsel and to the person entitled to legal assistance, including, where appropriate:

(a) Legal research and advice; and

(b) Appearing before a Chamber in respect of specific issues.

Regulation 78
Withdrawal of defence counsel

Prior to withdrawal from a case, defence counsel shall seek the leave of the Chamber.

Section 3
Legal representatives of victims

Regulation 79
Decision of the Chamber concerning legal representatives of victims

1. The decision of the Chamber to request the victims or particular groups of victims to choose a common legal representative or representatives may be made in conjunction with the decision on the application of the victim or victims to participate in the proceedings.

2. When choosing a common legal representative for victims in accordance with rule 90, sub-rule 3, consideration should be given to the views of the victims, and the need to respect local traditions and to assist specific groups of victims.

3. Victims may request the relevant Chamber to review the Registrar's choice of a common legal representative under rule 90, sub-rule 3, within 30 days of notification of the Registrar's decision.

Regulation 80
Appointment of legal representatives of victims by a Chamber

1. A Chamber, following consultation with the Registrar, may appoint a legal representative of victims where the interests of justice so require.

2. The Chamber may appoint counsel from the Office of Public Counsel for victims.

Regulation 81
Office of Public Counsel for victims

1. The Registrar shall establish and develop an Office of Public Counsel for victims for the purpose of providing assistance as described in sub-regulation 4.

2. The Office of Public Counsel for victims shall fall within the remit of the Registry solely for administrative purposes and otherwise shall function as a wholly independent office. Counsel and assistants within the Office shall act independently.

3. The Office of Public Counsel for victims may include a counsel who meets the criteria set out in rule 22 and regulation 67. The Office shall include assistants as referred to in regulation 68.

4. The Office of Public Counsel for victims shall provide support and assistance to the legal representative for victims and to victims, including, where appropriate:

(a) Legal research and advice; and

(b) Appearing before a Chamber in respect of specific issues.

Regulation 82
Withdrawal of legal representatives of victims

Prior to withdrawal from a case, legal representatives of victims shall seek the leave of the Chamber.

Section 4
Legal assistance paid by the Court

Regulation 83
General scope of legal assistance paid by the Court

1. Legal assistance paid by the Court shall cover all costs reasonably necessary as determined by the Registrar for an effective and efficient defence, including the remuneration of counsel, his or her assistants as referred to in regulation 68 and staff, expenditure in relation to the gathering of evidence, administrative costs, translation and interpretation costs, travel costs and daily subsistence allowances.

2. The scope of legal assistance paid by the Court regarding victims shall be determined by the Registrar in consultation with the Chamber, where appropriate.

3. A person receiving legal assistance paid by the Court may apply to the Registrar for additional means which may be granted depending on the nature of the case.

4. Decisions by the Registrar on the scope of legal assistance paid by the Court as defined in this regulation may be reviewed by the relevant Chamber on application by the person receiving legal assistance.

Regulation 84
Determination of means

1. Where a person applies for legal assistance to be paid by the Court, the Registrar shall determine the applicant's means and whether he or she shall be provided with full or partial payment of legal assistance.

2. The means of the applicant shall include means of all kinds in respect of which the applicant has direct or indirect enjoyment or power freely to dispose, including, but not limited to, direct income, bank accounts, real or personal property, pensions, stocks, bonds or other assets held, but excluding any family or social benefits to which he or she may be entitled. In assessing such means, account shall also be taken of any transfers of property by the applicant which the Registrar considers relevant, and of the apparent lifestyle of the applicant. The Registrar shall allow for expenses claimed by the applicant provided they are reasonable and necessary.

Regulation 85
Decisions on payment of legal assistance

1. In accordance with the procedure set out in the Regulations of the Registry, the Registrar shall decide within one month of the submission of an application or, within one month of expiry of a time limit set in accordance with the Regulations of the Registry, whether legal assistance should be paid by the Court. The decision shall be notified to the applicant together with the reasons for the decision and instructions on how to apply for review.

The Registrar may, in appropriate circumstances, make a provisional decision to grant payment of legal assistance.

2. The Registrar shall reconsider his or her decision on payment of legal assistance if the financial situation of the person receiving such legal assistance is found to be different than indicated in the application, or if the financial situation of the person has changed since the application was submitted. Any revised decision shall be notified to the person together with the reasons for the decision and instructions on how to apply for review.

3. Persons as referred to in sub-regulations 1 and 2 may seek review of the decisions described in those provisions by the Presidency within 15 days of notification of the relevant decision. The decision of the Presidency shall be final.

4. Subject to rule 21, sub-rule 5, where legal assistance has been paid by the Court and it is subsequently established that the information provided to the Registrar on the applicant's means was inaccurate, the Registrar may seek an order from the Presidency for recovery of the funds paid from the person who received legal assistance paid by the Court. The Registrar may seek the assistance of the relevant States Parties to enforce that order.

Chapter 5
Victims participation and reparations

Regulation 86
Participation of victims in the proceedings under rule 89

1. For the purposes of rule 89 and subject to rule 102 a victim shall make a written application to the Registrar who shall develop standard forms for that purpose which shall be approved in accordance with regulation 23, sub-regulation 2. These standard forms shall, to the extent possible, be made available to victims, groups of victims, or intergovernmental and nongovernmental organizations, which may assist in their dissemination, as widely as possible. These standard forms shall, to the extent possible, be used by victims.

2. The standard forms or other applications described in sub-regulation 1 shall contain, to the extent possible, the following information:

(a) The identity and address of the victim, or the address to which the victim requests all communications to be sent; in case the application is presented by someone other than the victim in accordance with rule 89, sub-rule 3, the identity and address of that person, or the address to which that person requests all communications to be sent;

(b) If the application is presented in accordance with rule 89, sub-rule 3, evidence of the consent of the victim or evidence on the situation of the victim, being a child or a disabled person, shall be presented together with the application, either in writing or in accordance with rule 102;

(c) A description of the harm suffered resulting from the commission of any crime within the jurisdiction of the Court, or, in case of a victim being an organization or institution, a description of any direct harm as described in rule 85 (b);

(d) A description of the incident, including its location and date and, to the extent possible, the identity of the person or persons the victim believes to be responsible for the harm as described in rule 85;

(e) Any relevant supporting documentation, including names and addresses of witnesses;

(f) Information as to why the personal interests of the victim are affected;

(g) Information on the stage of the proceedings in which the victim wishes to participate, and, if applicable, on the relief sought;

(h) Information on the extent of legal representation, if any, which is envisaged by the victim, including the names and addresses of potential legal representatives, and information on the victim's or victims' financial means to pay for a legal representative.

3. Victims applying for participation in the trial and/or appeal proceedings shall, to the extent possible, make their application to the Registrar before the start of the stage of the proceedings in which they want to participate.

4. The Registrar may request further information from victims or those presenting an application in accordance with rule 89, sub-rule 3, in order to ensure that such application contains, to the extent possible, the information referred to in sub-regulation 2, before transmission to a Chamber. The Registrar may also seek additional information from States, the Prosecutor and intergovernmental or non-governmental organizations.

5. The Registrar shall present all applications described in this regulation to the Chamber together with a report thereon. The Registrar shall endeavour to present one report for a group of victims, taking into consideration the distinct interests of the victims.

6. Subject to any order of the Chamber, the Registrar may also submit one report on a number of applications received in accordance with sub-regulation 1 to the Chamber seized of the case or situation in order to assist that Chamber in issuing only one decision on a number of applications in accordance with rule 89, sub-rule 4. Reports covering all applications received in a certain time period may be presented on a periodic basis.

7. Before deciding on an application, the Chamber may request, if necessary with the assistance of the Registrar, additional information from, *inter alia*, States, the Prosecutor, the victims or those acting on their behalf or with their consent. If information is received from States or the Prosecutor, the Chamber shall provide the relevant victim or victims with an opportunity to respond.

8. A decision taken by a Chamber under rule 89 shall apply throughout the proceedings in the same case, subject to the powers of the relevant Chamber in accordance with rule 91, sub-rule 1.

9. There shall be a specialised unit dealing with victims' participation and reparations under the authority of the Registrar. This unit shall be responsible for assisting victims and groups of victims.

Regulation 87
Information to victims

1. The Prosecutor shall notify the Pre-Trial Chamber as to information provided pursuant to rule 50, sub-rule 1, including the date the information was provided.

2. The Prosecutor shall inform the Registry of his or her decision not to initiate an investigation or not to prosecute pursuant to article 53, paragraphs 1 and 2, respectively, and shall provide all relevant information for notification by the Registry to victims in accordance with rule 92, sub-rule 2.

Regulation 88
Requests for reparations in accordance with rule 94

1. For the application of rule 94, the Registrar shall develop a standard form for victims to present their requests for reparations and shall make it available to victims, groups of victims, or intergovernmental and non-governmental organizations which may assist in its dissemination, as

widely as possible. This standard form shall be approved in accordance with regulation 23, sub-regulation 2, and shall, to the extent possible, be used by victims.

2. The Registrar shall seek all necessary additional information from a victim in order to complete his or her request in accordance with rule 94, sub-rule 1, and shall assist victims in completing such a request. The request shall then be registered and stored electronically in order to be notified by the unit described in regulation 86, sub-regulation 9, in accordance with rule 94, sub-rule 2.

APPENDIX V

Code of Professional Conduct for Counsel

Chapter 1
General provisions

Article 1
Scope

This Code shall apply to defence counsel, counsel acting for States, *amici curiae* and counsel or legal representatives for victims and witnesses practising at the International Criminal Court, hereinafter referred to as "counsel".

Article 2
Use of terms

1. Unless otherwise defined in this Code, all terms are used as defined in the Statute, the Rules of Procedure and Evidence and the Regulations of the Court.

2. In this Code:

- "Court" refers to the International Criminal Court;
- "associate" refers to lawyers who practise in the same law firm as counsel;
- "national authority" refers to the bar association of which counsel is a member or any other organ competent to regulate and control the activity of lawyers, judges, prosecutors or professors of law, or other qualified counsel according to rule 22, paragraph 1, of the Rules of Procedure and Evidence;
- "client" refers to all those assisted or represented by counsel;
- "defence team" refers to counsel and all persons working under his or her oversight; and
- "agreement" refers to the oral or written legal relationship which binds counsel to his or her client before the Court.

Article 3
Amendment procedure

1. States Parties, judges, the Registrar, counsel and independent organizations representing lawyers' associations and counsel may submit proposals for amendments to this Code. Any proposal for amendments to this Code shall be submitted to the Registrar, together with explanatory material, in one or both working languages of the Court.

2. The Registrar shall transmit the proposals to the Presidency, together with a reasoned report prepared after consultation with the Prosecutor and, as appropriate, with any independent organization representing lawyers' associations and counsel.

3. Any proposal to amend this Code, submitted by one or more States Parties, shall be transmitted by the Presidency to the Assembly of States Parties together with any comments the Presidency may have, taking into account the report of the Registrar.

4. Any proposal to amend this Code, other than one submitted by one or more States Parties, shall be transmitted by the Presidency to the Assembly of States Parties together with any comments the Presidency may have, taking into account the report of the Registrar. In such circumstances, the Presidency shall provide the Assembly of States Parties with the Presidency's reasoned recommendations as to whether or not any such proposal should be adopted. If the Presidency recommends adoption, it shall submit a draft amendment in relation to that proposal to the Assembly of States Parties for the purpose of adoption.

5. Amendments to this Code shall be adopted by the Assembly of States Parties in accordance with article 112, paragraph 7, of the Statute.

Article 4
Primacy of the Code of Professional Conduct for counsel

Where there is any inconsistency between this Code and any other code of ethics or professional responsibility which counsel are bound to honour, the terms of this Code shall prevail in respect of the practice and professional ethics of counsel when practising before the Court.

Article 5
Solemn undertaking by counsel

Before taking office, counsel shall give the following solemn undertaking before the Court: "I solemnly declare that I will perform my duties and exercise my mission before the International Criminal Court with integrity and diligence, honourably, freely, independently, expeditiously and conscientiously, and that I will scrupulously respect professional secrecy and the other duties imposed by the Code of Professional Conduct for Counsel before the International Criminal Court".

Article 6
Independence of counsel

1. Counsel shall act honourably, independently and freely.

2. Counsel shall not:

(a) Permit his or her independence, integrity or freedom to be compromised by external pressure; or

(b) Do anything which may lead to any reasonable inference that his or her independence has been compromised.

Article 7
Professional conduct of counsel

1. Counsel shall be respectful and courteous in his or her relations with the Chamber, the Prosecutor and the members of the Office of the Prosecutor, the Registrar and the members of the Registry, the client, opposing counsel, accused persons, victims, witnesses and any other person involved in the proceedings.

2. Counsel shall maintain a high level of competence in the law applicable before the Court. He or she shall participate in training initiatives required to maintain such competence.

3. Counsel shall comply at all times with the Statute, the Rules of Procedure and Evidence, the Regulations of the Court and such rulings as to conduct and procedure as may be made by the Court, including the enforcement of this Code.

4. Counsel shall supervise the work of his or her assistants and other staff, including investigators, clerks and researchers, to ensure that they comply with this Code.

Article 8
Respect for professional secrecy and confidentiality

1. Counsel shall respect and actively exercise all care to ensure respect for professional secrecy and the confidentiality of information in accordance with the Statute, the Rules of Procedure and Evidence and the Regulations of the Court.

2. The relevant provisions referred to in paragraph 1 of this article include, inter alia, article 64, paragraph 6 (c), article 64, paragraph 7, article 67, paragraph 1 (b), article 68, and article 72 of the Statute, rules 72, 73, and 81 of the Rules of Procedure and Evidence and regulation 97 of the Regulations of the Court. Counsel shall also comply with the relevant provisions of this Code and any order of the Court.

3. Counsel may only reveal the information protected under paragraphs 1 and 2 of this article to co-counsel, assistants and other staff working on the particular case to which the information relates and solely to enable the exercise of his or her functions in relation to that case.

4. Subject to paragraph 3 of this article, counsel may only disclose the information protected under paragraphs 1 and 2 of this article, where such disclosure is provided for by a particular provision of the Statute, the Rules of Procedure and Evidence, the Regulations of the Court or this Code or where such disclosure is ordered by the Court. In particular, Counsel shall not reveal the identity of protected victims and witnesses, or any confidential information that may reveal their identity and whereabouts, unless he or she has been authorized to do so by an order of the Court.

Article 9
Counsel-client relationship

1. Counsel shall not engage in any discriminatory conduct in relation to any other person, in particular his or her client, on grounds of race, colour, ethnic or national origin, nationality, citizenship, political opinions, religious convictions, gender, sexual orientation, disability, marital status or any other personal or economic status.

2. In his or her relations with the client, counsel shall take into account the client's personal circumstances and specific needs, in particular where counsel is representing victims of torture or of physical, psychological or sexual violence, or children, the elderly or the disabled.

3. Where a client's ability to make decisions concerning representation is impaired because of mental disability or for any other reason, counsel shall inform the Registrar and the relevant Chamber. Counsel shall also take the steps necessary to ensure proper legal representation of the client according to the Statute and the Rules of Procedure and Evidence.

4. Counsel shall not engage in any improper conduct, such as demanding sexual relations, coercion, intimidation, or exercise any other undue influence in his or her relations with a client.

Article 10
Advertising

Counsel may advertise provided the information is:

(a) Accurate; and

(b) Respectful of counsel's obligations regarding confidentiality and privilege.

Chapter 2
Representation by counsel

Article 11
Establishment of the representation agreement

The agreement is established when counsel accepts a request from a client seeking representation or from the Chamber.

Article 12
Impediments to representation

1. Counsel shall not represent a client in a case:

(a) If the case is the same as or substantially related to another case in which counsel or his or her associates represents or formerly represented another client and the interests of the client are incompatible with the interests of the former client, unless the client and the former client consent after consultation; or

(b) In which counsel was involved or was privy to confidential information as a staff member of the Court relating to the case in which counsel seeks to appear. The lifting of this impediment may, however, at counsel's request, be ordered by the Court if deemed justified in the interests of justice. Counsel shall still be bound by the duties of confidentiality stemming from his or her former position as a staff member of the Court.

2. In the case of paragraph 1 (a) of this article, where consent has been obtained after consultation, counsel shall inform the Chamber of the Court seized with the situation or case of the conflict and the consent obtained. Such notice shall be provided in a manner consistent with counsel's duties of confidentiality pursuant to article 8 of this Code and rule 73, sub-rule 1 of the Rules of Procedure and Evidence.

3. Counsel shall not act in proceedings in which there is a substantial probability that counsel or an associate of counsel will be called to appear as a witness unless:

(a) The testimony relates to an uncontested issue; or

(b) The testimony relates to the nature and value of legal services rendered in the case.

4. This article is without prejudice to article 16 of this Code.

Article 13
Refusal by counsel of a representation agreement

1. Counsel has the right to refuse an agreement without stating reasons.

2. Counsel has a duty to refuse an agreement where:

(a) There is a conflict of interest under article16 of this Code;

(b) Counsel is incapable of dealing with the matter diligently; or

(c) Counsel does not consider that he or she has the requisite expertise.

Article 14
Performance in good faith of a representation agreement

1. The relationship of client and counsel is one of candid exchange and trust, binding counsel to act in good faith when dealing with the client. In discharging that duty, counsel shall act at all times with fairness, integrity and candour towards the client.

2. When representing a client, counsel shall:

(a) Abide by the client's decisions concerning the objectives of his or her representation as long as they are not inconsistent with counsel's duties under the Statute, the Rules of Procedure and Evidence, and this Code; and

(b) Consult the client on the means by which the objectives of his or her representation are to be pursued.

Article 15
Communication between counsel and the client

1. Counsel shall provide the client with all explanations reasonably needed to make informed decisions regarding his or her representation.

2. When counsel is discharged from or terminates the agreement, he or she shall convey as promptly as possible to the former client or replacement counsel any communication that counsel received relating to the representation, without prejudice to the duties which subsist after the end of the representation.

3. When communicating with the client, counsel shall ensure the confidentiality of such communication.

Article 16
Conflict of interest

1. Counsel shall exercise all care to ensure that no conflict of interest arises. Counsel shall put the client's interests before counsel's own interests or those of any other person, organization or State, having due regard to the provisions of the Statute, the Rules of Procedure and Evidence, and this Code.

2. Where counsel has been retained or appointed as a common legal representative for victims or particular groups of victims, he or she shall advise his or her clients at the outset of the nature of the representation and the potential conflicting interests within the group. Counsel shall exercise all care to ensure a fair representation of the different yet consistent positions of his or her clients.

3. Where a conflict of interest arises, counsel shall at once inform all potentially affected clients of the existence of the conflict and either:

(a) Withdraw from the representation of one or more clients with the prior consent of the Chamber; or

(b) Seek the full and informed consent in writing of all potentially affected clients to continue representation.

Article 17
Duration of the representation agreement

1. Counsel shall advise and represent a client until:

(a) The case before the Court has been finally determined, including all appeals;

(b) Counsel has withdrawn from the agreement in accordance with article 16 or 18 of this Code; or

(c) A counsel assigned by the Court has been withdrawn.

2. The duties of counsel towards the client continue until the representation has ended, except for those duties which subsist under this Code.

Article 18
Termination of the representation

1. With the prior consent of the Chamber, counsel may withdraw from the agreement in accordance with the Regulations of the Court if:

(a) The client insists on pursuing an objective that counsel considers repugnant; or

(b) The client fails to fulfil an obligation to counsel regarding counsel's services and has been given reasonable warning that counsel will withdraw unless the obligation is fulfilled.

2. Where counsel withdraws from the agreement, he or she remains subject to article 8 of this Code, as well as any provisions of the Statute and the Rules of Procedure and Evidence relating to confidentiality.

3. Where counsel is discharged by the client, counsel may be discharged in accordance with the Regulations of the Court.

4. Where counsel's physical or mental condition materially impairs his or her ability to represent the client, counsel may be withdrawn by the Chamber at his or her request or at the request of the client or the Registrar.

5. In addition to complying with the duties imposed by article 15, paragraph 2, of this Code, counsel shall convey to replacement counsel the entire case file, including any material or document relating to it.

Article 19
Conservation of files

Following the termination of the representation, counsel shall keep files containing documents and records of work carried out in fulfilment of the agreement for five years. Counsel shall allow the former client to inspect the file unless he or she has substantial grounds for refusing to do so. After this time counsel shall seek instructions from the former client, his or her heirs or the Registrar on the disposal of the files, with due regard to confidentiality.

Article 20
Counsel's fees

Prior to establishing an agreement, counsel shall inform the client in writing of the rate of fees to be charged and the criteria for setting them, the basis for calculating the costs, the billing arrangements and the client's right to receive a bill of costs.

Article 21
Prohibitions

1. Notwithstanding article 22, counsel shall not accept remuneration, in cash or in kind, from a source other than the client unless the client consents thereto in writing after consultation and counsel's independence and relationship with the client are not thereby affected.

2. Counsel shall never make his or her fees contingent on the outcome of a case in which he or she is involved.

3. Counsel shall not mix funds of a client with his or her own funds, or with funds of counsel's employer or associates. Counsel shall not retain money received on behalf of a client.

4. Counsel shall not borrow monies or assets from the client.

Article 22
Remuneration of counsel in the framework of legal assistance

1. The fees of counsel where his or her client benefits from legal assistance shall be paid exclusively by the Registry of the Court. Counsel shall not accept remuneration in cash or in kind from any other source.

2. Counsel shall neither transfer nor lend all or part of the fees received for representation of a client or any other assets or monies to a client, his or her relatives, acquaintances, or any other third person or organization in relation to which the client has a personal interest.

3. Counsel shall sign an undertaking to respect the obligations under this article when accepting the appointment to provide legal assistance. The signed undertaking shall be sent to the Registry.

4. Where counsel is requested, induced or encouraged to violate the obligations under this article, counsel shall advise the client of the prohibition of such conduct.

5. Breach of any obligations under this article by Counsel shall amount to misconduct and shall be subject to a disciplinary procedure pursuant to this Code. This may lead to a permanent ban on practising before the Court and being struck off the list of counsel, with transmission to the respective national authority.

Chapter 3
Relations with the Court and others

Article 23
Communications with the Chambers and judges

Unless the judge or the Chamber dealing with a case permits counsel to do so in exceptional circumstances, counsel shall not:

(a) Make contact with a judge or Chamber relative to the merits of a particular case other than within the proper context of the proceedings; or

(b) Transmit evidence, notes or documents to a judge or Chamber except through the Registry.

Article 24
Duties towards the Court

1. Counsel shall take all necessary steps to ensure that his or her actions or those of counsel's assistants or staff are not prejudicial to the ongoing proceedings and do not bring the Court into disrepute.

2. Counsel is personally responsible for the conduct and presentation of the client's case and shall exercise personal judgement on the substance and purpose of statements made and questions asked.

3. Counsel shall not deceive or knowingly mislead the Court. He or she shall take all steps necessary to correct an erroneous statement made by him or her or by assistants or staff as soon as possible after becoming aware that the statement was erroneous.

4. Counsel shall not submit any request or document with the sole aim of harming one or more of the participants in the proceedings.

5. Counsel shall represent the client expeditiously with the purpose of avoiding unnecessary expense or delay in the conduct of the proceedings.

Article 25
Evidence

1. Counsel shall at all times maintain the integrity of evidence, whether in written, oral or any other form, which is submitted to the Court. He or she shall not introduce evidence which he or she knows to be incorrect.

2. If counsel, while collecting evidence, reasonably believes that the evidence found may be destroyed or tampered with, counsel shall request the Chamber to issue an order to collect the evidence pursuant to rule 116 of the Rules of Procedure and Evidence.

Article 26
Relations with unrepresented persons

1. When required in the course of representation, counsel may communicate with and meet an unrepresented person in the client's interest.

2. When counsel communicates with unrepresented persons he or she shall:

(a) Inform them of their right to assistance from counsel and, if applicable, to their right to legal assistance; and

(b) Without infringing upon the confidentiality of counsel-client privilege, inform them of the interest that counsel represents and the purpose of the communication.

3. If counsel becomes aware of a potential conflict of interest in the course of a communication or meeting with an unrepresented person, he or she shall, notwithstanding paragraph 1 of this article, refrain immediately from engaging in any further contact or communication with the person.

Article 27
Relations with other counsel

1. In dealing with other counsel and their clients, counsel shall act fairly, in good faith and courteously.

2. All correspondence between counsel representing clients with a common interest in a litigated or non-litigated matter and who agree on exchanging information concerning the matter, shall be presumed confidential and privileged by counsel.

3. When counsel does not expect particular correspondence between counsel to be confidential, he or she shall state clearly at the outset that such correspondence is not confidential.

Article 28
Relations with persons already represented by counsel

Counsel shall not address directly the client of another counsel except through or with the permission of that counsel.

Article 29
Relations with witnesses and victims

1. Counsel shall refrain from intimidating, harassing or humiliating witnesses or victims or from subjecting them to disproportionate or unnecessary pressure within or outside the courtroom.

2. Counsel shall have particular consideration for victims of torture or of physical, psychological or sexual violence, or children, the elderly or the disabled.

Chapter 4
Disciplinary regime

Article 30
Conflict with other disciplinary regimes

Subject to article 38 of this Code, the present chapter is without prejudice to the disciplinary powers of any other disciplinary authority that may apply to counsel subject to this Code.

Article 31
Misconduct

Counsel commits misconduct when he or she:

(a) Violates or attempts to violate any provisions of this Code, the Statute, the Rules of Procedure and Evidence and the Regulations of the Court or of the Registry in force imposing a substantial ethical or professional duty on him or her;

(b) Knowingly assists or induces another person to commit any misconduct, referred to in paragraph (a) of this article, or does so through the acts of another person; or

(c) Fails to comply with a disciplinary decision rendered pursuant to this chapter.

Article 32
Liability for conduct of assistants or other staff

1. Counsel shall be liable for misconduct under article 31 of this Code by his or her assistants or staff when he or she:

(a) Orders or approves the conduct involved; or

(b) Knows or has information suggesting that violations may be committed and takes no reasonable remedial action.

2. Counsel shall instruct his or her assistants or staff in the standards set by this Code.

Article 33
The Commissioner

1. A Commissioner responsible for investigating complaints of misconduct in accordance with this chapter shall be appointed for four years by the Presidency. The Commissioner shall be chosen from amongst persons with established competence in professional ethics and legal matters.

2. The Commissioner shall not be eligible for re-appointment. A Commissioner who is involved in an investigation when his or her mandate expires shall continue to conduct such an investigation until it is concluded.

Article 34
Filing a complaint of misconduct

1. Complaints against counsel regarding misconduct as referred to in articles 31 and 32 of this Code may be submitted to the Registry by:

(a) The Chamber dealing with the case;

(b) The Prosecutor; or

(c) Any person or group of persons whose rights or interests may have been affected by the alleged misconduct.

2. The complaint shall be made in writing or, if the complainant is unable to do so, orally before a staff member of the Registry. It shall identify the complainant and the counsel against whom the complaint is made and shall describe in sufficient detail the alleged misconduct.

3. The Registrar shall transmit the complaint to the Commissioner.

4. The Registrar may, on his or her own initiative, make complaints to the Commissioner regarding the misconduct referred to in articles 31 and 32 of this Code.

5. All complaints shall be kept confidential by the Registry.

Article 35
Limitation period

The right to file a complaint against counsel for misconduct shall lapse five years after the termination of the representation agreement.

Article 36
Composition and management of the Disciplinary Board

1. The Disciplinary Board shall comprise three members, two of whom shall be permanent and one *ad hoc*.

2. The members of the Disciplinary Board shall perform their functions under this Code in an independent and impartial manner.

3. The Registry shall make appropriate arrangements for the elections, provided for in paragraph 4 of this article, in consultation with counsel and, as appropriate, national authorities.

4. The two permanent members, as well as one alternate member who may serve as a replacement in accordance with paragraph 10 of this article, shall

be elected for four years by all counsel entitled to practise before the Court. They shall be chosen from amongst persons with established competence in professional ethics and legal matters.

5. The *ad hoc* member shall be a person appointed by the national authority competent to regulate and control the activities of counsel subject to the disciplinary procedure.

6. The permanent members shall not be eligible for re-election.

7. Notwithstanding paragraph 4 of this article, at the first election one of the permanent members shall be selected by lot to serve for a term of six years.

8. After each election and in advance of the first meeting of the newly-elected Disciplinary Board, the permanent and alternate members shall elect one of the permanent members as a chairperson.

9. All members of the Disciplinary Board shall have the same rights and votes. The Disciplinary Board shall decide by majority vote. An alternate member serving on a case pursuant to paragraph 10 of this article shall have the same rights and votes as permanent and *ad hoc* members serving on the same case.

10. If one of the permanent members is unavailable to deal with the case or serve on the Disciplinary Board, the chairperson or, where the chairperson is the permanent member concerned, the other permanent member, shall request the alternate member to serve as a replacement on the Disciplinary Board.

11. Permanent members or the alternate member whose mandates have expired shall continue to deal with the cases they already have under consideration until such cases are finally determined including all appeals.

12. The Registrar shall appoint a staff member of the Registry who will render secretariat services to the Disciplinary Board. Once appointed, the relevant staff member of the Registry shall act at arm's length from the Registry and, subject to article 44, paragraph 12 of this Code, solely as the secretariat of the Disciplinary Board.

Article 37
Preliminary procedures

1. If the complaint filed meets the requirements in article 34 of this Code, the Commissioner shall forward it to counsel subject to the disciplinary

procedure, who shall submit a response within sixty days from the date the complaint is forwarded.

2. The response shall indicate whether the alleged misconduct has been or is the subject of a disciplinary procedure before the national authority. If so, it shall include:

(a) The identity of the national authority deciding on the alleged misconduct; and

(b) A certified communication by the national authority stating the alleged facts that are the basis of the disciplinary procedure before it.

Article 38
Complementarity of disciplinary measures

1. The disciplinary procedure in this Code shall be applied by the Disciplinary Board.

2. The *ad hoc* member of the Disciplinary Board shall serve as the contact point with the relevant national authority for all communication and consultation regarding the procedure.

3. Counsel subject to the disciplinary procedure shall request the national authority dealing with the matter to inform the Disciplinary Board of the progress of any national disciplinary procedure concerning the alleged misconduct and of its final decision, and shall take all measures necessary to facilitate such communication.

4. When the alleged misconduct is the basis of a disciplinary procedure which has already been initiated before the relevant national authority, the procedure before the Disciplinary Board shall be suspended until a final decision is reached regarding the former procedure, unless:

(a) the national authority does not respond to communications and consultations in accordance with paragraph 2 of this article within a reasonable time;

(b) the Disciplinary Board considers that the information received is not satisfactory; or

(c) the Disciplinary Board considers that, in the light of the information received, the national authority is unable or unwilling to conclude the disciplinary procedure.

5. As soon as it receives the decision of the national authority, the Disciplinary Board shall:

(a) declare the procedure closed, unless the decision adopted does not adequately address a complaint of misconduct under this Code; or

(b) declare that the decision of the national authority does not cover or only partially covers the misconduct brought before the Disciplinary Board and that therefore the procedure is to be continued.

6. In the case of paragraphs 3 and paragraph 4 (b) of this article, the Disciplinary Board may ask counsel subject to the disciplinary procedure to provide detailed information about the procedure, including any minute or evidence which might have been submitted.

7. A decision by the Disciplinary Board based on this article may be appealed before the Disciplinary Appeals Board.

Article 39
Disciplinary procedure

1. The Commissioner conducting the investigation may dismiss a complaint without any further investigation if he or she considers on the basis of the information at his or her disposal that the allegation of misconduct is unfounded in fact or in law. He or she shall notify the complainant accordingly.

2. Should the Commissioner consider otherwise, he or she shall promptly investigate the counsel's alleged misconduct and decide either to submit a report to the Disciplinary Board or to bring the procedure to an end.

3. The Commissioner shall take into consideration all evidence, whether oral, written or any other form, which is relevant and has probative value. He or she shall keep all information concerning the disciplinary procedure confidential.

4. The Commissioner may try to find an amicable settlement if he or she deems it appropriate. The Commissioner shall report the outcome of any such efforts to reach an amicable settlement to the Disciplinary Board, which may take it into consideration. Any amicable settlement shall be without prejudice to the competence or powers of the Disciplinary Board under this Code.

5. The report of the Commissioner shall be submitted to the Disciplinary Board.

6. The Disciplinary Board hearing shall be public. However, the Disciplinary Board may decide to hold a hearing or parts of it in closed session, in

particular to safeguard the confidentiality of information in the report of the Commissioner or to protect victims and witnesses.

7. The Commissioner and the counsel subject to the disciplinary procedure shall be called and heard. The Disciplinary Board may also call and hear any other person deemed useful for the establishment of the truth.

8. In exceptional cases, where the alleged misconduct is of such a nature as to seriously prejudice the interests of justice, the Commissioner may lodge an urgent motion with the Chamber before which the counsel who is the subject of the complaint is appearing, so that it may, as appropriate, declare a temporary suspension of such counsel.

Article 40
Rights of counsel subject to the disciplinary procedure

1. Counsel subject to the disciplinary procedure shall be entitled to assistance from other counsel.

2. Counsel shall have the right to remain silent before the Disciplinary Board, which may draw any inferences it deems appropriate and reasonable from such silence in the light of all the information submitted to it.

3. Counsel shall have the right to full disclosure of the information and evidence gathered by the Commissioner as well as the Commissioner's report.

4. Counsel shall be given the time required to prepare his or her defence.

5. Counsel shall have the right to question, personally or through his or her counsel, any person called by the Disciplinary Board to testify before it.

Article 41
Decisions by the Disciplinary Board

1. The Disciplinary Board may conclude the procedure finding no misconduct on the basis of the evidence submitted to it or finding that counsel subject to disciplinary procedure committed the alleged misconduct.

2. The decision shall be made public. It shall be reasoned and issued in writing.

3. The decision shall be notified to counsel subject to the disciplinary procedure and to the Registrar.

4. When the decision is final, it shall be published in the Official Journal of the Court and transmitted to the national authority.

Article 42
Sanctions

1. When misconduct has been established, the Disciplinary Board may impose one or more of the following sanctions:

(a) Admonishment;

(b) Public reprimand with an entry in counsel's personal file;

(c) Payment of a fine of up to €30,000;

(d) Suspension of the right to practise before the Court for a period not exceeding two years; and

(e) Permanent ban on practising before the Court and striking off the list of counsel.

2. The admonishment may include recommendations by the Disciplinary Board.

3. The costs of the disciplinary procedure shall be within the discretion of the Disciplinary Board.

Article 43
Appeals

1. Sanctioned counsel and the Commissioner shall have the right to appeal the decision of the Disciplinary Board on factual or legal grounds.

2. The appeal shall be notified to the secretariat of the Disciplinary Board within thirty days from the day on which the decision has been delivered.

3. The secretariat of the Disciplinary Board shall transmit the notification of the appeal to the secretariat of the Disciplinary Appeals Board.

4. The Disciplinary Appeals Board shall decide on the appeal according to the procedure followed before the Disciplinary Board.

Article 44
Composition and management of the Disciplinary Appeals Board

1. The Disciplinary Appeals Board shall decide on appeals against decisions of the Disciplinary Board.

2. The members of the Disciplinary Appeals Board shall perform their functions under this Code in an independent and impartial manner.

3. The Registry shall make appropriate arrangements for the elections provided for in paragraph 5 of this article, in consultation with counsel and, as appropriate, national authorities.

4. The Disciplinary Appeals Board shall comprise five members:

(a) The three judges of the Court who take precedence under regulation 10 of the Regulations of the Court, not including:

(i) the judges dealing with the case from which the complaint subject to the disciplinary procedure arose; or

(ii) any members or former members of the Presidency who appointed the Commissioner.

(b) Two persons elected in accordance with paragraph 5 of this article.

5. The two members of the Disciplinary Appeals Board referred to in paragraph 4 (b) of this article, as well as an alternate member who may serve as a replacement in accordance with paragraph 6 of this article, shall be elected for four years by all counsel entitled to practise before the Court. They shall be chosen from amongst persons with established competence in professional ethics and legal matters.

6. If one of the elected members is unavailable to deal with the case or serve on the Disciplinary Appeal Board, the chairperson shall request the alternate member to serve as a replacement on the Disciplinary Appeals Board.

7. The functions of members of the Disciplinary Appeals Board are incompatible with those of members of the Disciplinary Board.

8. The elected members shall not be eligible for re-election.

9. The judge who takes precedence among the three judges referred to in paragraph 4 (a) of this article shall be the chairperson of the Disciplinary Appeals Board.

10. All members of the Disciplinary Appeals Board shall have the same rights and votes. The Disciplinary Appeals Board shall decide by majority vote. An alternate member serving on a case pursuant to paragraph 6 of this article shall have the same rights and votes as other members serving on the same case.

11. Members whose mandates have expired shall continue to deal with the cases they already have under consideration until such cases are finally determined.

12. The staff member of the Registry appointed by the Registrar pursuant to article 36, paragraph 12, of this Code to provide secretariat services to the Disciplinary Board shall also act as the secretariat of the Disciplinary Appeals Board. Once appointed, the relevant staff member of the Registry shall act at arm's length from the Registry.

Chapter 5
Final provisions

Article 45
Entry into force

This Code and any amendments to it shall enter into force 30 days after their adoption by the Assembly of States Parties in accordance with article 112, paragraph 2, of the Rome Statute.

Article 46
Publication

The Code adopted by the Assembly of States Parties shall be published in the Official Journal of the Court.

APPENDIX VI

Counsel Participation Form

This form is also available at: http://www.icc-cpi.int/Menus/ICC/Structure+of+the+Court/Victims/Office+of+Public+Counsel+for+Victims/Legal+Research+and+Advice.htm

Cour Pénale Internationale

International Criminal Court

Candidate application form list of counsel

Candidates are requested to fill in the form below and answer all the questions. The form and the required documents should be sent to the following address: Registry of the International Criminal Court, Division of Victims and Counsel, P.O. Box 19519, 2500 CM The Hague, The Netherlands, quoting "Reference: list of counsel".

Surname of candidate:	**Candidate's home address:**
First name(s):	
Sex: ☐ **M** ☐ **F**	**Candidate's office address:**
Other names used now or in the past (e.g. maiden name):	**Other addresses:**
Date of birth:	**Telephone number (home):**
Place and country of birth:	**Telephone number (office):**
Present nationality/nationalities:	**Mobile phone number:**
Candidate's father's full name:	**Fax number (home):**
Candidate's mother's full name:	**Fax number (office):**
	E-mail address:

Do you have any connection whatsoever with a member of the list of counsel and/or any investigator? ☐ Yes (please provide details) ☐ No	**Do you or any member of your family have any connection whatsoever with a person seeking representation before the Court?** ☐ Yes (please provide details) ☐ No
Do you have any connection whatsoever with a person seeking legal assistance from the Court? ☐ Yes (please provide details) ☐ No	**Do you have any connection whatsoever with a staff member of the Court?** ☐ Yes (please provide details) ☐ No

Language proficiency				
What is your mother tongue?				
Other languages **(Please indicate your level in each skill as follows: Basic/Intermediate/Advanced)**				
Language	**Written comprehension**	**Oral comprehension**	**Writing**	**Speaking**

Knowledge of law:	
How would you describe your knowledge of the common law system? ☐ Excellent ☐ Good ☐ Quite good ☐ Basic (please provide details)	**How would you describe your knowledge of international law and procedure?** ☐ Excellent ☐ Good ☐ Quite good ☐ Basic (please provide details):
How would you describe your knowledge of the civil law system? ☐ Excellent ☐ Good ☐ Quite good ☐ Basic (please provide details)	**How would you describe your knowledge of criminal law and procedure?** ☐ Excellent ☐ Good ☐ Quite good ☐ Basic (please provide details)

Education	
Secondary and university education. Please give details of diplomas, degrees and merits obtained, specifying the year, university, institute or other institution attended, and area of specialisation. Please provide the full address and contact details of the institutions attended, specifying the name of a contact person in each case.	Other studies: Other significant information:
Computer skills	
How would you describe your computer skills? ☐ Excellent ☐ Good ☐ Quite good ☐ Basic **Have you ever used computer tools for document management?** ☐ Yes (please provide details) ☐ No **Would you describe your knowledge of computerised case management systems as:** ☐ Excellent ☐ Good ☐ Quite good ☐ Basic (please provide details)	Please list the computer tools or computer equipment that you use in your work: Please list any computer programs you use:

If you are a judge, lawyer or prosecutor, please indicate:	
Years of experience in criminal proceedings: **Your field of expertise and years of experience in that field:** **Total number of years of experience:** **Other activities related to criminal proceedings:**	**Have you worked or are you currently working for an international criminal court?** ☐ Yes (please provide details) ☐ No **Have you ever appeared before a court as an expert witness?** ☐ Yes (please provide details) ☐ No **Have you ever appeared before a court as *amicus curiae*?** ☐ Yes (please provide details) ☐ No **Have you ever appeared before a court as a legal representative of a victim or victims?** ☐ Yes (please provide details) ☐ No

If you are an academic in law, please indicate:	
Your field of expertise: **Total number of years of experience:** **Please list any significant publications relating to international criminal law, international humanitarian law or human rights of which you are the author:** **Other activities related to criminal proceedings:**	**Have you ever appeared before a court as an expert witness?** ☐ Yes (please provide details) ☐ No **Have you ever appeared before a court as *amicus curiae*?** ☐ Yes (please provide details) ☐ No **Have you ever appeared before a court as a legal representative of a victim or victims?** ☐ Yes (please provide details) ☐ No

Additional information	
Name, telephone number, fax number, e-mail address of the bar association(s) and/or the controlling administrative authority with which you are registered:	**Have you ever been the subject of a disciplinary sanction by the bar association(s) or the controlling administrative authority with which you are registered or by an international criminal court?** ☐ Yes (please provide details) ☐ No **Are you eligible for appointment as counsel at an international criminal court?** ☐ Yes (please provide details) ☐ No **Have you ever been convicted of a criminal offence, excluding minor traffic violations?** ☐ Yes (please provide details) ☐ No **Are any criminal proceedings currently being brought against you?** ☐ Yes (please provide details) ☐ No

Please enclose the following with this form:

1. **Detailed *curriculum vitae,***
2. **Original or certified copy of the certificate issued by the bar association and/or the controlling administrative authority with which you are registered,**
3. **Completed "certificate of good standing for candidates to the list of counsel",**
4. **A certificate issued by the relevant authority of the State(s) in which you are domiciled, stating the existence, if any, of criminal convictions,**
5. **Valid practicing certificate,**
6. **Copy of your professional insurance policy,**
7. **Legible copy of your birth certificate,**
8. **Legible copy of your passport/travel document,**
9. **Two passport-size photographs (colour).**

N.B.: The original version of all these documents must be submitted. If the original version is in neither English nor French, it must be accompanied by a certified translation.

In the event that you are admitted to the list of counsel, would you object to the list being published, inter alia on the Court website?

☐ Yes
☐ No

If your answer to the previous question is negative, would you object to your contact information also being posted on the "list of counsel" page of the Court website.

☐ Yes
☐ No

Please specify if you have ever been or are a member of a disciplinary body or if you have specific responsibilities relating to ethics.

Please specify if you have any preferences in respect of an eventual appointment.

Preferences:

None	Defence	Victims	Other
☐	☐ Yes ☐ No	☐ Yes ☐ No	☐ (please provide details)

In the event that you are appointed, would you be willing to use an electronic signature?

☐ Yes

☐ No (please provide additional information)

Would you object to the Registry contacting the professional authority with which you are registered, and/or the institutions and persons mentioned on this form?

☐ Yes

☐ No (please provide additional information)

Please provide below any information that you consider ought to be brought to the attention of the International Criminal Court.

I certify on my honour that I have verified the information in this form and that it is true and correct. I hereby undertake to inform the Court in the event of a change in my circumstances.

I understand that any decision to appoint me at the Court will be based on the information provided herein. I also understand that, should any item of information herein prove to be incorrect or false, the Court would be at liberty to terminate my appointment without notice. I hereby undertake to inform the Court of any future criminal proceedings that may be initiated against me.

I undertake not to enter into any fee-splitting arrangement with any person seeking representation or relative, friend or associate of the same.

Date: **Signature:**

APPENDIX VII

Victim Participation Form

This form is also available at: http://www.icc-cpi.int/Menus/ICC/Structure+of+the+Court/Victims/Office+of+Public+Counsel+for+Victims/Contribution+Form+regarding+the+Participation+of+Victims+in+the+Proceedings.htm

**Cour
Pénale
Internationale**

**International
Criminal
Court**

STANDARD APPLICATION FORM TO PARTICIPATE IN PROCEEDINGS BEFORE THE INTERNATIONAL CRIMINAL COURT FOR INDIVIDUAL VICTIMS AND PERSONS ACTING ON THEIR BEHALF

FORM PARTICIPATION-1

Please complete this Application Form if you believe you have suffered harm as a result of a crime under the jurisdiction of the International Criminal Court (ICC) and wish to participate in the proceedings before the ICC by putting forward your observations, views or concerns, or if you are acting on behalf of such a person.

The purpose of this Application Form is to collect information to help a Chamber of Judges in the ICC decide whether you are entitled to participate in proceedings before the Court. Your completion of this Application Form will not automatically lead to your participation in the proceedings before the ICC.

The information provided in the Application Form will be forwarded to a Chamber of Judges in the ICC which will consider your application. Please be advised that criminal proceedings take time and it may be some time before the Court makes decisions on your application.

Please review the accompanying Booklet before completing the Application Form as it will help you fill it in correctly. The Booklet contains explanations regarding:

- What the International Criminal Court is
- The purpose of this Application Form and what will happen to it
- Instructions on how to complete each section of the Application Form. Please note that each Part of this Application Form corresponds to the same Part of the Booklet.

Who should use this Application Form?

A victim who is seeking to participate in proceedings before the ICC
For the purposes of the ICC, a victim is a person who has suffered harm as a result of the commission of a crime within the jurisdiction of the Court.

☞ Victims that are organizations or institutions should use FORM PARTICIPATION-2.

A person acting on behalf of a victim
Where a victim is a child, or has a disability that prevents the victim from acting on her or his own behalf, someone else may make an application on their behalf. Where a victim is deceased, someone else may also make the application. In addition, a person may make the application with the consent of a victim. In any of above circumstances, the person making the application should complete Part B.

A person assisting a victim
Where a victim or a person acting on behalf of a victim is filling in this Application Form, they may be assisted in filling in the Application Form by another person. This would be the case, for example, if either the victim or the person acting on behalf of the victim is unable to read or to write. Where a person assists in filling in this Application Form, she or he should complete Part I.

Please note that one Application Form should be filled in per applicant.

NOTE

This Application Form and the process of applying are free of charge. The ICC, as a matter of practice, does not charge any fee at any stage of the application process.

Instructions:

Please take into account the following instructions when completing this Application Form:

- Please fill in this Application Form to the extent possible.
- Please type or write your answers clearly.
- Please attach answers to the questions on a separate sheet of paper if you need more space.
- You must sign your Application Form, or add your thumbprint or other mark where indicated at the end of Part J.
- Please also put initials of the applicant in the box located at the bottom of each page of this Application Form as well as any other documents accompanying it. This will help prevent pages of the Application Form from being lost.
- Please provide photocopies of documents requested to the extent possible. If you do not have the documentation requested your application will still be considered. If possible, please staple all the pages of the Application Form and the accompanying documents. Do not send original documents at this time, but please take good care of original documents, which the Court may request at a later stage.

If you seek help in filling in this Application Form, you may contact the ICC or an ICC Field Office which will put you in touch with someone near you to help you fill in this Application Form.

Note regarding disclosure of information:

The information contained in your Application Form may be forwarded to the Defence and the Prosecutor. In addition, part or all of the information may be made available to the general public in the course of proceedings. If you do not wish for part or all of the information in the form to be disclosed or made public for reasons related to your security or well-being, you should tick the relevant boxes in Part H of the Application Form and provide the information requested. The Chamber of Judges will decide on the request, and their decision will be communicated to you.

The Application Form should be sent directly to one of the following addresses:

ICC HEADQUARTERS

International Criminal Court
Victims Participation and Reparations Section (VPRS)
P.O. Box 19519, 2500 CM The Hague
The Netherlands
Fax: + 31 70 515 9100
Email: vprsapplications@icc-cpi.int

ICC FIELD OFFICES

ICC Field Office in Kampala
Victims Participation and Reparations Section (VPRS)
P.O. Box 72735 - Kampala
Telephone: + 256 77 2 706062

ICC Field Office in Kinshasa
Victims Participation and Reparations Section (VPRS)
Telephone: + 243 998011426, + 243 998011403

PART A

PERSONAL INFORMATION ABOUT THE VICTIM. *See Part A of the Booklet.*

Have you already submitted an application for participation or reparations to the ICC?

☐ Yes ☐ No

If yes, when?

Day ______ Month ______ Year ______

If you have a registration number, please indicate it:

VPRS- ☐☐/☐☐ - ☐☐/☐☐

1. **Surname(s):** ______

2. **Other name(s):** ______

3. **Please provide the following information as far as relevant:**

   Father's name: ______

   Mother's name: ______

   Name of next of kin or, if you are under 18 years old, guardian: ______

4. **Sex:** ☐ Female ☐ Male

5. **Age** or, if not known, approximate age: ☐☐

   or **date of birth**, or if not known, approximate date of birth:

   Day ______ Month ______ Year ______

6. **Place of birth:** ______

7. **Nationality (ies):** ______

8. **What is your tribe/ethnic group?**

______

______

Initials of applicant

NOTE: This Application Form and the process of applying are free of charge.

9. What is your occupation?

- ☐ Agriculture (crops, livestock)
- ☐ Seller (self-employed, trade)
- ☐ State employee
- ☐ Teacher
- ☐ Medical worker
- ☐ Artisan/skilled labor/ casual worker
- ☐ Work for NGO or UN
- ☐ Unemployed
- ☐ Other - Specify:

____

10. What is your marital status?

- ☐ Single
- ☐ Married
- ☐ Divorced
- ☐ Widow/widower
- ☐ Other (such as abandoned spouse, co-habitee)

____

11. How many dependants do you have? *Please write number.*

____

12. If you have a disabilty or disabilities, please specify.

____

____

____

Initials of applicant

13. Which of the following proof of identity do you have? *Please indicate the number or other reference and attach a photocopy if possible. Please note that one of the following is sufficient. If you have no documentation your application will still be considered.*

Type of proof of identity	Number or other reference
☐ Passport	
☐ Driver's licence	
☐ Identity card (such as students, employees)	
☐ Letter from Local Authority	
☐ Camp registration card	
☐ Card from humanitarian agency (such as UNHCR, WFP)	
☐ Tax document	
☐ Voting card	
☐ Other. *Please specify and provide number or other reference:*	
☐ None	

14. Where do you currently live? *Please complete all that apply to you.*

Street: Number/Plot:

Camp/Zone/Sector/Cell:

Village/Parish/Subcounty/Town:

County/District:

P.O. Box: Postal Code:

Country:

If you have been displaced from your home, please indicate your place of origin:

Village/Parish/Subcounty/Town:

County/District:

Country:

Initials of applicant

15. Where would you like to be contacted? *Please tick as appropriate.*

☐ Please use the address mentioned in question 14.

☐ Please contact me through a person acting on my behalf.
If you tick this box, please fill in Part B of this Application Form as appropiate.

☐ Please use the following address. *Please complete all that apply to you:*

C/O: ______

Street: ______ Number/Plot: ______

Camp/Zone/Sector/Cell: ______

Village/Parish/Subcounty/Town: ______

County/District: ______

P.O. Box: ______ Postal Code: ______

Country: ______

☐ Please use the following telephone number (*please give area code*):

______

☐ Please use the following mobile phone number:

______

☐ Please use the following fax number (*please give area code*):

______

☐ Please use the following e-mail address:

______

16. Which languages do you speak?

______

______

17. In which of the following languages are you able to understand written correspondence?

☐ English

☐ French

☐ Other language. *Please specify:* ______

☐ Cannot read

Initials of applicant

PART B

INFORMATION ABOUT A PERSON ACTING ON BEHALF OF THE VICTIM. *See Part B of the Booklet.*

If this Application Form is being completed by a person acting on behalf of the victim (as outlined on page 1 of the Application Form), that person should provide her or his details below.

1. **Surname(s):** ____________________

2. **Other name(s):** ____________________

3. **Sex:** ☐ Female ☐ Male

4. **Age** or, if not known, approximate age: ____________________

   or **date of birth**, or if not known, approximate date of birth:

   Day ☐ Month ☐ Year ☐

5. **Which of the following proof of identity do you have?** *Please indicate the number or other reference and attach a photocopy if possible. Please note that one of the following is sufficient. If you have no documentation your application will still be considered.*

Type of proof of identity	Number or other reference
☐ Passport	
☐ Driver's licence	
☐ Identity card (such as students, employees)	
☐ Letter from Local Authority	
☐ Camp registration card	
☐ Card from humanitarian agency (such as UNHCR, WFP)	
☐ Tax document	
☐ Voting card	
☐ Other. *Please specify and provide number or other reference:*	
☐ None	

Initials of applicant

6. Contact details. *Please complete all that apply to you.*

Street: ______________________ Number/Plot: ______________________

Camp/Zone/Sector/Cell: ______________________

Village/Parish/Subcounty/Town: ______________________

County/District: ______________________

P.O. Box: ______________________ Postal Code: ______________________

Country: ______________________

Telephone number. *Please give area code:* ______________________

Mobile phone number: ______________________

Fax number. *Please give area code:* ______________________

E-mail address: ______________________

7. Which languages do you speak?

____

____

8. In which of the following languages are you able to understand written correspondence?

☐ English

☐ French

☐ Other language. *Please specify:*

____

☐ Cannot read

9. In what capacity are you making this application? *Please tick as appropiate.*

I am making this application because:

ⓐ ☐	The victim is a child	
ⓑ ☐	The victim is a person with a disability	Nature of disability: ______________
ⓒ ☐	The victim is deceased	Date of death: Day ☐ Month ☐ Year ☐ Is there a death certificate, court document granting entitlement or the equivalent? ☐ Yes ☐ No *If yes, please provide a photocopy.*
ⓓ ☐	The victim gave her/his consent	*The victim must indicate her or his consent by signing in Part J of this Application Form.*

Initials of applicant

10. What is your relationship to the victim? ______________________

Do you have proof of the relationship (such as marriage certificate, birth certificate, family registration booklet, will or testament or court document)?

☐ Yes ☐ No

If yes, please provide a photocopy.

PART C

STAGE OF PARTICIPATION. *See Part C of the Booklet.*

1. During which of the following stages of the proceedings do you wish to participate?

☐ Preliminary Examination Stage

☐ Pre-Trial Stage

☐ Trial Stage

☐ Appeal Stage

PART D

INFORMATION ABOUT THE ALLEGED CRIME(S). *See Part D of the Booklet.*

Please attach answers to this section on a separate sheet of paper if necessary.

1. Please give a detailed description of the alleged crime(s) which form the basis of this application (please explain in detail what happened to you).

____

When did the event or events occur? If possible, please specify day(s), month(s) and year(s).

____

Initials of applicant

Where did the event or events take place? If necessary you may attach a drawing or a map of the location.

2. **Who do you believe is responsible for the event or events and why do you believe this?** *Please answer to the extent possible.*

3. **Were there any other victims of the event or events?**

☐ Yes ☐ No

If yes (and if you can), please give their names and addresses, unless you know that they wish to remain anonymous, or it would put the applicant or anyone else at risk.

4. **Were there any witnesses?**

☐ Yes ☐ No

If yes (and if you can), please give their names and addresses, unless you know that they wish to remain anonymous or it would put the applicant or anyone else at risk.

5. **Do you have any relationship with these witnesses (are they family members, neighbours, friends, etc.)?**

☐ Yes ☐ No

If yes, please indicate:

Initials of applicant

PART E

INFORMATION ABOUT THE INJURY, LOSS OR HARM SUFFERED. *See Part E of the Booklet.*

1. **Please describe the injury, loss or harm you have suffered, and give brief descriptions (such as physical injuries, mental pain and anguish, loss of or damage to property).**

2. **Were you examined by a doctor after the event or events occurred?**

   ☐ Yes ☐ No

3. **Did you receive any medical or psychological treatment?**

   ☐ Yes ☐ No

4. **If yes, do you have (or have access to) any records regarding any medical or phychological treatment?** *If yes, please tick as appropriate and provide a photocopy, if availiable.*

   ☐ Medical report from doctor, hospital or health center

   ☐ X-rays

   ☐ Prescriptions/Invoices for medicines

   ☐ Other. *Please specify:*

   ☐ None

5. **Does your condition persist today?**

   ☐ Yes ☐ No

   If yes, please give details:

PART F

NOT APPLICABLE. *See Part F of the Booklet.*

Initials of applicant

PART G

LEGAL REPRESENTATION. *See Part G of the Booklet.*

A victim may be represented before the ICC by a legal representative. A victim is free to choose her or his legal representative before the ICC, who must be a person with 10 years' relevant experience as a criminal lawyer, judge or prosecutor, and be fluent in one of the Court's working languages (English or French).

1. Do you have a legal representative?

☐ Yes ☐ No

If yes, please provide her/his name, and contact details:

Name: ______________________________

Address:

Street: ______________ Number/Plot: ______________

Camp/Zone/Sector/Cell: ______________________________

Village/Parish/Subcounty/Town: ______________________________

County/District: ______________________________

P.O. Box: ______________________________

Country: ______________________________

Telephone number. *Please give area code:* ______________________________

Mobile phone number: ______________________________

Fax number. *Please give area code:* ______________________________

Email address: ______________________________

2. If no, would you like assistance from the Court to obtain legal representation?

☐ Yes ☐ No

Note regarding victims' legal representation:

The ICC can help victims find a legal representative by providing a list of qualified counsel.

Although the Court's resources for legal aid are limited, the Court may be able to provide some financial assistance. If you believe you will not be able to afford legal representation, a separate form for requesting legal assistance paid by the Court is available at the ICC Field Offices and the website at www.icc-cpi.int

Where there are many victims, a Chamber of Judges may ask victims to choose a common legal representative, in order to make the proceedings more efficient. If for any reason the victims are unable to choose one, the Chamber of Judges may ask the Registrar to do so. If the victims are not happy with the Registrar's choice, they may ask a Chamber of Judges to review it.

Please note that the Office of Public Counsel for Victims within the Court may also be appointed to represent victim(s) or a group of victims free of charge. Such Office provides support and assistance to victims and legal representatives of victims, including legal advice and representation before a Chamber.

Initials of applicant

PART H

REQUEST FOR NON-DISCLOSURE OF INFORMATION. *See Part H of the Booklet.*

Completing this section does not automatically mean that your request for non-disclosure will be accepted. Please note that a Chamber of Judges will decide on this request.

1. Please tick one or more boxes if you wish to request that your identity be kept from:

☐ The Prosecutor ☐ The Defence ☐ The general public ☐ State or other participant

2. Please tick one or more boxes if you wish to request that any information provided in this Application Form other than your identity be kept from:

☐ The Prosecutor ☐ The Defence ☐ The general public ☐ State or other participant

If yes, which information?

____

____

____

If you have ticked either box, please give reasons:

____

____

____

3. Have you or your family been in contact with any person or organization to discuss your concerns regarding security as a result of filling in this Application Form?

☐ Yes ☐ No

If yes, please give details:

____

____

____

PART I

INFORMATION ABOUT A PERSON ASSISTING IN FILLING IN THIS APPLICATION FORM.
See Part I of the Booklet.

If you are assisting the victim or assisting a person acting on behalf of the victim, please fill in this part.

1. Surname(s): ________________________________

2. Other name(s): ________________________________

☐ *Initials of applicant*

3. Address. *Please complete all that apply to you.*

Street: Number/Plot:

Camp/Zone/Sector/Cell:

Village/Parish/Subcounty/Town:

County/District:

P.O. Box: Postal Code:

Country:

Telephone number. *Please give area code:*

Mobile phone number:

Fax number. *Please give area code:*

E-mail address:

4. Occupation, place of employment and job title:

5. Which languages do you speak?

6. Which language did you use in communicating with the victim?

7. Was an interpreter present?

☐ Yes ☐ No

If yes, please provide his/her name:

Initials of applicant

PART J

SIGNATURES. *See Part J of the Booklet.*

SIGNATURE OF THE VICTIM

You should sign or add your thumbprint or other mark and date this Application Form, whether or not someone is acting on your behalf or assisting you in filling in this Application Form.

I hereby declare that, to the best of my knowledge and belief, the information I have given in the present Application Form is correct.

Signature, thumbprint or other mark of the victim

Day ______ Month ______ Year ______

Location: ______________________

Witnessed by:

Name: ______________________

Signature: ______________________

Initials of applicant

SIGNATURE OF THE PERSON ACTING ON BEHALF OF THE VICTIM AND CONSENT OF THE VICTIM

If you ticked box ⓓ on page 8 (Question 9, Part B — *if the victim has consented to you making this application on her or his behalf*): ☞ *The victim must sign the consent below, or add her or his thumbprint or other mark, and the person acting on the victim's behalf should also sign where indicated.*	**If you ticked box ⓐ, ⓑ or ⓒ on page 8** (Question 9, Part B — *if the victim is a child, disabled or deceased*): ☞ *The person acting on behalf of the victim must sign below.*

Consent of the victim:

I, ________________________________

Print name of the victim

consent to

____

Print name of the person acting on behalf of the victim

to act on my behalf in making this application.

Signature, thumbprint or other mark of the victim

Signature, thumbprint or other mark of a person acting on behalf of the victim

Day ______ Month ______ Year ______

Location: ________________________________

Witnessed by:

Name: ________________________________

Signature: ________________________________

Initials of applicant

NOTE: This Application Form and the process of applying are free of charge.

REMINDER

Before submitting this Application Form, please review it and tick the following as appropriate:

☐ I have attached the following documents in support of this Application Form:

1. ____________________

2. ____________________

3. ____________________

☐ I have initialed every page of this Application Form as well as any other documents accompanying it.

Please indicate total number of pages of this Application Form including additional pages and photocopies of documentation: ________

If you are the victim:	If you are a person acting on behalf of the victim:
☐ I have provided a photocopy of proof of identity in response to Question 13 of Part A.	☐ I have provided a photocopy of proof of identity in response to Question 5 of Part B.
☐ I have provided contact information in response to Question 15 of Part A.	☐ I have provided contact information in response to Question 6 of Part B.
☐ I have signed or made my mark in the first box in Part J.	☐ I have provided a death certificate, court document granting entitlement or the equivalent if the victim is deceased.
	☐ I have provided a photocopy of proof of relationship to the victim as requested in Question 10 of Part B.
	☐ I have signed or made my mark in the second box in Part J.

What will happen to your application?

Once the ICC receives your Application Form, you will receive an acknowledgement. This acknowledgement will provide you with a registration number that you should use when communicating with the Court. If you send additional information to the Court, please use this registration number to ensure your application is properly updated. Please note that criminal proceedings take time and it may be a while before a Chamber of Judges make a decision on your application.

Initials of applicant

APPENDIX VIII

Reparations Form

This form is also available at: http://www.icc-cpi.int/Menus/ICC/Structure+of+the+Court/Victims/Reparation/Standard+application+form+for+reparations+before+the+International+Criminal+Court+for+victims+which.htm

Cour Pénale Internationale

International Criminal Court

STANDARD APPLICATION FORM FOR REPARATIONS BEFORE THE INTERNATIONAL CRIMINAL COURT FOR INDIVIDUAL VICTIMS AND PERSONS ACTING ON THEIR BEHALF

FORM REPARATIONS-1

Please complete this Application Form if you believe you have suffered harm as a result of a crime under the jurisdiction of the International Criminal Court (ICC) and wish to submit a request for reparations to the ICC, or if you are acting on behalf of such a person.

The purpose of this Application Form is to collect information to help a Chamber of Judges in the ICC decide on matters relating to reparation. Completion of this form will not automatically lead to reparation awards by the ICC.

The information provided in the Application Form will be presented to a Chamber of Judges in the ICC which will consider your request. Please be advised that criminal proceedings take time and it may be some time before the Court makes decisions on reparations.

Please review the accompanying Booklet before completing the Application Form as it will help you fill it in correctly. The Booklet contains explanations regarding:

- What the International Criminal Court is
- The purpose of this Application Form and what will happen to it
- Instructions on how to complete each section of the Application Form. Please note that each Part of this Application Form corresponds to the same Part of the Booklet.

Who should use this Application Form?

A victim who is seeking to submit a request for reparations to the ICC
For the purposes of the ICC, a victim is a person who has suffered harm as a result of the commission of any crime within the jurisdiction of the Court.

☞ Victims that are organizations or institutions should use FORM REPARATIONS-2.

A person acting on behalf of a victim
Where a victim is a child, or has a disability that prevents the victim from acting on her or his own behalf, someone else may make an application on their behalf. Where a victim is deceased, someone else may also make the application. In addition, a person may make the application with the consent of a victim. In any of above circumstances, the person making the application should complete Part B.

A person assisting a victim
Where a victim or a person acting on behalf of a victim is filling in this Application Form, they may be assisted in filling in the Application Form by another person. This would be the case, for example, if either the victim or the person acting on behalf of the victim is unable to read or to write. Where a person assists in filling in this Application Form, she or he should complete Part I.

NOTE

This Application Form and the process of applying are free of charge. The ICC, as a matter of practice, does not charge any fee at any stage of the application process.

Instructions:

Please take into account the following instructions when completing this Application Form:

- Please fill in this Application Form to the extent possible.
- Please type or write your answers clearly.
- Please attach answers to the questions on a separate sheet of paper if you need more space.
- You must sign your Application Form, or add your thumbprint or other mark where indicated at the end of Part J.
- Please also put initials of the applicant in the box located at the bottom of each page of this Application Form as well as of any other documents accompanying it. This will help prevent pages of the Application Form from being lost.
- Please provide photocopies of documents requested to the extent possible. If you do not have the documentation requested your application will still be considered. If possible, please staple all the pages of the Application Form and the accompanying documents. Do not send original documents at this time, but please take good care of original documents, which the Court may request at a later stage.

If you seek help in filling in this Application Form, you may contact the ICC or an ICC Field Office which will put you in touch with someone near you to help you fill in this Application Form.

Note regarding disclosure of information:

The information contained in your Application Form may be forwarded to the Defence and other interested persons, including States, at the relevant stage. In addition, part or all of the information may be made available to the general public in the course of proceedings. If you do not wish for part or all of the information in the form to be disclosed or made public for reasons related to your security or well-being, you should tick the relevant boxes in Part H of the Application Form and provide the information requested. The Chamber of Judges will decide on the request, and their decision will be communicated to you.

The Application Form should be sent directly to one of the following addresses:

ICC HEADQUARTERS

International Criminal Court
Victims Participation and Reparations Section (VPRS)
P.O. Box 19519, 2500 CM The Hague
The Netherlands
Fax: + 31 70 515 9100
Email: vprsapplications@icc-cpi.int

ICC FIELD OFFICES

ICC Field Office in Kampala
Victims Participation and Reparations Section (VPRS)
P.O. Box 72735 - Kampala
Telephone: + 256 77 2 706062

ICC Field Office in Kinshasa
Victims Participation and Reparations Section (VPRS)
Telephone: + 243 998011426, + 243 998011403

PART A

PERSONAL INFORMATION ABOUT THE VICTIM. *See Part A of the Booklet.*

Have you already submitted an application for participation or reparations to the ICC?

☐ Yes ☐ No

If yes, when?

Day ______ Month ______ Year ______

If you have a registration number, please indicate it:

VPRS- ☐☐/☐☐ - ☐☐/☐☐

1. **Surname(s):** ____________________

2. **Other name(s):** ____________________

3. **Please provide the following information as far as relevant:**

   Father's name: ____________________

   Mother's name: ____________________

   Name of next of kin or, if you are under 18 years old, guardian: ____________________

4. **Sex:** ☐ Female ☐ Male

5. **Age** or, if not known, approximate age: ☐☐

   or **date of birth**, or if not known, approximate date of birth:

   Day ______ Month ______ Year ______

6. **Place of birth:** ____________________

7. **Nationality (ies):** ____________________

8. **What is your tribe/ethnic group?**

   ____

   ____

Initials of applicant

NOTE: This Application Form and the process of applying are free of charge.

9. What is your occupation?

☐ Agriculture (crops, livestock)

☐ Seller (self-employed, trade)

☐ State employee

☐ Teacher

☐ Medical worker

☐ Artisan/skilled labor/ casual worker

☐ Work for NGO or UN

☐ Unemployed

☐ Other - Specify:

____

10. What is your marital status?

☐ Single

☐ Married

☐ Divorced

☐ Widow/widower

☐ Other (such as abandoned spouse, co-habitee)

____

11. How many dependants do you have? *Please write number.*

____

12. If you have a disabilty or disabilities, please specify.

____

____

____

Initials of applicant

13. Which of the following proof of identity do you have? *Please indicate the number or other reference and attach a photocopy if possible. Please note that one of the following is sufficient. If you have no documentation your application will still be considered.*

Type of proof of identity	**Number or other reference**
☐ Passport	
☐ Driver's licence	
☐ Identity card (such as students, employees)	
☐ Letter from Local Authority	
☐ Camp registration card	
☐ Card from humanitarian agency (such as UNHCR, WFP)	
☐ Tax document	
☐ Voting card	
☐ Other. *Please specify and provide number or other reference:*	
☐ None	

14. Where do you currently live? *Please complete all that apply to you.*

Street: ______ Number/Plot: ______

Camp/Zone/Sector/Cell: ______

Village/Parish/Subcounty/Town: ______

County/District: ______

P.O. Box: ______ Postal Code: ______

Country: ______

If you have been displaced from your home, please indicate your place of origin:

Village/Parish/Subcounty/Town: ______

County/District: ______

Country: ______

Initials of applicant

15. Where would you like to be contacted? *Please tick as appropriate.*

☐ Please use the address mentioned in question 14.

☐ Please contact me through a person acting on my behalf.
If you tick this box, please fill in Part B of this Application Form as appropiate.

☐ Please use the following address. *Please complete all that apply to you*:

C/O: ______

Street: ______ Number/Plot: ______

Camp/Zone/Sector/Cell: ______

Village/Parish/Subcounty/Town: ______

County/District: ______

P.O. Box: ______ Postal Code: ______

Country: ______

☐ Please use the following telephone number (*please give area code*):

______

☐ Please use the following mobile phone number:

______

☐ Please use the following fax number (*please give area code*):

______

☐ Please use the following e-mail address:

______

16. Which languages do you speak?

______

______

17. In which of the following languages are you able to understand written correspondence?

☐ English

☐ French

☐ Other language. *Please specify:* ______

☐ Cannot read

Initials of applicant

PART B

INFORMATION ABOUT A PERSON ACTING ON BEHALF OF THE VICTIM. *See Part B of the Booklet.*

If this Application Form is being completed by a person acting on behalf of the victim (as outlined on page 1 of the Application Form), that person should provide her or his details below.

1. **Surname(s):** ______________________________

2. **Other name(s):** ______________________________

3. **Sex:** ☐ Female ☐ Male

4. **Age** or, if not known, approximate age: ______________________________

   or **date of birth**, or if not known, approximate date of birth:

   Day ☐ Month ☐ Year ☐

5. **Which of the following proof of identity do you have?** *Please indicate the number or other reference and attach a photocopy if possible. Please note that one of the following is sufficient. If you have no documentation your application will still be considered.*

Type of proof of identity	Number or other reference
☐ Passport	
☐ Driver's licence	
☐ Identity card (such as students, employees)	
☐ Letter from Local Authority	
☐ Camp registration card	
☐ Card from humanitarian agency (such as UNHCR, WFP)	
☐ Tax document	
☐ Voting card	
☐ Other. *Please specify and provide number or other reference:*	
☐ None	

Initials of applicant

6. **Contact details.** *Please complete all that apply to you.*

Street: ______________________ Number/Plot: ______________

Camp/Zone/Sector/Cell: ______________________

Village/Parish/Subcounty/Town: ______________________

County/District: ______________________

P.O. Box: ______________________ Postal Code: ______________

Country: ______________________

Telephone number. *Please give area code:* ______________________

Mobile phone number: ______________________

Fax number. *Please give area code:* ______________________

E-mail address: ______________________

7. **Which languages do you speak?**

____

____

8. **In which of the following languages are you able to understand written correspondence?**

☐ English

☐ French

☐ Other language. *Please specify:*

____

☐ Cannot read

9. **In what capacity are you making this application?** *Please tick as appropiate.*

I am making this application because:

ⓐ ☐	The victim is a child	
ⓑ ☐	The victim is a person with a disability	Nature of disability: ______________
ⓒ ☐	The victim is deceased	Date of death: Day ☐ Month ☐ Year ☐ Is there a death certificate, court document granting entitlement or the equivalent? ☐ Yes ☐ No *If yes, please provide a photocopy.*
ⓓ ☐	The victim gave her/his consent	*The victim must indicate her or his consent by signing in Part J of this Application Form.*

☐

Initials of applicant

10. What is your relationship to the victim? ______________________

Do you have proof of the relationship (such as marriage certificate, birth certificate, family registration booklet, will or testament or court document)?

☐ Yes ☐ No

If yes, please provide a photocopy.

PART C

NOT APPLICABLE. *See Part C of the Booklet.*

PART D

INFORMATION ABOUT THE ALLEGED CRIME(S). *See Part D of the Booklet.*

Please attach answers to this section on a separate sheet of paper if necessary.

1. **Please give a detailed description of the alleged crime(s) which form the basis of this application (please explain in detail what happened to you).**

When did the event or events occur? If possible, please specify day(s), month(s) and year(s).

Initials of applicant

Where did the event or events take place? If necessary you may attach a drawing or a map of the location.

____

____

____

____

____

2. **Who do you believe is responsible for the event or events and why do you believe this?**
Please answer to the extent possible.

____

____

____

____

____

____

3. **Were there any other victims of the event or events?**

☐ Yes ☐ No

If yes (and if you can), please give their names and addresses, unless you know that they wish to remain anonymous, or it would put the applicant or anyone else at risk.

____

____

____

4. **Were there any witnesses?**

☐ Yes ☐ No

If yes (and if you can), please give their names and addresses, unless you know that they wish to remain anonymous or it would put the applicant or anyone else at risk.

____

____

____

5. **Do you have any relationship with these witnesses (are they family members, neighbours, friends, etc.)?**

☐ Yes ☐ No

If yes, please indicate:

____

____

Initials of applicant

PART E

INFORMATION ABOUT THE INJURY, LOSS OR HARM SUFFERED. *See Part E of the Booklet.*

1. **Please describe the injury, loss or harm you have suffered, and give brief descriptions (such as physical injuries, mental pain and anguish, loss of or damage to property).**

2. **Were you examined by a doctor after the event or events occurred?**

   ☐ Yes ☐ No

3. **Did you receive any medical or psychological treatment?**

   ☐ Yes ☐ No

4. **If yes, do you have (or have access to) any records regarding any medical or phychological treatment?** *If yes, please tick as appropriate and provide a photocopy, if availiable.*

   ☐ Medical report from doctor, hospital or health center

   ☐ X-rays

   ☐ Prescriptions/Invoices for medicines

   ☐ Other. *Please specify:*

   ☐ None

5. **Does your condition persist today?**

   ☐ Yes ☐ No

   If yes, please give details:

Initials of applicant

PART F

Reparations. *See Part F of the Booklet.*

1. **Which of the following forms of reparations would you like to claim?** *Please see the accompanying Booklet for descriptions of the terms listed below. You may tick more than one box.*

   - [ ] Compensation
   - [ ] Restitution
   - [ ] Rehabilitation
   - [ ] Other form of reparations - Specify:

   ____

   ____

2. **Physical injuries**

   What physical injuries have you suffered as a result of the alleged crime(s) (such as dismemberment, disfigurement, loss or limitation of use of a body organ, member, function or system, including sexual/ reproductive health problems)?

   ____

   ____

   ____

3. **Mental pain and anguish**

   Do you experience any of the following reactions as a result of the alleged crime(s)?
   You may tick more than one box.

Type of harm	Description
☐ Emotional problems (such as anxiety, anguish and guilt, shame, sadness, nightmares, irritability and anger, defeat and apathy, feeling overwhelmed)	
☐ Mental problems (such as intrusive images and thoughts, slowing of thought process, concentration problems, memory dysfunction, confusion)	
☐ Physical reactions and behavioural changes (such as aches and pains, sleep disturbances, excessive sweating, breathing problem, increased heart rate)	
☐ Pain, complaints and/or concerns related to experiences of sexual violence	

Initials of applicant

4. Loss of or damage to property

Have you lost or suffered damage to any of the following as a result of the alleged crime(s)? *You may tick more than one box.*

Type of loss	Description
☐ Home(s)	
☐ Land	
☐ Personal property, including household goods	
☐ Animal(s)	
☐ Other	

5. Other damage

Have you lost any of the following as a result of the alleged crime(s)? *You may tick more than one box.*

Type of loss	Description
☐ Loss of income, unpaid salaries, loss of support and any other losses connected to employment. *Please explain impact of the loss on how you sustain your life.*	
☐ Loss of savings at banks, stocks and other securities	
☐ Social status	
☐ Legal rights	
☐ Other	

Initials of applicant

6. If resources are available (from a person convicted by the ICC or from the ICC's Trust Fund for Victims), what would help you and your community the most?

____

____

____

____

____

____

PART G

LEGAL REPRESENTATION. *See Part G of the Booklet.*

A victim may be represented before the ICC by a legal representative. A victim is free to choose her or his legal representative before the ICC, who must be a person with 10 years' relevant experience as a criminal lawyer, judge or prosecutor, and be fluent in one of the Court's working languages (English or French).

1. Do you have a legal representative?

☐ Yes ☐ No

If yes, please provide her/his name, and contact details:

Name: ______________________________

Address:

Street: ______________ Number/Plot: ______________

Camp/Zone/Sector/Cell: ______________________________

Village/Parish/Subcounty/Town: ______________________________

County/District: ______________________________

P.O. Box: ______________________________

Country: ______________________________

Telephone number. *Please give area code:* ______________________________

Mobile phone number: ______________________________

Fax number. *Please give area code:* ______________________________

Email address: ______________________________

☐

Initials of applicant

2. If no, would you like assistance from the Court to obtain legal representation?

☐ Yes ☐ No

Note regarding victims' legal representation:

The ICC can help victims find a legal representative by providing a list of qualified counsel.

Although the Court's resources for legal aid are limited, the Court may be able to provide some financial assistance. If you believe you will not be able to afford legal representation, a separate form for requesting legal assistance paid by the Court is available at the ICC Field Offices and the website at www.icc-cpi.int

Where there are many victims, a Chamber of Judges may ask victims to choose a common legal representative, in order to make the proceedings more efficient. If for any reason the victims are unable to choose one, the Chamber of Judges may ask the Registrar to do so. If the victims are not happy with the Registrar's choice, they may ask a Chamber of Judges to review it.

Please note that the Office of Public Counsel for Victims within the Court may also be appointed to represent victim(s) or a group of victims free of charge. Such Office provides support and assistance to victims and legal representatives of victims, including legal advice and representation before a Chamber.

PART H

REQUEST FOR NON-DISCLOSURE OF INFORMATION. *See Part H of the Booklet.*

Completing this section does not automatically mean that your request for non-disclosure will be accepted. Please note that a Chamber of Judges will decide on this request.

1. Please tick one or more boxes if you wish to request that your identity be kept from:

☐ The Prosecutor ☐ The Defence ☐ The general public ☐ State or other participant

2. Please tick one or more boxes if you wish to request that any information provided in this Application Form other than your identity be kept from:

☐ The Prosecutor ☐ The Defence ☐ The general public ☐ State or other participant

If yes, which information?

____

____

____

If you have ticked either box, please give reasons:

____

____

____

3. Have you or your family been in contact with any person or organization to discuss your concerns regarding security as a result of filling in this Application Form?

☐ Yes ☐ No

If yes, please give details:

____

____

____

Initials of applicant

PART I

INFORMATION ABOUT A PERSON ASSISTING IN FILLING IN THIS APPLICATION FORM.
See Part I of the Booklet.

If you are assisting the victim or assisting a person acting on behalf of the victim, please fill in this part.

1. **Surname(s):** ____________________

2. **Other name(s):** ____________________

3. **Address.** *Please complete all that apply to you.*

   Street: ____________ Number/Plot: ____________

   Camp/Zone/Sector/Cell: ____________________

   Village/Parish/Subcounty/Town: ____________________

   County/District: ____________________

   P.O. Box: ____________ Postal Code: ____________

   Country: ____________________

   Telephone number. *Please give area code:* ____________________

   Mobile phone number: ____________________

   Fax number. *Please give area code:* ____________________

   E-mail address: ____________________

4. **Occupation, place of employment and job title:** ____________________

5. **Which languages do you speak?** ____________________

6. **Which language did you use in communicating with the victim?** ____________________

7. **Was an interpreter present?**

   ☐ Yes ☐ No

   If yes, please provide his/her name:

   ____

Initials of applicant

PART J

SIGNATURES. *See Part J of the Booklet.*

SIGNATURE OF THE VICTIM

You should sign or add your thumbprint or other mark and date this Application Form, whether or not someone is acting on your behalf or assisting you in filling in this Application Form.

I hereby declare that, to the best of my knowledge and belief, the information I have given in the present Application Form is correct.

Signature, thumbprint or other mark of the victim

Day ______ Month ______ Year ______

Location: ______________________

Witnessed by:

Name: ______________________

Signature: ______________________

Initials of applicant

SIGNATURE OF THE PERSON ACTING ON BEHALF OF THE VICTIM AND CONSENT OF THE VICTIM

If you ticked box ⓓ on page 8 (Question 9, Part B — *if the victim has consented to you making this application on her or his behalf):* ☞ *The victim must sign the consent below, or add her or his thumbprint or other mark, and the person acting on the victim's behalf should also sign where indicated.*	**If you ticked box ⓐ, ⓑ or ⓒ on page 8** (Question 9, Part B — *if the victim is a child, disabled or deceased):* ☞ *The person acting on behalf of the victim must sign below.*

Consent of the victim:

I, ______________________________

Print name of the victim

consent to

____

Print name of the person acting on behalf of the victim

to act on my behalf in making this application.

Signature, thumbprint or other mark of the victim

Signature, thumbprint or other mark of a person acting on behalf of the victim

Day ______ Month ______ Year ______

Location: ______________________________

Witnessed by:

Name: ______________________________

Signature: ______________________________

Initials of applicant

NOTE: This Application Form and the process of applying are free of charge.

REMINDER

Before submitting this Application Form, please review it and tick the following as appropriate:

☐ I have attached the following documents in support of this Application Form:

1. ______________________________
2. ______________________________
3. ______________________________

☐ I have initialed every page of this Application Form as well as any other documents accompanying it.

Please indicate total number of pages of this Application Form including additional pages and photocopies of documentation: ________

If you are the victim:	**If you are a person acting on behalf of the victim:**
☐ I have provided a photocopy of proof of identity in response to Question 13 of Part A.	☐ I have provided a photocopy of proof of identity in response to Question 5 of Part B.
☐ I have provided contact information in response to Question 15 of Part A.	☐ I have provided contact information in response to Question 6 of Part B.
☐ I have signed or made my mark in the first box in Part J.	☐ I have provided a death certificate, court document granting entitlement or the equivalent if the victim is deceased.
	☐ I have provided a photocopy of proof of relationship to the victim as requested in Question 10 of Part B.
	☐ I have signed or made my mark in the second box in Part J.

What will happen to your application?

Once the ICC receives your Application Form, you will receive an acknowledgement. This acknowledgement will provide you with a registration number that you should use when communicating with the Court. If you send additional information to the Court, please use this registration number to ensure your application is properly updated. Please note that criminal proceedings take time and it may be a while before a Chamber of Judges make a decision on your application.

Initials of applicant

Table of Authorities

International Statutes, Protocols, Covenants, Reports, Conventions, and Charters

ICC Rulings and Filings*

* Please note that the citation styles used herein are not necessarily uniform; instead, they track how the issuing Chamber styled the ruling.

Other Cases

ICC Legal Provisions

Rome Statute Articles

Rules

Regulations of the Court

Index